THE
BUDAPEST GALLERY

THE BUDAPEST GALLERY

PAINTINGS IN THE MUSEUM OF FINE ARTS

KLÁRA GARAS

CORVINA PRESS

Translated from the Hungarian
A Szépművészeti Múzeum képei (Corvina, 1973)
by Lili Halápy
Revised by Elisabeth West

Photographs in black and white by courtesy of the Budapest Museum of Fine Arts. Colour photography by Alfréd Schiller, Károly Szelényi and János Huschit

Second edition

ISBN 963 13 7290 1
Printed in Hungary, 1977
Kossuth Printing House, Budapest

CONTENTS

THE HISTORY OF THE MUSEUM

The Museum of Fine Arts was opened in 1906, so it is only comparatively recently that the works assembled there have been brought together. Some of the collections from which they came, however, have a history which can be traced for several centuries, and the antecedents of the Museum are closely linked to the development of art collections in Hungary.

Unlike the majority of great European collections the Budapest museum is not the descendant of a royal collection, for very few of the works of art collected by Hungarian kings have survived the tempests of history. King Matthias Corvinus (1440–90) collected many treasures for the royal castle in his capital city of Buda, including the magnificently illuminated manuscripts of the Corvina library and Renaissance sculptures and paintings presented to him by Italian rulers, but after his death these were dispersed or destroyed; a Leonardo *Madonna*, sent by Lodovico Sforza, and a Verrocchio relief of Darius from Lorenzo de' Medici, were among the works lost without trace. The conditions which prevailed during the Turkish attack on Buda and the consequent fall of the capital in 1541, the division of the country into three parts and the ensuing hundred-and-fifty years of Turkish occupation scarcely favoured the maintenance or increase of art collections. The Habsburg Emperor, who was at the same time King of Hungary, had his residences in Vienna and Prague. It was in these cities that the Imperial collection came into being, and to it most of the finest works of art left in Hungary were transferred. By bequest or confiscation, the collections of a number of Hungarian aristocrats finally became part of the Imperial collection, and it was thus that, along with less significant collections, the Emperor acquired the contents of the Sárvár gallery owned by the Chief Justice, Ferenc Nádasdy, who was beheaded in 1671. It was not until the eighteenth century, when Hungary had been liberated and the Turks forced to flee the country, that conditions were established in which it was once more possible to patronize the arts and build up great collections.

The first Hungarian public collection was that of the Hungarian National Museum, which was opened in 1802. It was founded by Count Ferenc Széchényi and was primarily intended for the display of historic relics of Hungary through the ages, but it was not long before the range was extended. The acquisition of the collection of Miklós Jankovich between 1832 and 1836 brought to the Museum for the first time a number of significant works of art. But the donation that really laid the foundations of the Gallery of the National Museum came in 1836, when János László Pyrker, Archbishop of Eger, gave the National Museum his valuable collection of 192 paintings. Most of them were works by Italian masters which he had collected in Italy during the first quarter of the nineteenth century, when he had been Patriarch of Venice, and among them were many important and significant paintings – Gentile Bellini's portrait of Caterina Cornaro, Giorgione's *Portrait of a Man*, the *Crucifixion* by Hans Memling, Paolo Veronese's *Allegory of Venice*, Giovanni Battista Tiepolo's *The Virgin with Six Saints* and a great many notable examples of Italian Renaissance painting.

In 1848, during the War of Independence, the collection was further enriched by the gift of yet another collection of important pictures. By order of the liberal leader, Lajos Kossuth,

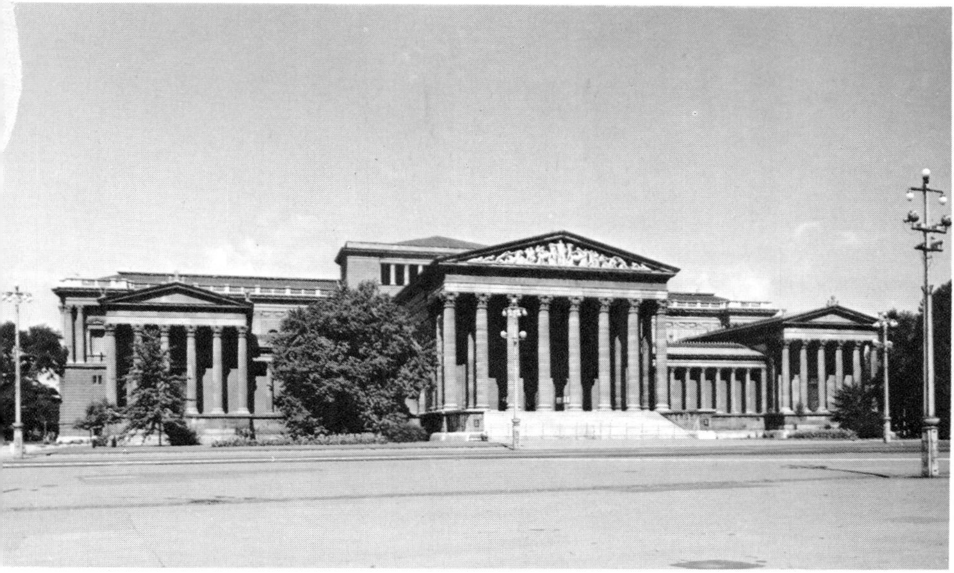

The façade of the Museum of Fine Arts

The main entrance to the Museum

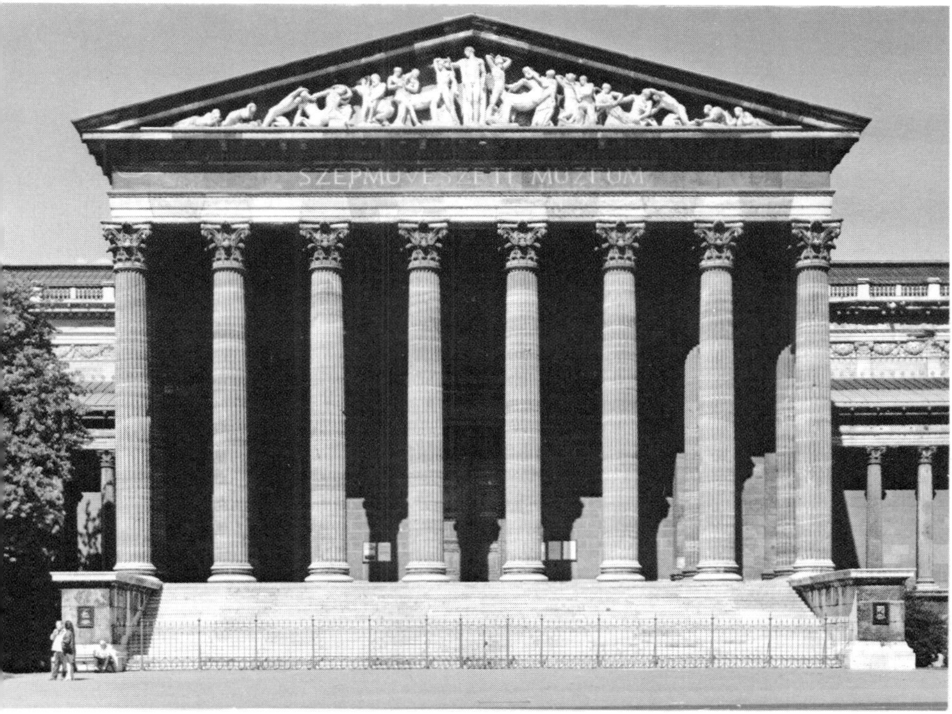

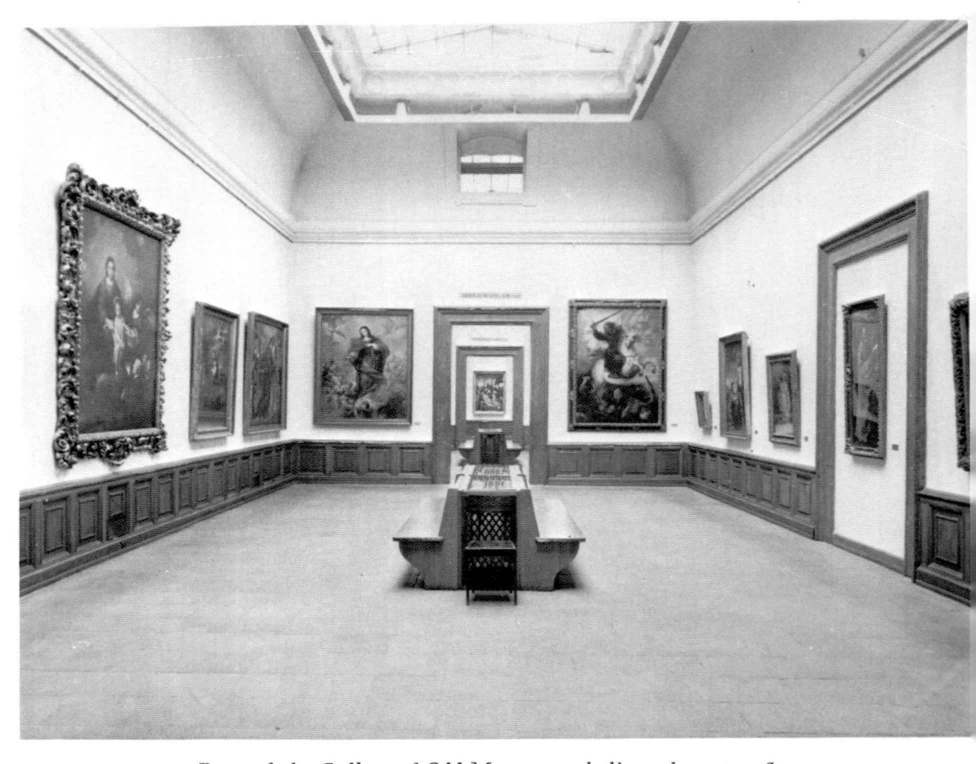

Part of the Gallery of Old Masters, a hall on the upper floor displaying Spanish paintings

seventy-eight paintings were transferred to the National Museum from the Buda residence of the former President of the Treasury and were thus placed under public ownership. This collection included many exceedingly valuable works: the history of some can be traced from the great Venetian and English collections of the early seventeenth century to the collection formed in Brussels by Archduke Leopold Wilhelm, the governor of the Spanish Netherlands, and later transferred to Vienna, whence some were taken to Buda. Among them were Dürer's *Portrait of a Man*, several masterpieces by Lucas Cranach the Elder, Lorenzo Lotto's painting of *The Sleeping Apollo* (a recent discovery), the *Self-portrait* by Giorgione, Palma Vecchio's enchanting *Betrothed Couple* and a great many other precious works of the Italian and Netherlandish schools.

In Pest – Buda's twin city – was a counter-attraction to the National Museum: the Esterházy collection, which was brought from Vienna in the 1860s. In the seventeenth century the Esterházy princes, heads of the wealthiest of the Hungarian noble families, had already acquired many valuable paintings, but the bulk of the collection came into being in the second half of the eighteenth century during the life of Prince Nicholas the Magnificent (1714–90), and, particularly, around the turn of the century during that of his grandson, Prince Miklós (1765–1833), who, during the course of his travels abroad, studied the famous collections and bought important works in Italy, England and France. In 1819 and 1821 he acquired the collection of Count Edmund Burke, former Danish ambassador to Spain, and thus laid the foundation of the uniquely valuable Spanish collection which was to become the pride of the gallery. In 1820 he bought some outstanding works at the auction of the Kaunitz collection in Vienna, amongst them Goya's *Water Seller* and *The Knife-Grinder* and Ribera's *Martyrdom of St Andrew*. For a time the

Esterházy collection was kept in the family's country houses at Eszterháza, Pottendorf and, later, at Laxenburg, but after 1814 it was exhibited in their palace in Mariahilf in Vienna. From that time on, the collection was considered to be one of the sights of Vienna; detailed accounts of it were printed in the contemporary reviews, travelogues were devoted to the gallery (which was open to the public three times a week), and, through the medium of a printed catalogue, the most famous exhibits found their way into the literature of universal art history.

From 1860 onwards the Hungarian people showed a growing interest in the Esterházy collection, and more and more widely the hope began to be expressed that it might be exhibited in Hungary to replace the many collections lost to the country for ever. In 1865, in response to these requests, Prince Pál Esterházy had the collection temporarily housed in the newly-erected building of the Hungarian Academy of Sciences.

In 1870, the Esterházy family, having run into financial difficulties, put the collection up for sale and the Hungarian Government paid 1,100,000 forints in gold for 636 paintings and a splendid collection of prints and drawings. Once this collection had been acquired, the government was able, in 1872, to establish the National Gallery, which formed the nucleus of the great collection now owned by the state.

The paintings from the Esterházy collection which found their way first to the National Gallery and then to the Museum of Fine Arts are still among the most valuable works of art in Hungary today. The Italian paintings were particularly notable, for among them were such masterpieces as Raphael's *Esterházy Madonna* and his portrait of Pietro Bembo, Correggio's *Madonna del Latte*, Crivelli's *Madonna and Child Enthroned*, Veronese's *Crucifixion* and Tiepolo's *St James the Greater*. The collection also included many famous paintings of the Flemish and Dutch schools, notably *Mucius Scaevola before Porsenna*, which is the joint work of Rubens and Van Dyck, the *Parable of the Hidden Treasure* by Rembrandt and Gerard Dou, Rembrandt's *Old Rabbi* and Jordaens's *Portrait of a Man*, as well as many fine landscapes, genre-paintings and still-lifes. The Spanish section contained three paintings by Murillo, one of them being *The Infant Jesus Distributing Bread to Pilgrims*, two by Cano and the two Goya masterpieces already mentioned, while among the French paintings were Simon Vouet's *Apollo and the Muses*, Claude Lorrain's *Villa in the Roman Campagna* and La Hire's *Theseus and Aethra*.

In 1872 the National Gallery was enriched with yet another important collection. Bishop Arnold Ipolyi, one of the first art historians in Hungary, donated sixty-four paintings, mainly works by Italian Primitives, a school not yet represented in the Gallery of the National Museum or among the Esterházy pictures, which widened the existing collection and gave it a more comprehensive character. Most of Ipolyi's paintings had originally been owned by Johann Anton Ramboux, one of the first painters of the nineteenth century to be attracted by the works of the Italian Primitives of the fourteenth and fifteenth centuries, and it was at the auction of the Ramboux collection in Cologne in 1869 that Ipolyi had acquired Sassetta's enchanting panel *St Thomas Aquinas before the Altar of the Virgin* as well as works by Spinello Aretino, Giovanni di Paolo, Sano di Pietro, Ambrogio Lorenzetti and a number of other Florentine or Sienese masters.

The National Gallery gradually assumed importance as a centre of European art, and the urgency of the need for the establishment of an organized collection became increasingly apparent. The works in the National Museum were incorporated into the National Gallery and this enlarged collection was still further expanded during the last decades of the century as a result of a policy of systematic acquisition. From the art dealers of Milan, Florence and Paris, Károly Pulszky, the new Director of the gallery, purchased many important works for the collection, among them the *Portrait of a Man*, believed at that time to be the work of Raphael but now attributed to Sebastiano del Piombo, Barend van Orley's splendid portrait of the Emperor Charles V, Rembrandt's *Dream of St Joseph* and a great many masterpieces of the Italian Renaissance and the seventeenth-century Dutch school. Unique among Pulszky's acquisitions is the precious series of north Italian frescoes removed from the walls on which they were painted and transferred onto canvas, still one of the rarities of the Museum. Pulszky was fortunate in the purchases he was able to make, and he transformed the random character of an amalgam of various private collections into a well-balanced national collection of European painting, while also performing the same service for the sculpture gallery and the collection of Hungarian art.

The National Gallery collection increased to such an extent that by the end of the century it was no longer possible to house all the acquisitions, and it became essential to find premises where all the paintings could be stored: premises, moreover, worthy of such valuable works of art. In 1896, during the celebrations of the thousandth anniversary of the foundation of Hungary, a decision was taken to allocate public funds for the provision of a new building to house the collection: a decision confirmed at the millenary session of Parliament. The site was decided upon, tenders were invited, the designs of Albert Schickedanz and Fülöp Herczog approved, and construction was soon under way. The huge building, with its Neoclassic façade, was completed by 1906 on a site bordering the City Park, at the end of what was then known as Sugár út (the Avenue). In the fashion of the period plaster casts of classical, medieval and Renaissance sculpture were displayed in the imposing halls of the ground floor, while the paintings were exhibited in the rooms upstairs. The valuable collection of prints and drawings was separately displayed.

This splendid new institution, to be known as the Museum of Fine Arts, was formally opened to the public in 1906. During the years which have passed since its inauguration, the Museum has seen tremendous developments which have made it one of the most significant art collections in Europe. Quite apart from the acquisitions, the collection has greatly increased in size and value as a result of bequests and donations. One of the most important was from Count János Pálffy, who in 1912 left the gallery 121 valuable old masters and added 56 works to the Department of Modern Art. It is to the Pálffy bequest that the Museum owes, among other works, Titian's fine *Doge Marcantonio Trevisani*, Boltraffio's *Lodi Madonna*, Veronese's distinguished *Portrait of a Man*, Petrus Christus' *Virgin and Child* and numerous paintings of the seventeenth-century Dutch School.

With the acquisition of the collection of the German archaeologist Paul Arndt in 1908 and 1913, the Department of Classical Antiquities became firmly established. In 1914 the collection of sculpture, established by Károly Pulszky's purchases towards the end of the nineteenth century, was considerably increased when the Museum purchased the bronze sculptures collected during the first decades of the nineteenth century, mainly in Italy, by the Hungarian Neoclassical sculptor, István Ferenczy; the value of this collection will be appreciated from the fact that it included the world-famous bronze horseman, attributed to Leonardo, which is now one of the treasures of the Museum of Fine Arts.

In spite of ever graver financial difficulties experienced in the period between the two world wars, the Museum continued to make valuable acquisitions, though by no means so many as formerly, and during these years it received a number of important gifts. Marcell Nemes, a famous collector living in Munich, presented the *Portrait of Ferenc Rákóczi II, Reigning Prince of Transylvania* by Ádám Mányoki, a picture of considerable national significance, as well as *Mary Magdalene*, an early work by El Greco. Jenő Boross, a Hungarian who had settled in America, donated a masterpiece by Jacopo Bassano, *Christ Carrying the Cross*, as well some other remarkable Italian paintings.

Another important donation was received in the 'thirties from Pál Majovszky whose Budapest collection included a number of supremely beautiful French graphic works, among them drawings by Manet, Renoir and Degas, and especially Delacroix' watercolour, *Horse Frightened by Lightning*. The Department of Sculpture was also enlarged during this period by the acquisition of some outstanding statues (for instance, a *Madonna* from the workshop of Tilman Riemenschneider) and the Hungarian collection was similarly strengthened, developing rapidly into a comprehensive exposition of the development of Hungarian painting and sculpture during the nineteenth and twentieth centuries.

The Second World War was, of course, calamitous for the Museum, for the building received a direct hit from a bomb, and the glass roof was totally destroyed. The contents of the Museum were safely preserved for a while, but in the last phase of the war the most significant works were hastily loaded in waggons and taken to Germany. It was not until several years after the end of the war that it became possible to retrieve them, with the exception of a number of small paintings.

The period immediately after the war was spent in repairing and rebuilding the Museum, so that it was only in the late nineteen-forties, when the works of art stored in Germany had been returned, that the Museum was able to resume its normal activities.

There followed a period of rapid expansion when whole collections of considerable value and parts of others were taken over by the Museum. Thus, in 1951, a number of precious paintings were transferred to the Museum with the Ráth collection, which had previously been treated as a separate foundation. The greater part of the collection had been bought by György Ráth from dealers in Paris and Vienna during the second half of the nineteenth century, and it included a number of outstanding works, among them Rembrandt's *The Slaughtered Ox*, the *Portrait of a Girl* by Sebastiano del Piombo and Dirck Hals' brilliant little garden scene, *A Merry Party*. Over a hundred more pictures, including a triptych by Taddeo di Bartolo and Moroni's portrait of Jacopo Foscarini, were added when the Zichy collection was taken over from the city of Budapest. Built up in Vienna in the nineteenth century by Count Ödön Zichy and left to the capital by one of his descendants, this collection was especially important because it contained a fine selection of Baroque paintings – particularly seventeenth- and eighteenth-century German and Austrian works – which greatly enriched the one section of the Museum of Fine Arts which, up to then, had been relatively weak.

The collection was also considerably augmented by the transfer of items which were more appropriate to the Museum of Fine Arts than to the other museums or institutions where they had previously been housed. By this means important additions were made to the Egyptian collection, while the Department of Hungarian Art received Hungarian paintings and sculptures dating from between the eleventh and eighteenth centuries. On the other hand, Hungarian works of the nineteenth and twentieth centuries were transferred to the Hungarian National Gallery, established in 1957.

A systematic policy of acquisition has enabled the Museum to increase considerably its collection of antique vases, modern prints and drawings, and early sculpture, and also to make some outstanding additions both to the Gallery of Old Masters and to the Department of Modern Art. New acquisitions of particular note are Zurbarán's masterpiece, *St Andrew*, and five paintings by El Greco: *The Holy Family with St Elizabeth*, *The Disrobing of Christ*, *The Agony in the Garden*, *St Andrew* and *Study of a Man*. Together with many other remarkable works these paintings came from the Herzog collection in Budapest, having been previously owned by Marcell Nemes. The most notable acquisitions in the gallery of French art are *The Rest on the Flight into Egypt*, believed to be an early painting of Poussin, Chardin's *Still-life with Turkey*, Corot's *Woman with Daisies*, Renoir's *Portrait of a Girl*, Monet's *Fishing Boats* and Courbet's large canvas entitled *The Wrestlers*. The collection of eighteenth-century Venetian painting has been greatly enlarged and is now almost fully representative since the acquisition of three paintings by Sebastiano Ricci, Bellotto's *The Kaunitz Palace and Garden in Vienna* and works by Giovanni Domenico Tiepolo, the Guardi brothers and others, while important additions have also been made to the eighteenth-century German and Austrian paintings.

Well-chosen acquisitions have thus successfully closed gaps in the collection which is now almost fully representative in every department. During more than a hundred-and-fifty years of its existence, the Budapest Museum of Fine Arts has become one of the most important collections in central Europe: a collection which includes a series of masterpieces clearly illustrating the development of European art.

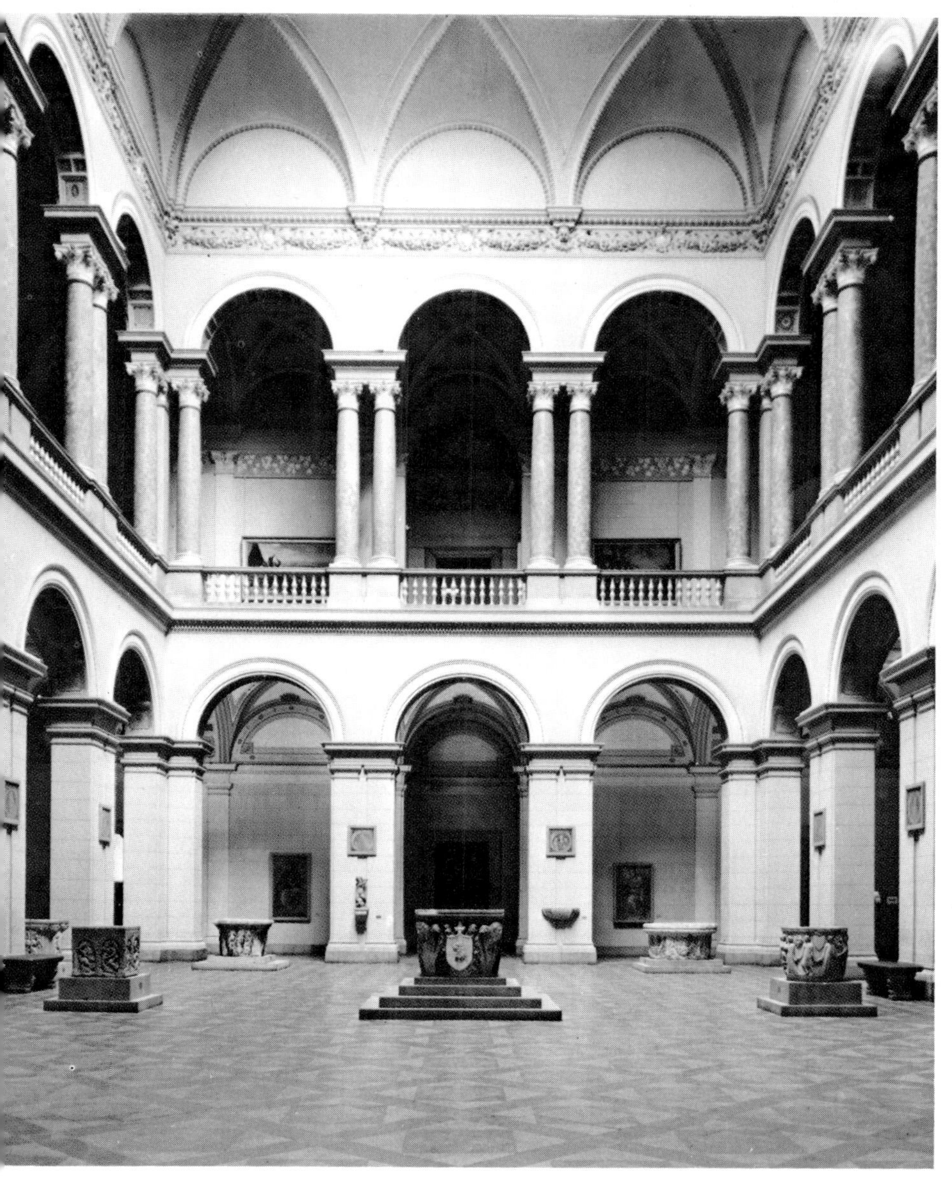

The Renaissance Hall, situated on the ground floor, holds a collection of Italian wells and frescoes of the period

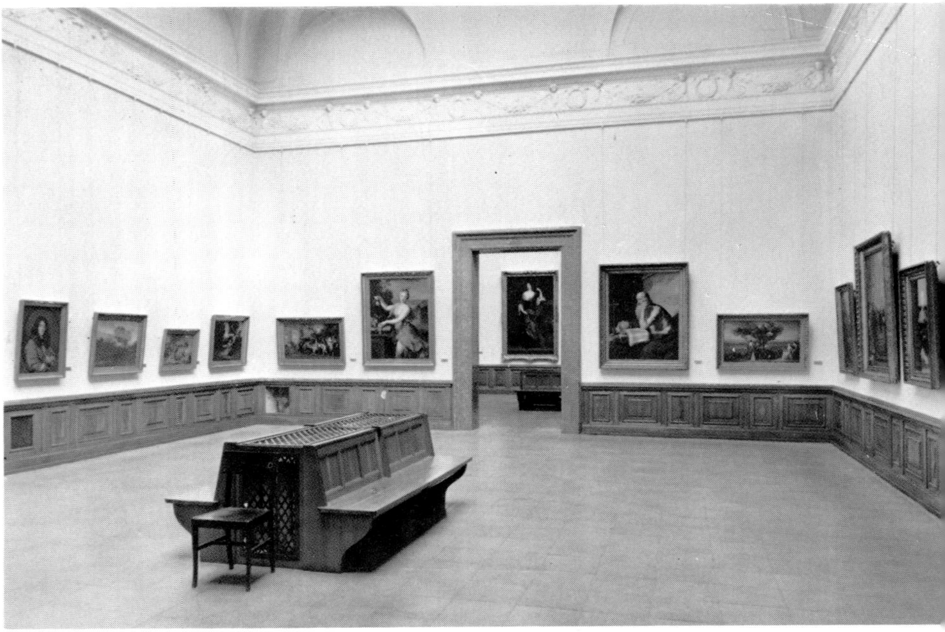

An upper-floor hall of the Gallery of Old Masters

A ground-floor hall showing part of the Greek collection

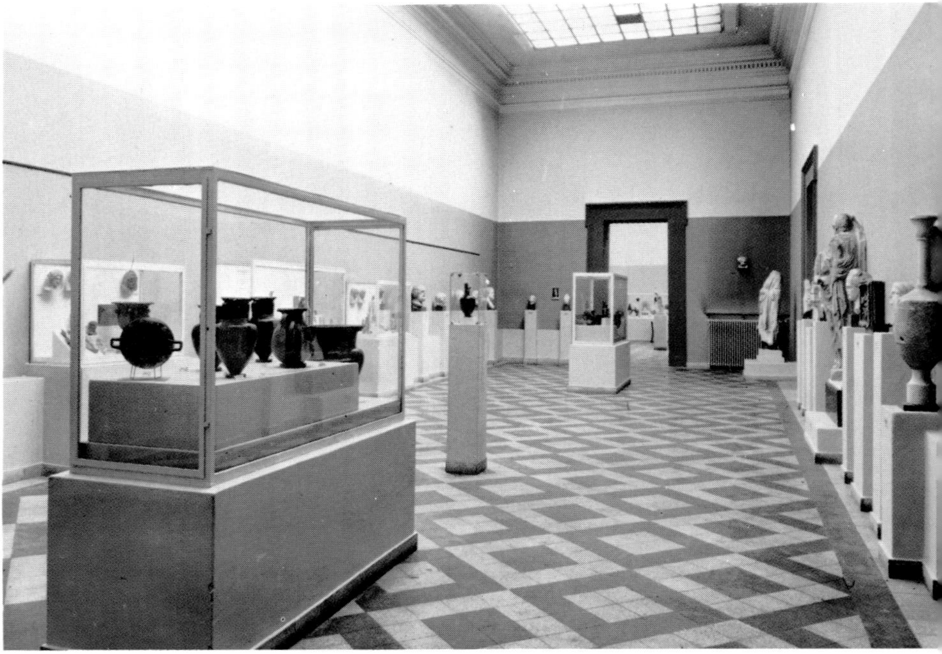

THE COLLECTIONS

The tripartite Neoclassical façade of the huge building of the Museum of Fine Arts overlooks Hősök tere (Heroes' Square). A wide flight of steps leads to the impressive portico, the pediment of which is decorated with a copy of the group on the pediment of the Temple of Zeus at Olympia. On the ground floor are several vast galleries, designed in imitation of earlier styles, which, when the Museum was first opened, contained plaster copies of famous sculptures of antiquity, the Middle Ages and the Renaissance; in recent decades, however, these have gradually been replaced by original works. Also on the ground floor is the Egyptian collection where we find items connected with the cult of the dead, mummies and grave-stelae, jewellery and objects of everyday use, and also some valuable sculptures such as a limestone head of a man dating from 1300 BC and a bronze cat of 1000 BC. This gallery gives a comprehensive picture of Egyptian art and culture from the Old Kingdom up to the Roman conquest.

The Graeco-Roman collection extends over four large rooms of the ground floor and, although this department of the Museum has been developed more recently than the others, it presents a vivid and interesting exposition of the history of the arts in the pre-Christian era. The collection of Bronze Age and Early Iron Age vases from Cyprus is particularly remarkable and so are some of the Greek sculptures, for instance the monumental marble sepulchre with three figures and the famous statue known as the Budapest Dancer; there is a rich series of tanagra figurines and also some splendid Black- and Red-figure Greek vases, the famous Grimani jug, which is one of the most outstanding Greek bronzes of the fifth century BC, and some excellent Roman copies of original Greek sculpture.

Selected examples of the different periods of Hungarian art are also exhibited on the ground floor: medieval sculptures, in both stone and wood, Gothic polyptychs, Renaissance and Baroque paintings, the *Visitation* by the Master MS (a picture of idyllic beauty), the statue of St Dorothy from Barka, Ádám Mányoki's portraits and Jakab Bogdány's still-lifes. In the future these works will be added to the collection in the Hungarian National Gallery and transferred to Buda Castle, where there will be a comprehensive exhibition of the history of art in Hungary.

Also on the ground floor we find a collection of European sculpture from the beginning of the nineteenth century to the present day, but while there are splendid examples of individual schools and periods, the collection is unfortunately not completely representative. Early nineteenth-century Neoclassicism is exemplified by the Danish sculptor, Bertel Thorwaldsen, Romanticism by a number of lesser-known Germans and Austrians and the Russian Paul Trubetskoi. The more interesting and valuable exhibits are, though, French. There are works by Jean-Baptiste Carpeaux and Jules Bastien-Lepage, but the most important works are by the greatest sculptor of the nineteenth century, Auguste Rodin: the Museum of Fine Arts is the proud owner of no fewer than six of his sculptures, among them such masterpieces as *Eternal Spring*, *The Golden Age*, *The Kiss* and *The Sculptor Falguière*. As there are also three small bronzes by Aristide Maillol, the *Portrait of a Woman* by Charles Despiau and a modern composition by André Bloc, the collection illustrates the development of French sculpture to the present day. The Museum also contains some splendid examples of the work of the Belgian Constantin Meunier who, during the latter half of the nineteenth century, became famous for creations based on the theme of work and the working man. In the section devoted to twentieth-century sculpture particular attention should be given to the work of the Jugoslav Ivan Meštrović, the German Fritz Cremer, the Italian Medardo Rosso, the Belgian George Minne and the Russian Manyizer, each represented by a single example. The department of contemporary sculpture, and also the collection of medals, are being continually enlarged as a result of acquisitions.

In the ground-floor gallery of graphic art there are each year three or four temporary exhibitions of items from the collection of Prints and Drawings, which, comprising 10,000 drawings and 100,000 prints, is certainly one of the most important in Europe. The basis of the collection was a selection of works which came to the Museum with the Esterházy collection. At the end of the eighteenth century and the beginning of the nineteenth, Miklós Esterházy managed to acquire some very important collections of drawings, for example, the Poggi collection from Paris and the Nowohratsky-Kolowrat collection from Prague, and thus became the owner of priceless drawings by Leonardo, Raphael and Rembrandt. But the drawings from the Esterházy collection provided only a nucleus which was continually added to as a result of purchases, donations and bequests. István Delhaes, a Hungarian painter who worked in Vienna, left a number of seventeenth- and eighteenth-century drawings and prints to the museum, while Pál Majovszky's bequest included a superb array of drawings by the French Impressionists.

The Museum's collection of drawings is particularly rich in Italian Renaissance works, including drawings by Raphael,

Veronese, Tintoretto, Correggio and Leonardo da Vinci, and there is also a selection of works by almost all the important Flemish and Dutch masters of the sixteenth and seventeenth centuries, including fifteen Rembrandts. There are outstanding examples by Dürer and Altdorfer among the German artists and some notable French works by Poussin, Watteau and Fragonard, besides Delacroix's watercolour *Horse Frightened by Lightning* and a number of masterpieces by Manet, Renoir, Picasso and Degas. The print collection serves to illustrate almost every stage in the development in Europe of the techniques of woodcut, engraving, etching, mezzotint and lithography, and includes series of works by Dürer, Lucas van Leyden, Rembrandt and Goya.

The Gallery of Old Masters is housed on the upper floors where about 600 works out of more than 2,000 owned by the Museum are permanently on view. These magnificent examples of European painting between the thirteenth and eighteenth centuries are, of course, the most valuable items in the Museum's collection.

In the Italian section nearly every school and practically every significant trend and master of Italian painting from the fourteenth century to the School of Venice in the eighteenth century is represented. The pictures are arranged chronologically and, where possible, grouped according to the region of origin (though this was not always possible with the cabinets in which the smaller works are displayed). The first exhibits are panel paintings by thirteenth-century Tuscan masters, followed by Florentine works of the fourteenth and early fifteenth centuries, which include Madonnas by Ambrogio Lorenzetti and Jacopo di Cione, *The Coronation of the Virgin* by Giotto's pupil, Maso di Banco, a huge altar-piece by Giovanni dal Ponte depicting *The Mystic Marriage of St Catherine*, and a section of a wing from

Spinello Aretino's polyptych from Monteoliveto; pictures by Giovanni di Paolo, Sano di Pietro and Sassetta, and some *biccherna* panels (painted covers of account books) give some idea of the lyrical approach of the Sienese masters. The Florentine School, perhaps the most significant of the fifteenth century, is represented by Domenico Ghirlandaio's brilliantly coloured *St Stephen*, an enchanting *St John the Baptist* from Botticelli's workshop and the *Virgin and Child Enthroned with Saints* from Verrocchio's workshop. Piero di Cosimo, the Umbrian Giovanni Boccati, Luca Signorelli and Giovanni Santi are also represented. Two exquisite pictures of music-making figures from the Ferrara School, *Ceres Enthroned* by Michele Pannonio, *Venus* by the Bolognese Lorenzo Costa and a *Crucifixion* by Francesco Francia demonstrate the immensely varied qualities and themes of other fifteenth-century Italian Schools.

A succession of masterpieces illustrates Venetian painting of the Quattrocento and Cinquecento. Several versions of the *Virgin and Child Enthroned* by Paolo da Venezia, Michele Giambono, Antonio Vivarini and Carlo Crivelli are followed by a sequence of outstanding Renaissance portraits, which begins with Gentile Bellini's famous *Caterina Cornaro*, and encompasses Giorgione's *Portrait of a Man*, Titian's *Doge Marcantonio Trevisani* and portraits of unknown sitters by Paolo Veronese and Sebastiano del Piombo.

It can truly be said that the Italian Renaissance is worthily represented in the Museum of Fine Arts, for, besides the Venetian works already mentioned, the collection includes a portrait of Pietro Bembo and the *Esterházy Madonna* by Raphael, a *Virgin and Child* thought to be the joint work of Leonardo and his pupil Giovanni Antonio Boltraffio, and works by Correggio, Palma Vecchio, Tintoretto, Jacopo Bassano and others: some of the greatest creations of a period so far unsurpassed in the history of art. Other aspects and trends of the time may be studied in the portraits and mythological and historical compositions of the North-Italian masters.

Mannerism, the transitional style bridging the art of the Renaissance and the Baroque, is represented in a gallery devoted mainly to works by the Florentine masters, Angelo Bronzino, Girolamo Macchietti and Battista Naldini, but also containing fine examples of the art of Ferrara and Rome.

As space is limited, there are not so many works of seventeenth-century Italian painting on view. It has been possible to hang only the most outstanding works of the great Baroque masters: Annibale Carracci's *Christ and the Woman of Samaria*, Guercino's *The Scourging of Christ*, the principal work of Furini's early years, *Venus Mourning Adonis*, some monumental compositions by Bernardo Strozzi, the lovely *Sleeping Girl* and *The Blind Leading the Blind* attributed to Domenico Fetti and a painting by Bartolomeo Manfredi.

The huge Baroque gallery also contains splendid eighteenth-century paintings, the most important being a *chef-d'œuvre* of Giovanni Battista Tiepolo, *St James the Greater*, and several large paintings by the Neapolitan Solimena and the Venetians Sebastiano Ricci and Bernardo Bellotto.

Early Netherlandish painting is represented by relatively fewer works, and some of the greatest names are missing; but Petrus Christus' *Virgin and Child*, Gerard David's youthful masterpiece, *The Nativity*, an old copy of Jan van Eyck's lost panel, *The Road to Calvary*, or Hans Memling's small triptych all give some idea of the superb craftsmanship and the perfect representation of nature found in this school. There is, however, a much wider selection of sixteenth-century painting which includes Barend van Orley's portrait of Emperor Charles V, *St John the Baptist Preaching* by Pieter Bruegel the Elder and works by Pieter Aertsen, Jan van Hemessen, Jacob Grimmer and others.

Dutch and Flemish paintings of the seventeenth century are displayed in four large galleries and nine cabinets. Here even the greatest of the Dutch masters are represented by several masterpieces. There are two excellent portraits by Frans Hals, and works by Rembrandt include *The Old Rabbi*, a beautiful and noble painting in greyish-brown tones, his dramatic composition *The Dream of St Joseph*, *The Slaughtered Ox*, and also a picture he painted with his pupil Gerard Dou, *The Parable of the Hidden Treasure*. Rembrandt's pupils and followers are also well represented and there are characteristic works by Nicolas Maes, Gerbrandt van den Eeckhout and Aert de Gelder among others. The Museum also has a very large number of works by minor Dutch masters – portraits, landscapes, genre-paintings and still-lifes – of which only a few carefully selected examples can be permanently displayed. But when we consider that it is possible to see works by such masters as Salamon and Jacob van Ruisdael, Jan van Goyen, Aert van der Neer, Pieter de Hooch, Adriaen van Ostade, Jan Steen, Paulus Potter, Meindert Hobbema and Jan van Huysum, it will be realized that visitors to the Museum can study every aspect of Dutch art and almost every important artist of the Dutch School.

The collection of seventeenth-century Flemish painting is almost as comprehensive, although works by Rubens are too few to be truly representative of his art; the *Study of a Man's Head* and *Portrait of a Man* do not adequately illustrate his gift for portraiture, and the history painting *Mucius Scaevola before Porsenna*, painted jointly with Van Dyck, scarcely reveals the buoyancy of his compositions or his expressive range. There are, however, some splendid Van Dycks, *Portrait of a Married Couple* and *St John the Evangelist*, an outstanding group of paintings by Jordaens and an interesting selection of seventeenth-century Flemish landscapes, genre-paintings and still-lifes by, amongst others, Adriaen Brouwer, Jan Siberechts, Jan Wildens, David Teniers the Younger and David Ryckaert.

The seventeenth- and eighteenth-century French paintings form a relatively modest collection. It is true that there are a number of masterpieces – Claude Lorrain, Simon Vouet, Laurent de La Hire and Pierre Mignard are each represented by splendid works and recent additions include *Rest on the Flight into Egypt* by Poussin and a *Still-life with Turkey* by Chardin – but the absence of the great masters of French Rococo severely limits the representation of French painting as a whole.

The collection of German and Austrian painting is particularly rich. Thanks to the acquisitions made during the last few decades, works from every significant school and style between the fifteenth and the late eighteenth centuries are now on view in four spacious rooms. The most important of the early panel paintings and fragments of polyptychs is the large panel by Hans Holbein the Elder depicting the death of the Virgin, and there are a number of significant works by the greatest masters of the Renaissance in Germany – Dürer's *Portrait of a Man*, Hans Baldung Grien's *Adam* and *Eve*, three pictures by Albrecht Altdorfer and eight by Lucas Cranach – which give a comprehensive picture of the golden age of German painting in the sixteenth century. Greater interest in seventeenth-century German art in recent years has led to increased research and to acquisitions of works by Johann Heinrich Schönfeld, Nicolaus Knüpfer and Christoph Paudiss. Even richer and more complete is the section devoted to eighteenth-century German and Austrian masters: here we find altar-pieces, sketches for ceilings, portraits and landscapes by Paul Troger, Daniel Gran, F. A. Maulbertsch, Angelica Kauffmann and Anton Raphael Mengs.

British painting, which for so long remained apart from the European mainstream but which developed rapidly from the eighteenth century onwards, can be studied in few European museums outside the British Isles. For this reason the collection in the Budapest museum is especially important, for it includes excellent examples of the most famous British artists of the eighteenth century. It is possible to trace the development of the British portrait painting from Lely and Kneller onwards, through the works of Hogarth, Gainsborough, Reynolds, Hoppner, Raeburn, Lawrence and Opie.

The most significant section of the Gallery of Old Masters is the justly famous Spanish collection. This comprises about eighty works, most of which were originally in the Esterházy collection, and illustrates the development of Spanish painting from the fifteenth century up to the beginning of the nineteenth. Primitive masters are represented as well as the great painters of the golden age, and a particularly interesting feature is that it includes not only masterpieces by Velázquez, Murillo, Ribera, Zurbarán and Goya but also remarkable works by artists little known outside Spain, such Luis Tristán, Vicente Carducho, Pedro Orrente, Francisco de Herrera, Mateo Cerezo and others. Because of this wide range, the Budapest gallery contains one of the richest collections of Spanish painting in the world, perhaps second only to the Prado in Madrid. There are seven El Grecos, from the early painting of *Mary Magdalene* up to the expressive vision of *The Agony in the Garden*. Velázquez is represented by an early genre-painting, *Peasants at Table* and the work of Ribera, who painted in Naples, can be studied in his beautiful *Martyrdom of St Andrew*. Three remarkable works by another outstanding Spanish painter of the seventeenth century, Zurbarán, can also be seen: the dramatic *St Andrew*, as well as the gentle and intimate *Holy Family* and *The Immaculate Conception* which date from his last years. Among the pictures by Murillo, *The Infant Jesus Distributing Bread to Pilgrims* is especially significant, while Goya's *Water Seller* and his portrait of Señora Bermúdez rank among his most important works.

On the first floor, next to the Gallery of Old Masters can be found the Department of Modern Art. This collection is as yet neither so splendid nor so comprehensive as its neighbour and is particularly deficient in the field of contemporary art, but it is an attractive collection which includes numerous good examples of the art of individual artists and schools. There is, for example, a good selection of Austrian Biedermeier and German nineteenth-century painting which includes numerous portraits, landscapes and genre-paintings and one characteristic work each by Ferdinand Georg Waldmüller, Franz Eybl, Friedrich von Amerling, Adolf Menzel, Wilhelm Leibl and Arnold Böcklin. The collection of nineteenth-century French painting is particularly fine. Romanticism is represented by an animated composition by Delacroix, *A Moroccan and His Horse*, and a small painting of a dancer by Theodore Chassériau. There are two landscapes of the Barbizon School, by Charles-François Daubigny and Narcisse Diaz, a figure painting of singular beauty, *Woman with Daisies*, by Corot, while Courbet, the great master of French Realism, is represented by some fine landscapes and by his masterpiece, *The Wrestlers*, of 1853. Jean-François Millet, Théodule Ribot and Eugène Carrière represent the period of transition before the emergence of Impressionism. The Budapest museum contains some outstanding works by the French Impressionists, for instance Manet's picture *Lady with Fan* (depicting Baudelaire's mistress, Jeanne Duval), Pissarro's *Pont-Neuf*, Monet's *Fishing Boats* and *The Harbour at Trouville*, an early landscape by Gauguin, and a later work, *Black Pigs*, dating from the Tahiti period. Renoir's *Portrait of a Girl*,

Toulouse-Lautrec's fresh and witty picture *Ces Dames*, Cézanne's *The Sideboard* and several pictures by Bonnard and Utrillo complete the section devoted to French paintings. Unfortunately, there is only a random selection of nineteenth- and twentieth-century works from other countries, giving merely a fragmentary idea of their painting, and these are the most incomplete sections of the Museum, where acquisitions are most needed.

On the mezzanine between the first and second storeys and in the second floor galleries is the Sculpture Gallery, which contains European sculpture dating from the thirteenth to the eighteenth centuries. In recent years the department has been considerably expanded and in particular the collection now provides a comprehensive survey of the development of Italian, German and Austrian sculpture of various periods. One of the most important early works in the collection was acquired only recently – a wooden crucifix, monumental in its very simplicity, which is the work of a thirteenth-century Spoleto master. Notable fourteenth- and fifteenth-century works include a statuette of the Madonna by Andrea Pisano, the *Archangel Gabriel* by Agostino di Duccio and works by Neroccio and Francesco di Giorgio. Pieces by Luca della Robbia, Desiderio da Settignano, Benedetto da Maiano and Antonio Rossellino represent the Florentine Renaissance, but even more important than these are the *Putto with Dolphin* from Verrocchio's workshop and the recently discovered *Pietà* by Verrocchio himself. The pride of the collection, however, is the small but well-known bronze rider, widely believed to be the work of Leonardo da Vinci. The schools of Padua and of Venice are represented by The *Rape of Europa*, a small and very beautiful bronze by Andrea Riccio, a monumental *Madonna* by Jacopo Sansovino and fire-dogs by Tiziano Aspetti.

Nearly every trend of German sculpture from the fourteenth to the eighteenth centuries – the Rhenish, Austrian, Swabian and Frankish Schools – are represented by some significant work. Three of the most important sculptures in this group are: a fine *Madonna* from Riemenschneider's workshop, a *Virgin and Child* from Multscher's workshop and a monumental *St John the Evangelist* by a master of Cologne. Other works of considerable value acquired during the last few decades are *St James the Apostle* and *St Barbara* and *St Catherine*, and some characteristic sculptures of the medieval Spanish, French and Netherlandish Schools.

The galleries on the mezzanine are devoted to Baroque sculpture of the seventeenth and eighteenth centuries. Here we find works by Italian and French masters, *Hercules with the Hydra* by Alessandro Algardi, one of the leading masters of the School of Rome, Jean-Baptiste Pigalle's *Amor*, and other works. Some of the most important German and Austrian Baroque works are the *Elisabeth* by Meinhard Guggenbichler, two remarkable lead reliefs by Georg Rafael Donner, who worked in Vienna and Pozsony (Bratislava), and a bust of Márton György Kovachich by Franz Xaver Messerschmidt.

ORGANIZATION AND PUBLICATIONS

The Museum of Fine Arts comprises seven major departments – the Department of Egyptian Art, the Graeco-Roman Department, the Gallery of Old Masters, the Department of Hungarian Art, the Sculpture Gallery, the Department of Prints and Drawings and the Department of Modern Art – besides which there are restoration and reference departments and a library. The most important works are always on view at the permanent exhibition. The remainder of the collection is in storage where part of the paintings, hung on screens, and the sculptures, placed on shelves, are readily accessible to both experts and students. In addition the Museum, from its own resources or with the help of other collections in Budapest, regularly mounts temporary exhibitions of paintings, prints and drawings, to illustrate some chosen theme, the subject of a monograph or the work of a particular school, or to celebrate some anniversary, as well as arranging temporary exchanges of treasures with foreign museums.

The task of classification and cataloguing goes steadily ahead (the collections contain no fewer than 110,000 items). Andor Pigler's two-volume catalogue of the Gallery of Old Masters was published in Hungarian in 1954 and in German in 1967, and there is also a single volume on the North-Italian drawings. Catalogues covering the fifteenth- and sixteenth-century Netherlandish drawings, the collection of Greek vases and the Sculpture Gallery are in preparation. Separate volumes are published on each section of the permanent collection of paintings, many of which are available in English, French, German and Russian, as well as Hungarian, and catalogues of the temporary exhibitions are also published regularly, providing much detailed and scholarly information for visitors to the Museum. Albums in several languages containing reproductions of works from the Gallery of Old Masters and the Department of Prints and Drawings are also available.

Lectures and conducted tours of the various collections are organized in order to attract more visitors to the Museum, and already the number of visitors has risen to nearly 400,000 a year and continues to increase. Except on Mondays, the Museum is open daily from 10 a.m. to 6 p.m., but when some particular exhibition is very popular these hours are extended.

THE PLATES

MASO DI BANCO Florentine, active 1320–53
The Coronation of the Virgin
Panel 20 1/8″ × 20 3/8″ (51.2 × 51.7 cm.) Inv. No. 7793

Formerly ascribed to Giotto but, as a result of recent research, now attributed to Maso di Banco, one of his most gifted pupils. This panel, with others now at Chantilly and in Berlin which also represent scenes from the life of the Virgin, is thought to have decorated the side of a reliquary and to date from the second quarter of the fourteenth century. As in his frescoes (for example, the *Coronation of the Virgin* in the church of Santa Croce in Florence), Maso di Banco makes use of the pictorial principles and structural solutions found in the work of his master: this indebtedness is apparent in the tiered construction of the throne and the spatial arrangement of the semicircle of figures, seen either in profile or from the back. However, the lyrical approach, loose grouping and especially the vigorous and pure colour are peculiar to Maso di Banco himself. The firm outlines and the monumental effect of solid areas of colour without any shadows convey to perfection the solemnity of the event. The pose of the two principal figures, enclosed in a severe central block, and the movement with which Christ bestows the crown on Mary convey the great achievement of Giotto and the early Tuscan painters in depicting human emotions and activities.

This picture was presented to the Museum of Fine Arts by Lord Rothermere in 1940 and was formerly in the British collections of W. Fuller Maitland and W.Y. Ottley.

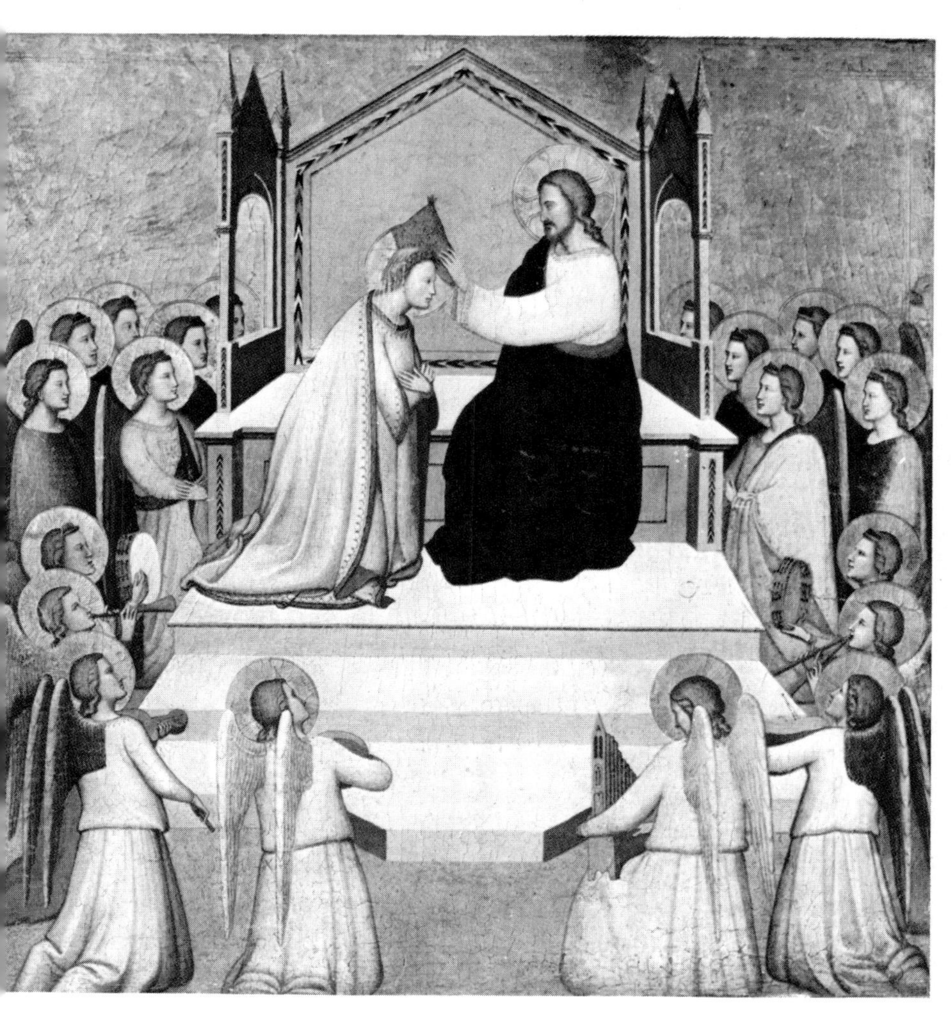

TADDEO DI BARTOLO Sienese, 1362/3–1422

Virgin and Child with St John the Baptist and St Andrew

Triptych. Centre panel 44 7/8″ × 28 3/8″ (114 × 72 cm.) wings, each 41 3/8″ × 17″ (105 × 43 cm.) Inv. No. 53.500

Taddeo of Siena was the pupil of a local master, Bartolo di Fredi, but he was most influenced by the leading Tuscan artists of the time, primarily the Lorenzetti brothers and Simone Martini. Though in his altar-pieces he employed the traditional forms of the fourteenth century, the marked plasticity of his figures, and their vivacity, foreshadow the trends of the fifteenth century.

The central panel of the triptych portrays the *Madonna dell' Umiltà*, a type of representation popular in fourteenth-century Siena. Mary, seated on a brocade carpet, is about to give the breast to her Child, while hovering angels hold a crown above her head. St John the Baptist and St Andrew are depicted in the wing panels, and in the lower part seven more saints can be seen. An inscription on the picture informs us that the altar was commissioned by Signora Datuccia, widow of Andrea de Campigli, to commemorate the dead members of her family: another part of the inscription, now lost, recorded the name of the master: 'Thadeus Bartholi de Senis pinxit hoc Anno Domini 1395'.

Until the beginning of the nineteenth century the triptych remained in its original place in a chapel of the church of S. Francesco, Pisa. In 1859 it was sold at auction in Vienna, as part of the collection of Sámuel Festetics, and was bought by Count Ödön Zichy. It found its way to Budapest with the collection of Count Jenő Zichy.

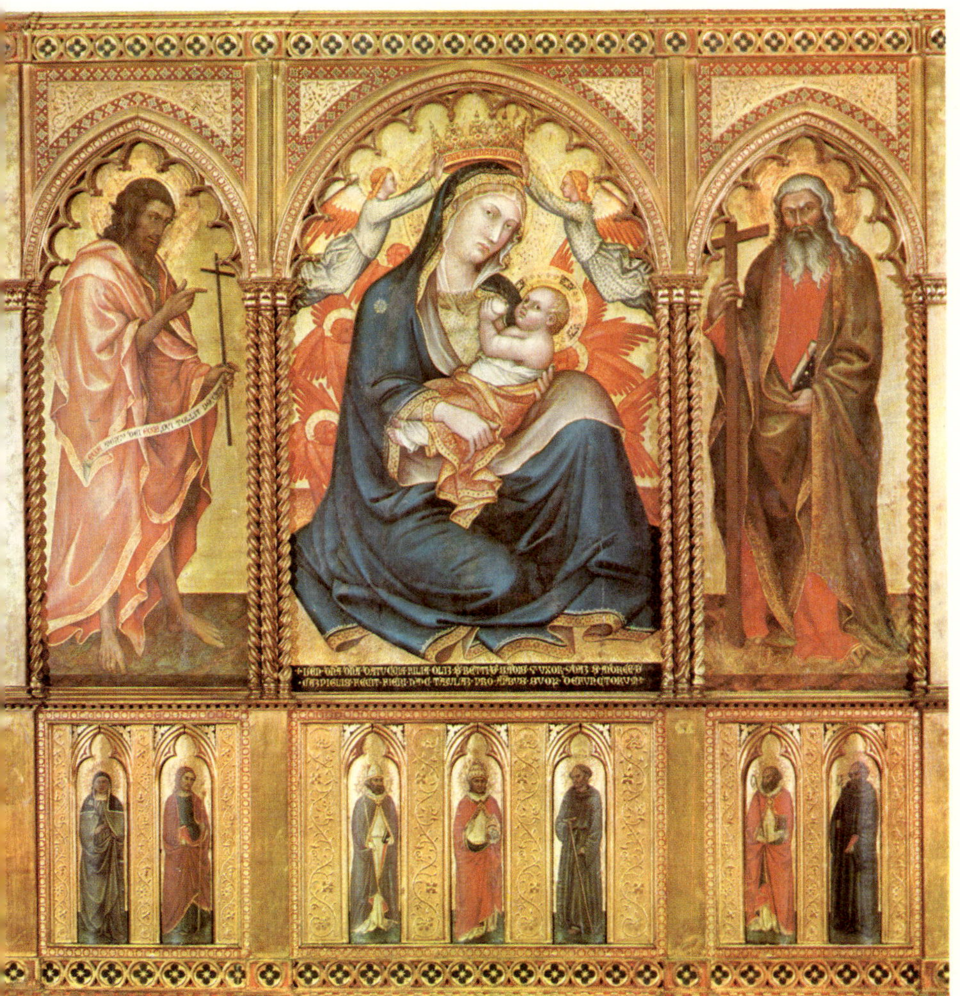

GIOVANNI DAL PONTE (GIOVANNI DI MARCO)
Florentine, 1385–1437
The Mystic Marriage of St Catherine
Panel 57 7/8″ × 66 3/8″ (147 × 168.5 cm.) Inv. No. 1139

Particularly in his late works the Florentine Giovanni dal Ponte applied the lesson he had learned from his masters, Spinello Aretino and Lorenzo Monaco, and successfully combined the pictorial traditions of the late Gothic style with the bolder and more realistic approach of early fifteenth-century art. The large altar-piece in Budapest is one of his major works and, according to the contemporary inscription on the frame, was painted in 1421, to a commission from the master saddler Jacopo di Tommaso. The central picture, which extends to almost the full width of the altar, represents the often-depicted scene of the mystic marriage of Catherine of Alexandria to Jesus; however, unlike popular versions of later date, this picture shows not the infant Jesus but a fully-grown man. Beside the monumental principal figures and the group of angels accompanying them are the kneeling figures of the donors, the saddler and his wife, depicted on a smaller scale as was the custom of the period. In the painting of the donor, seen in sharp profile with folded hands and dressed in a grey hood, there are unmistakable indications of realistic representation and individual characterization. A similar interest in everyday reality and the fascination of incident are revealed in the animated scenes from the legend of the saint on the predella.

We have no data about the original site of the altar-piece. It was acquired for the Museum in Florence in 1894.

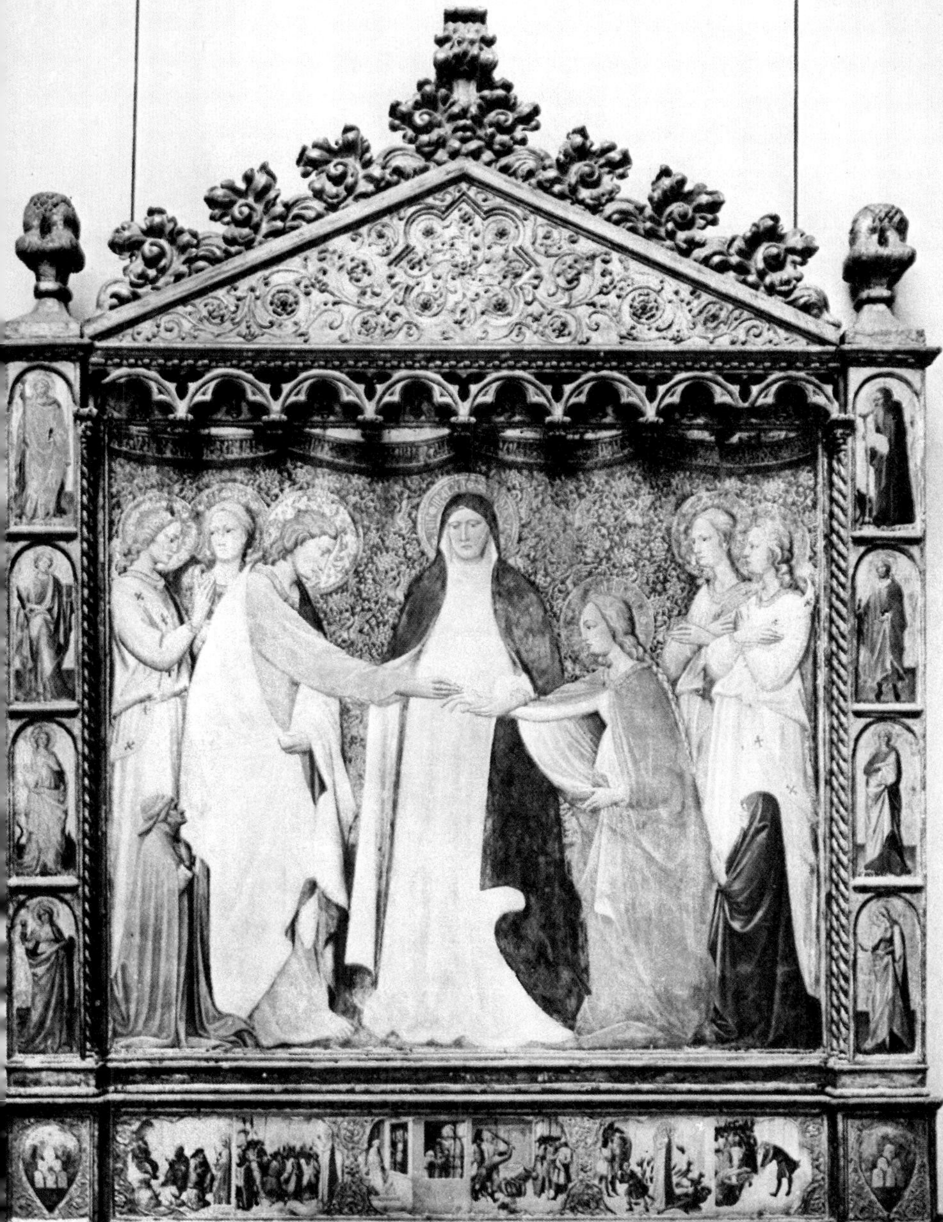

SASSETTA (STEFANO DI GIOVANNI)
Sienese, *c.* 1392–*c.* 1450
St Thomas Aquinas before the Altar of the Virgin
Panel 9 1/4″ × 15 3/8″ (23.6 × 39 cm.) Inv. No. 32

Stefano di Giovanni, known as Sassetta, is perhaps the most popular of fifteenth-century Sienese masters and certainly one of the most attractive. His pictures of the Virgin and the saints are all characterized by a charming grace, his paintings of Biblical stories are freshly observed and rich in narrative detail. He understood and applied the discoveries made by the great Florentine masters of the early fifteenth century, particularly Masolino and Masaccio, especially the new methods of depicting space and nature. But at the same time – and this makes his work especially attractive – he succeeded in preserving the softer lines, the tender expression and the fresh and delicate colouring of the Sienese painters.

This painting, representing with easy spontaneity the interior of a chapel with St Thomas Aquinas kneeling before the altar of the Virgin, was part of the predella of one of Sassetta's masterpieces, the altar of the Arte della Lana. The guild of wool-weavers, the Arte della Lana, of Siena, commissioned this altar in 1423 for their chapel in the church of S. Pellegrino. It remained in its original site from 1426 until the beginning of the nineteenth century when it was divided up and sold. Today, unfortunately, it is known only from fragments which can be seen in different collections all over the world. Other parts of the predella (the lower section of the altar), with scenes from the life of St Thomas, are in the Vatican Gallery in Rome and the Bowes Museum at Barnard Castle.

The Budapest panel was the gift of Arnold Ipolyi, who acquired it from the Ramboux collection in Cologne.

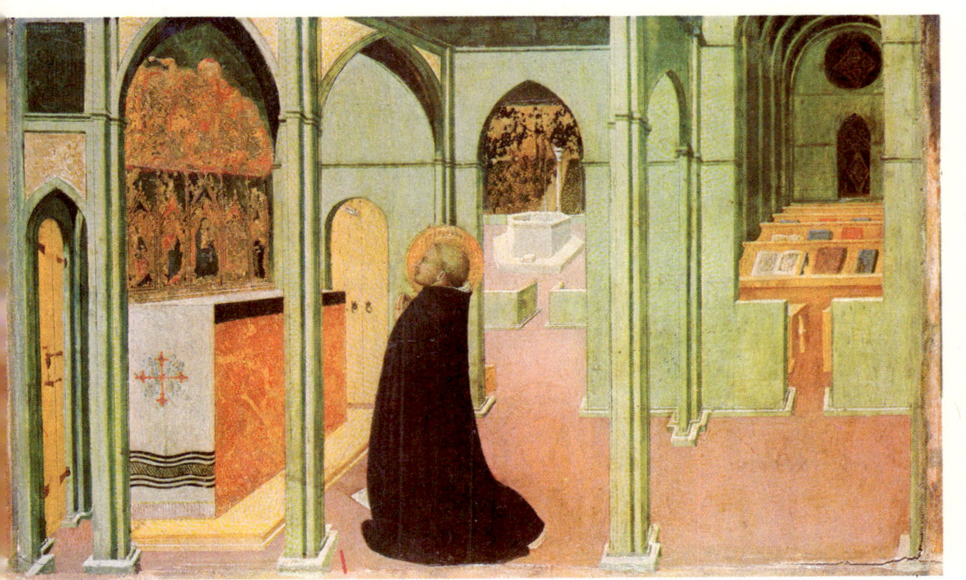

GIOVANNI BOCCATI Umbrian, *c.* 1420–after 1480
Virgin and Child Enthroned with Saints and Angels
Panel 73 3/8″ × 63 3/4″ (186.5 × 162 cm.) Inv. No. 1209

Originating from the Chapel of St Sabinus in Orvieto Cathedral, this altar-piece is one of the most important paintings of the fifteenth-century Umbrian School. From 1445 onwards, Giovanni Boccati worked mainly in Perugia and was influenced partly by the Florentine masters Benozzo Gozzoli and Filippo Lippi but also by Piero della Francesca. He went on to develop a style of his own in which the interpretation is more lyrical and the means of expression more naïve and immediate than those of his masters. His compositions, however, remained traditional, and in many of his paintings we find only slight variations of the arrangement seen in the Budapest picture. The Madonna is seen seated on a gorgeous throne in the centre, with saints and angels, symmetrically arranged on both sides, enclosing the strictly frontal composition like a living wall. In strange contrast to the solemnity of the atmosphere and the dignity and tranquillity of the main figures there is a refreshing naturalness in the details – in the charming and playful movements of the Infant and the two chubby *putti* in the foreground.

This altar-piece, dated 1473, found its way from Orvieto Cathedral to the chapel in the house of the Pietrangeli family. Stripped of its predella it was bought from a Florentine dealer for the Budapest Museum in 1895.

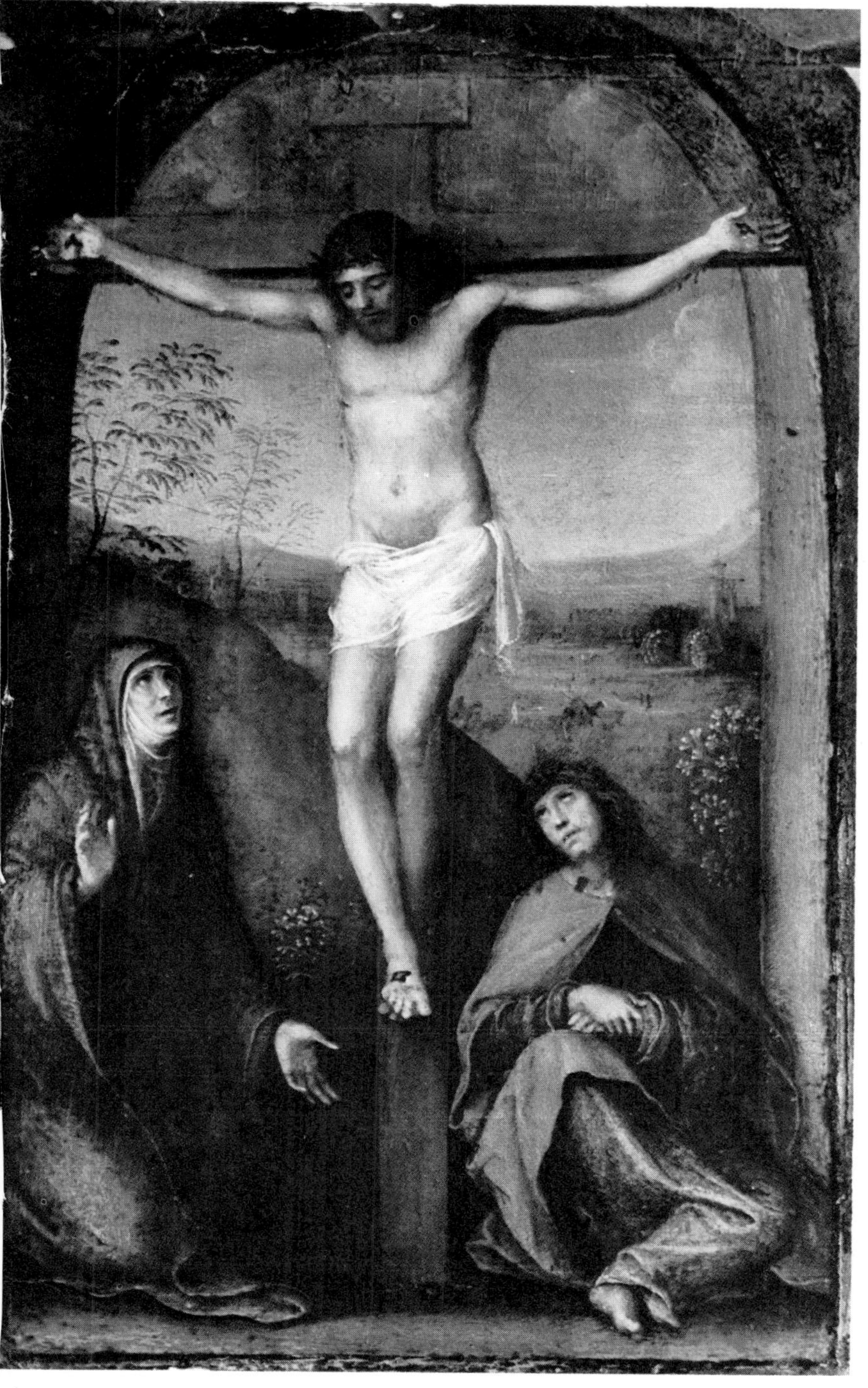

DOMENICO GHIRLANDAIO (DOMENICO DI TOMMASO BIGORDI) Florentine, 1449–94

St Stephen

Panel 75 1/4″ × 22″ (191 × 56 cm.) Inv. No. 4914

Domenico Ghirlandaio belonged to the second great generation of Florentine painters of the fifteenth century. Having studied under Alesso Baldovinetti, he followed in the footsteps of Andrea del Castagno, Paolo Uccello and Andrea del Verrocchio – the pioneers of the Renaissance who discovered the secret of realistic representation of the human body, movement and space – using their discoveries wherever he created his frescoes and altar-pieces. He was one of the most truthful and gifted chroniclers of Florence in the time of the Medicis, the city's golden age, recording in his frescoes of Biblical scenes the life of his native town and the features of his famous contemporaries. He was given commissions by the ruling classes of the city, and it was the banker Giovanni Tornabuoni, a relative of the Medicis, who commissioned for the church of Santa Maria Novella a large polyptych of which the picture of St Stephen now in Budapest once formed a part.

According to Vasari this altar-piece was partly executed by members of the Ghirlandaio workshop after the master's death. He describes the standing figures of saints on the front section of the altar as painted by Ghirlandaio himself, and this attribution is supported by the powerful characterization and sure touch in the plastic forms and in the superb colouring of the picture.

In the early nineteenth century, when the altar came to be divided and sold, the wings depicting St Stephen and St Peter were acquired for the collection of Lucien Bonaparte; the painting of St Stephen passed through a number of French collections and was acquired by the Museum in 1914.

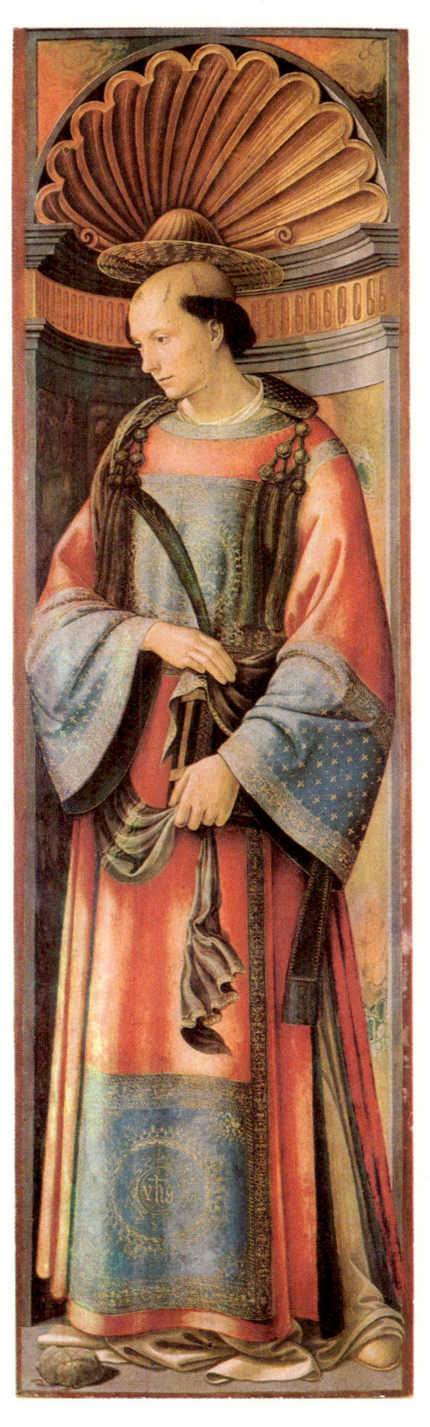

FILIPPINO LIPPI Florentine, 1457–1504
St Anthony of Padua Commends a Friar to the Patronage of the Virgin
Panel 22 1/2″ × 16 3/8″ (57 × 41.5 cm.) Inv. No. 1140

Fra Filippo Lippi, a former Carmelite monk, and his son Filippino, were both important figures in the history of fifteenth-century Florentine painting. While an altar-piece, *The Virgin Enthroned with Saints*, is the only example of the elder Lippi's work in the Budapest Museum (and this is considered to be a workshop picture), his son is represented by this extremely attractive and significant painting. Filippino studied under Botticelli, as well as his father, and developed into an equally outstanding painter of murals and panels. A tempestuous and passionate artist, he conveyed with a singular sensitivity the restless atmosphere and doubting mood of Florence at the end of the fifteenth century. Like most artists of this generation he turned towards the past and evoked, by means of tenderly expressed feelings and a disquieting interplay of lines, the world of late Gothic art. His figures are fragile and gracefully elongated, like the Madonna of this picture, his colours are pale, and the whimsical, vibrating contours reveal inner tension. In this work of lyrical beauty, the gentle quality of the landscape, an important expressive element in his work, serves to strengthen the atmosphere suggested by the theme.

Unfortunately no details are known about the origin of this picture. Károly Pulszky purchased it for the Museum from a Venetian dealer in 1894.

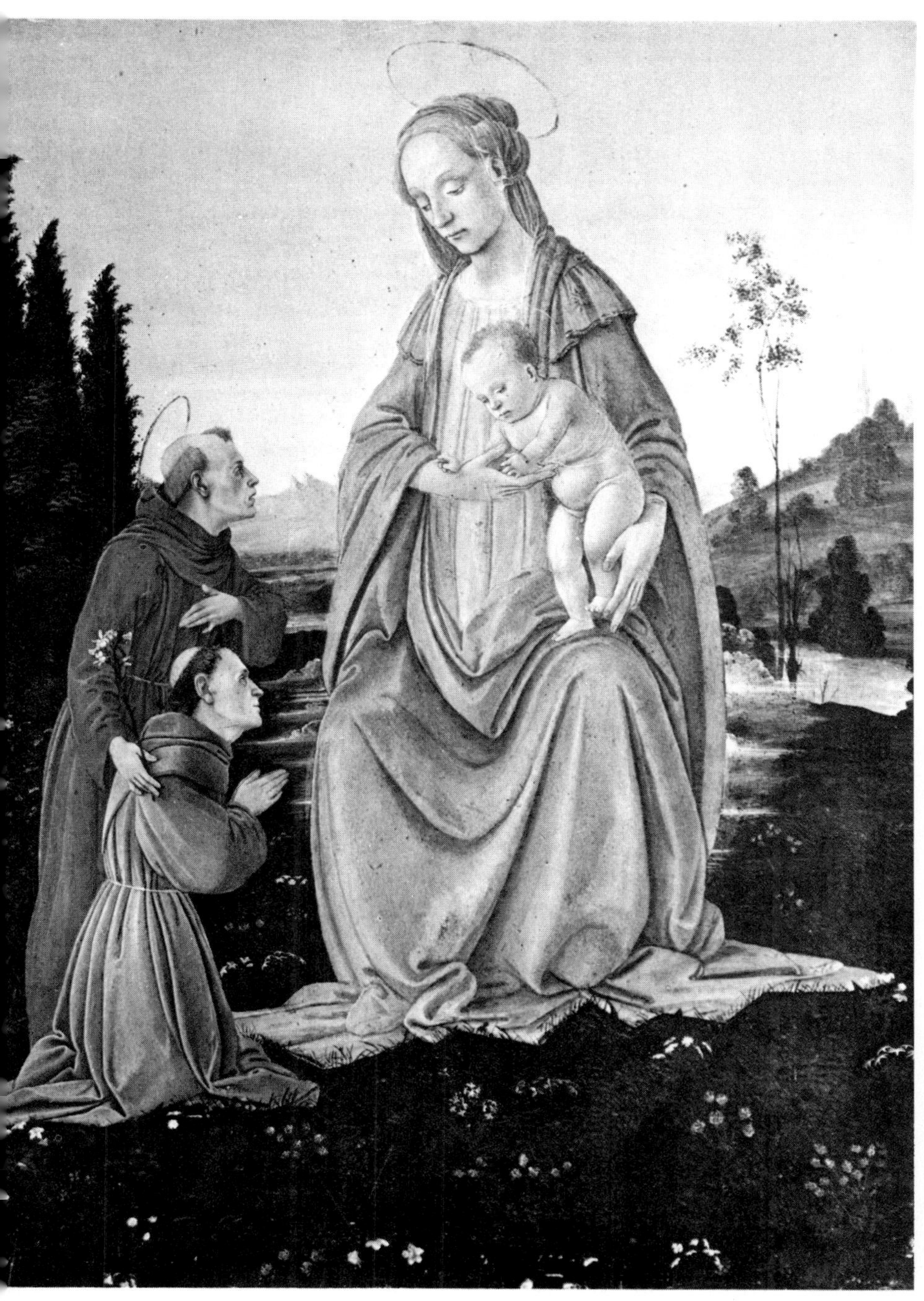

CARLO CRIVELLI Venetian, 1430/5–1493
Virgin and Child Enthroned
Panel 41 7/8" × 21 3/4" (106.5 × 55.3 cm.) Inv. No. 75
Signed on the step of the throne: OPVS CAROLI CRIVELLI VENETI

Crivelli was one of the busiest painters in Venice during the second half of the fifteenth century and was responsible for many altarpieces in small churches in the Veneto and in the Marches. Adapting himself to the conservative taste of his patrons, he painted in an archaic style based on Gothic tradition; his Madonnas are usually frontally posed and seen against a gold background of Byzantine splendour. There is but little movement and few details from nature, the composition being solemn and strictly linear. Only the pure and sure design of the faces and the lavishly applied festoons of flowers and fruits testify to Crivelli's being a master of the fifteenth century, a Renaissance artist with a style of his own.

Virgin and Child Enthroned was formerly the central panel of a polyptych in the church of S. Domenico at Ascoli Piceno and may have been painted around 1476. The representations of saints from the wings were acquired by the National Gallery, London. The Budapest painting was in the Esterházy collection before 1820.

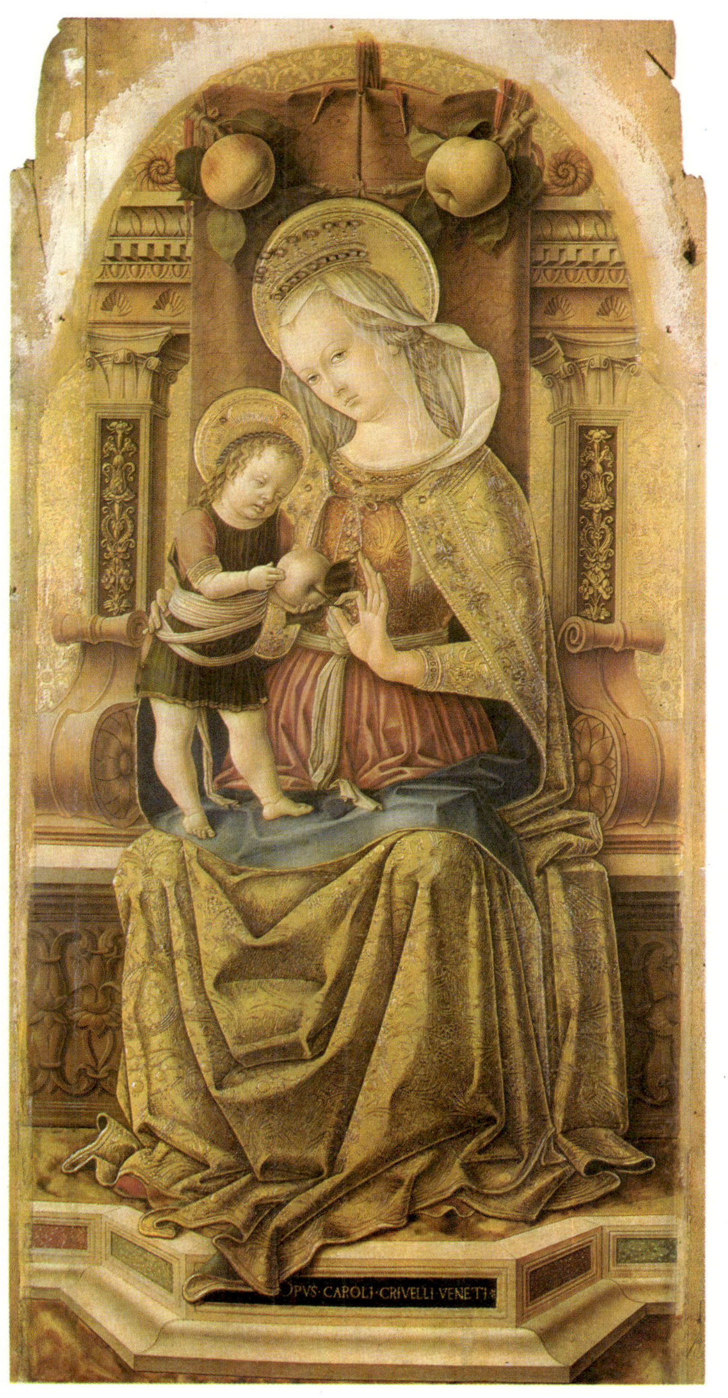
OPVS·CAROLI·CRIVELLI·VENETI

GENTILE BELLINI Venetian, 1429–1507
Caterina Cornaro
Panel 24 3/4″ × 19 1/4″ (63 × 49 cm.) Inv. No. 101
Signed in the inscription at top left

Caterina Cornaro, a Venetian lady of noble birth and widow of the King of Cyprus, abdicated her kingdom in favour of the Republic of Venice in 1489. From that time onwards she lived in seclusion at Asolo, in the neighbourhood of Venice. Gentile Bellini, who followed events in the life of Venice as faithfully as any chronicler, painted a likeness of the ex-Queen on more than one occasion. In his great composition painted in 1500, *The Miracle of the True Cross* (Accademia, Venice), she is seen kneeling on the left, her face in profile and her posture almost the same as in the Budapest picture. In both paintings she is wearing the same dress and it is almost certain that the half-length portrait was painted from the life during that same year. It is one of the most important works by Gentile Bellini and especially notable as an example of an Italian portrait of the fifteenth century – a time when portraiture was just developing in that country.

The painting represents an interesting transitional stage between the fifteenth-century approach and the way of representing the human figure typical of the Renaissance. The artist paid great attention to detail, recording every wrinkle on the face and minutely copying the pattern of the garment. But his intention went beyond the reproduction of life-like details: he tried to summarize the physical realities, creating a work of art which would reveal the character and personality of the sitter. Gentile Bellini's greatest gift, from which comes the strength of his work, was an objective and sober clear-sightedness. This is what made him one of the most sought-after painters of his time; the Signoria of Venice overwhelmed him with official commissions, the Emperor made him a nobleman and he was also greatly favoured by Sultan Mehmet II, whose portrait he painted in Constantinople between 1479 and 1481.

The portrait of Caterina Cornaro came originally from Venice and was part of Archbishop Pyrker's bequest to the Museum in 1836.

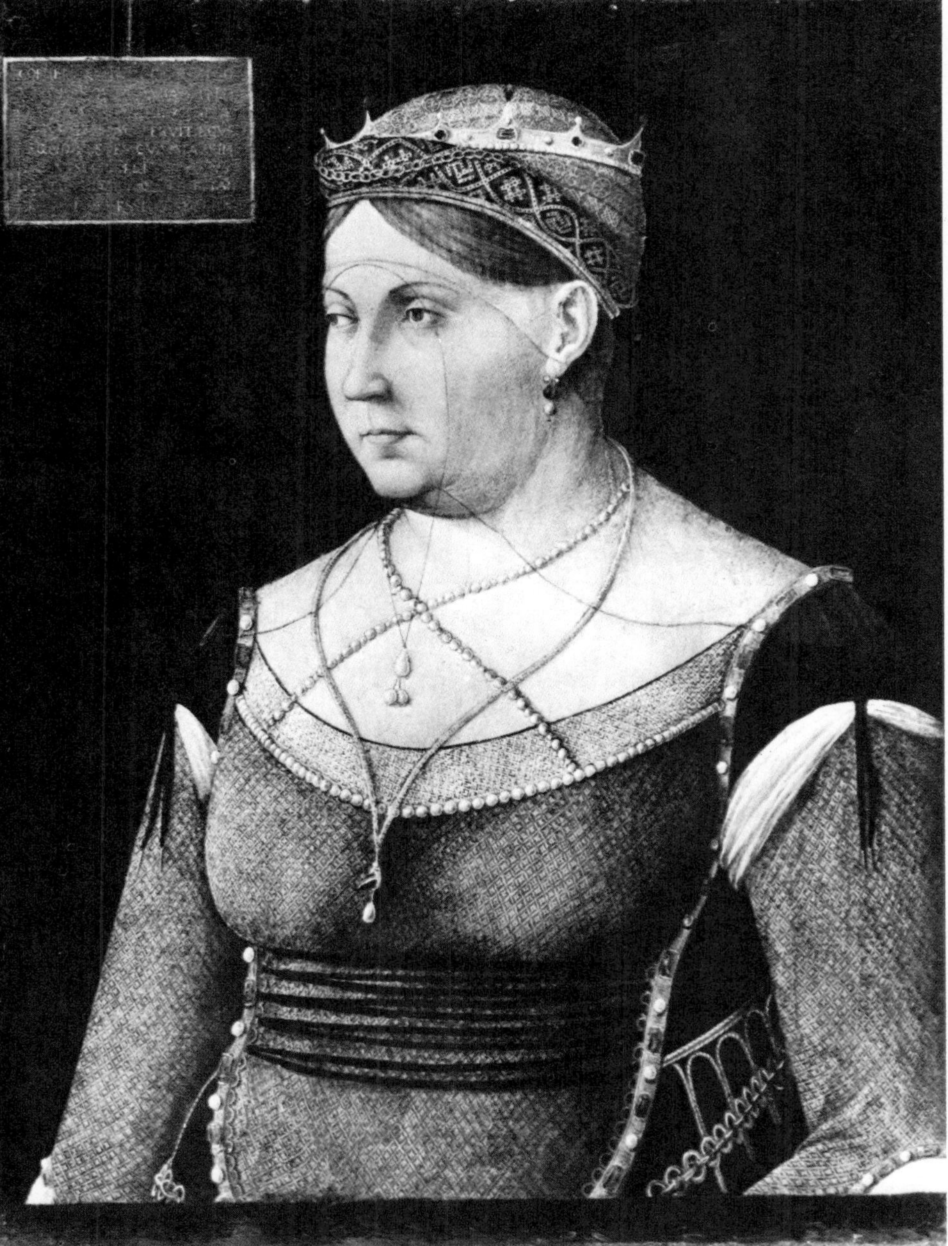

GIOVANNI ANTONIO BOLTRAFFIO Milanese, 1467–1516
The Virgin and Child
Panel 32 $^5/_8$" × 25" (83 × 63.5 cm.) Inv. No. 52

Of all Leonardo's pupils and followers it is Boltraffio whose work is most clearly related to that of the master in style. He is recorded as having worked for some years after 1491 in Leonardo's studio in Milan, and in his own works he often made use of compositions, sketches and drawings by the master – to whom more than one of his pictures has at some time been attributed. At the beginning of the last century the half-length Madonna in the Esterházy collection was so attributed, and it certainly shows an unmistakably close link with Leonardo, the surviving series of whose drawings demonstrate that he was occupied with the idea of a composition in which the infant Jesus stretches out his arms towards flowers in a vase. Nor is it only in the type of picture that the Budapest Madonna is related to Leonardo. The subtlety of the detail, for instance the beauty of Mary's hands, the tender pose of the heads and the accomplished execution of the rich drapery, all provide evidence that the link with Leonardo is more than a matter of inspiration or the borrowing of motifs.

Scholars and art historians now believe that the master himself made some contribution to this work and this belief is supported by the fact that the half-length Madonna is a much finer work than the other painting by Boltraffio in Budapest – the *Lodi Madonna* (p. 249), which was painted after 1508. This, too, follows a Leonardo composition, the *Virgin of the Rocks*, but, with its hard and linear execution and dry handling, has much less affinity with Leonardo's work than the harmonious *Virgin and Child.*

From the Esterházy collection.

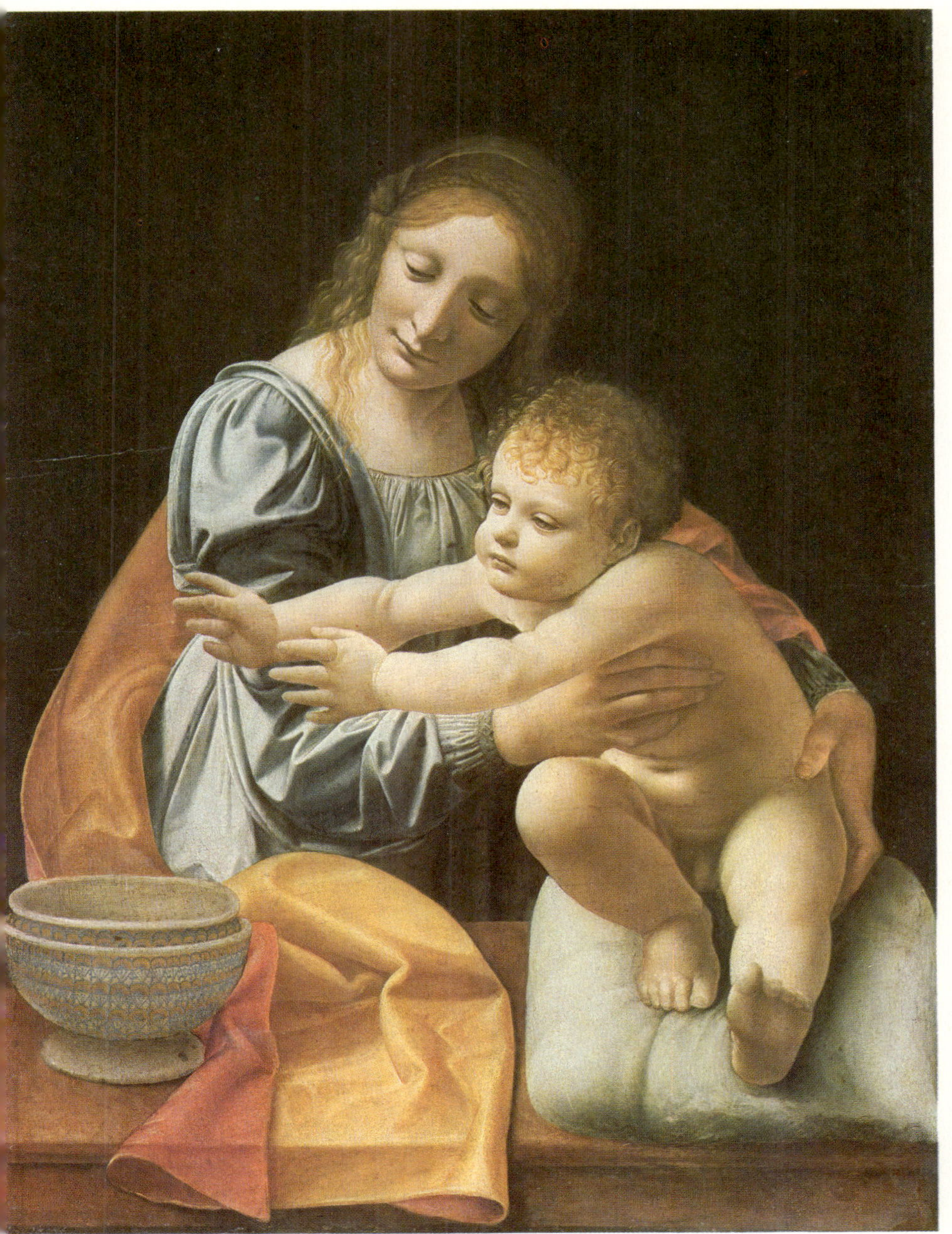

BERNARDINO LUINI Milanese, 1480–1531/2
Virgin and Child with St Catherine and St Barbara
Panel 37″ × 28 3/8″ (94 × 72 cm.) Inv. No. 58

Leonardo worked in Milan for about twenty years and decisively influenced the development of the Lombard School of painting. Apart from Boltraffio, Bernardino Luini, a native of the Lake Maggiore region, was the most significant and certainly the most prolific of his followers. Luini painted frescoes and altar-pieces for the churches and monastic orders of Lombardy, continually repeating types and compositions created by Leonardo and making use of his master's technique of soft modelling by means of light and shade and his gentle, lyrical approach.

Luini's female figures are delicate and charming, witness the graceful saints of the Budapest picture, and there is a soft continuity of line. His colours are warm and richly tinted and the tender, oval faces, the finely drawn hands and the singular suppleness and rhythm of the movements lend a rare beauty and poetry to his works.

This picture and his *Virgin and Child with St Elizabeth and the Young St John the Baptist* (p. 249) were acquired as part of the Esterházy collection. In the 1812 catalogue of the Esterházy collection this painting was attributed to Leonardo da Vinci.

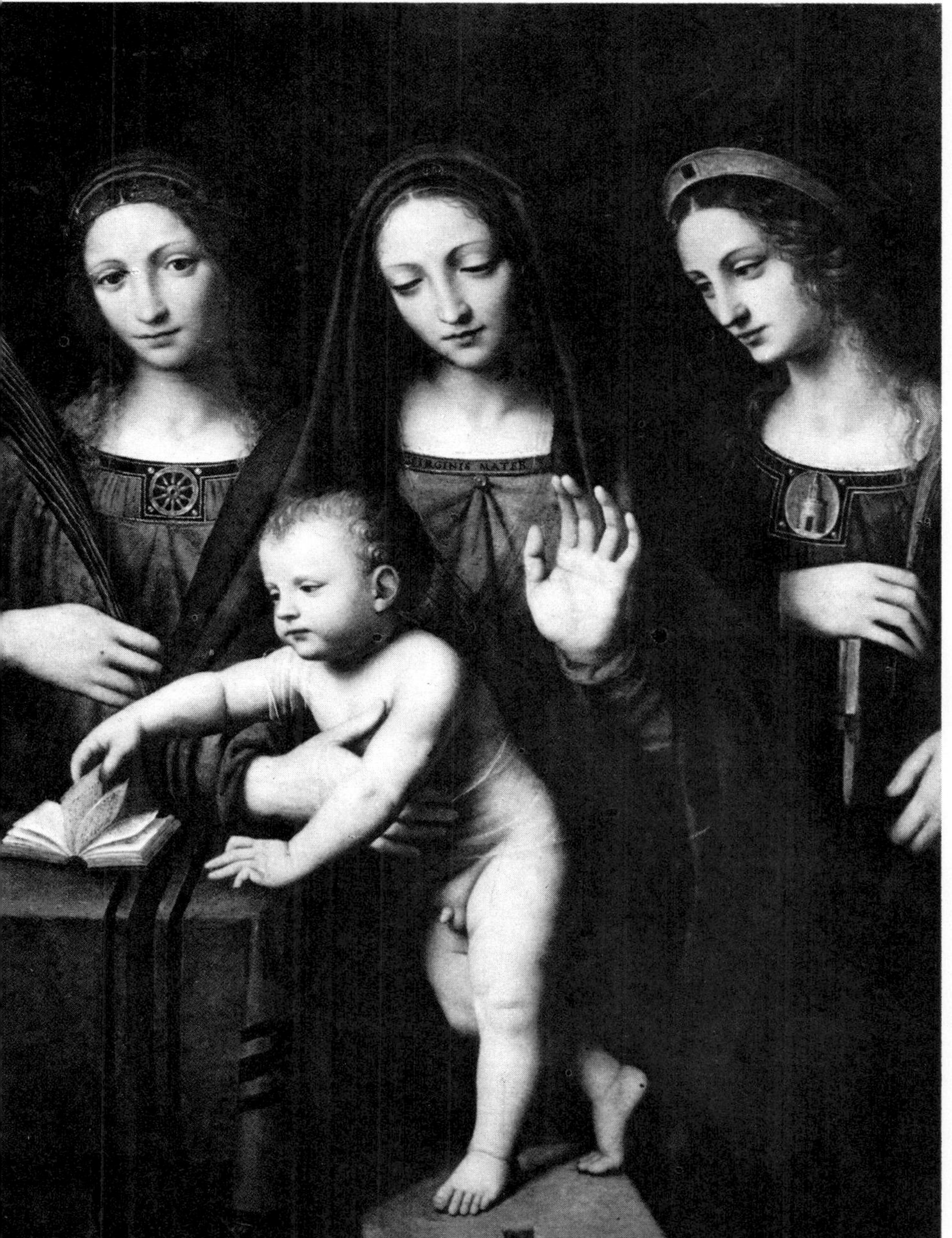

GIORGIONE (GIORGIO DA CASTELFRANCO)
Venetian, *c.* 1478–1510
Portrait of a Man
Canvas 28 $^1/_2$″ × 21$^1/_4$″ (72.5 × 54 cm.) Inv. No. 94
Inscribed on the parapet: ANTONIVS BROKARDVS MAR...

This beautiful painting is one of the most problematical pictures in the history of art and a constant subject of debate. The identity of the painter is still in question and, while the majority of experts ascribe it to Giorgione, there are a number of scholars who believe it was painted by Giovanni Cariani (an artist much influenced by Giorgione) or by some other Venetian painter active around 1510. Any decision is rendered more difficult by the fact that the painting has come down to us in a very bad condition: the window-opening on the left and the landscape in the background, for example, are so faded that they are scarcely visible to the naked eye. X-ray photographs reveal alterations to both the eyes and the hands, made while the picture was being painted, similar to modifications in other paintings by Giorgione. Certainly there are several features – the extraordinarily fine painterly approach, the intimacy of the expression, the inclusion of the parapet and the window-opening – which support the belief that *Portrait of a Man* was painted by Giorgione himself, possibly not long before his death in 1510.

The emblems on the parapet – the small hat with a V on it, the female triple head, the tiny tablet and the inscription – have been variously interpreted. One explanation, the most frequent and perhaps the most acceptable, is that this picture is a portrait of the poet Antonio Broccardo.

From the Pyrker collection. Ascribed to Orazio Vecellio when acquired by Archbishop Pyrker in Venice at the beginning of the nineteenth century.

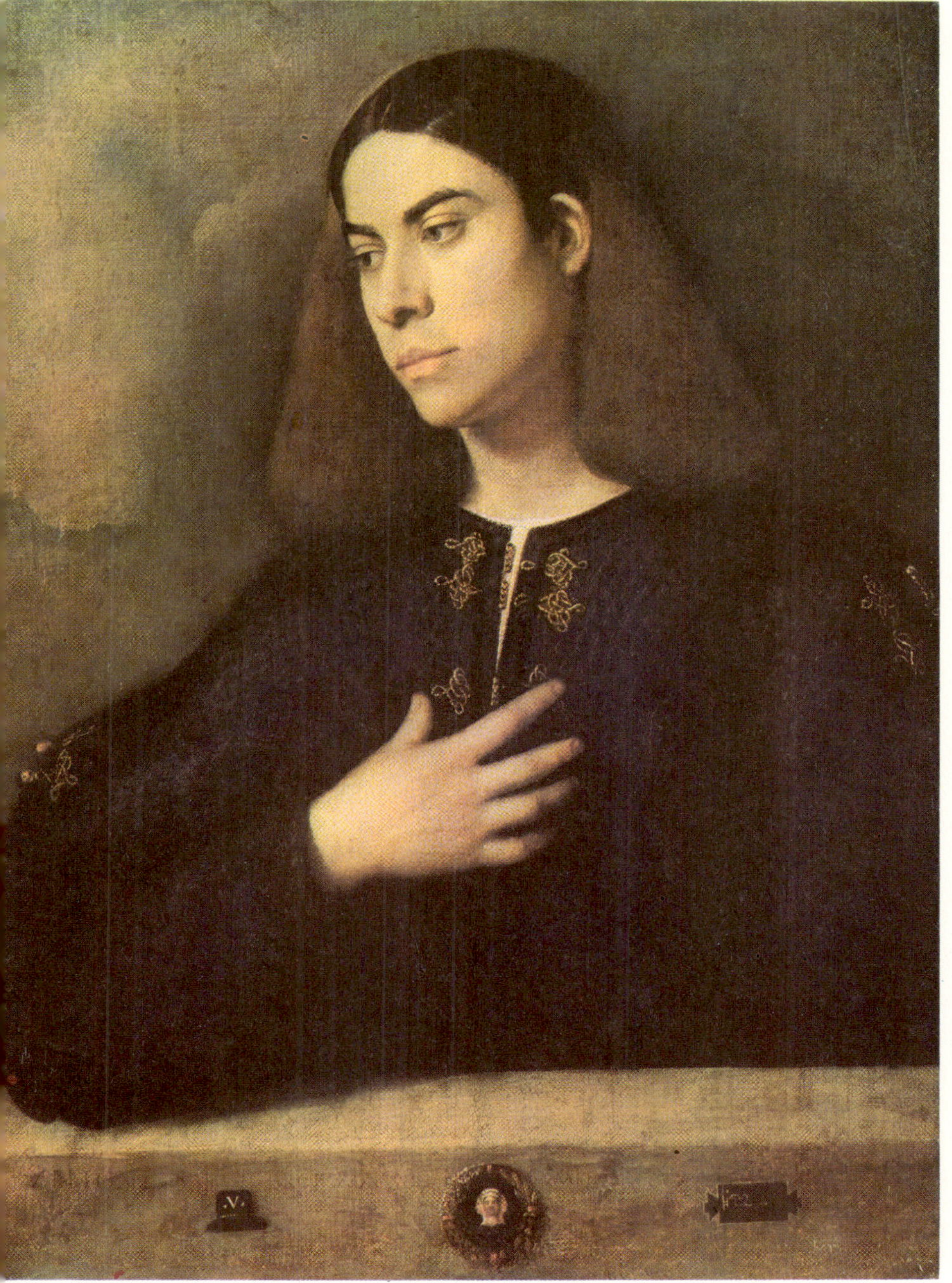

SEBASTIANO DEL PIOMBO (SEBASTIANO LUCIANI)
Venetian and Roman, *c.* 1485–1547
Portrait of a Man
Panel 45 1/4" × 37" (115 × 94 cm.) Inv. No. 1384

Sebastiano Luciani was born in Venice, where he worked as the pupil and follower of Giovanni Bellini and later of Giorgione. After 1511 he moved to Rome, where he came under the influence of Raphael and Michelangelo, who were working there at that time, and he gradually abandoned the soft, picturesque Venetian style of his early work to become one of the most important representatives of the School of Rome. He was frequently commissioned to paint portraits of the Roman nobility. In 1531 he was given the sinecure of *Piombatore Papale* (keeper of the Papal seals) and thereafter called himself Sebastiano del Piombo.

His works in the Budapest Museum enable us to study each phase of his development: the Venetian period is represented by the *Portrait of a Girl* (p. 249), the early Roman years by *Portrait of a Man* and his late period by the austere and dramatic *Christ Carrying the Cross.* When *Portrait of a Man* was bought for the Museum in 1895, it was generally believed to be a portrait of the poet Antonio Tebaldeo by Raphael; in the Ducal Gallery of Modena, too, it had been attributed to Raphael. But at the beginning of the twentieth century it was decided that this picture and several other paintings of the same type, also attributed to Raphael, were in fact the work of Piombo – the main reason for the decision being the Venetian character of the landscape background. The posture and clothes of the sitter indicate that the portrait was painted in Rome between 1515 and 1520.

Purchased in 1895 from the Scarpa collection of Motta di Livenza.

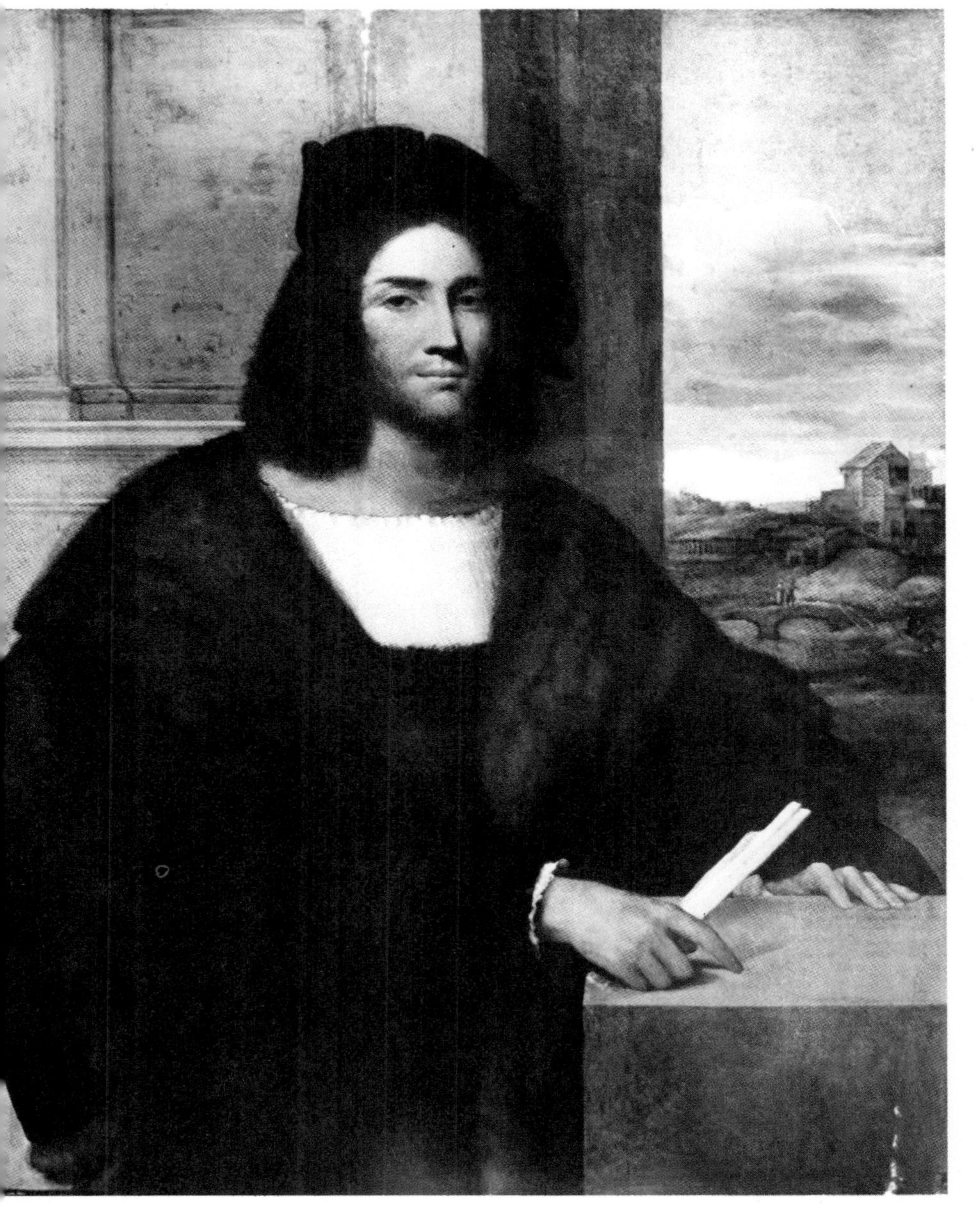

RAPHAEL (RAFFAELLO SANTI)
Umbrian, Florentine and Roman, 1483–1520
Pietro Bembo
Panel 21 1/4″ × 15 3/8″ (54 × 39 cm.) Inv. No. 72

Raphael began his career by working with his father, Giovanni Santi, court painter of Urbino, and later studied under the most popular master in Umbria, Perugino. In 1504 he moved to Florence where he came under the influence of the great Tuscan masters of the Renaissance, especially Leonardo da Vinci. The late Gothic traditions of Umbrian painting disappeared from his work as he began to respond to these new sources of inspiration and were replaced by the closer structure and the firmer lines of Renaissance painting.

The portrait of Pietro Bembo, one of Raphael's earliest portraits, represents his art at the very beginning of the sixteenth century, the period of transition between his early work in the Umbrian style and that of his Florentine period. The youth in red gown and cap is seen against a landscape background depicting the gentle, hilly countryside of Umbria. The hair, hanging in long locks as was the fashion at that time, frames a gentle face; both hands rest on the parapet and in his right hand is a folded sheet of paper. Because of its general resemblance to the early *Self-portrait* in Florence, this picture was for some time thought to be another self-portrait, while some scholars believed it to be the portrait of a young cardinal. Recent research has, however, identified it as the picture once seen by the Venetian Marcantonio Michiel in the *studiolo* of Pietro Bembo in Padua, representing Bembo in his youth. It was painted by the young Raphael when he met Bembo at the court of Urbino in 1506.

From the Esterházy collection. In the 1812 catalogue of the Esterházy gallery and in later inventories the painting was described as a portrait of Raphael by Bernardino Luini.

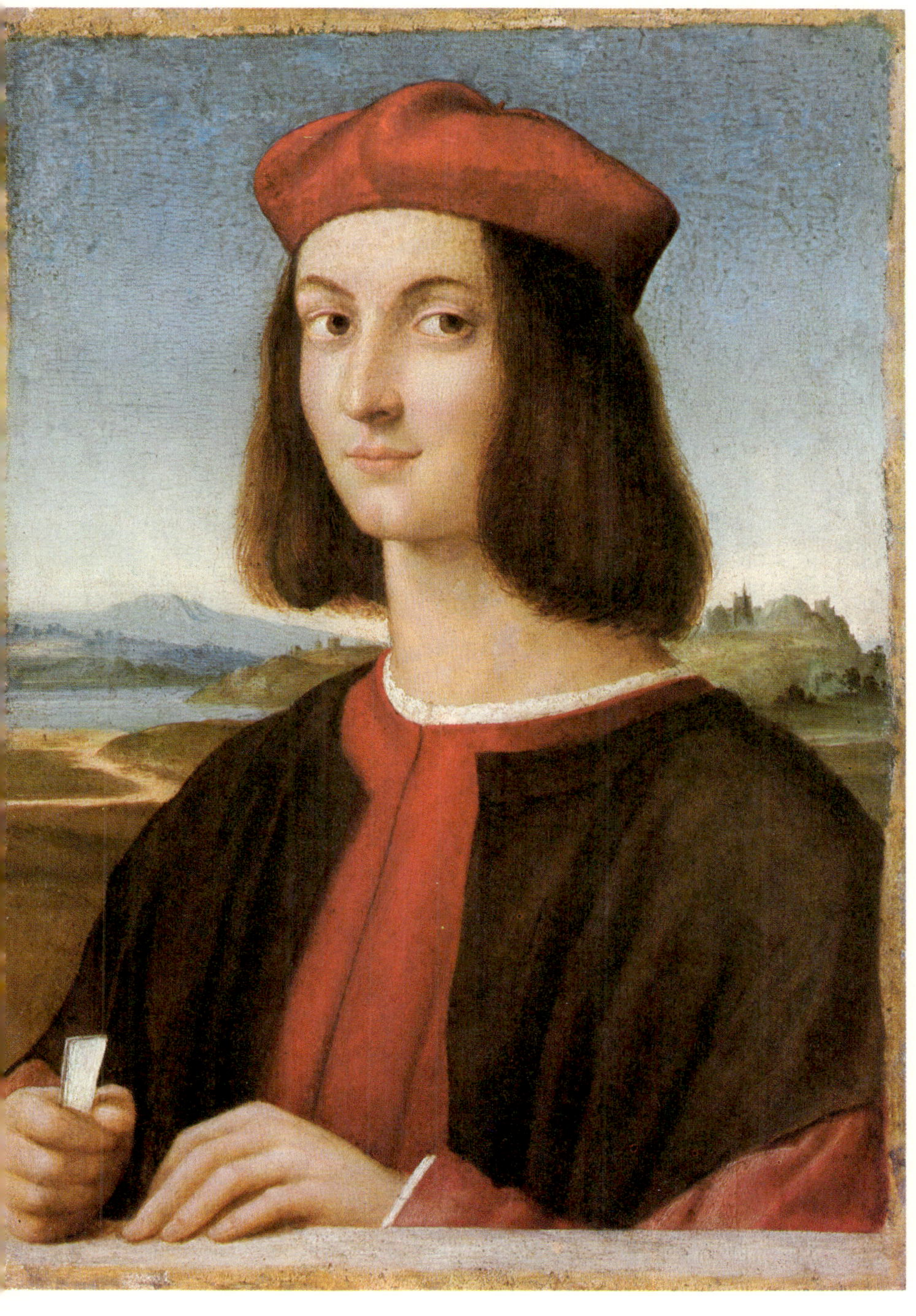

RAPHAEL (RAFFAELLO SANTI)
Umbrian, Florentine and Roman, 1483–1520
The Esterházy Madonna
(Virgin and Child with the Young St John the Baptist)
Panel 11 1/4″ × 8 1/2″ (28.5 × 21.5 cm.) Inv. No. 71

Raphael, perhaps the most popular and widely appreciated master of Renaissance Italy, was a man of many talents. He succeeded Bramante as architect of St Peter's and was surveyor of excavations of the antiquities of Ancient Rome, as well as producing monumental frescoes and outstanding religious compositions and portraits. It is as a painter of Madonnas, however, that he is most widely known, and his unrivalled popularity with succeeding generations has been mainly due to the harmony and beauty of these paintings. He depicted Mary as a heavenly being who was yet flesh and blood: in half-length or full-length pictures she is seen enthroned or floating through the heavens, against a landscape background or in some interior scene, alone with her Child or in the company of saints.

The panel now in Budapest, known as *The Esterházy Madonna*, is a small painting, still in its original frame, that has been in the Esterházy collection since the eighteenth century. It is particularly interesting in that it has been left unfinished – as we can see in the figures of Jesus and the young St John where the drawn lines showing on the light ground allow us an insight into Raphael's technique. We do not know how the picture came to be painted, or for whom, but the style, the gentle forms and the firm composition indicate that it must have been executed about 1508, when Raphael moved from Florence to Rome. A study for this painting, a pen drawing, is in the Uffizi Gallery in Florence.

From the Esterházy collection. According to a former inscription on the back of the picture it was a gift from Pope Clement XI to Empress Elisabeth, wife of the Emperor Charles III. Later it became part of the Kaunitz collection and was finally acquired by the Esterházy family.

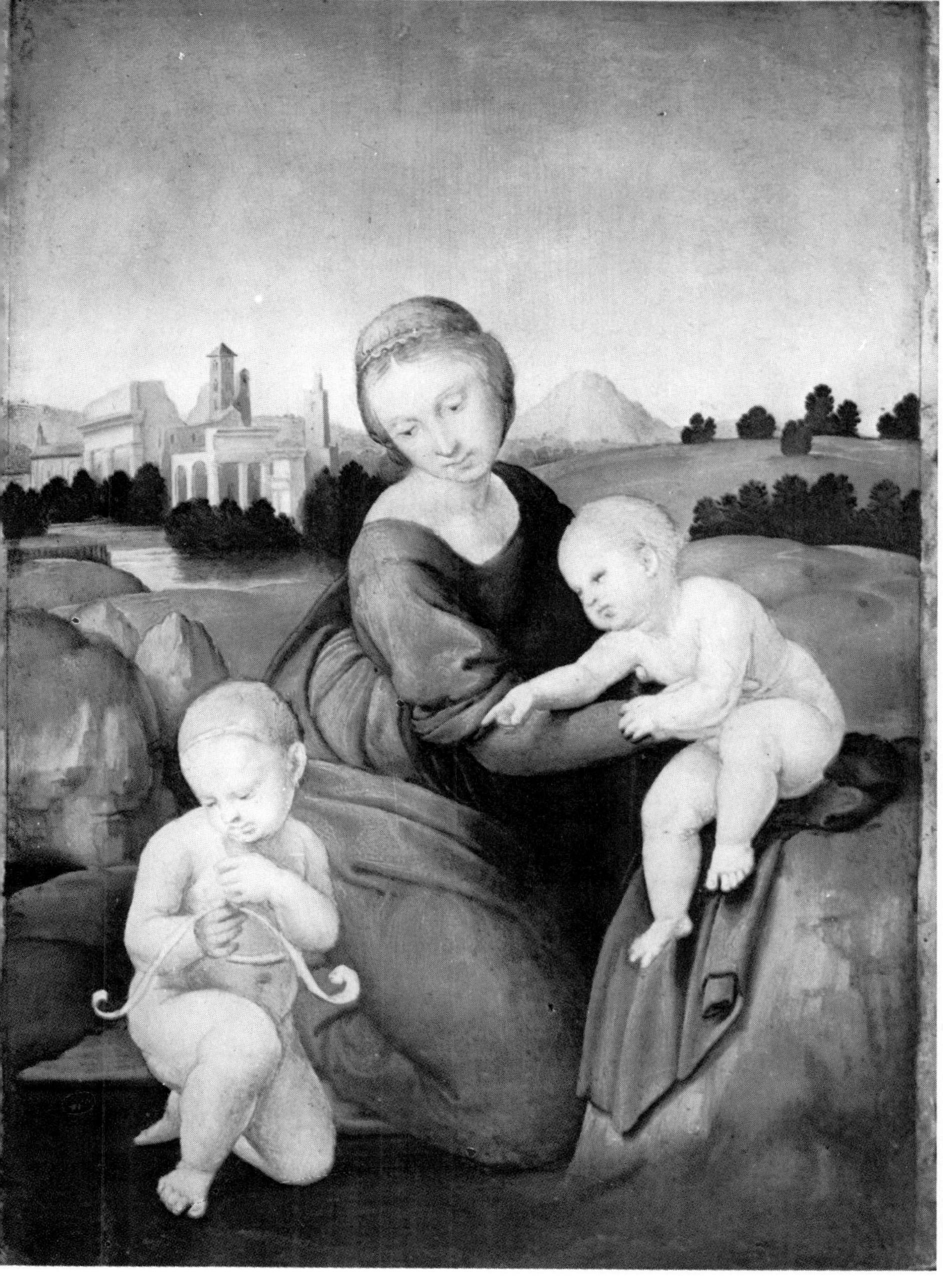

TITIAN (TIZIANO VECELLIO)
Venetian, 1477 or 1488/90–1576
Doge Marcantonio Trevisani
Canvas 39 3/8″ × 34″ (100 × 86.5 cm.) Inv. No. 4223

Titian, a man of legendary longevity and a notably prolific artist, painted about five hundred portraits; in fact he painted the likeness of almost every eminent man of his time, from the poet Aretino to the Emperor Charles V and Pope Paul III. His achievement in this field is uniformly superb, whether we consider his half-length portraits, full-length figures in sumptuous interiors, portraits of children, equestrian studies or portrait groups. He depicted the sitter first and foremost as a human being but sometimes added details such as the emblems of power, office or occupation appropriate to the subject's public personality. All his portraits reveal a penetrating insight into the character of the sitter which enabled him to create enduring memorials to a Venetian nobleman, a dictatorial ruler, a servile courtier, or a pope in his declining years.

As the official painter of the Venetian Republic, it was Titian's duty to paint a portrait of each doge when he took office. He painted several portraits of Marcantonio Trevisani, Doge in 1553–4. In 1577 a fire in the Palazzo Ducale destroyed one of these, and the only surviving portrait is that now in Budapest; characterized by golden tones and subtle delineation, it is an example of Titian's mature period.

From the Pálffy bequest. Formerly in the Vienna collections of F. Sterne and Sámuel Festetics.

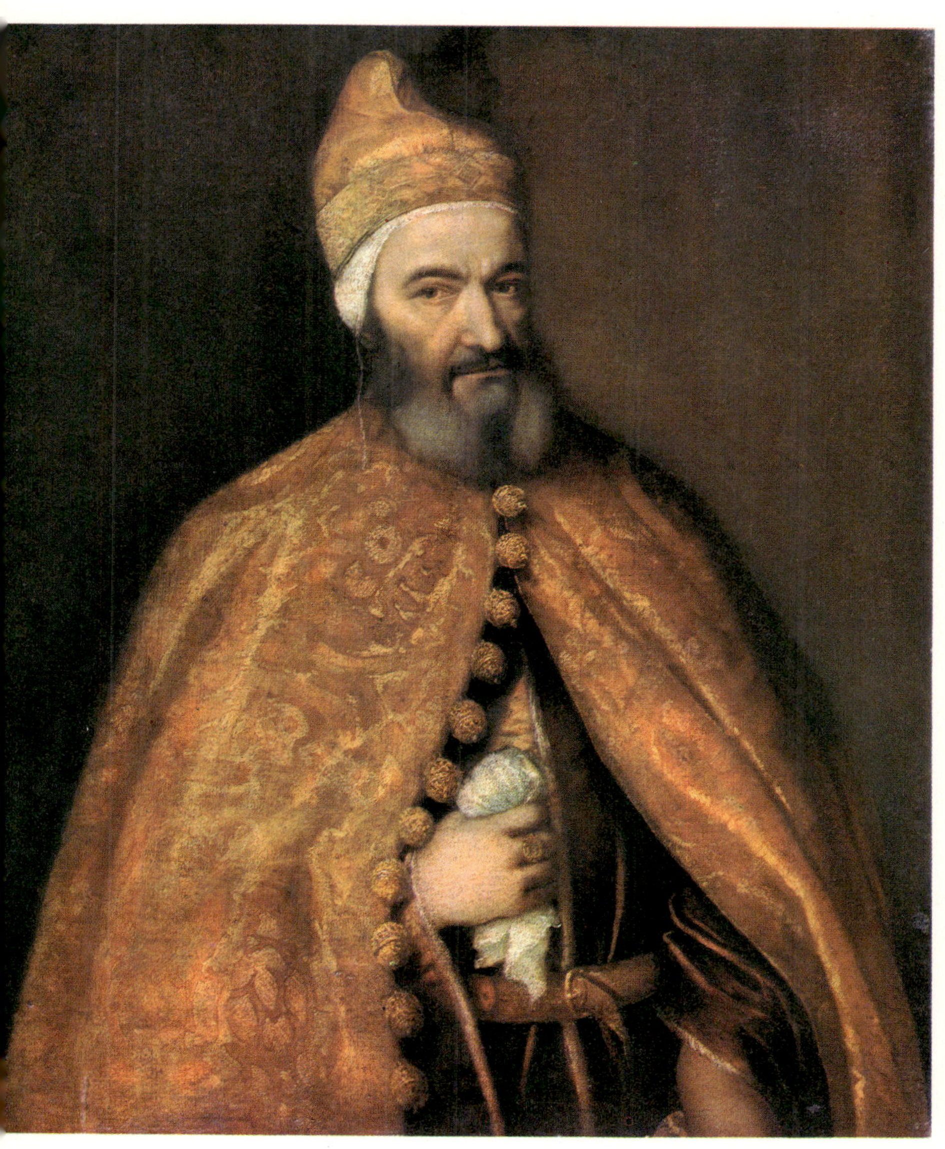

PALMA VECCHIO (JACOPO D'ANTONIO NEGRETI)
Venetian, *c.* 1480–1528
Bust of a Girl
Panel 15 1/4″×11 1/4″ (38.8×28.5 cm.) Inv. No. 939

Jacopo d'Antonio Negreti, known to art history as Palma Vecchio (Palma the Elder), left Serinalta, near Bergamo, while still a youth and went to Venice. Although a pupil of Giovanni Bellini, his early work reveals the powerful influence of Giorgione. In spite of research, little is known about the early years of his career, but this small bust and its companion-piece (p. 249) which are jointly known as *Portraits of a Betrothed Couple* are considered to be early works.

In the early seventeenth century this portrait of a young girl with flowing silky hair, and its counterpart, depicting a smooth-faced youth crowned with a garland, were considered to be the work of Giorgione. Indeed this attribution is most understandable, for the paintings have something of the intimate and lyrical atmosphere associated with Giorgione; on the other hand the placing of the figures in a landscape setting, the blue sky and the generally light colouring, are all reminiscent of Giovanni Bellini. Recent research, therefore, suggests that the pictures were painted by Palma Vecchio, an artist who was close to both these painters, and they are now assumed to date from the beginning of the sixteenth century. It may well be that the two likenesses had a symbolic meaning, for in seventeenth-century Venetian records they are listed as *Portraits of a Roman Consul and His Wife*.

Before 1636 part of the Bartolomeo della Nave collection in Venice, the pictures were later acquired by the Duke of Hamilton in England, whence they passed, via the collection of Archduke Leopold Wilhelm, to the Imperial collection in Vienna. In 1848 they were transferred from Buda Castle to the Museum.

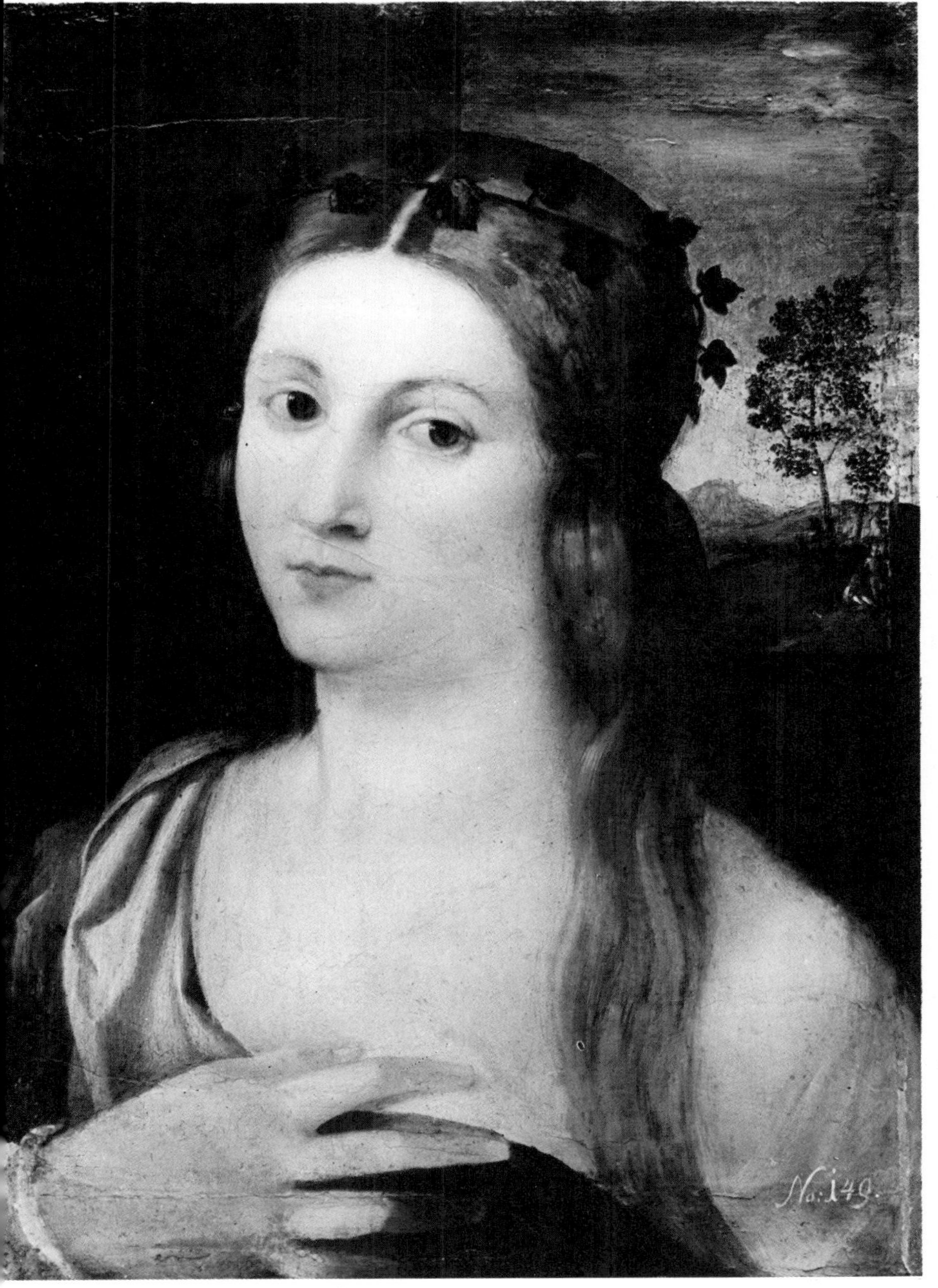
No: 149

TINTORETTO (JACOPO ROBUSTI) Venetian, 1518–94
The Supper at Emmaus
Canvas 61 3/8″ × 83 1/2″ (156 × 212 cm.) Inv. No. 111

Tintoretto began his career as one of Titian's pupils and was later much influenced by Parmigianino and Michelangelo, but his own art, dramatic and animated, passionate and visionary, kept a highly individual note that was in many respects totally original. His pictures in Budapest, *Hercules Expelling the Faun from Omphale's Bed* (p. 252), *Doge Pietro Loredano*, *Portrait of a Man* (p. 252) and *The Supper at Emmaus*, give some idea of the different phases of his art, as well as the variety of his subjects.

The *Supper at Emmaus* is considered by experts to have been painted in about 1540, when he was a young man. Unlike his paintings of the Last Supper – a frequent subject of his later years – this painting is a more balanced composition in the Renaissance style, with the figures arranged parallel to the picture plane. The figures are relatively large and statuesque, and there is not such effective use of contrasting light and shade or spatial arrangement as in the more mature works. It is primarily by means of gestures and vigorous poses that the painter conveys the dramatic and tense atmosphere inherent in the scene.

Acquired by the Museum as part of the Esterházy collection.

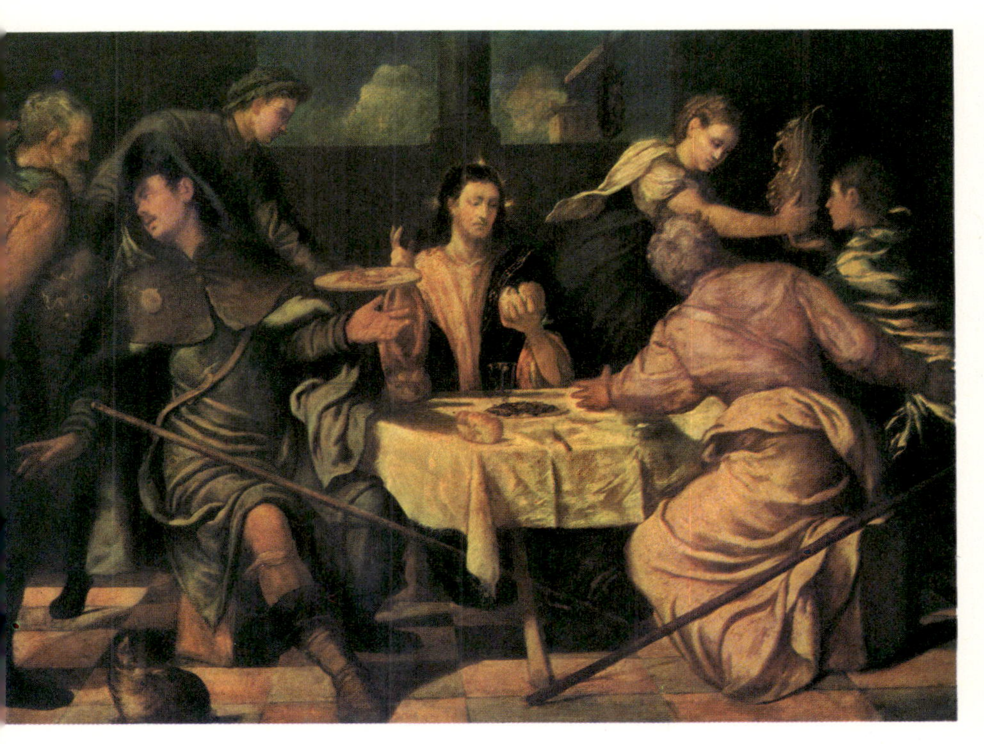

PAOLO VERONESE (PAOLO CALIARI) Venetian, 1528–88
The Crucifixion
Canvas 58 5/8″ × 35 3/8″ (149 × 90 cm.) Inv. No. 117

Paolo Caliari, born in Verona and therefore known by the name of Veronese, was one of the most famous painters in Venice during the second half of the sixteenth century. His principal work was essentially decorative: he adorned the churches, palaces and villas of Venice and the surrounding countryside with large pictures, frescoes and panel-paintings as animated as they were lavish. It was in the representation of spectacular and animated scenes that he could best make use of a many-sided talent – draughtsmanship which is exceptional in its sureness of touch and colours that are both brilliant and silky, are alike characteristic of his religious, mythological and allegorical compostions. His paintings in Budapest, *Allegory of Venice*, *Portrait of a Man* and *The Crucifixion* demonstrate various aspects and phases of his art. Certainly his *Portrait of a Man* (p. 252), a likeness in which there is nobility as well as beauty, should be regarded as an early work, and the allegorical ceiling painting (p. 252), originally in the Palazzo Ducale, may have been executed during the 1570s.

The Crucifixion is usually believed to be one of his late works. Recently cleaned and restored so that the delicate tints can now be appreciated, the painting is noteworthy for the unusual lighting and the dramatic contrast between the dark, stormy clouds in the background and the radiant body of Christ.

From the Esterházy collection.

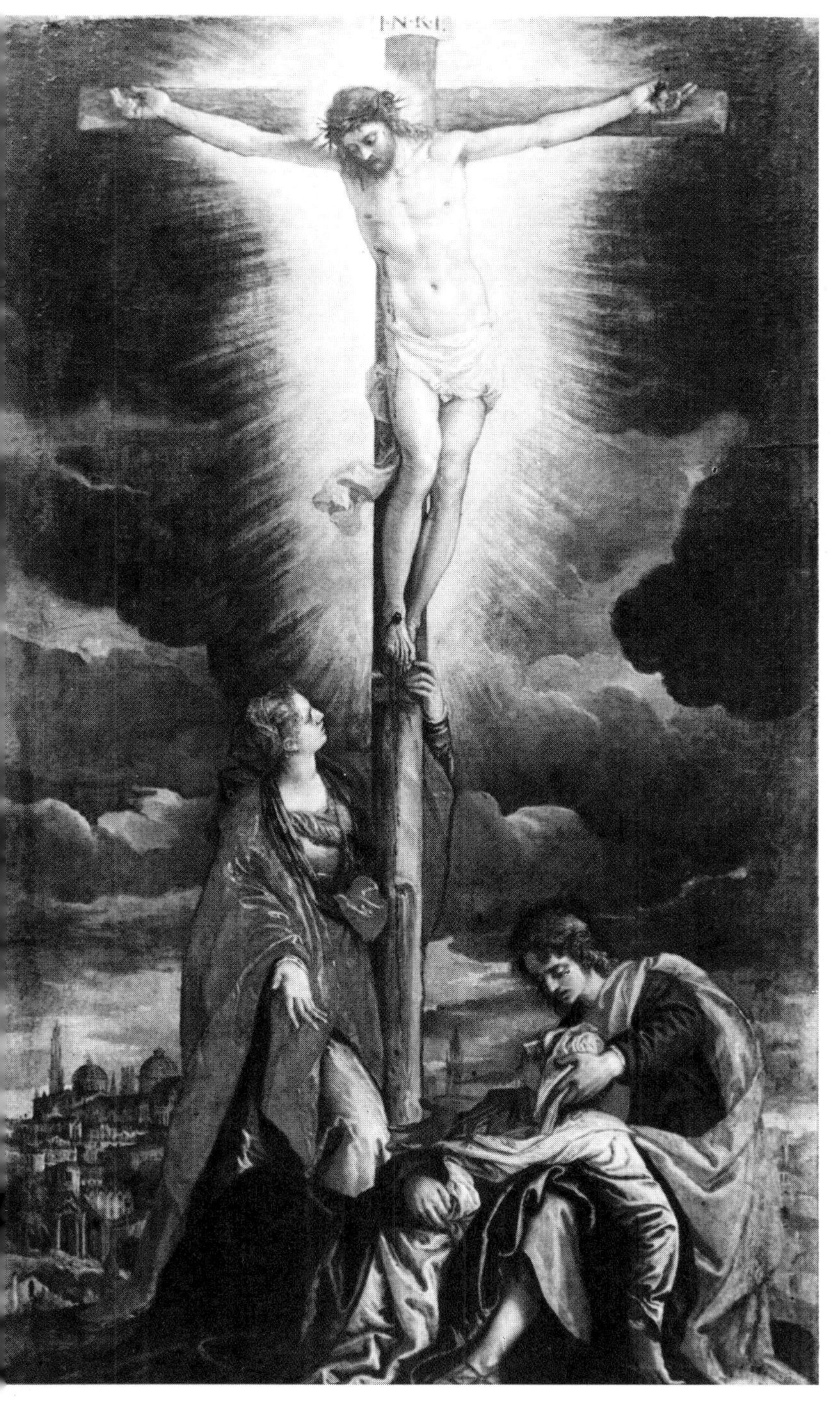
I·N·R·I

JACOPO BASSANO (JACOPO DA PONTE)
Venetian, *c.* 1510–92
Christ Carrying the Cross
Canvas 37″ × 44 7/8″ (94 × 114 cm.) Inv. No. 5879

The da Ponte family from Bassano produced several painters, of whom Jacopo was the most famous. He began his career in Bassano as one of his father's pupils and remained there for the greater part of his life. Early in his career, however, he went to Venice, where he came under the influence of such great masters as Titian, Veronese and Tintoretto, and was soon initiating a new style of his own: he made use of the glowing colours and rich pictorial construction of the Venetian School but introduced a new range of themes. He broke away from restrictive traditions surrounding the representation of Biblical subjects and introduced aspects of everyday human activity, scenes from the local countryside, animals and still-life details, into his pictures. He was in fact one of the creators of Italian genre-painting.

Christ Carrying the Cross, a work of great concentration, yet lively and dramatic, is one of the master's most remarkable paintings. Though at one time thought to be the work of Andrea Schiavone, it has now been definitely attributed to Jacopo Bassano and dates from the 1550s.

Given to the Museum in 1922 by Jenő Boross.

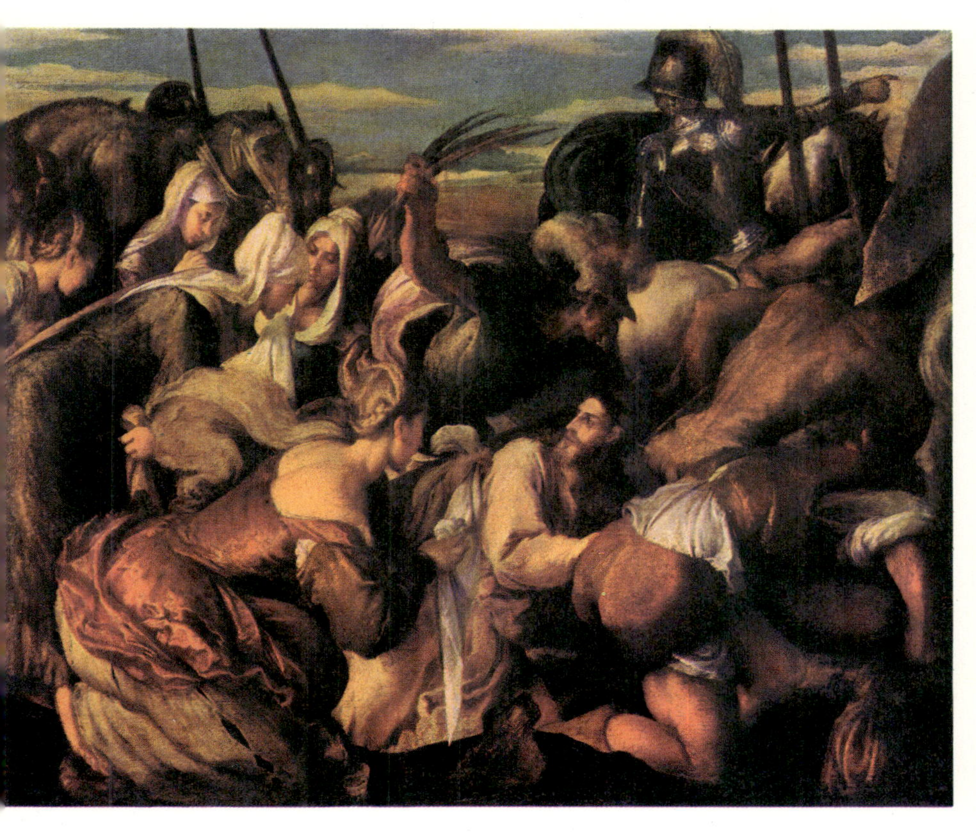

LORENZO LOTTO Venetian, *c.* 1480–1556
The Sleeping Apollo
Canvas 17 1/2" × 29 1/8" (44.5 × 74 cm.) Inv. No. 947

Lorenzo Lotto was a most prolific painter of religious compositions, mythological scenes and portraits, and in 1953 the long list of his known works was increased when an attractive painting, then in the reserves of the Museum of Fine Arts, was identified and attributed to him by Andor Pigler.

The subject is allegorical – while Apollo is asleep and his lyre silent, the Muses disperse and Fame flies away – and there is a charm in Lotto's work which matches this poetic thought. The painting has a fresh lyricism which catches a mood by the use of fresh spots of colour and small animated figures.

According to the painter's account book this work was in a lottery at Ancona in 1550. In the early seventeenth century it was taken from Venice to England for the collection of the Duke of Hamilton; later it formed part of Archduke Leopold Wilhelm's famous collection which was transferred from Brussels to Vienna. At that time it was complete and the missing right-hand section, on which there were another four muses, was damaged or destroyed only after 1659. Thus this poetic composition, probably intended for a music room, or at any rate for a setting associated with the arts in some way, was originally a third as wide again, though no higher than at present.

Formerly in the Imperial collection in Vienna; transferred to the Museum from Buda Castle.

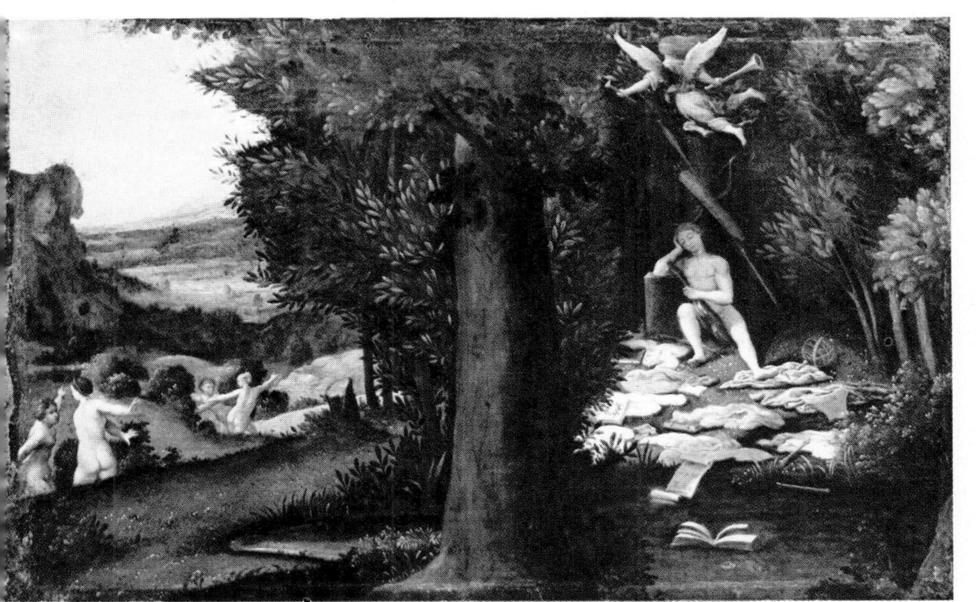

GIROLAMO ROMANINO Brescian, 1484/7–1562
Portrait of a Man
Panel 32 1/2″ × 28 1/8″ (82.5 × 71.5 cm.) Inv. No. 1254

Romanino studied under the local masters of Brescia but his art was decisively influenced by his famous contemporaries in Venice: Giorgione, Titian and Palma Vecchio. His compositions are large, the structure firm and harmonious, the colours warm and varied. He was greatly concerned with expressing emotion and mood, and his work contains a certain romantic and poetic element.

His *Portrait of a Man* depicts a young man, wearing a gold brocade coat and a gold-coloured hat and posed against a dark green curtain, who looks rather wistfully into the distance, lost in thought; though his right hand rests on the hilt of his sword, the pose is that of someone both relaxed and meditative. The identity of the sitter is not known (he may have been a member of one of the ruling families of Brescia); the same sitter appears in a smaller fragmentary version now in the Accademia Carrara in Bergamo.

Bought in Venice in 1895. Traditionally believed to have been the property of the Fenaroli family in Brescia.

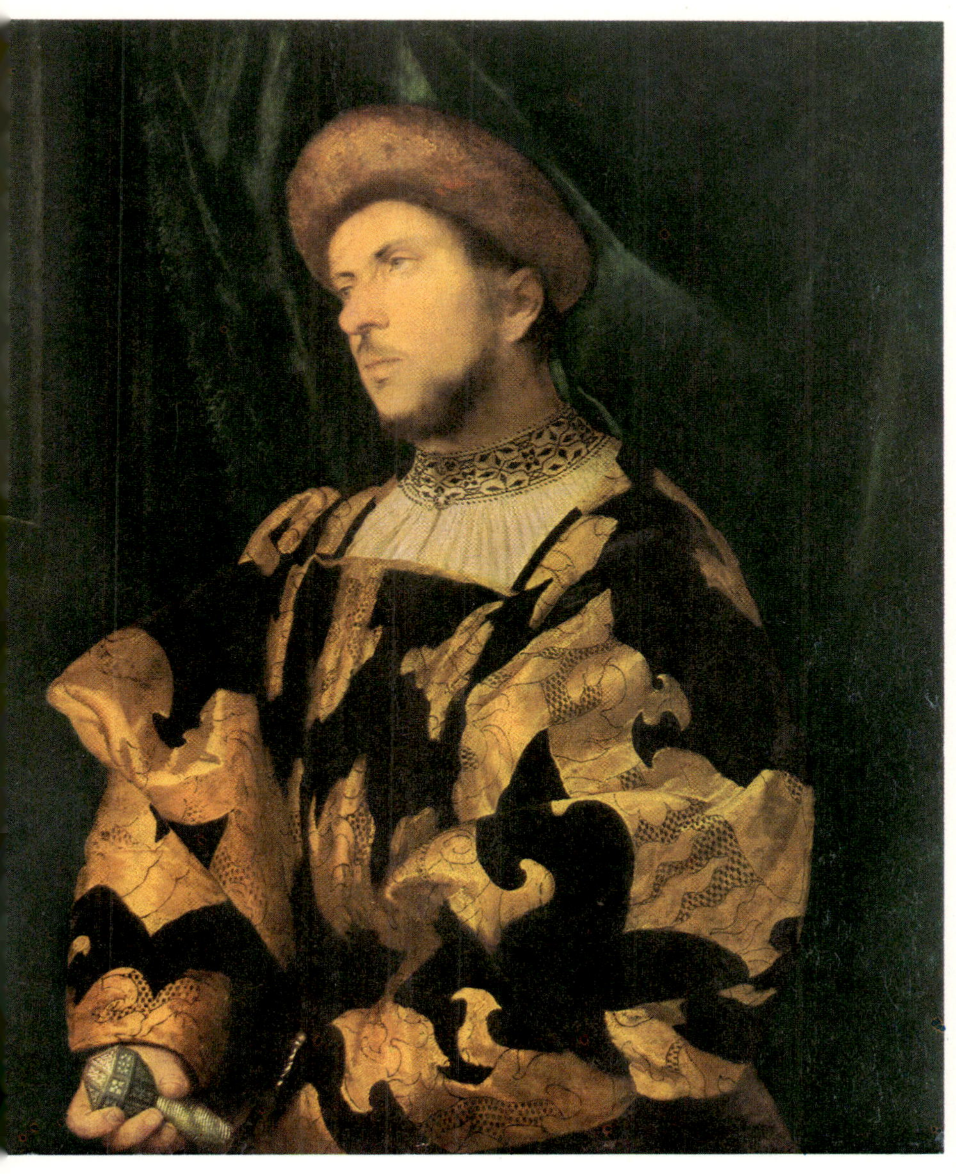

GIOVANNI BATTISTA MORONI Bergamasque, 1520/5–1578
Jacopo Foscarini
Canvas 41 3/8″ × 32 7/8″ (105 × 83.5 cm.) Inv. No. 53.501
Signed at bottom right: Jo: Bap: Moronus. p. MDLXXV

The reputation of Giovanni Battista Moroni of Bergamo rests primarily on his numerous portraits although, like his master, Moretto da Brescia, he also painted altar-pieces and religious compositions (one of his Madonnas is illustrated on p. 250). His models were, for the most part, the patricians, bourgeois scholars and artisans living in the small towns of northern Italy. Usually he painted them at work with the tools of their particular trade: the scholar is seen holding a book or writing implements, the tailor is about to cut his cloth.

According to a later inscription at the top right, this is a portrait of Jacopo Contarini, *Podestà* of Padua. However, Padua never had a *Podestà* of this name and, since it is known that Jacopo Foscarini filled that office when the picture was painted, we can only assume that the inscription is inaccurate and that the portrait is indeed of Foscarini. He is shown as a distinguished man of middle age with an air of seriousness that commands respect. Only the serene harmony of greys and reds resolves the sombre mood of the painting.

From the Zichy bequest. Formerly in Vienna in the Gsell, Galvagni and Sámuel Festetics collections.

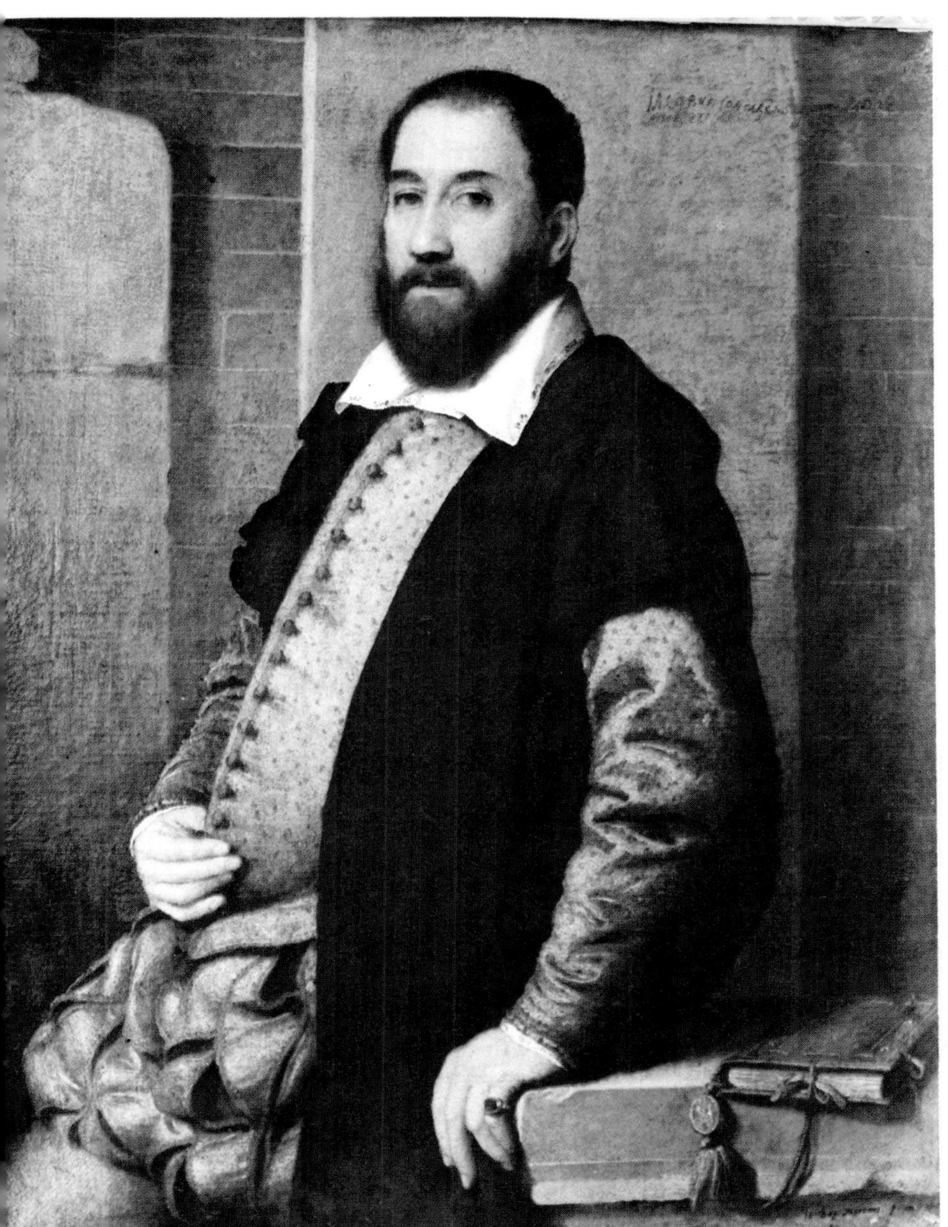

CORREGGIO (ANTONIO ALLEGRI) Parmesan, 1489/94–1534
The Virgin and Child with an Angel (Madonna del Latte)
Panel 27″ × 22 3/8″ (68.5 × 56.8 cm.) Inv. No. 55

Antonio Allegri, born in and known by the name of Correggio, lived and worked in Parma, a relatively quiet town, remote from the great centres of art. Tradition has it that he was the pupil of Francesco Bianchi Ferrari, a local master, but in reality his artistic development was most profoundly influenced by Mantegna and Leonardo, as well as by the Bolognese painters Lorenzo Costa and Francesco Francia. He was well known as a fresco-painter and virtuoso draughtsman, and his religious and mythological frescoes in the churches of Parma are notable for their charm and poetic quality.

His *Madonna del Latte* was extraordinarily popular for several centuries, and many versions, engravings and copies of it have survived. However, the quality of the Budapest picture, especially the tender modelling and expressive beauty of the faces and hands, have led scholars to believe that this must be the original painting so greatly treasured in seventeenth-century Rome, and reproduced in a contemporary engraving by F. Spierre. The landscape background seen in the engraving is hardly visible in the painting, which has darkened considerably with age.

From the Esterházy collection. Bought by Prince Miklós Esterházy from the Crivelli family in Naples at the end of the eighteenth century.

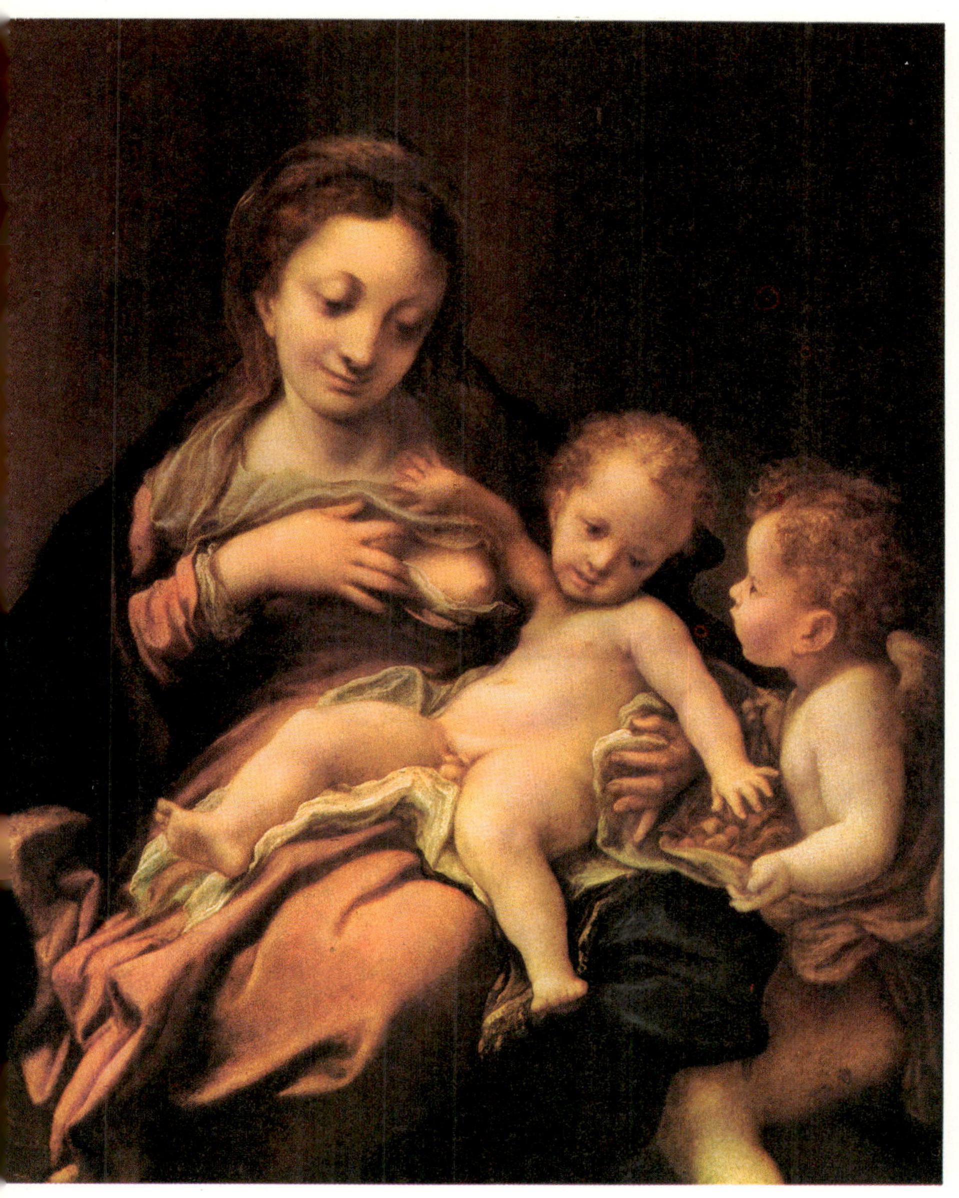

BRONZINO (ANGELO DI COSIMO DI MARIANO)
Florentine, 1503–72
Venus, Cupid and Jealousy
Panel 75 5/8″ × 55 7/8″ (192 × 142 cm.) Inv. No. 163
Signed on the vase on the right: IL BRÕZINO FIOR. F.

Bronzino, a pupil of Pontormo, was one of the leading masters of Florentine Mannerism. His art was determined by the requirements of the ruling classes and the ostentation of the Tuscan court, where he was employed as court painter. In his large religious and allegorical compositions and particularly in his portraits, of which there are a great many, the approach is dignified and reserved, the poses solemn and forbidding and the colours cool.

This large allegorical composition depicts Venus and Cupid, here seen in the guise of a youth, with the figure of Jealousy in the background. There is a similar composition in the National Gallery, London, in which Venus, Cupid and Jealousy are accompanied by a figure representing Time.

The picture was presented to the Museum by Count István Keglevich in 1863; formerly in the Kaunitz collection in Vienna.

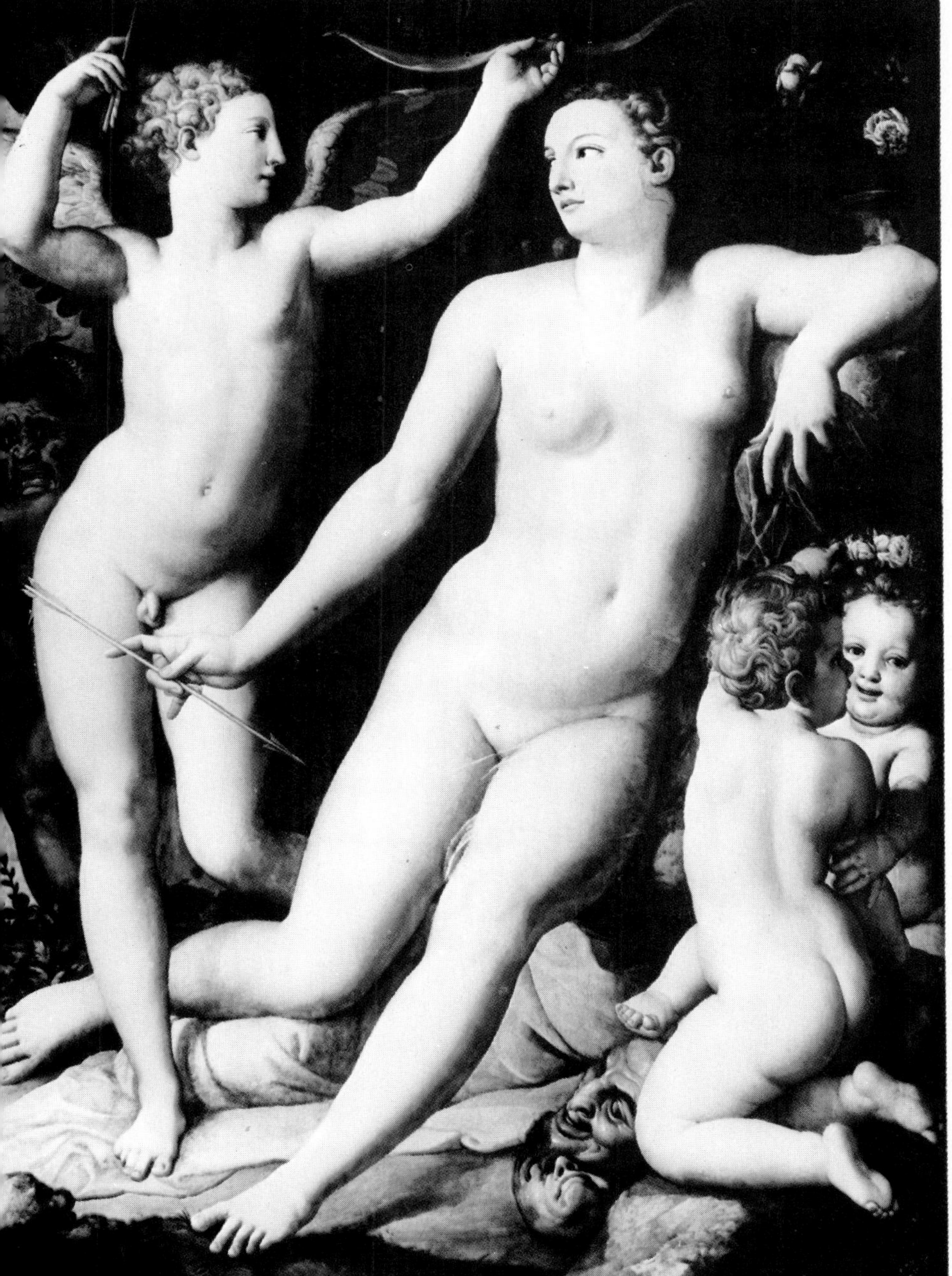

ANNIBALE CARRACCI Bolognese, 1560–1609
Christ and the Woman of Samaria
Canvas 30 1/8" × 25" (76.5 × 63.5 cm.) Inv. No. 3823

The Carracci family, Annibale, his uncle Lodovico and his brother Agostino, played an important role in the development of Baroque art both through their personal achievements and through the teaching academy they set up in Bologna; through their pupils, amongst them Domenichino, Reni and Guercino, they had a lasting influence on the development of Italian painting in the seventeenth century.

After travelling in northern Italy and studying the work of Correggio and the School of Venice, Annibale, the most talented member of the family, moved to Rome where his work was more highly appreciated and sought after than that of any other artist. He was a painter with a very wide range of talent; his exceptional gift for composition, his keen observation and subtle characterization can be seen alike in the frescoes with which he adorned Roman palaces, his monumental altar-pieces and brilliant drawings.

The story of Christ meeting the woman of Samaria at the well (described in St John, chapter 4) is a theme represented in several of his pictures. One version in the Brera, Milan, is more dramatic and agitated than the Budapest picture, and the version in Vienna, recently attributed to Domenichino, is cooler and more reserved.

Possibly dating from around 1590, and originally owned by the Oddi family in Perugia; in the eighteenth century it was in the collection of the Duke of Orleans in Paris. Purchased in 1908 from an Amsterdam dealer.

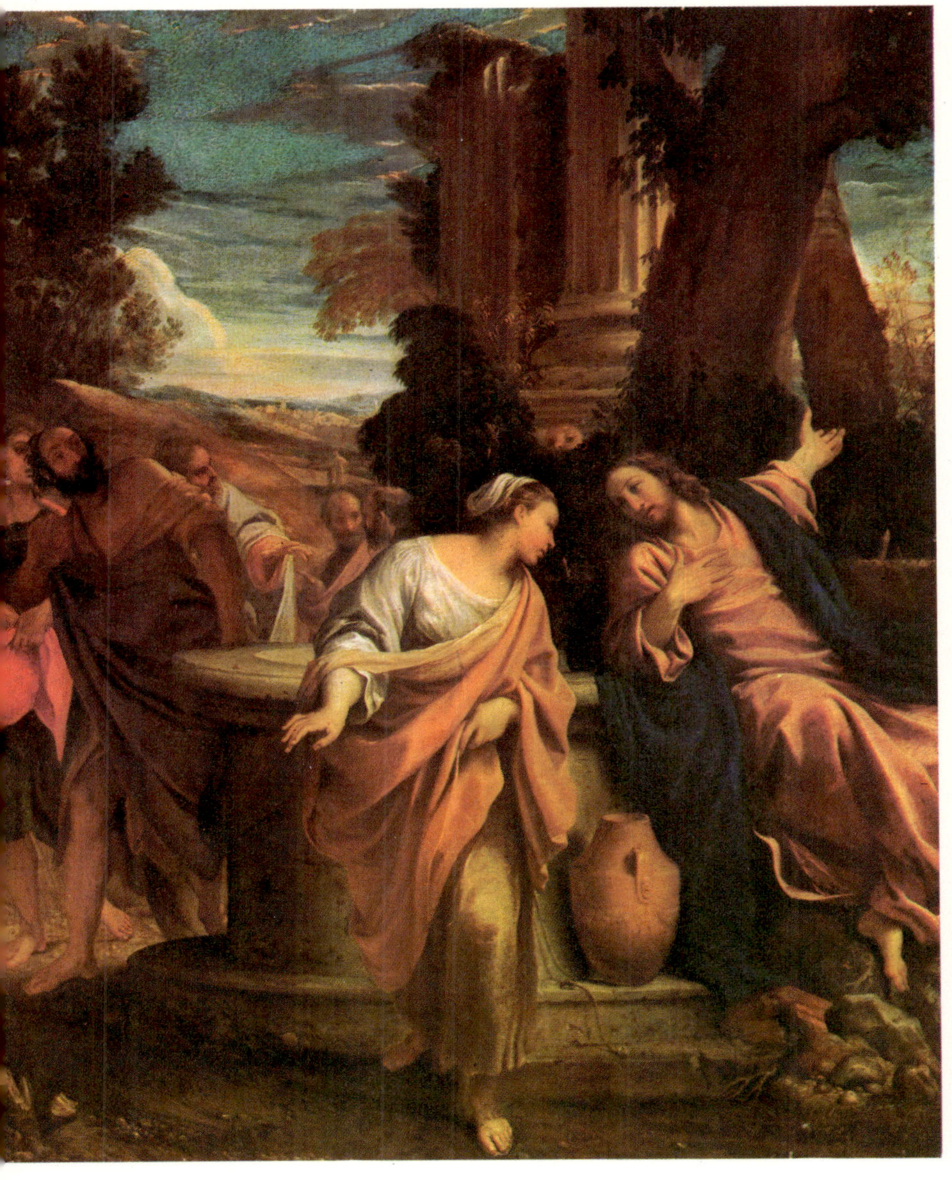

GUIDO RENI Bolognese, 1575–1642
David and Abigail
Canvas 60 1/4" × 63 3/8" (153 × 161 cm.) Inv. No. 490

Reni began his studies under Denys Calvaert, a Flemish master working in Bologna, but his artistic development was determined by the years he spent in the Carracci workshop. He worked a great deal in his home town, but around 1601, when he began to be famous, he went to Rome. Overwhelmed with commissions for frescoes, altar-pieces, portraits, mythological and allegorical compositions, he became one of the most fêted masters of seventeenth-century Italy. Even during his lifetime his pictures found their way to practically every part of Europe, and patrons and collectors paid extraordinarily high prices for his work.

So great was the demand for his paintings that Reni followed the practice, usual at that time, of painting numerous variations on the same theme. He painted several versions of David and Abigail with half-length figures; one of them, similar to the painting in Budapest, may be seen in the Chrysler Collection in New York, and another is in Toulouse. The slight but detectable changes made in the course of the execution of the painting *(pentimenti)* make it likely that the Budapest picture, a superb work in vivid colours, may be an early version.

From the Esterházy collection. The picture was acquired by the Esterházys from the Nuremberg collection of Paul Praun, who bought most of his pictures in the early seventeenth century in Bologna where he was personally acquainted with Reni. Seventeenth- and eighteenth-century sources and travel books mention Reni's painting as one of the sights of Nuremberg.

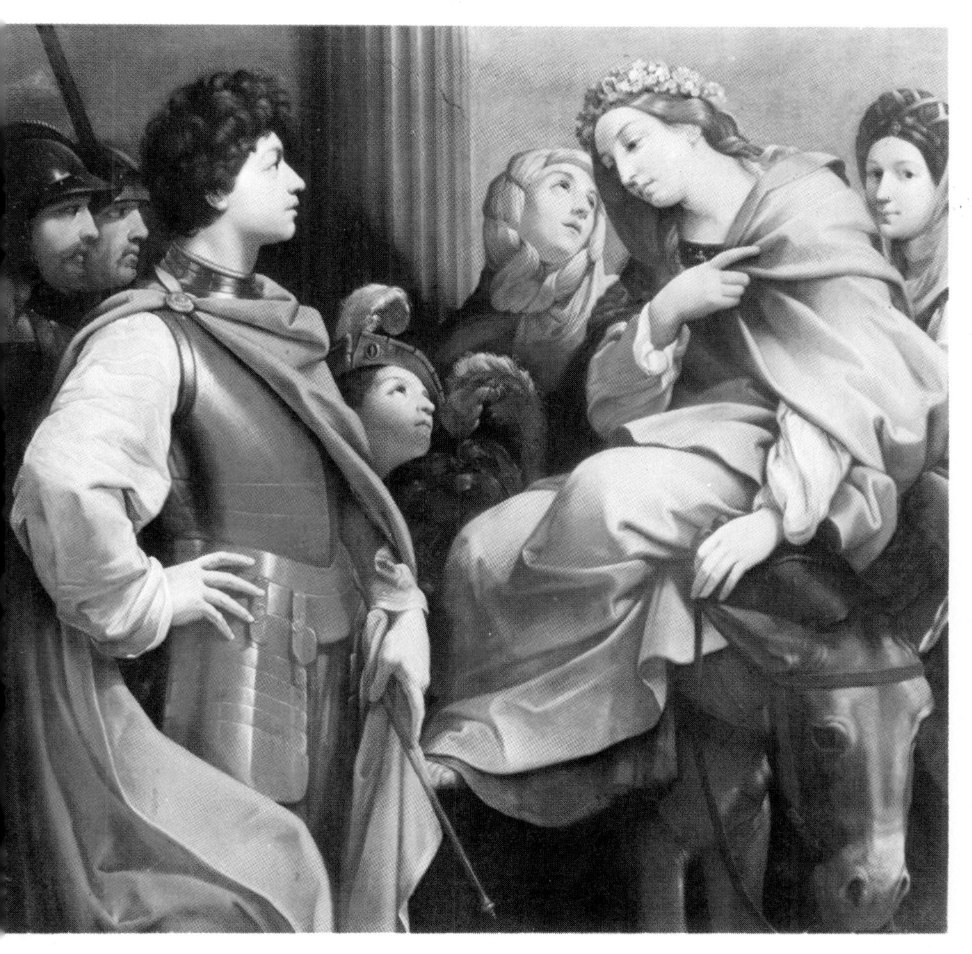

SALVATOR ROSA Neapolitan, 1615–73
Seaport with Ruins
Canvas 30 7/8″×43 3/4″ (78.5×111 cm.) Inv. No. 535
Signed on the plank at bottom centre: ROSA

Salvator Rosa, painter, poet, etcher and musician, was one of the most interesting artists of the Italian Baroque. He worked in Naples, Florence and Rome, painting mostly Graeco-Roman historical scenes, allegories, landscapes and battle scenes. He himself thought most highly of his figure compositions because of their moral and philosophic content, but even his contemporaries found these works too intricate and contrived, preferring his romantic and beautiful landscapes and violent battle scenes.

This landscape, together with its companion-piece (p. 253), was transferred to the National Museum from Buda Castle in 1848, but it was only recently recognized as a signed and authentic work by Rosa. Both pictures were yellow and darkened, with age, but cleaning restored them to their original beauty, and the signature, once believed to be a forgery, turned out to be genuine. When compared with Rosa's early landscapes in the galleries of Florence and Modena, similarities of style and subject are evident.

The painting is mentioned in contemporary records and is known to have been acquired from the artist's friend Francesco Cordini for the Ambras collection by Ferdinand Charles, Archduke of Tyrol, along with several other works by Rosa. It later passed to the Imperial collection in Vienna before being transferred to Buda Castle.

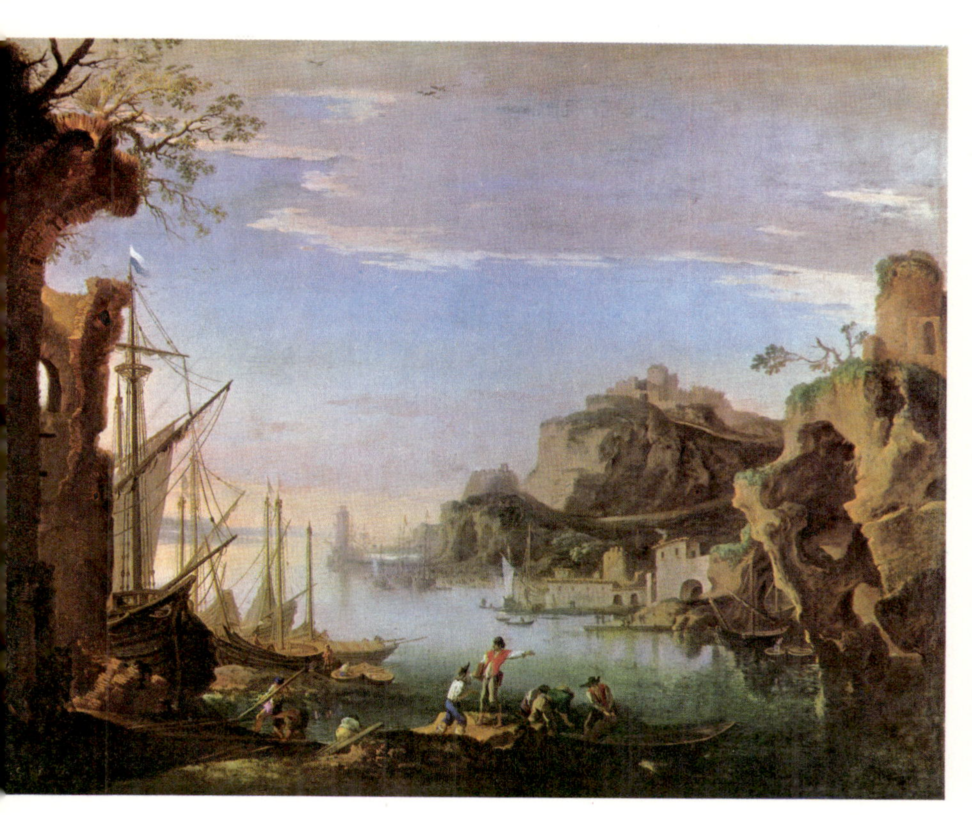

LUCA GIORDANO Neapolitan, 1632–1705
The Flight into Egypt
Canvas 79 1/2″ × 114 1/8″ (202 × 290 cm.) Inv. No. 528

Luca Giordano was known to his contemporaries as *Luca fa presto* ('Luke, do it quickly') and, from the quantity of his surviving work, we can realize something of the speed at which he must have worked, as well as appreciating his virtuoso technique. He worked mainly in his native town of Naples but stayed for varying periods of time in nearly all the larger towns in Italy, including Venice, Florence and Rome. He painted frescoes, altar-pieces, mythological compositions and ponderously Baroque allegorical works, as well as portraits and still-lifes, and his paintings and sketches may be seen in practically every gallery in the world.

The most attractive of the three in Budapest, and the most important, is *The Flight into Egypt*. Unlike most representations of the subject, the picture does not show the Virgin riding on an ass but the episode, less frequently painted, in which angels assist the Family into a boat to cross a river and escape the massacre at Bethlehem. Giordano's poetic approach is expressed in the fresh, light colours and fluid handling. The other two paintings by him in Budapest, *Venus, Adonis and Cupid* and the allegory *Justice Disarmed*, are earlier works, more plastic and Baroque in style.

From the Esterházy collection.

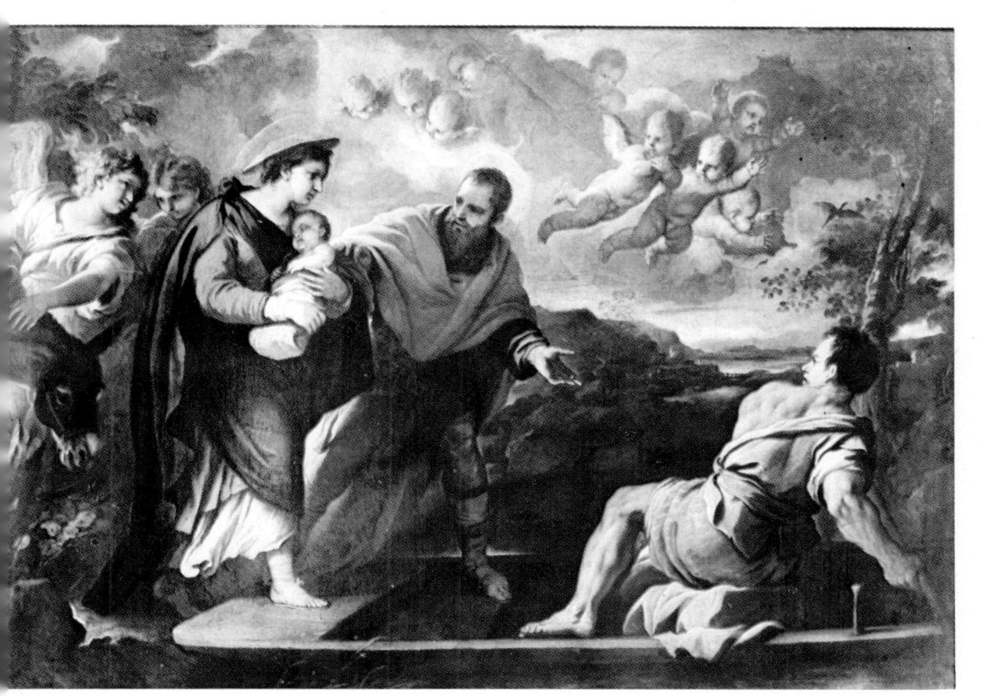

BERNARDO STROZZI Genoese, 1581–1644
The Annunciation
Canvas 57 1/8 ″ × 47 1/4 ″ (145 × 120 cm.) Inv. No. 596

At the age of seventeen the Genoese Bernardo Strozzi became a Capuchin monk (hence his nicknames of 'Il Capucino' or 'Il Prete Genovese'), but in 1610 he left his convent in order to support his mother and sister by his work as a painter. When the former died and the latter married he was recalled to his order but disobeyed and, to escape imprisonment, fled to Venice where he spent the rest of his life. Influenced to some extent by the painters of Venice but mainly by Caravaggio and Rubens, Strozzi was a versatile and extraordinarily prolific artist, whose work comprises nearly every kind of painting – frescoes, altar-pieces, genre scenes and portraits. His approach was natural and robust, his forms vigorous and his colours warm, even fiery. There are six of his paintings in the Museum of Fine Arts, of which the large *Annunciation*, painted during his Venetian period, is the most beautiful. This composition and *The Tribute Money* (p. 254) vividly reveal his dynamic manner of composition and brilliant colouring.
From the Esterházy collection.

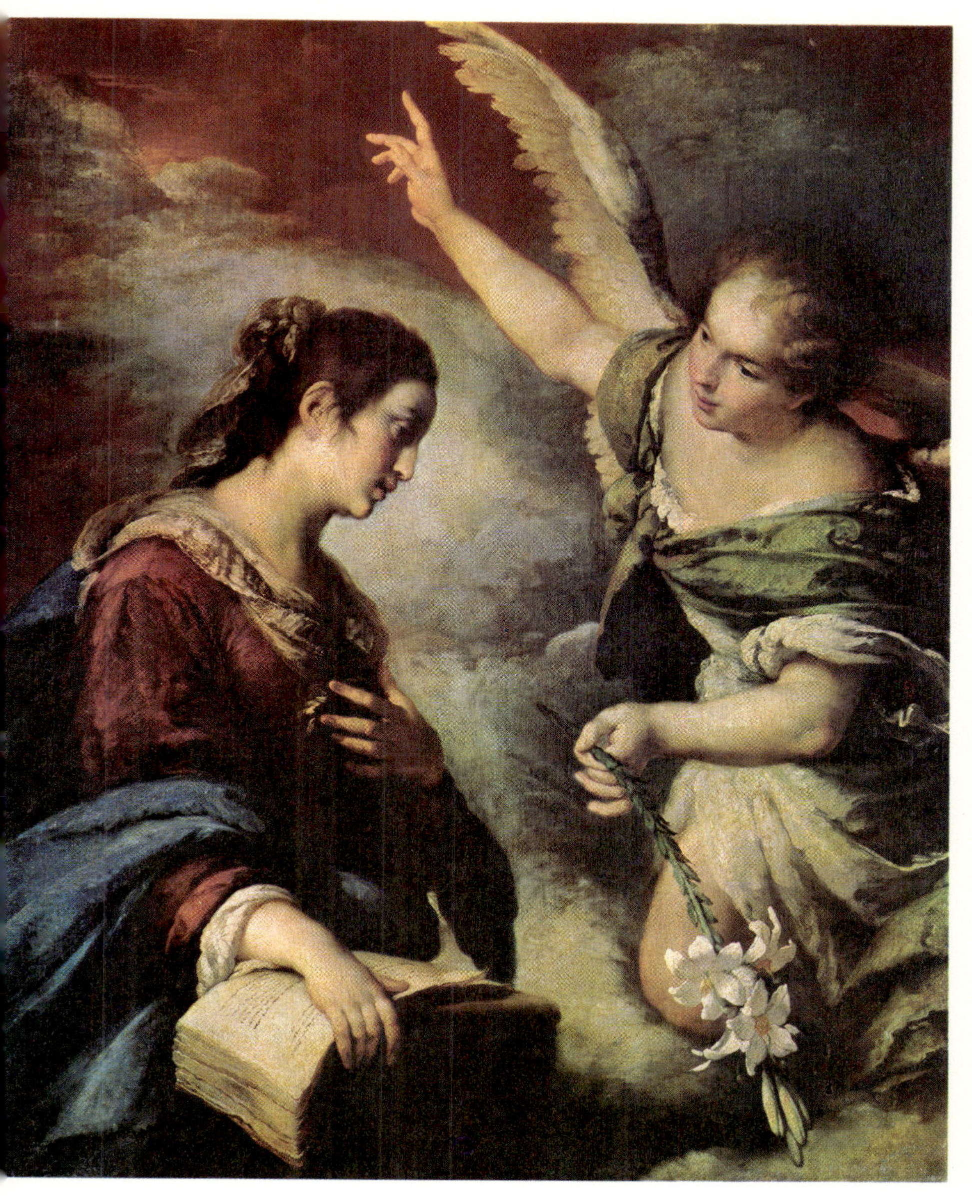

ALESSANDRO MAGNASCO Lombard and Genoese, 1667–1749
The Inquisition
Canvas 17 3/8″ × 33 1/2″ (44 × 85 cm.) Inv. No. 594

The Genoese Alessandro Magnasco was taught by his father Stefano and a little known Milanese painter, Filippo Abbiati, and began by painting in a conventional seventeenth-century style. During his stay in Florence at the beginning of the eighteenth century, however, he became acquainted with the work of Salvator Rosa and the etchings of Callot, and under their influence developed a content and style of his own. His themes were bizarre, different from anything to be seen in Genoa, Milan, or indeed anywhere in Italy; nor did his manner of painting resemble that of any other artist in Italy. He depicted imaginary scenes, *capriccios* in many of which monks are seen in strange settings or tiny figures in stormy landscapes. In his paintings, which are usually small, the figures are oddly elongated, the strokes of the brush vibrating and restless; indeed, everything seems to be in flickering movement. He also painted scenes in which he showed up the anxieties of his age, as for instance in this picture, which depicts a torture-chamber of the Inquisition. He borrowed some of his motifs from Callot's etchings, but the expressive arrangement and flowing rhythm of the groups are a reflection of his own highly individual and original style. A larger and later version of the same composition is in the Vienna Gallery.

From the Esterházy collection.

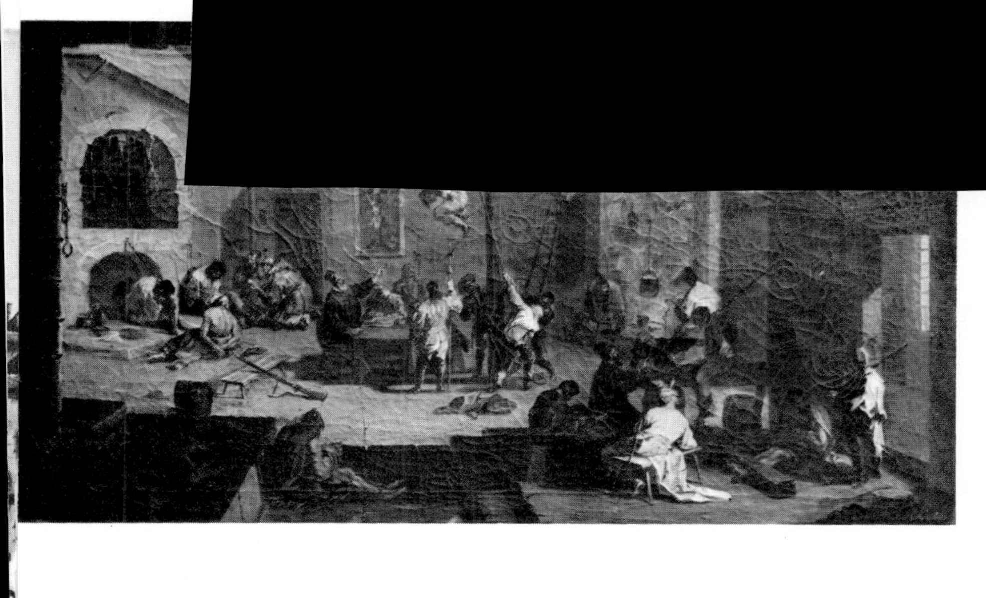

Like many of his contemporaries, Sebastiano Ricci spent a large part of his life in travelling about Europe, painting works commissioned by secular and ecclesiastical authorities. After studying in Venice Ricci worked in Bologna, Parma and Rome, Milan and Florence, and was invited to the Imperial court in Vienna, where he worked on the Schönbrunn Palace. In 1712 he went to England where he decorated Chelsea Hospital Chapel and began work on Burlington House. The latter was finished by Kent when in 1716, reputedly angered at failing to obtain the commissions for decorating St Paul's Cathedral and Hampton Court, Ricci returned to Venice. He worked there for the rest of his life, embellishing the churches, religious houses and villas of the city and surrounding countryside with lavish works in gay colours.

The Museum of Fine Arts owns four significant works by Ricci. The two large Biblical compositions, *Bathsheba Bathing* and *Moses Defending the Daughters of Jethro* (p. 255), as well as *Venus and the Satyr*, are thought to have been painted between 1720 and 1730. *The Assumption* is one of Ricci's latest works, painted shortly before his death in 1734 for the Karlskirche, the most beautiful Baroque church in Vienna. The sketch for this composition, also acquired by the Museum as part of the Esterházy collection, is an exquisite and poetic work, delicately executed with light strokes of the brush.

From the Esterházy collection.

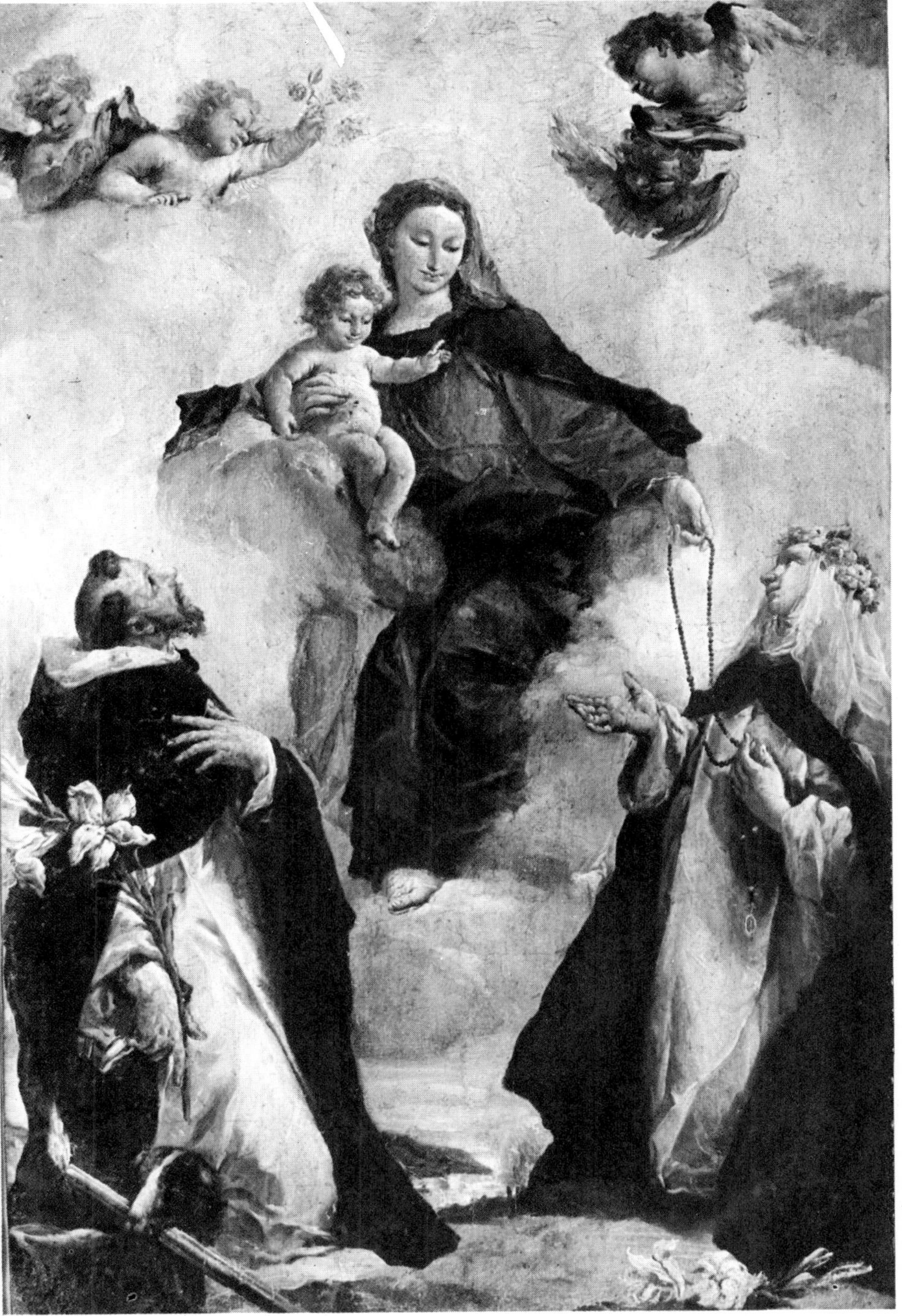

FRANCESCO GUARDI Venetian, 1712–93
Bridge at Dolo
Cardboard 5 3/4″×7 1/4″ (14.5×18.5 cm.) Inv. No. 4252

The city view, or *veduta*, is a genre specifically associated with eighteenth-century Venetian painting. Travellers from abroad were eager to buy pictures of Venice as souvenirs, and Canaletto and Luca Carlevaris painted large views of the city, executed with great topographical accuracy, which were particularly popular with the English. There was another type of *veduta*, however, in which the artist tried to record a mood or fleeting impression, at the same time introducing bizarre or imaginary elements into a real scene. One of the most successful masters of this latter genre, known as the *veduta ideata* or *capriccio*, was Francesco Guardi. After the death of his elder brother, Giovanni Antonio, Francesco developed independently, abandoned figure painting and devoted his time exclusively to *vedute*. The Museum of Fine Arts has four of his works, depicting lagoons, bridges and churches in the countryside near Venice.

From the Pálffy bequest.

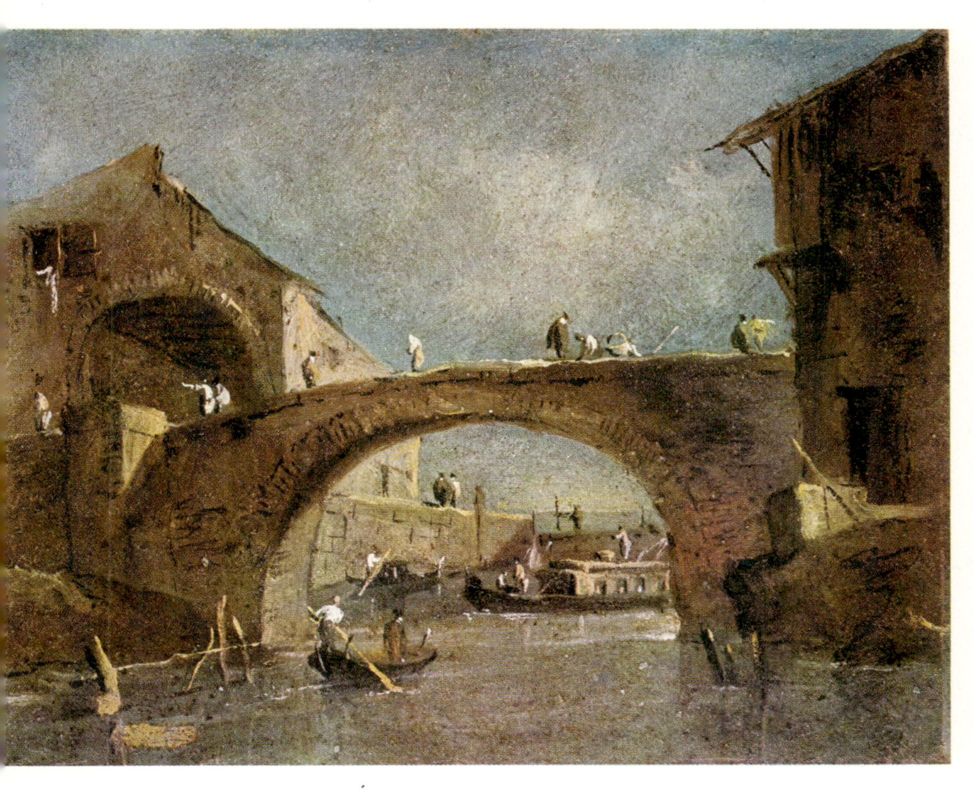

EL GRECO (DOMENIKOS THEOTOCOPOULOS)
Spanish, 1541–1614
Mary Magdalene
Canvas 61 5/8″ × 47 5/8″ (156.5 × 121 cm.) Inv. No. 5640

The young Cretan painter studied in Venice, where he was chiefly influenced by his great contemporaries, Titian, Jacopo Bassano and Tintoretto; for a short time he worked in Parma, Rome and Naples, but around 1576 he moved on to Spain for reasons which are still not clear.

In this relatively early picture the Magdalene, represented as a woman of mature beauty with an oval face and auburn hair falling to her shoulders, is closely related to Titian's female figures, and the picturesque still-life of book and skull, as well as the atmosphere of the landscape in the background, show a clear Venetian influence. Yet, in the expressive power and the colours, the young El Greco is already revealing a number of individual characteristics of style: the curve of the hands indicating internal tension, the light, flickering in the landscape, which conveys a strange restlessness. But the most striking feature is the colouring: a peculiar disharmony of yellows and blues, so different from the warmth of the Venetians.

Like five of the other six El Grecos in the Museum of Fine Arts (pp. 115, 117, 257), *Mary Magdalene* was formerly owned by the Hungarian collector, Marcell Nemes. During the early years of the twentieth century, he was one of the first connoisseurs to discover El Greco, who had been scarcely known until then, and one of the first collectors to buy his works in Spain.

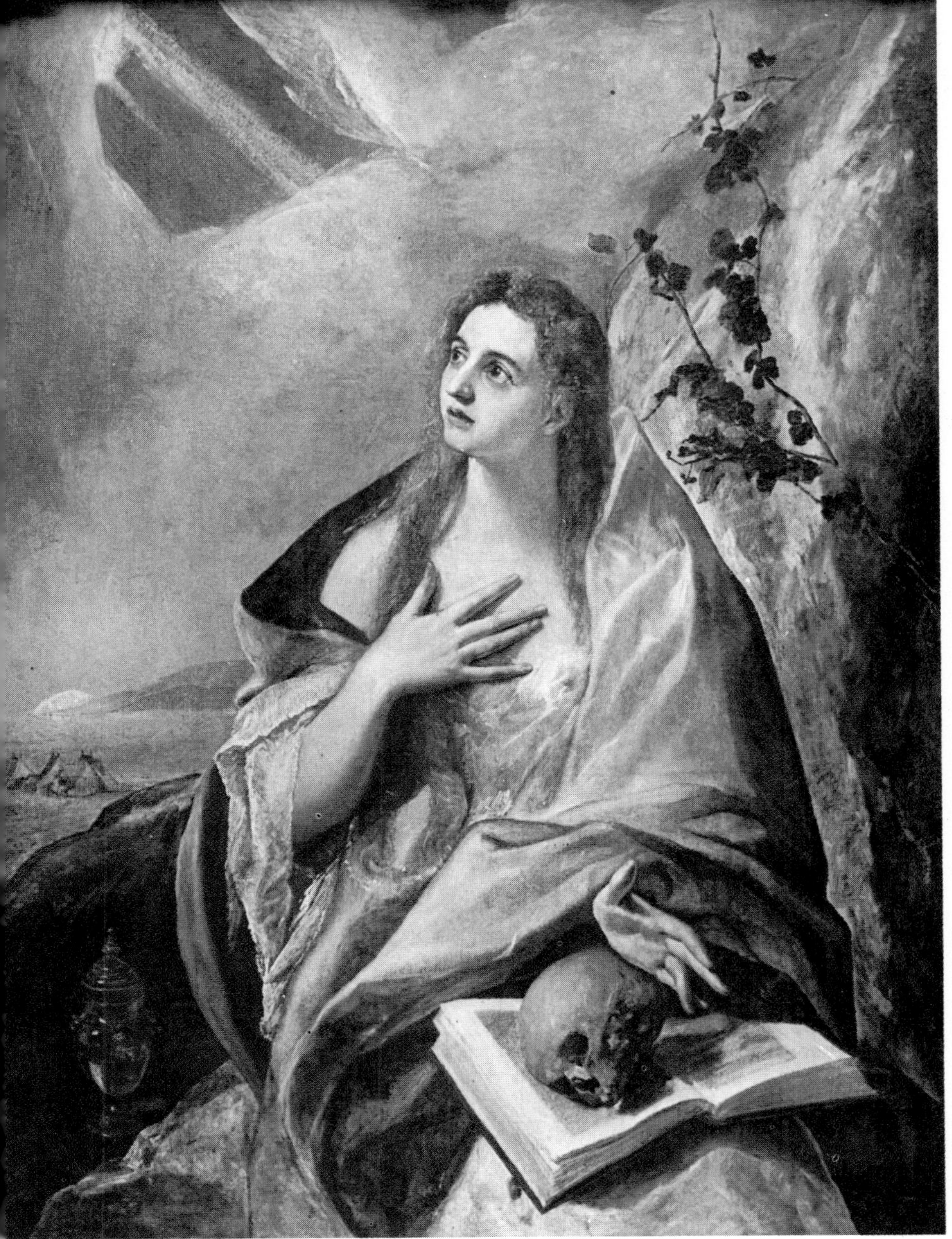

EL GRECO (DOMENIKOS THEOTOCOPOULOS)
Spanish, 1541–1614
The Agony in the Garden
Canvas 66 7/8″×44 1/4″ (170×112.5 cm.) Inv. No. 51.2827
Signed at bottom right in Greek characters

When the young El Greco went to Spain, he settled in Toledo, carrying out a number of ecclesiastical commissions including his famous *Disrobing of Christ* in the cathedral. Between 1580 and 1583 he painted *The Martyrdom of St Maurice* for Philip II, but this extravagant, passionate and uneasy painting was not approved by the King, who preferred the calm and ordered style of Titian and the Italian High Renaissance. El Greco therefore found it impossible to settle in court circles and returned to Toledo, the centre of the Church in Spain, where for the rest of his life he painted mainly works commissioned for churches and monastic orders.

In his religious compositions and portraits he frequently repeated themes from his major works, with slight alterations, to meet different commissions. He broke away from the Renaissance tradition and ceased to depict reality and nature. In order to convey mystic emotions and to imbue his work with passion he distorted and elongated the forms and used stridently blazing colours to express the transcendental. *The Agony in the Garden* is one such mystic interpretation representative of El Greco's late years and mature style.

From the collections of Lipót M. Herzog and Marcell Nemes.

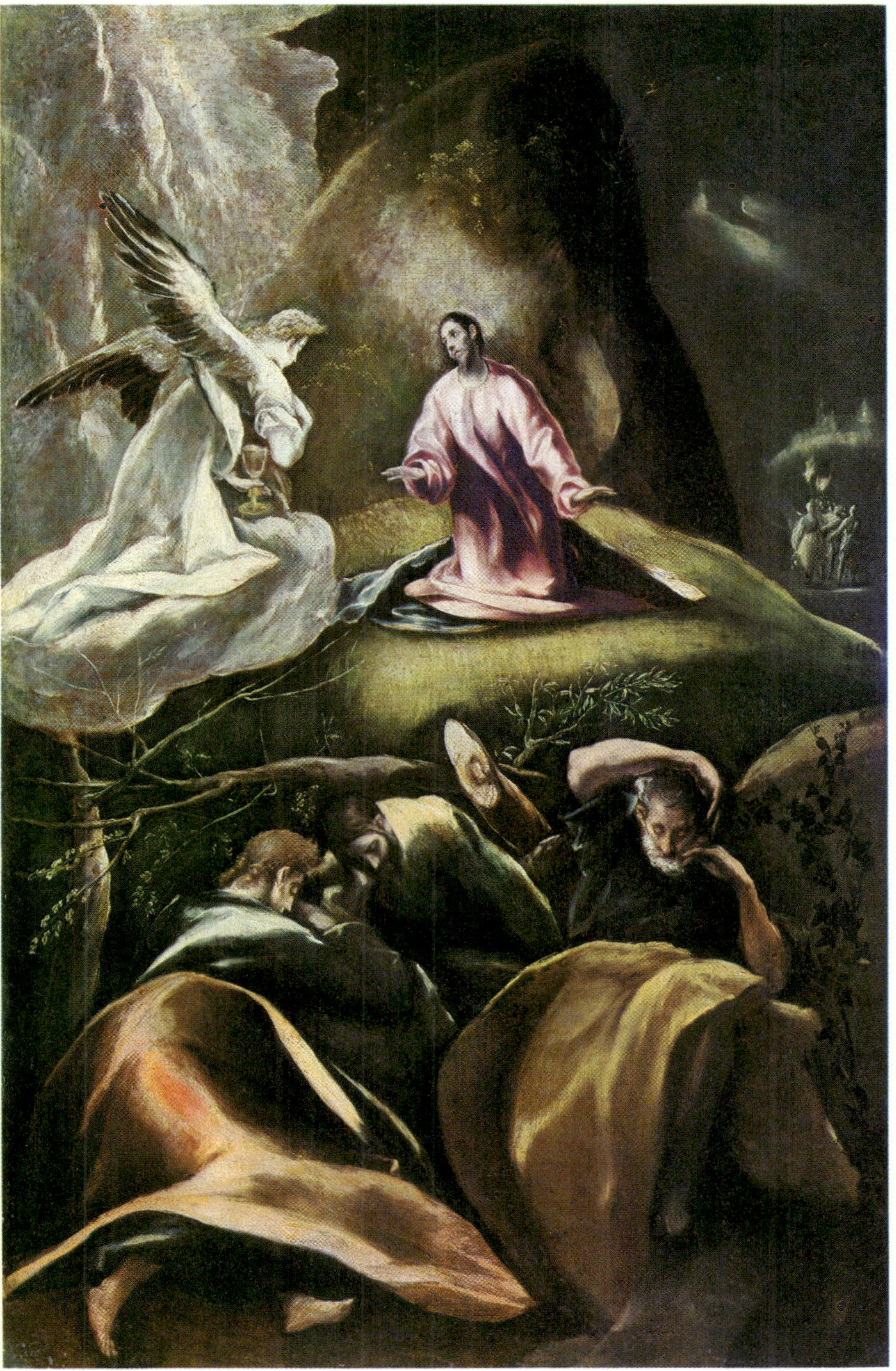

EL GRECO (DOMENIKOS THEOTOCOPOULOS)
Spanish, 1541–1614
Study of a Man
Canvas 19 1/2″ × 16 3/4″ (49.5 × 42.5 cm.) Inv. No. 9048

Likenesses have a special place in El Greco's work. Although he was primarily interested in painting religious subjects for ecclesiastical commissions, he also produced some outstanding portraits, often inserting them into his religious compositions, as for example in the famous *Burial of Count Orgaz* in Toledo. His formal portraits and studies from life are characterized by an element of drama and a penetrating insight into the character of the sitter. He was not interested in depicting the background, nor in the insignia of rank or office which would indicate the subject's worldly status or occupation, and his sitters nearly always face the spectator – and their faces reveal the soul within.

No doubt the *Study of a Man* is a likeness, though we do not know the identity of the model nor in what connection it came to be produced. The sketchy greenish-purplish draperies and the cloud-streaked blue background are a perfect foil for the thin ascetic face with its sparse beard. The picture was usually believed to represent El Greco himself, but as a result of recent research it is now thought to be one of a series of likenesses of the Apostles – painted from an unknown model in Toledo.

From the collections of Lipót M. Herzog and Marcell Nemes.

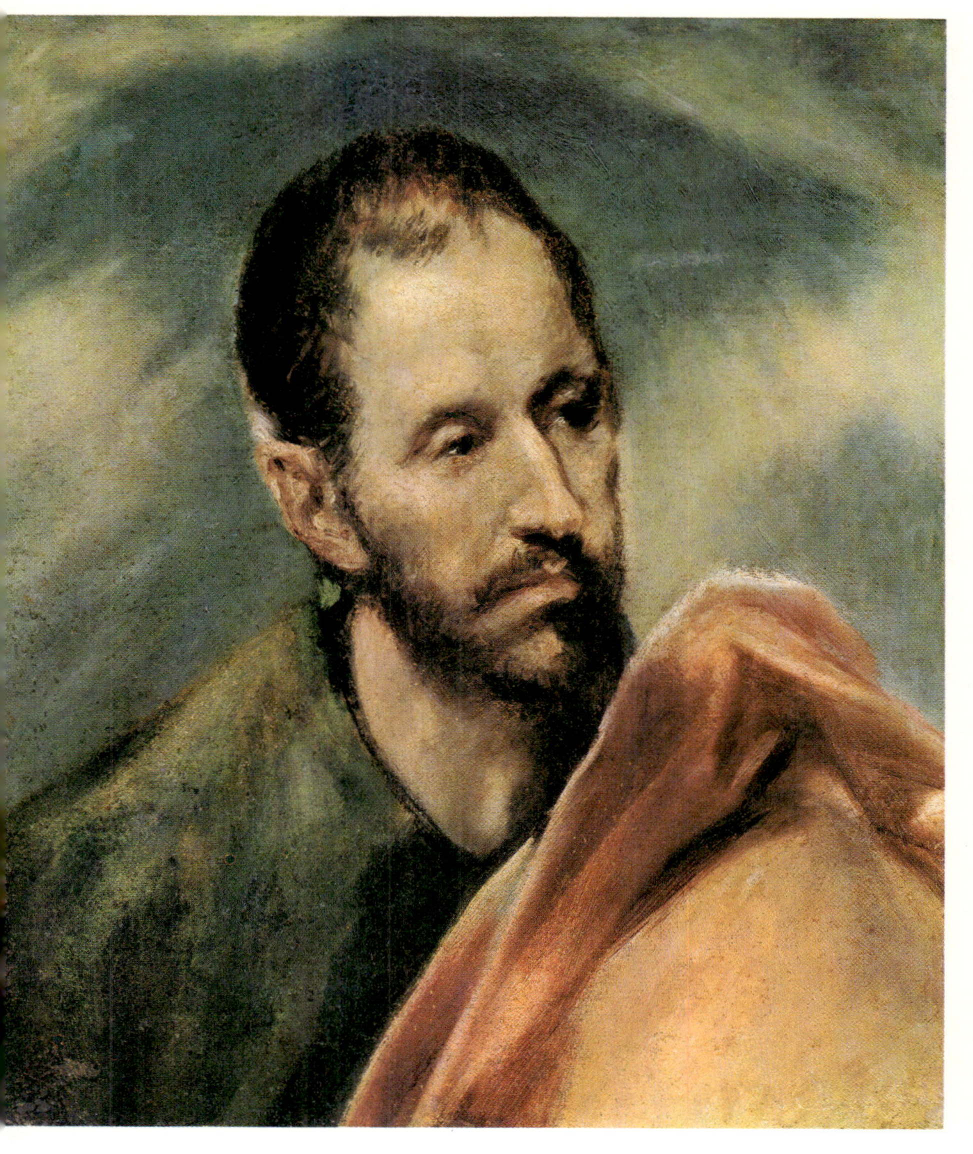

JUSEPE DE RIBERA (LO SPAGNOLETTO) Spanish, 1591–1652

The Martyrdom of St Andrew

Canvas 82 1/4″ × 72″ (209 × 183 cm.) Inv. No. 523

Signed bottom right

Jusepe de Ribera studied in Francisco Ribalta's workshop in Valencia, but when still young he went to Naples, then under Spanish rule, where he worked for the rest of his life. He obtained most of his commissions from the Spanish Viceroy and his entourage, but he also completed a good many paintings for the churches and religious houses of the city.

The influence of that bold innovator, Caravaggio, was felt throughout southern Italy and there can be little doubt that Ribera was the artist with the strongest and most independent personality of all his followers. Ribera represented crude reality boldly and without embellishment. The construction of his pictures is monumental and he reveals a strong sense of drama, emphasized by means of strongly contrasting light and shade. The poor inhabitants of Naples and the peasants of southern Italy were his models, and he depicted them without flattery or idealization as enormous figures clothed in rags. Dating from 1628, *The Martyrdom of St Andrew*, with its powerful forms, effective diagonal composition and dramatic lighting embodies all that is most specific and characteristic in Baroque painting as it developed under the influence of Caravaggio.

From the Esterházy collection. Formerly in the Kaunitz collection in Vienna.

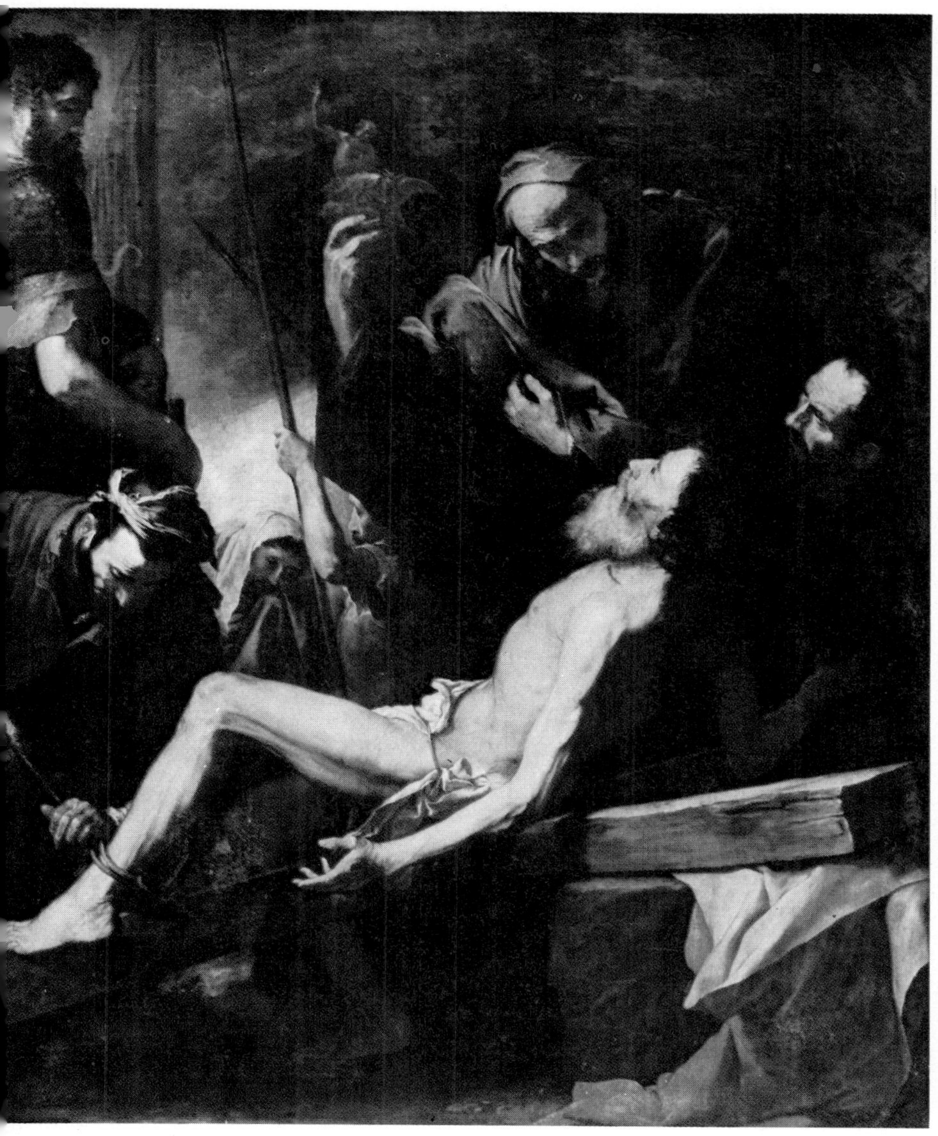

DIEGO RODRÍGUEZ DE SILVA Y VELÁZQUEZ
Spanish, 1599–1660
Peasants at Table
Canvas 37 3/4″ × 44 1/8″ (96 × 112 cm.) Inv. No. 3820

Having mastered the rudiments of painting under Francisco Herrera and his father-in-law, Francisco Pacheco, Velázquez worked for a time in his native Seville. He was primarily attracted by the characteristic figures of the locality and the everyday scenes of Seville: the old water-carrier who walked the streets with his huge clay jar, an old woman cooking her broth and peasants at their simple meals.

Peasants at Table is one of his finest early pieces of the type known in Spain as a *bodegón*, a combination of conversation piece and still-life. Velázquez studied his models with loving attention, depicting them as faithfully as any portraitist. We can see from the types he chose, their gestures and expressions, that he had a marked gift for portraying both national and individual characteristics. This is complemented by clean, simple lines and a lucidly constructed composition. There is another version of *Peasants at Table* in the Hermitage in Leningrad.

Purchased from a British private collection in 1908.

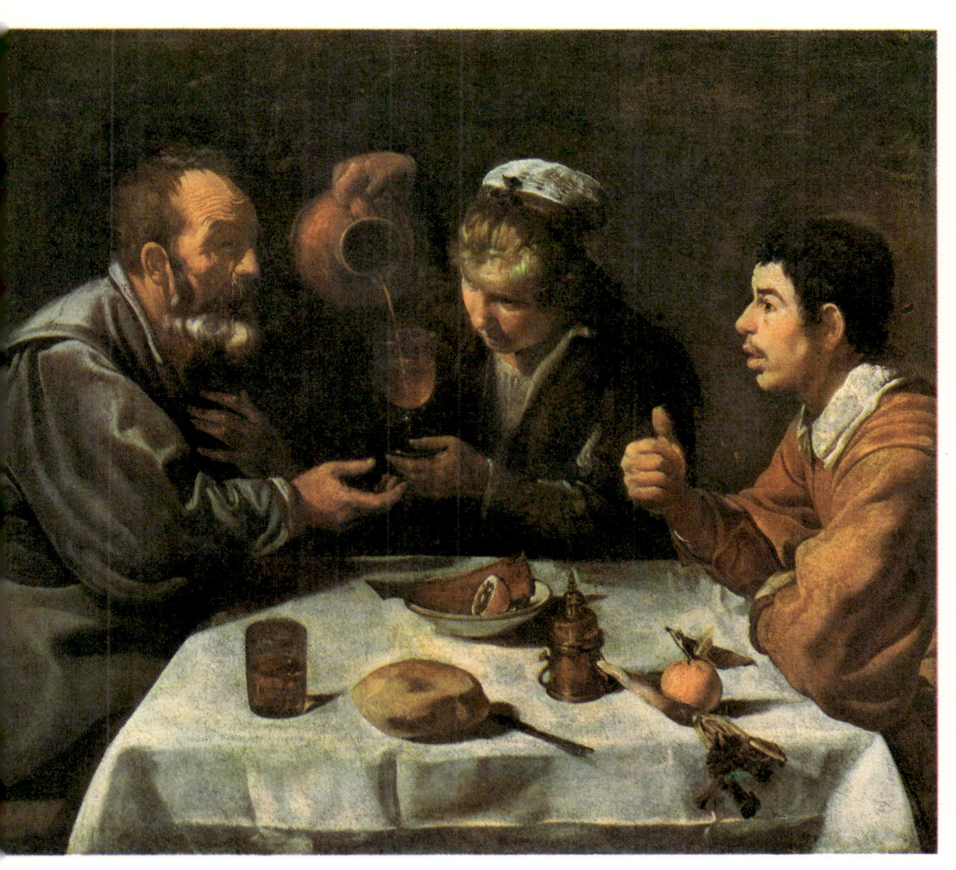

BARTOLOMÉ ESTEBAN MURILLO Spanish, 1618–82
The Infant Jesus Distributing Bread to Pilgrims
Canvas 86 1/4" × 71 5/8" (219 × 182 cm.) Inv. No. 777

Murillo, like Velázquez, began his career in Seville, where he was taught by a local master, Juan del Castillo. Then he went to Madrid where he saw the works by the great Italian and Flemish masters in the royal collection. In 1645 he returned to his native city and in 1660 was one of the founders and the first president of the important and influential Seville Academy. He was chiefly occupied in executing commissions for religious houses and churches in Seville, so that most of his work therefore was of a religious nature. His fame as an artist, in his own lifetime and ever since, has rested mainly on his Madonnas, where he uses the tender female figures of Andalusia as models, introduces starry-eyed children and depicts saints in some intimate, contemporary milieu.

This large picture, which he painted in 1678 for the refectory of an alms-house, was commissioned by Canon Justino de Neve, whom we see in the kneeling group of pilgrims in the bottom corner. Like so many of Murillo's paintings this composition is characterized by delicately-shaded, warm colouring and a harmonious structure and is full of his special charm and lyricism.

From the Esterházy collection.

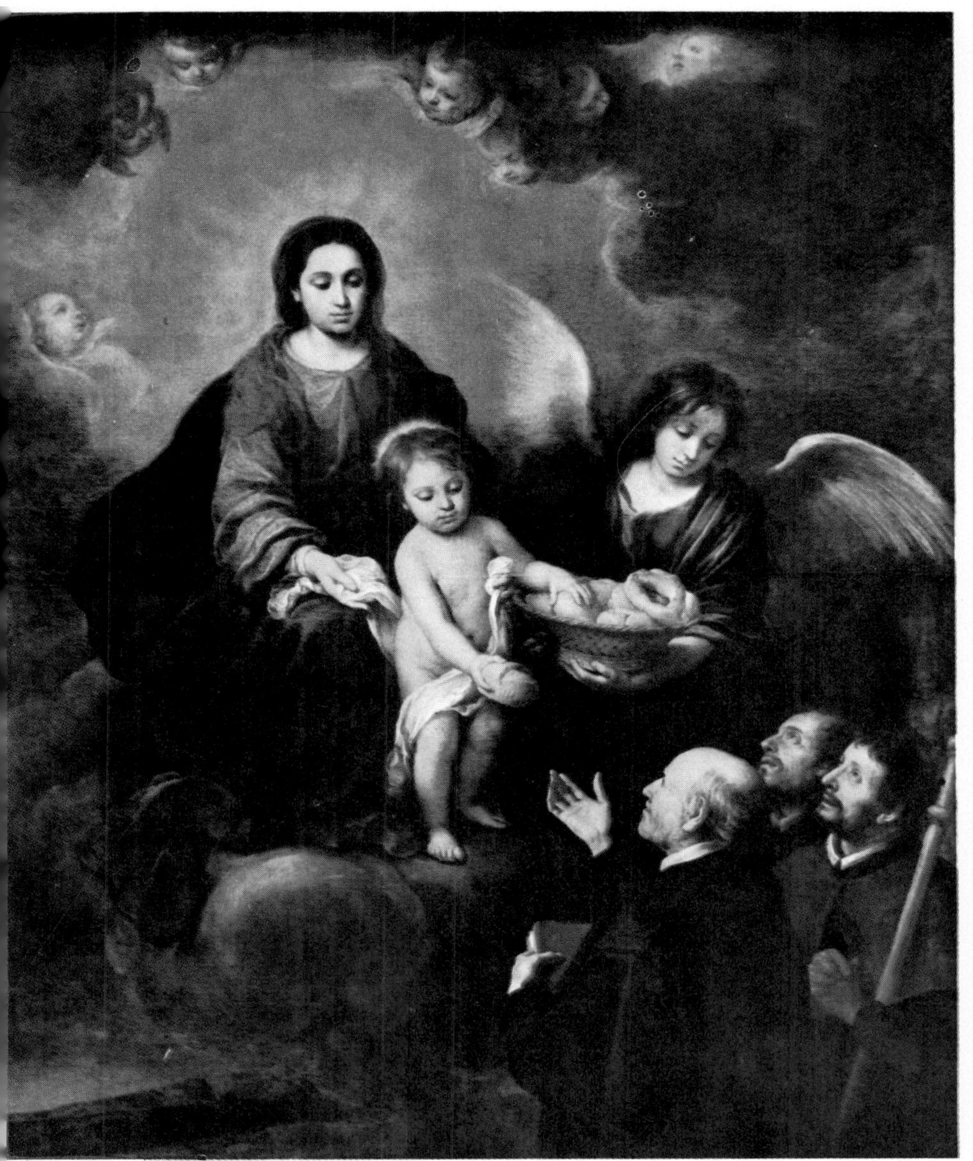

ALONSO CANO Spanish, 1601–67

Noli me Tangere

Canvas 55 3/4″ × 43 1/8″ (141.5 × 109.5 cm.) Inv. No. 787

Signed at bottom right: ALO · CANO · F

Alonso Cano was a painter, sculptor and architect and worked for varying periods in nearly every large town in Spain – Madrid, Seville, Valencia and Toledo. He was a pupil of the famous sculptor Juan Martinez Montañés and learned the rudiments of painting in the studios of Juan del Castillo, Francisco Pacheco and Francisco Herrera the Elder. His *œuvre* is very rich, though more restricted in range than that of Velázquez or Murillo, for he painted almost exclusively religious subjects, keeping strictly to the accepted ecclesiastical tradition.

The Budapest Museum of Fine Arts has three works by Cano: the gentle *Head of the Virgin*, the large *St John the Evangelist on Patmos* and this painting, which dates from around 1640. Cano never went to Italy but was strongly influenced by the Italian masterpieces in the Spanish royal collection. The composition of his *Noli me tangere* owes much to the inspiration of Correggio's painting of the same subject, which was in Madrid at that time, and the colouring shows the influence of the Venetian masters, especially Titian.

From the Esterházy collection; before 1820 in the collection of Count Edmund Burke, Danish Ambassador to Spain.

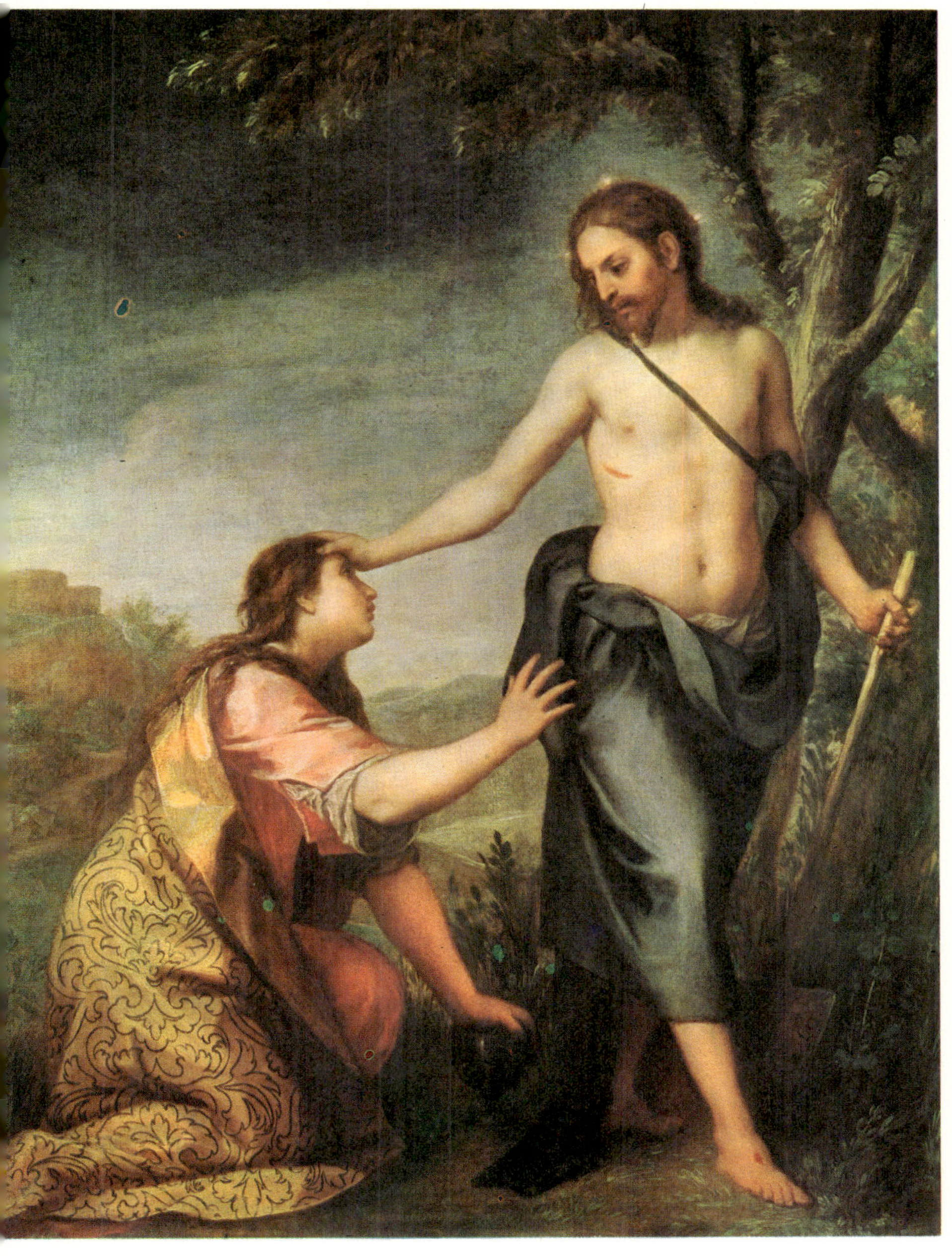

FRANCISCO DE ZURBARÁN Spanish, 1598–1664
The Holy Family
Canvas 47 7/8″ × 38 1/8″ (121.5 × 97 cm.) Inv. No. 2536
Signed on the manger at the bottom: Franco De Zurbaran f. 1659

Whereas the names and works of Velázquez and Murillo were known and appreciated by European connoisseurs at a relatively early date, Zurbarán was scarcely known outside Spain, and even now there are not very many of his works to be found in European galleries. Born in Fuente de Cantos, a small village in Estremadura, he studied in Seville and most of his work, almost exclusively commissions for monastic orders and churches, was done there. These circumstances determined his themes and the way he treated them: he painted hardly anything but religious subjects, mostly scenes from the lives of the saintly or monastic visionaries. His pictures are generally characterized by a severe structure, vigorous forms, rustic models and a close and detailed observation of nature.

During the last years of his life Zurbarán worked in Madrid where, mainly under the influence of Murillo, his interpretation became softer, his way of expression more lyrical and his colours lighter. *The Holy Family*, signed and dated 1659, is a remarkable example of this late period: a simple composition of half-length figures with an intimate charm and emotionalism strongly reminiscent of Murillo.

Bought from a Paris dealer in 1904.

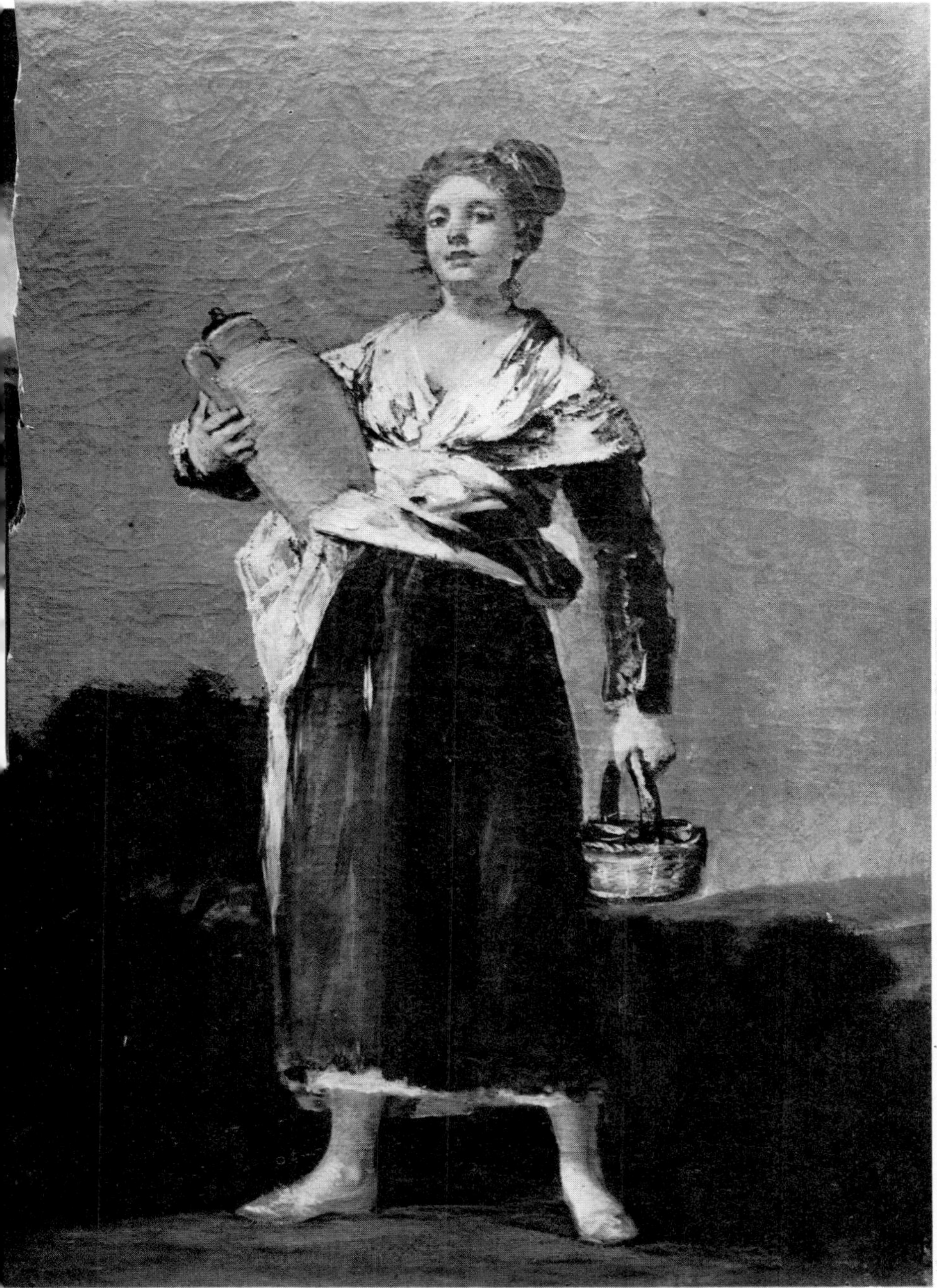

FRANCISCO DE GOYA Spanish, 1746–1828
Señora Bermúdez
Canvas 47 5/8″ × 33 1/4″ (121 × 84.5 cm.) Inv. No. 3792

Goya was one of the boldest and most brilliant portraitists in the history of painting. His insight into character, as seen in the group-painting of the royal family in Madrid, his portrait of the Duchess of Alba or his study of the overbearing Godoy, has hardly ever been equalled. Nonetheless, in spite of the fact that he neither flattered nor beautified his sitters he was one of the most popular portraitists of his period. The artistic qualities of his works and his unfailing ability to convey the personality of his sitters, made them forget all that their vanity would otherwise have demanded.

This portrait, painted in the early 1790s, is a ravishing and astonishing achievement, yet it is the likeness of a young Spanish woman with rather insignificant features. The sitter, the wife of Goya's friend, the writer Ceán Bermúdez, is represented as being neither beautiful nor particularly intelligent as she looks at us wonderingly, somewhat timidly, her hands resting on the embroidery on her lap. The painter has broken up the rather dark tone of the painting with greens and touches of red and white to give a translucent appearance to her lace gown, silk shawl and flowery head-dress.

Bought from a Vienna dealer in 1908. Formerly in the collection of the Marqués de Casa Torres in Madrid.

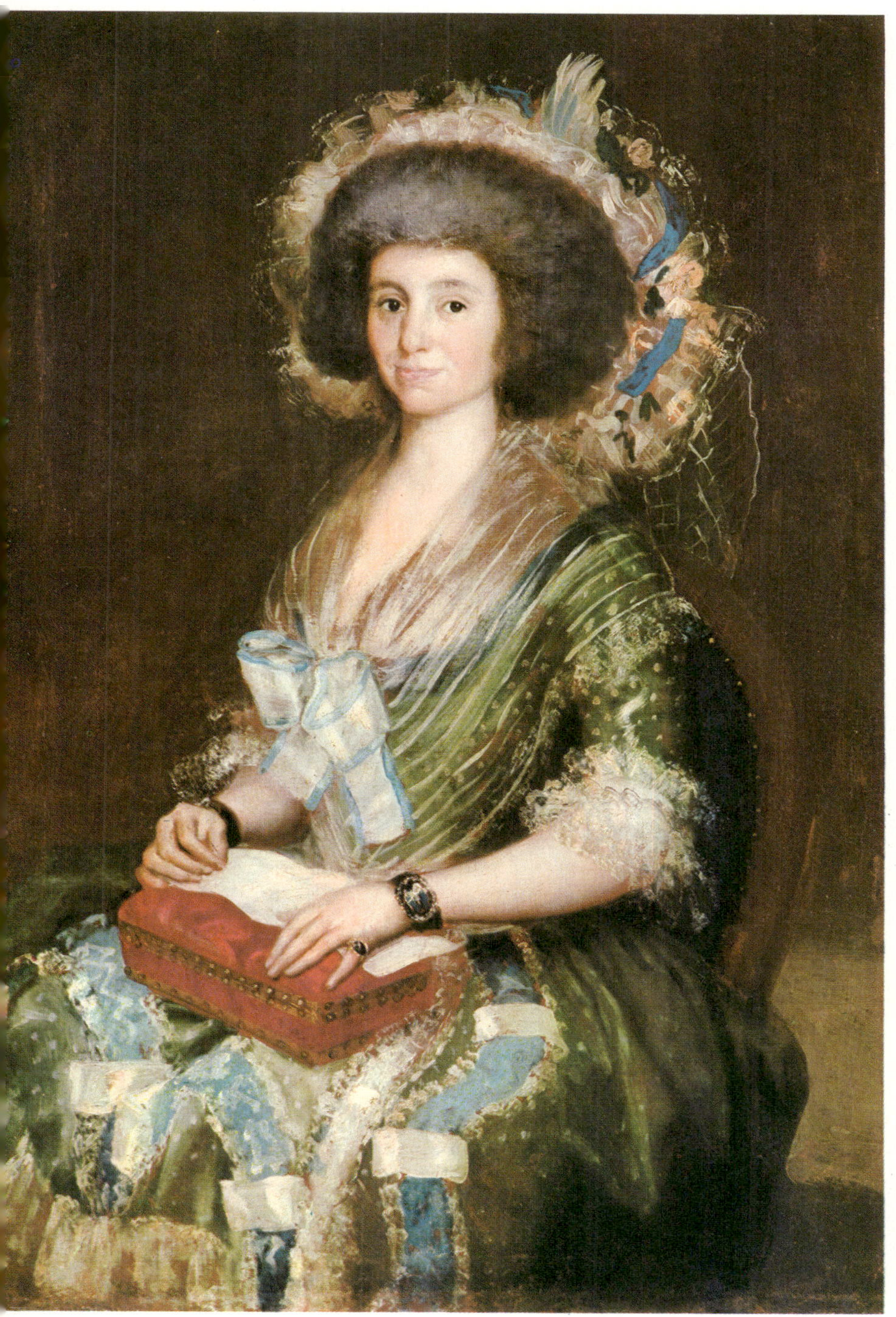

PETRUS CHRISTUS Netherlandish, d. 1472/3
The Virgin and Child
Panel 21 7/8″ × 12 3/8″ (55.5 × 31.5 cm.) Inv. No. 4324

We know very little about the life of Petrus Christus, though it is certain that in 1444 he obtained the citizenship of Bruges, then the richest town in Flanders and its main artistic centre. He may have been the pupil of Jan van Eyck, and in his surviving panel paintings we can see that his solutions to problems of composition and his figure types are similar to those of his predecessor. Indeed Christus's delicately wrought and brilliantly coloured works served to popularize the technique and manner of Van Eyck.

Some fifteen to twenty works by Christus are known, one of which is *The Virgin and Child*, probably the surviving part of a triptych for home devotion. Framed by a semi-circular arch resting on slender columns and with a pleasant landscape in the background, the Virgin looks tenderly down at the naked Infant supported on her arm. Every detail has been painted with meticulous care – the minute wrinkles on the Infant's face, the foliage of the trees in the distance and the statuette of Adam and Eve on the columns at the sides, which, in alluding to the Fall, emphasize the coming Redemption through Christ. Other versions and copies have survived, indicating the popularity of this picture over the years, but unfortunately none of them give any clue as to when it was painted or who commissioned it.

From the Pálffy bequest.

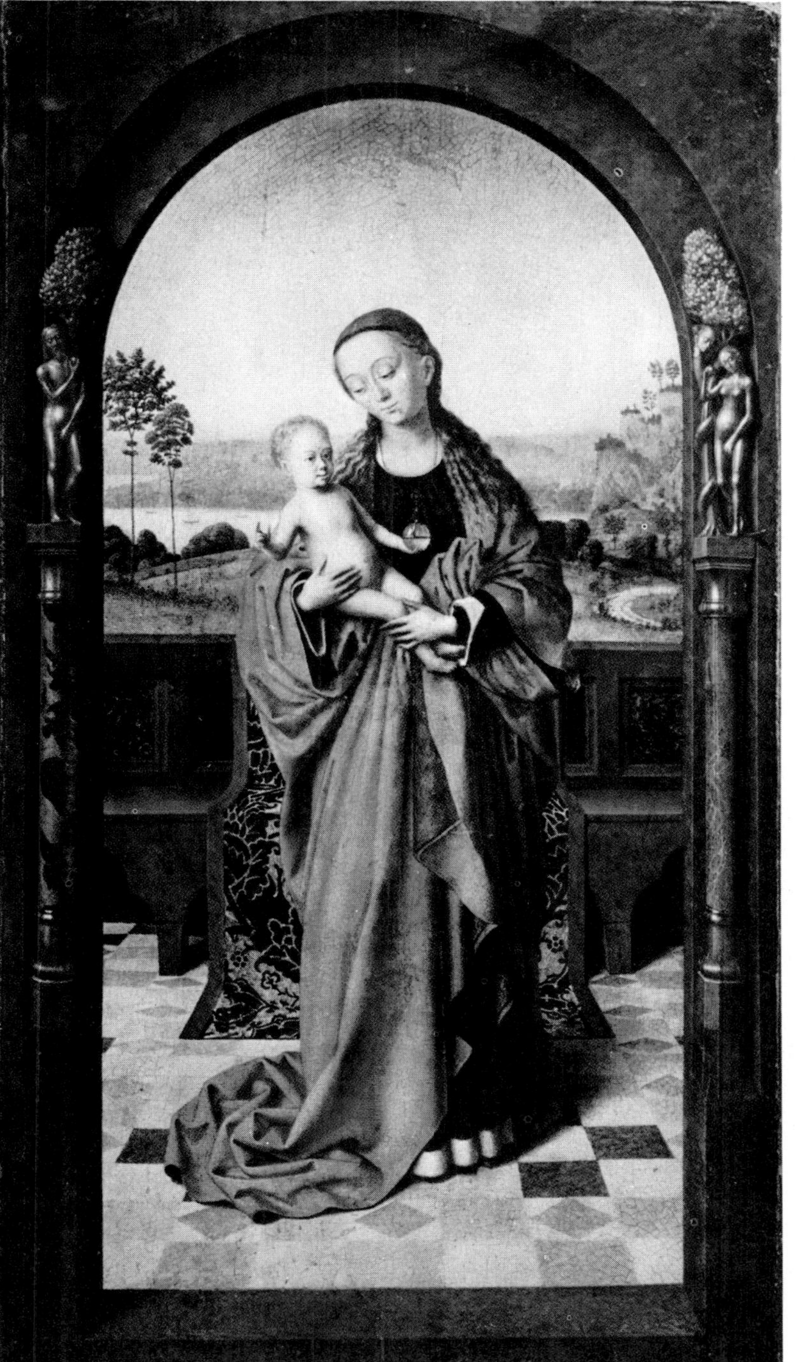

GERARD DAVID Netherlandish, *c.* 1460–1523
The Nativity
Panel 30 1/8″ × 22″ (76.5 × 56 cm.) Inv. No. 1336

Gerard David, one of the most important of the Netherlandish painters, was born in Oudewater in the northern province of Holland, but in 1484 he settled in the south, in Bruges. When this city began to lose its importance as a trading centre he moved on to Antwerp, where he is recorded as a member of the painters' guild in 1515. His *œuvre* provided a link between the late Gothic art of the earlier Netherlandish masters and the new Renaissance style; in it we see a felicitous combination of the vigour characteristic of the northern masters and the brilliant technique and feeling for form seen in the work of those of the southern provinces. He painted mostly altar-pieces, Madonnas and saints, striving to make the figures lifelike and including many natural, intimate details. In this *Nativity* the shepherds, ungainly in their clumsy boots, look as if they scarcely dare to approach the Infant (the figure in the background opening is usually believed to be a self-portrait) and the streets and houses of the town in the background are depicted with the detailedclarity of a topographer. One of David's early works, the picture is believed to have been executed about 1490.

Bought from the Bourgeois Brothers in Cologne in 1894.

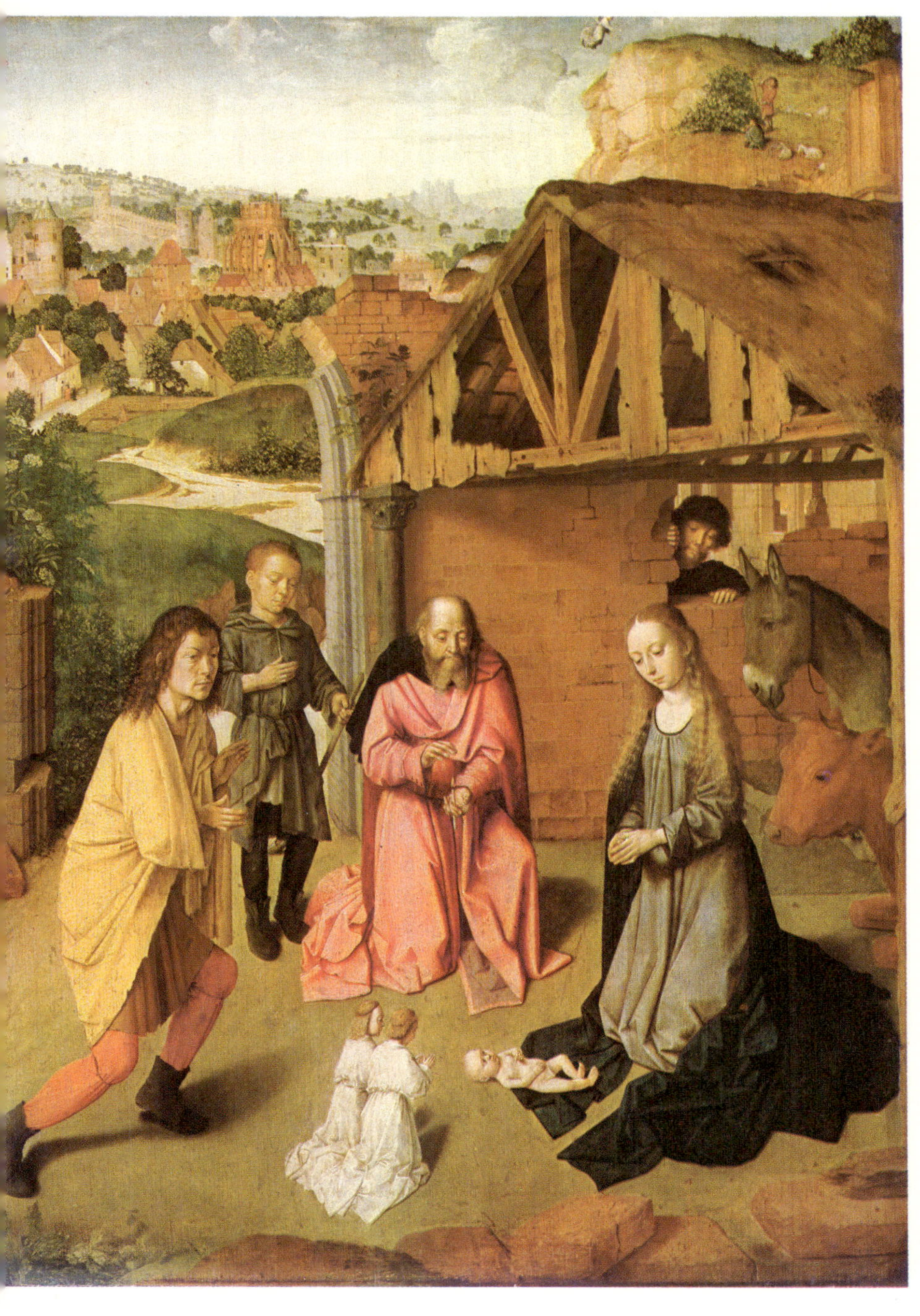

JOOS VAN CLEVE Netherlandish, *c.* 1485–1540

The Virgin and Child

Panel 20 5/8″ × 16 1/2″ (52.5 × 42 cm.) Inv. No. 4329

Very little has been discovered as yet about the life and activity of Joos van Cleve, also known as Joos van der Beke, although some of his most important paintings have been firmly attributed and the sphere of his activity outlined, at least approximately. At one time he was known only as the Master of the Death of the Virgin, after a large altar in Cologne, and, since there were several painters surnamed van Cleve, his pictures have often been confused with their work. Joos was born in Bruges in the 1480s and worked in Antwerp from 1511 onwards. His altar-pieces and portraits were known and appreciated beyond the boundaries of the Netherlands, and he spent some time as a portrait painter at the court of Francis I, King of France. He was influenced by Leonardo and the Italian Renaissance painters, but in his religious compositions he mostly adhered to the great tradition of early Netherlandish painting handed down from Van Eyck and Rogier van der Weyden. This half-length Madonna is a late Gothic type, frequently found also in Memling's works. She faces the spectator and gives to her Child a glass of red wine symbolic of the Redemption. The colouring is brilliant, the fresh green of the landscape and the fiery red of the Virgin's mantle creating a lovely harmony.

From the Pálffy bequest.

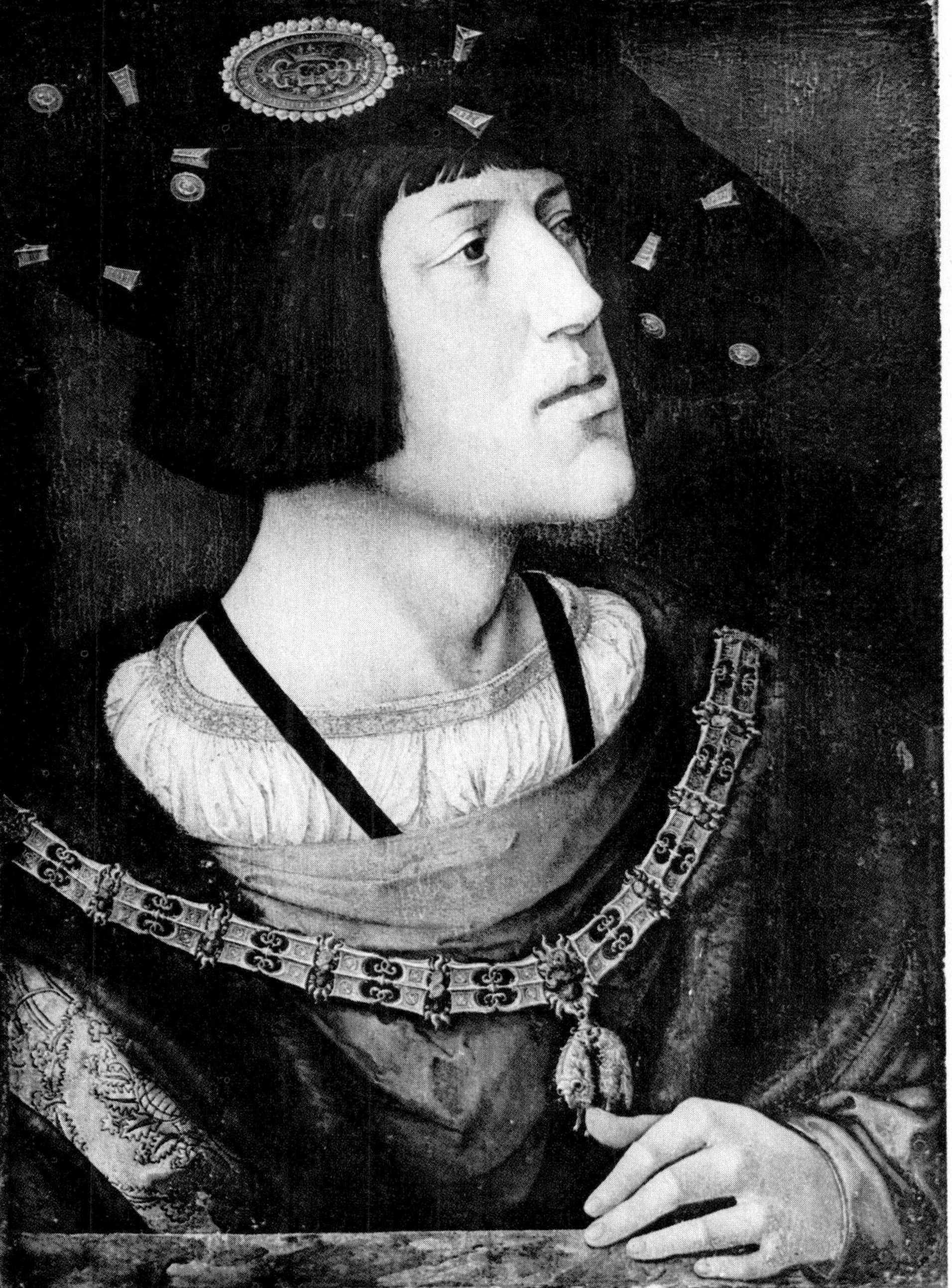

PIETER BRUEGEL THE ELDER Netherlandish, *c.* 1522–69
St John the Baptist Preaching
Panel 37 3/8″ × 63 1/8″ (95 × 160.5 cm.) Inv. No. 2829
Signed at bottom right: BRVEGEL M.D. LXVI

Karel van Mander, in his lives of the Netherlandish painters, has described how Pieter Bruegel would regularly visit a village wedding or a fair, mixing with the crowd and making sketches of the people and their manners and clothes. He made use of these studies in his pictures of Biblical episodes, which, for the most part, served only as a pretext for depicting the everyday life of Flanders.

In this picture of St John the Baptist we recognize a village preacher at one of the religious congregations which were a feature of the Reformation. The figure of St John, however, is almost lost in the heart of the picture, the principal subject being the motley and colourful crowd – a haphazard congregation of believers, or people merely curious to see what was going on, some attentive, some bored. An abundance of detail combined with dramatic intensity, integration of figures with landscape and an expressive power unequalled in its vividness are the principal characteristics of this masterpiece. Numerous copies made by Bruegel's sons testify to its popularity through the ages.

Acquired for the Museum of Fine Arts in 1951, originally from the Batthyány Castle at Nagycsákány. Probably identical with the *Sermon of St John the Baptist* recorded with about the same dimensions in the 1633 inventory of Isabella, Regent of the Netherlands, in Brussels.

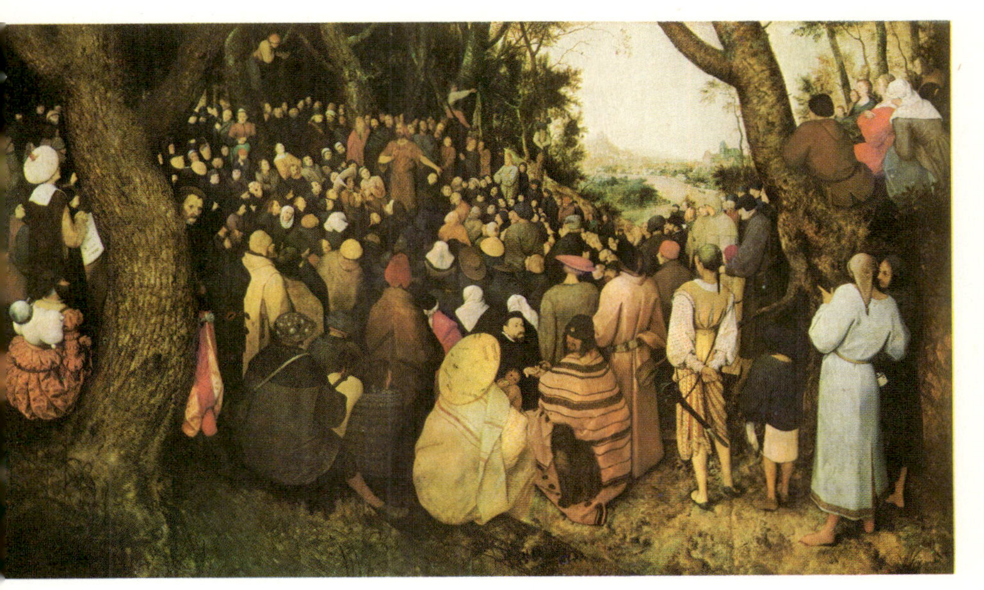

PIETER AERTSEN Netherlandish, 1508–75
Market Scene
Panel 66 7/8″ × 32 5/8″ (170 × 82.8 cm.) Inv. No. 1337
Dated 1561

Genre-painting, as an independent subject, originated in the Netherlands in the sixteenth century. Before then scenes from everyday life had often been depicted in the background of pictures with a primarily religious content, but it was only after about the middle of the sixteenth century that many painters began to feel their principal task was to represent everyday life for its own sake. With Pieter Bruegel the Elder, also called Peasant Bruegel, genre-painting came to be generally accepted and found a great many adherents in the Netherlands. Pieter Aertsen, who was born in Amsterdam and worked mainly in his native city and in Antwerp, was one of the most eminent of these. Most of his works depict market vendors, scenes at fairs or kitchen interiors, with an abundance of carefully painted still-life motifs.

In this painting he depicts an old Dutch peasant taking his produce to the market, on his head a heavy tub, in his right hand a brace of mallard and a basket of eggs. A peasant girl in the background kneels by a tray of pasties or loaves. The painter has achieved an effect of monumentality by using large spots of colour and clear outlines and by enclosing his powerfully modelled figures within the confines of a narrow space. Aertsen's great virtue lies in his sincerity and simplicity, particularly noticeable if we compare his work with later genre-scenes.

Bought in 1894 from the Bourgeois Brothers in Cologne.

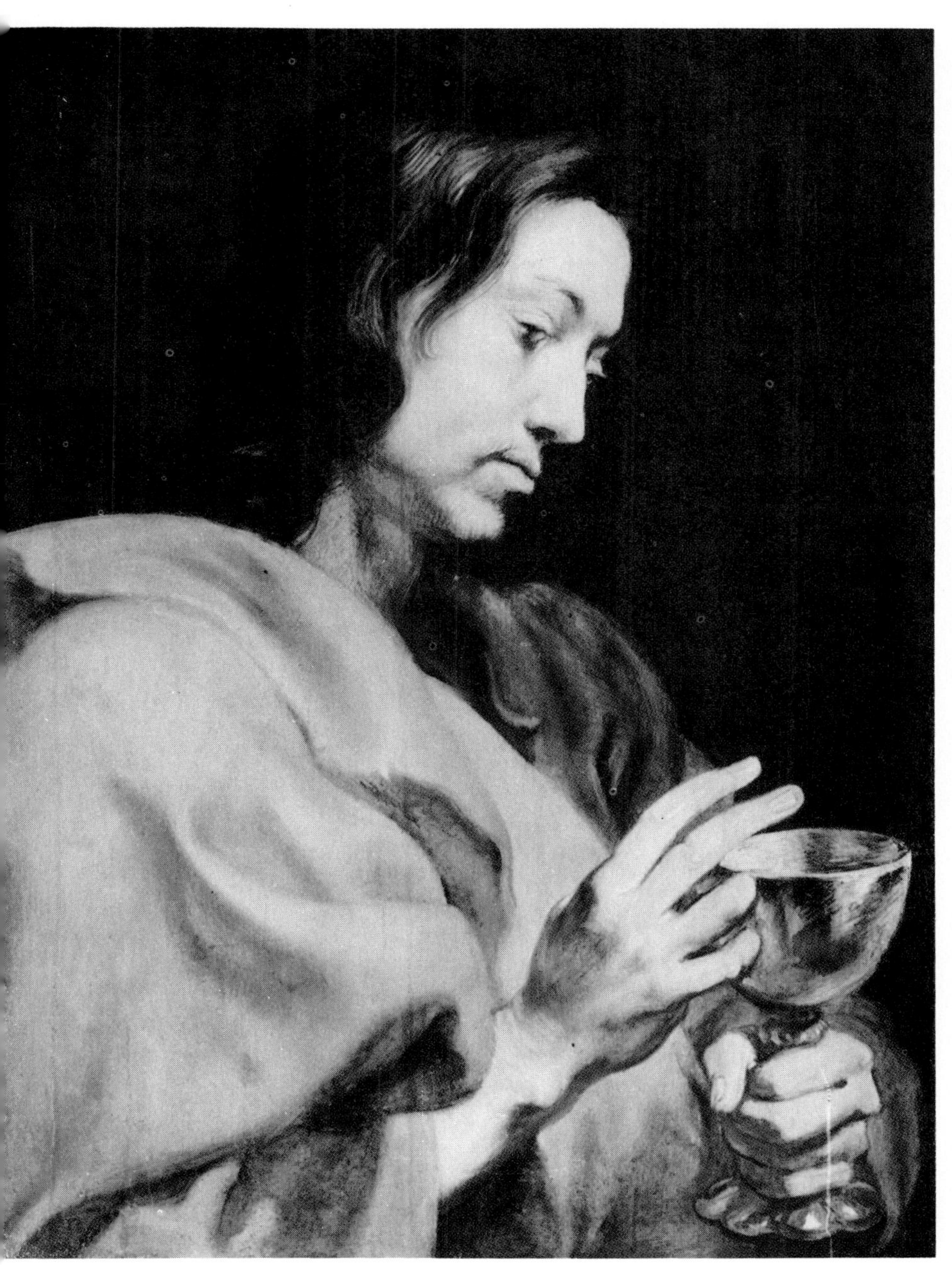

SIR ANTHONY VAN DYCK Flemish, 1599–1641
Portrait of a Married Couple
Canvas 44 1/8″ × 51 5/8″ (112 × 131 cm.) Inv. No. 754

After the years of studying in Rubens's workshop and a sojourn in Italy, Van Dyck settled in his native city of Antwerp and soon became one of the most popular portraitists of the wealthy bourgeoisie. For the most part he painted full-length official likenesses, or else family portraits with the sitters posed in settings of homely intimacy. He devised many different arrangements and poses, suiting them to the character and rank of the sitter, but the effect was always serious, noble and distinguished, and the impression of solemnity and reserve was enhanced by the dark costumes – high-necked black garments with starched ruffs – as in the portrait of the couple in Budapest.

In this picture attention is focused on the sharply characterized faces and expressive, delicately depicted hands, while the black and white of the clothes, the red of the armchair, and the gold of the gloves provide a marvellously harmonious background. We do not know the identity of the married couple, unfortunately, and to discover their connection with any particular Antwerp family seems hardly possible today.

From the Esterházy collection. Formerly in the Kaunitz collection in Vienna.

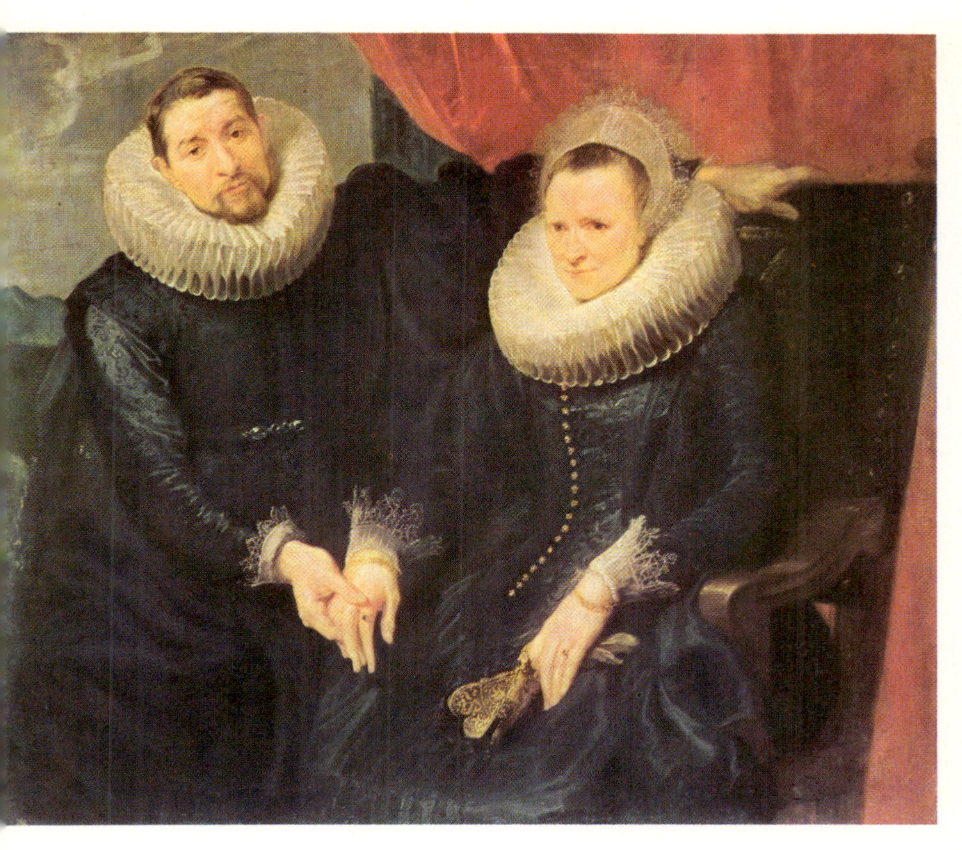

JACOB JORDAENS Flemish, 1593–1678

The Peasants and the Satyr

Canvas 74 3/4″ × 65″ (190 × 165 cm.) Inv. No. 738

Although his career was not so brilliant nor the range of his activity so wide as those of Rubens and Van Dyck, Jacob Jordaens was the next most significant master in seventeenth-century Flanders. His art was more deeply rooted in the popular Flemish tradition and he stayed in his native city of Antwerp all his life. Overwhelmed with both secular and ecclesiastical commissions, particularly after the death of Rubens, he painted large altar-pieces, religious, historical and mythological compositions, allegories and portraits – but he felt most at ease as a genre-painter, depicting scenes from everyday life. His pictures are peopled with ruddy, buxom wenches, heavy old women and Flemish peasants even though many of his pictures have a narrative element and illustrate myths or legends of saints.

Jordaens liked, and often painted, Aesop's fable about the satyr who was surprised when his peasant host first breathed on his hands to warm them and then breathed on his soup to cool it. He created a fascinating, lively picture in which the simplicity of the setting, the intimacy of the interior and the charming figures of the peasants are contrasted with the goat-footed mythological creature. The picture is generally thought to be one of Jordaens's early works, possibly dating from between 1620 and 1630.

This painting, together with another important work by Jordaens was acquired as part of the Esterházy collection.

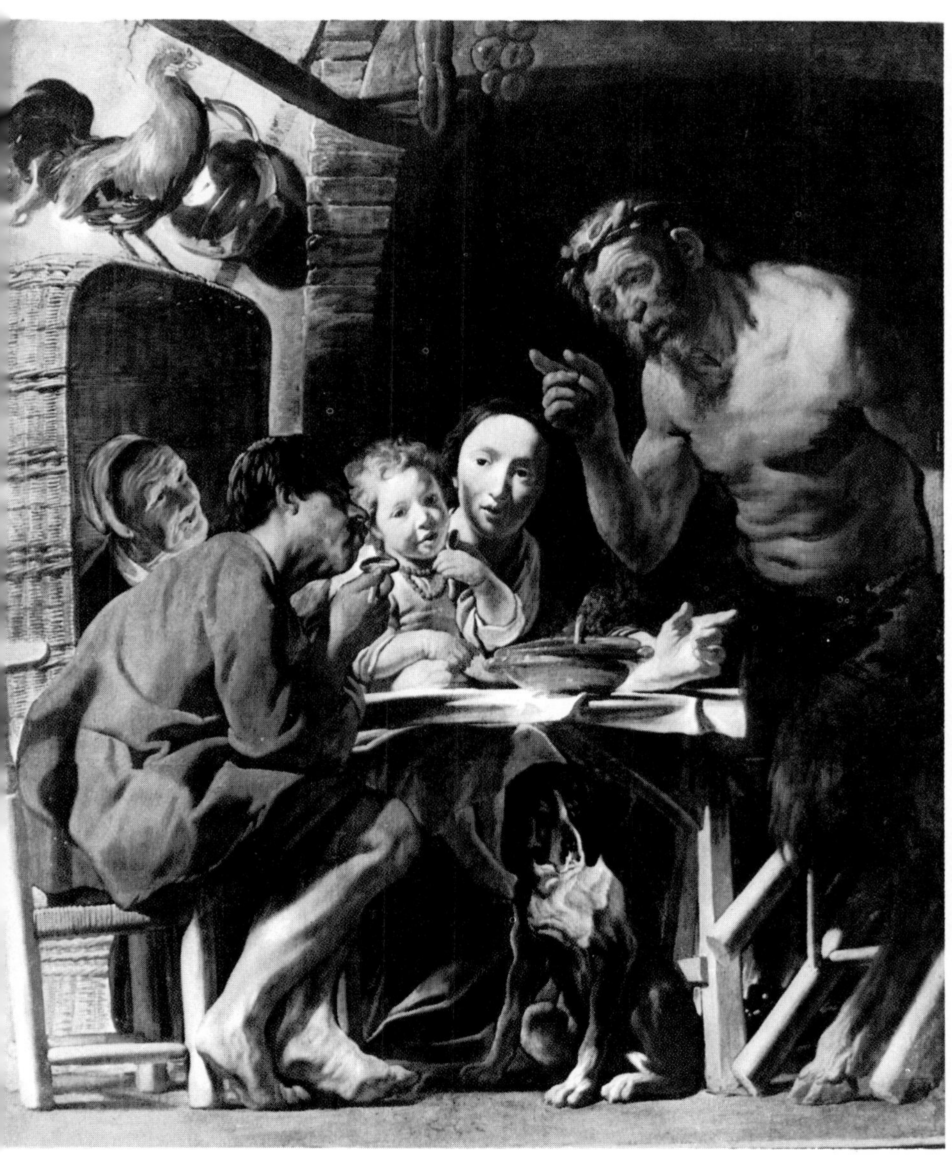

JAN SIBERECHTS Flemish, 1627–1703
The Ford
Canvas 28 1/4″ × 23 1/2″ (71.8 × 59.6 cm.) Inv. No. 1226
Signed at bottom left: J. Siberechts en. anvers. 1672

The painters of the Netherlands have always found in their own countryside an almost inexhaustible treasury of themes. Fertile fenland stretching into the distance, carefully maintained farmsteads, fords, meandering lanes with carts stuck in the mud, bluish waterfronts – these are the motifs repeatedly found in the works of Jan Siberechts, one of the most popular of the Flemish landscape painters. And these landscapes are peopled with figures closely associated with the toil of the land: a buxom country woman sits on a milking stool in front of a barn, a girl with her skirt tucked up drives a cart across a ford, a young herdsman rests while his flock grazes. In these contemplative paintings the mood is gentle; their appeal lies in the sparse arrangement of the motifs, the harmonious structure and bluish-grey colouring. In this picture, with its low horizon, light plays a very important role in connecting the foreground with the depths of the picture. It conveys movement and change and creates a feeling of harmony between man, beast and landscape.

Purchased in Cologne in 1896.

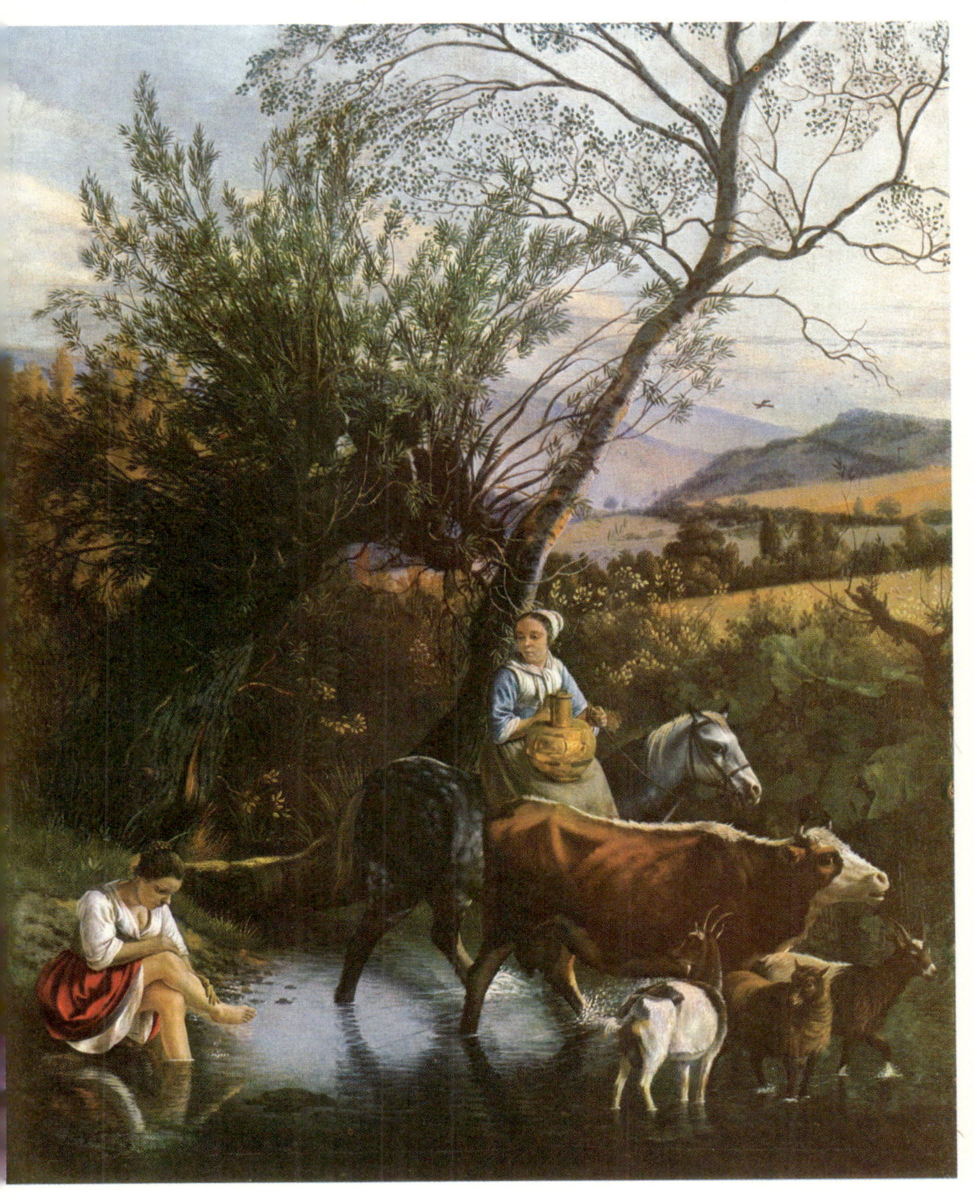

CORNELIS VAN HAARLEM (CORNELIS CORNELISZ.)
Dutch, 1562–1638
The Golden Age
Canvas 61 7/8" × 76 1/8" (157 × 193.5 cm.) Inv. No. 2062
Signed: CvH 1614

The Mannerists of the Netherlandish School frequently chose Graeco-Roman myths and complex allegories as subjects for their pictures and were particularly fond of representing nudes. Most of Cornelis van Haarlem's work consists of such paintings, three of which are now in the Budapest Museum. The earliest is *Jupiter Punishing Lara*, painted in 1597, *The Judgment of Paris* (p. 263), painted in 1628 and *The Golden Age*, dated 1614. In this latter work the painter depicted a company of nude figures feasting in the open air. There are innumerable versions of this scene variously entitled *The Feast of Gods*, *Bacchanalia* or *The Wedding of Peleus and Thetis*, and in some of them, as here, there are details indicating that the painter's intention was to illustrate the myth of the legendary golden age. But the Dutch painter's interpretation of this classical and idyllic theme is almost vulgar – even clumsy. The heavy nudes are not beautiful. The still-life motifs and genre-like details reflect the profound influence of Netherlandish realism, an artistic approach radically different from the classical tradition.

Bought from a Budapest dealer in 1902.

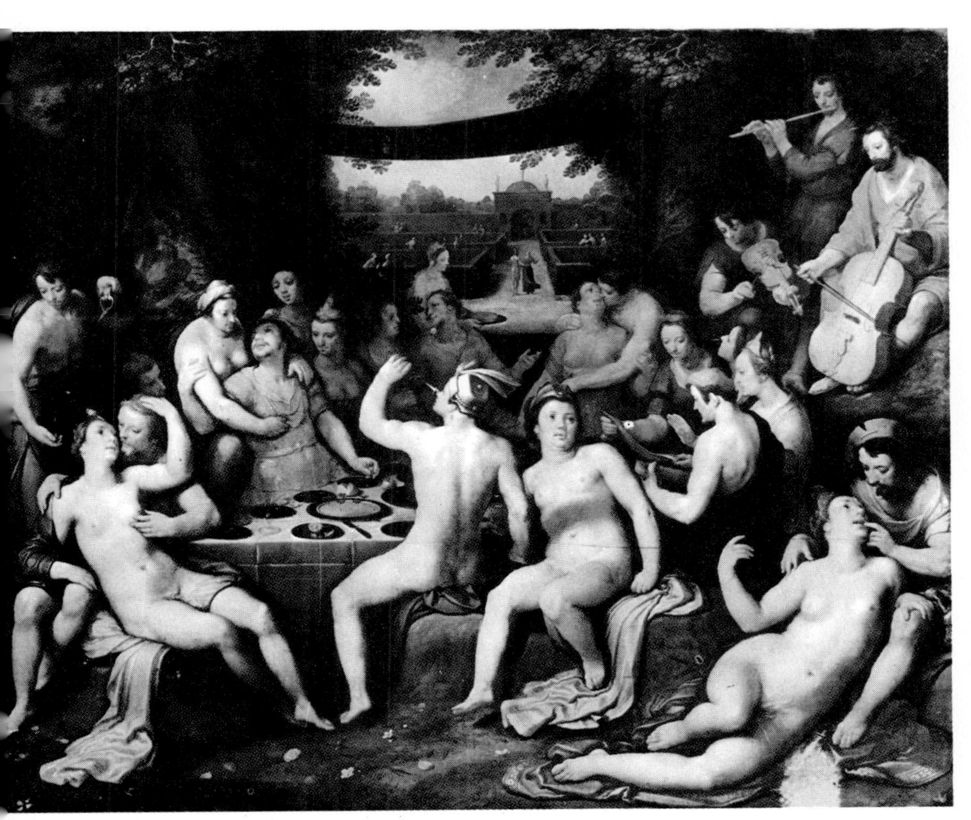

FRANS HALS Dutch, 1580/1–1666

The Painter Jan Asselyn

Canvas 25 3/8″ × 18 1/4″ (64.5 × 46.3 cm.) Inv. No. 277

Frans Hals lived and worked in Haarlem, and it was as a result of his achievements that the Haarlem School became one of the leading schools of painting in the Netherlands. He studied under the Mannerist painter Karel van Mander but, unlike his master, eschewed Biblical or mythological subjects and specialized in genre-scenes and, especially, portraits. In the early seventeenth century portraiture became the predominant and most flourishing branch of painting in Holland; after the heroic struggle for national independence the Dutch merchants, who had laid the foundation of the country's wealth, were disposed to have their portraits painted – singly or in groups – for presentation to their families, their heirs or some society.

In Frans Hals's work we can see almost every type of portrait: full-length, half-length, group portraits, studies of heads. Background detail is almost non-existent, the pictures usually being of a summary simplicity with figures in dark clothes and neutral backgrounds. Interpretation of character and expression is the dominant feature, and by means of effective poses and masterly brushwork, made up of black and white and grey strokes, the artist expressed the essence of his sitter's personality. In most cases we do not even know who the sitters were, and it is only recently that the dashing figure in this picture has been identified as the painter Jan Asselyn.

From the Esterházy collection.

REMBRANDT HARMENSZ. VAN RIJN and GERARD DOU
Dutch, 1606–69 and 1613–75
The Parable of the Hidden Treasure
Panel 27 3/4″ × 35 3/8″ (70.5 × 90 cm.) Inv. No. 342

Contemporary sources tell us that Rembrandt and his young pupil Gerard Dou worked together in Leyden between 1628 and 1631, and several jointly executed paintings are recorded in inventories and other documents. Very few of these works are known today, and for this reason *The Parable of the Hidden Treasure* is of special interest.

Set against a flat, gloomy landscape, the vigorous figure of the man with the satchels and the golden vessels before him vividly calls to mind Matthew 14, verse 44: 'The kingdom of heaven is like unto treasure hid in a field; the which when a man hath found, he hideth, and for joy thereof goeth and selleth all that he hath, and buyeth that field.' In the style and handling of the figure, the anxious expression on the face and the eloquence of the movement there is unmistakable evidence of the hand of Rembrandt – indeed the same head is to be seen in several of his other paintings and drawings. On the other hand the still-life in the foreground, meticulously and delicately wrought, is characteristic of Gerard Dou, and similar representations may be seen in many of his early works. This could even conceivably be the painting, described as the joint work of Dou and Rembrandt, that was listed in the estate of the Amsterdam merchant Johannes de Renialme in 1657.

From the Esterházy collection.

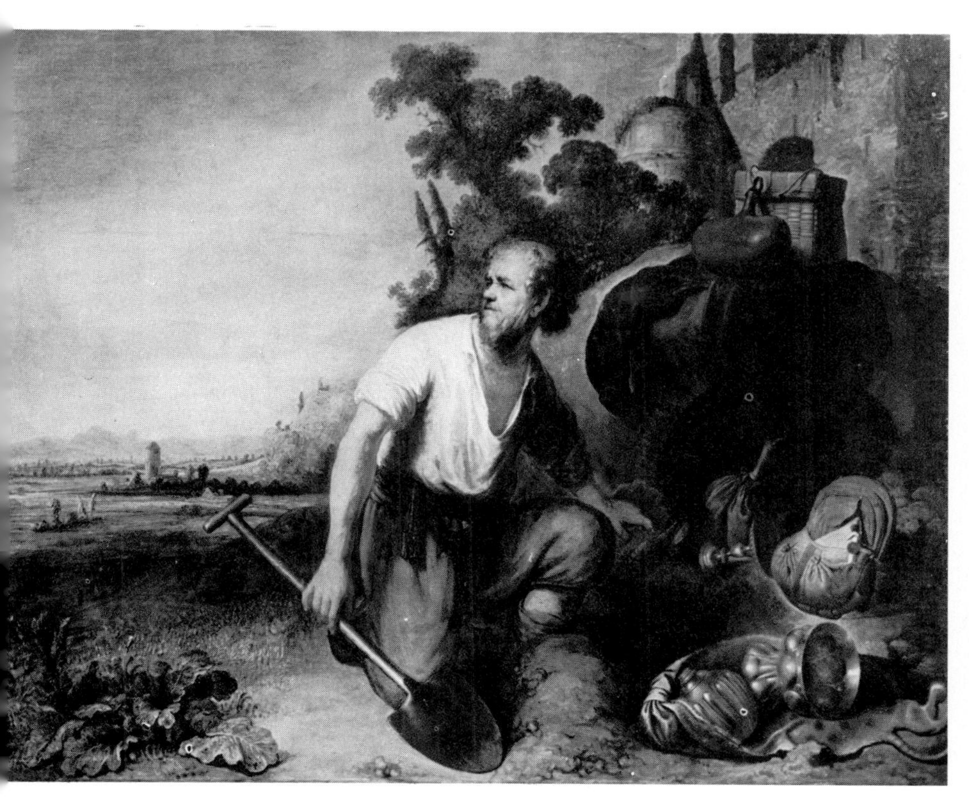

REMBRANDT HARMENSZ. VAN RIJN Dutch, 1606–69
The Dream of St Joseph
Canvas 41 3/8″ × 32 5/8″ (105 × 83 cm.) Inv. No. 236

Figures or scenes from the New Testament are relatively rare in the works of seventeenth-century Dutch painters. For Rembrandt, however, the Bible was an inexhaustible source of inspiration, providing him with innumerable examples of human joys and sorrows. He depicted his Biblical characters in the prosaic environment of ordinary Dutch people of his time, showing them as protagonists in the eternal human drama, moved by love, anxiety, wrath, treachery, humility or pride.

This picture is a reference to the dream in which St Joseph was warned by an angel to flee into Egypt so that Jesus might escape the Massacre of the Innocents (Matthew 2 : 13). The Holy Family is shown resting in a dim stable; Mary is protected from the cold by a large shawl which she has also folded round the Infant on her lap so that only his tiny face is visible. Joseph, depicted as a clumsy Dutch peasant, is seen awakening from the sleep of exhaustion, dazed by a brilliant apparition which puts a hand on his shoulder as a sign of heavenly comfort, support and encouragement for the weak. The angel is the source of the warm golden light suffusing the whole group. It is generally believed that this poetic and beautiful work was painted early in the 1650s; the preliminary study for the painting, a pen-drawing with wash, dating from the same period, is in the Berlin Kupferstichkabinett.

It appears from inventories that the painting was sold by auction in Amsterdam in 1775. It was acquired by the Museum of Fine Arts from the Munich collection of Alois Hauser in 1885.

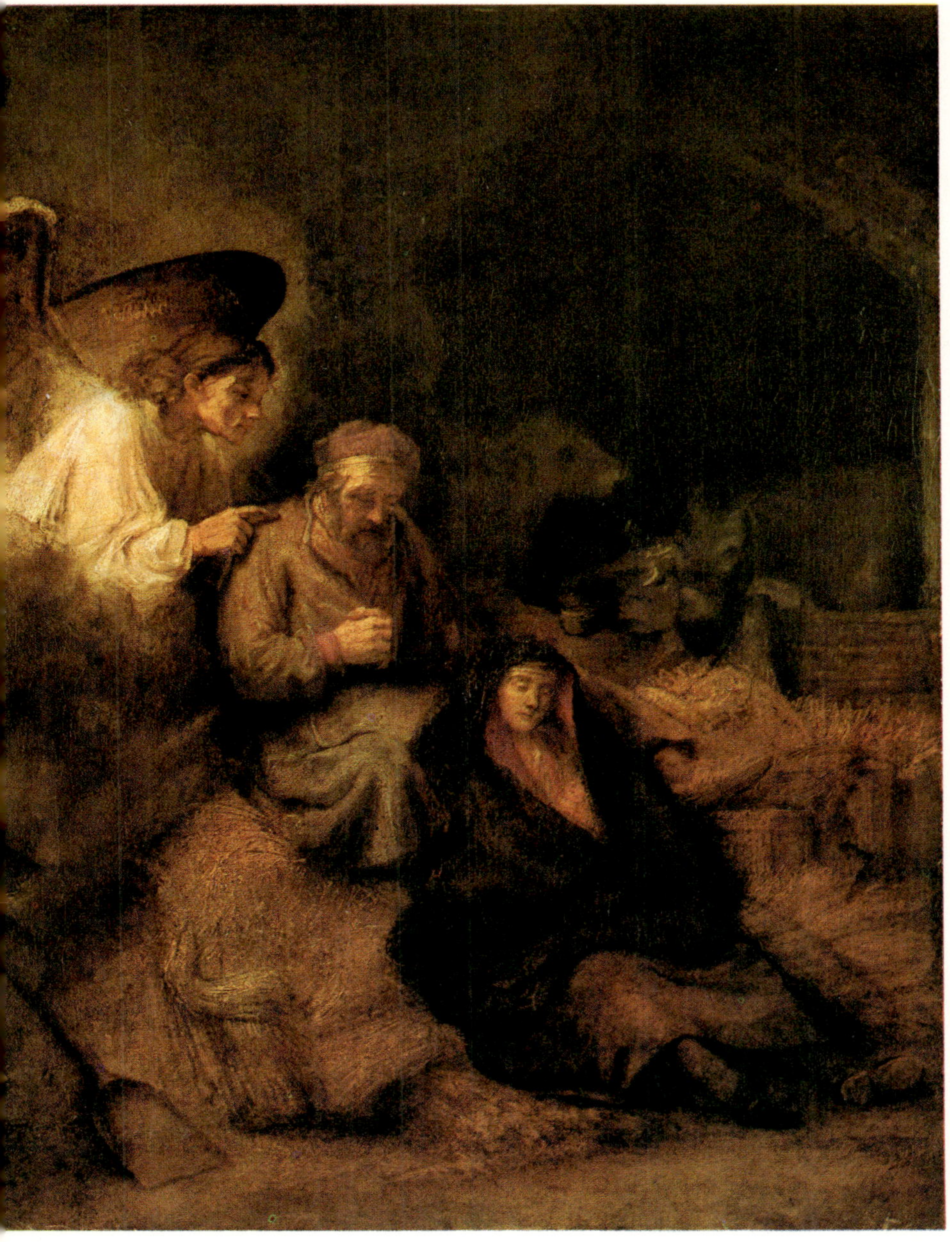

NICOLAES MAES Dutch, 1632–93
Christ before Pilate
Canvas 85″ × 68 1/2″ (216 × 174 cm.) Inv. No. 229

For four years, between 1648 and 1652, Nicolaes Maes, a native of Dordrecht, was one of Rembrandt's pupils; indeed, he was one of his most distinguished pupils. At the beginning of his career he faithfully followed his master – like Rembrandt he painted Biblical subjects, developed an intimate manner of expression and employed warm colouring – but later, disengaging himself from Rembrandt's entourage, he became popular with the citizens of Dordrecht as a painter of genre scenes and portraits. His portrayal became more elegant but at the same time more superficial, his use of lines harder, his colouring cooler.

This picture is an early work which, when it was acquired for the Esterházy collection at the beginning of the nineteenth century, was ascribed to Rembrandt. It is an unusual example of Maes's work, partly because the subject has been taken from the New Testament – not the artist's usual practice. The two works which come closest to this picture are *Christ Blessing Children* in the National Gallery in London and *Christ Mocked*, once in Leningrad, and we know of no other works by the artist which show any relationship to this picture. There is no reliable evidence as to the circumstances in which it was painted, though, hypothetically, it might be the painting by Maes mentioned by seventeenth-century sources as being in collections in Amsterdam and Dordrecht.

From the Esterházy collection.

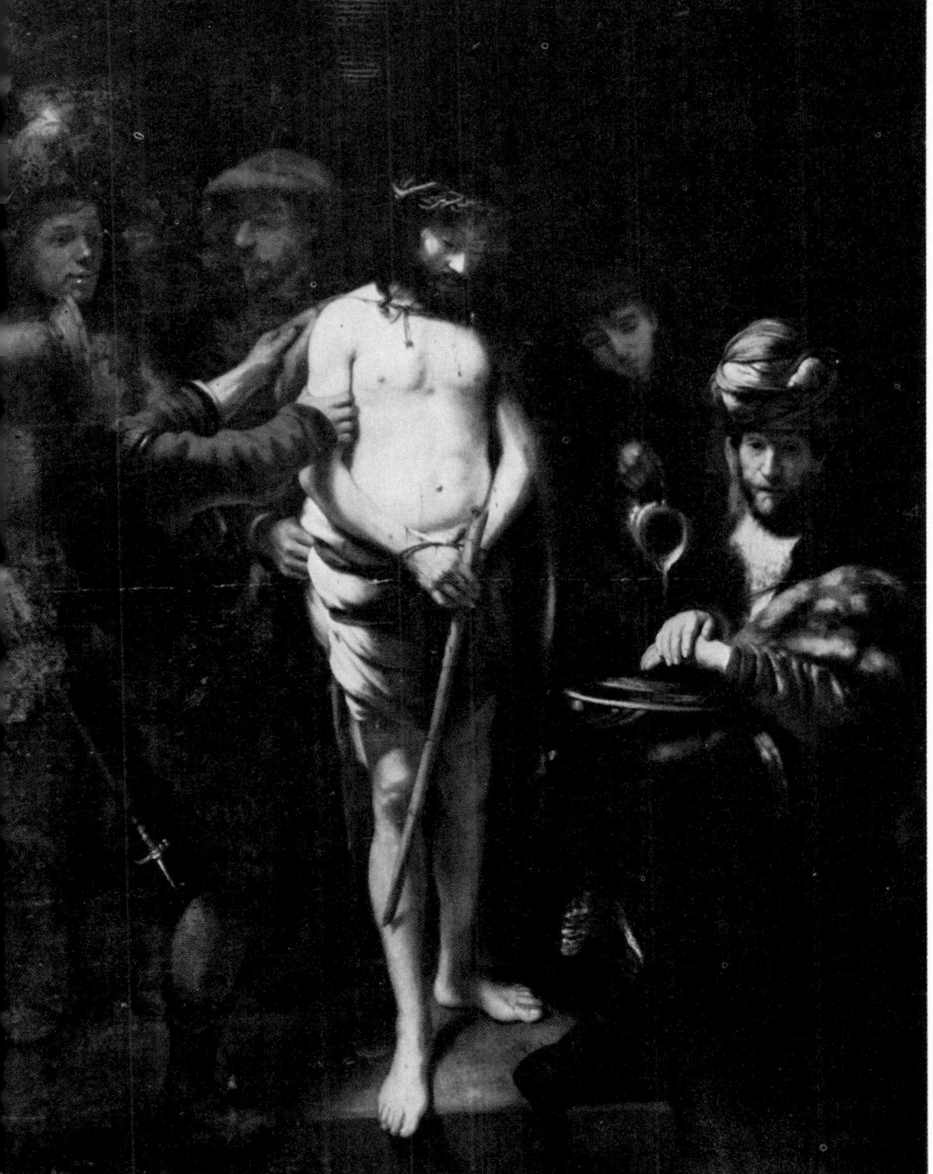

AERT DE GELDER Dutch, 1645–1727
Esther and Mordecai
Canvas 36 5/8″ × 58 1/2″ (93 × 148.5 cm.) Inv. No. 1342
Signed at top right: A. De Gelder f. 1685

Aert de Gelder was one of Rembrandt's last pupils and continued to work in the spirit and style of his master long after other pupils, for instance, Maes, Gerbrand van den Eeckhout and Jan Lievens, had succumbed to the fashionable trend towards smooth and perfunctory painting. He painted large compositions with two or three figures, mostly based on the Old Testament subjects so favoured by Rembrandt. Like his master, he loved rich properties and colourful draperies – the eighteenth-century historiographer Van Houbraken records that his studio was a veritable gallery of antiques, full of ancient weapons, silks and all kinds of utensils – and he used manikins for the sake of greater authenticity, carefully dressing them to suit the requirements of his theme. He painted with broad strokes of the brush, as Rembrandt had, and created warm tonalities and colour harmonies.

Esther and Mordecai, dating from 1685, is one of de Gelder's most valuable and characteristic works. The Old Testament book of Esther is summarized here into a single dramatic moment, the internal tension being conveyed through the structure of the composition and through the gestures. De Gelder painted several versions of this subject differing in various degrees; the version now in the Providence Museum of Art, Rhode Island, also depicting half-length figures, is particularly close to the painting in Budapest.

Bought from the Bourgeois Brothers in Cologne in 1894.

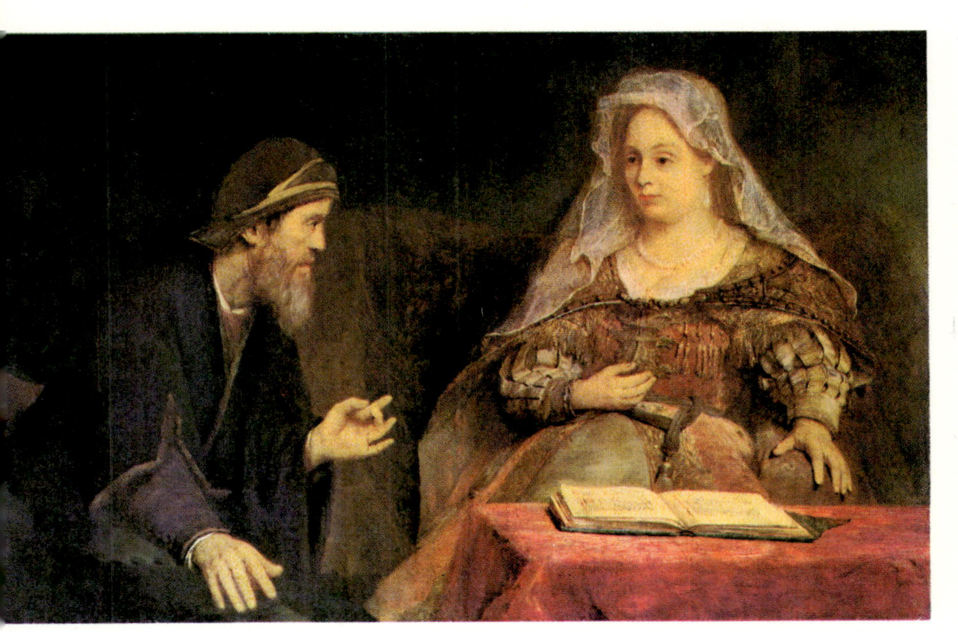

Attributed to JAN VERMEER VAN DELFT Dutch, 1632–75
Portrait of a Woman
Canvas 32 1/4″ × 25 5/8″ (82 × 65 cm.) Inv. No. 316

Jan Vermeer van Delft was one of the most remarkable Dutch genre-painters of the seventeenth century. His paintings were small, the colours luminous and delicately vibrating, and his most usual subjects were interiors, with couples engaged in music-making or conversation, or housewives at their daily tasks – pouring out the milk or stooping over their embroidery-frames. He painted an exquisite townscape of Delft and a few allegories and studies of heads, but no authentic portrait by him has survived; portraiture seems not to have attracted him.

It is for this reason that the attribution to him of the portrait of a young Dutch woman in the Budapest Museum has recently been questioned. Although the experts agree that the picture is a splendid creation, the work of a significant master, it has so far been impossible to identify the painter with certainty. The composition is severe and the monochrome, dark tone is quite unlike Vermeer's serene colouring, and, moreover, the monumentality and sombre mood of the figure are also alien to him. At the beginning of the last century, when it was in the Esterházy collection, the portrait was listed under Rembrandt's name, and even today there are a great many experts who ascribe it to Rembrandt's circle, largely because of the absorbed expression of the sitter and the colouring. However, neither analysis of the materials nor examination of the style have enabled us to identify with any degree of certainty either the artist or the sitter.

From the Esterházy collection.

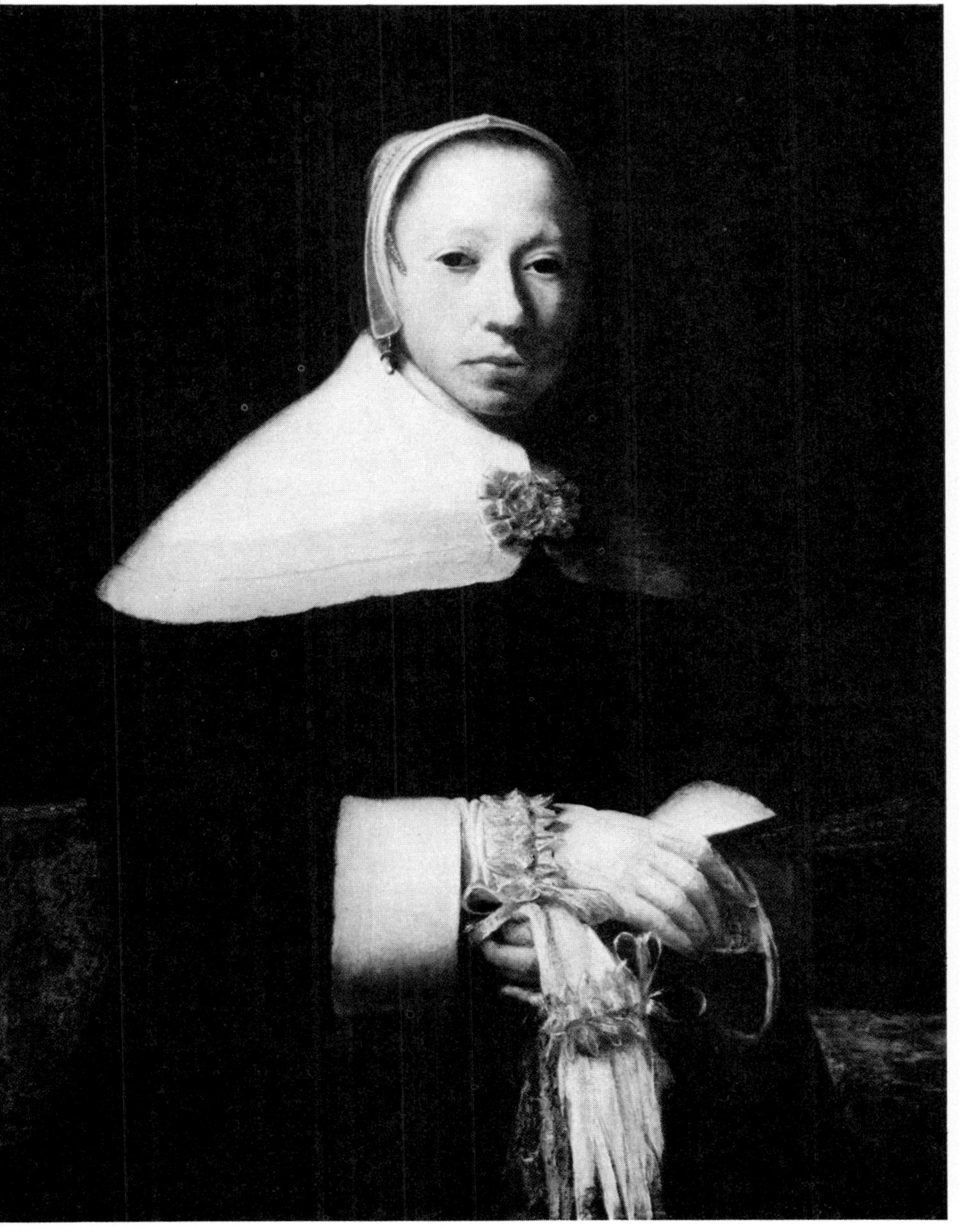

PIETER DE HOOCH Dutch, 1629–after 1683
Woman Reading a Letter
Canvas 21 5/8″ × 21 5/8″ (55 × 55 cm.) Inv. No. 5933
Signed at bottom right: P de Hoogh 1664

Pieter de Hooch depicts for us incidents in the lives of women at home with their children: the mother watching over the cradle, serving her family at table, reading a letter or working in her kitchen. Some of his paintings show guests arriving in a spotlessly clean room or courtyard, taking a glass of wine, listening to music or conversing together. The keynote of every single picture is an intimate simplicity; the painter conducts us into a calm and quiet world, both clean and orderly, inhabited by the well-to-do. Patrons whose preference was for something livelier, for gay and colourful peasant scenes, bought pictures by the Ostades, Jan Steen or Jan Miense Molenaer, but de Hooch was popular in the narrower circle of those who appreciated his distinctive approach and delicacy of execution. The magic of his works lies not so much in his subjects as in the means by which he interpreted them: the lucid and balanced composition, the feeling of space and the warm glow of his colours.

Purchased in 1923.

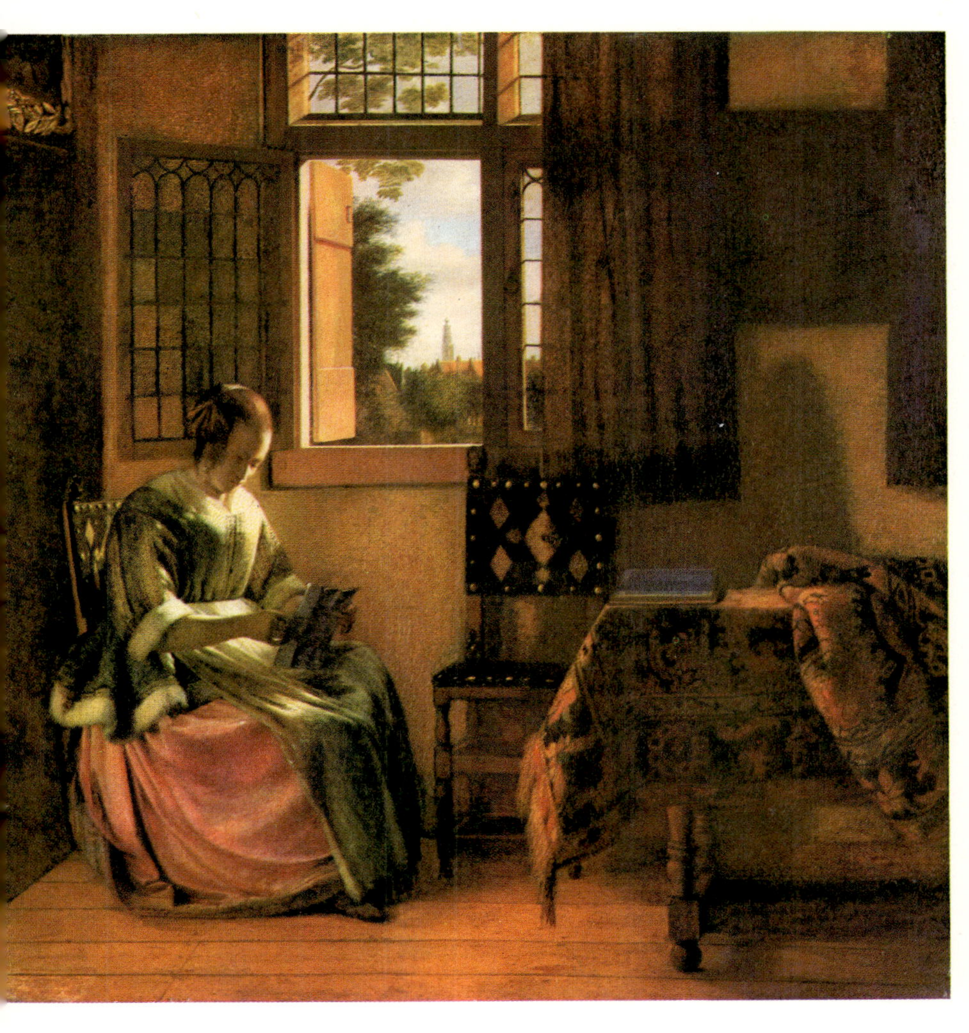

ADRIAEN VAN OSTADE Dutch, 1610–84
The Fishwife
Panel 11 3/8″ × 10 3/8″ (29 × 26.5 cm.) Inv. No. 306

Adriaen van Ostade, a native of Haarlem, is said to have been a pupil of Frans Hals. Certainly one can see the master's influence in his choice of subjects and in his approach, particularly in his early work, but he created an artistic idiom of his own and his development was essentially individual. He painted genre-scenes, recording the lives of ordinary Dutch townsfolk and peasants; in his pictures we see the interiors of cottages and poor village schools, crowded taverns and workshops. But he often depicted single figures as well: everyday characters such as the baker, the fishmonger or the barber-surgeon. Market scenes were a favourite subject of his, and this picture – an ugly fishwife in a red bodice cleaning fish at her stall while, beyond her, the crowd mills round the other stalls – captures the atmosphere of a street market with the freshness of a snapshot. Van Ostade was in the habit of painting several versions of a favourite motif, and a larger version, now in the Rijkmuseum in Amsterdam, bears the date 1672. The Budapest painting may have been produced at about the same time, and is probably the latest of the master's six works now in the Budapest Museum.

From the Esterházy collection.

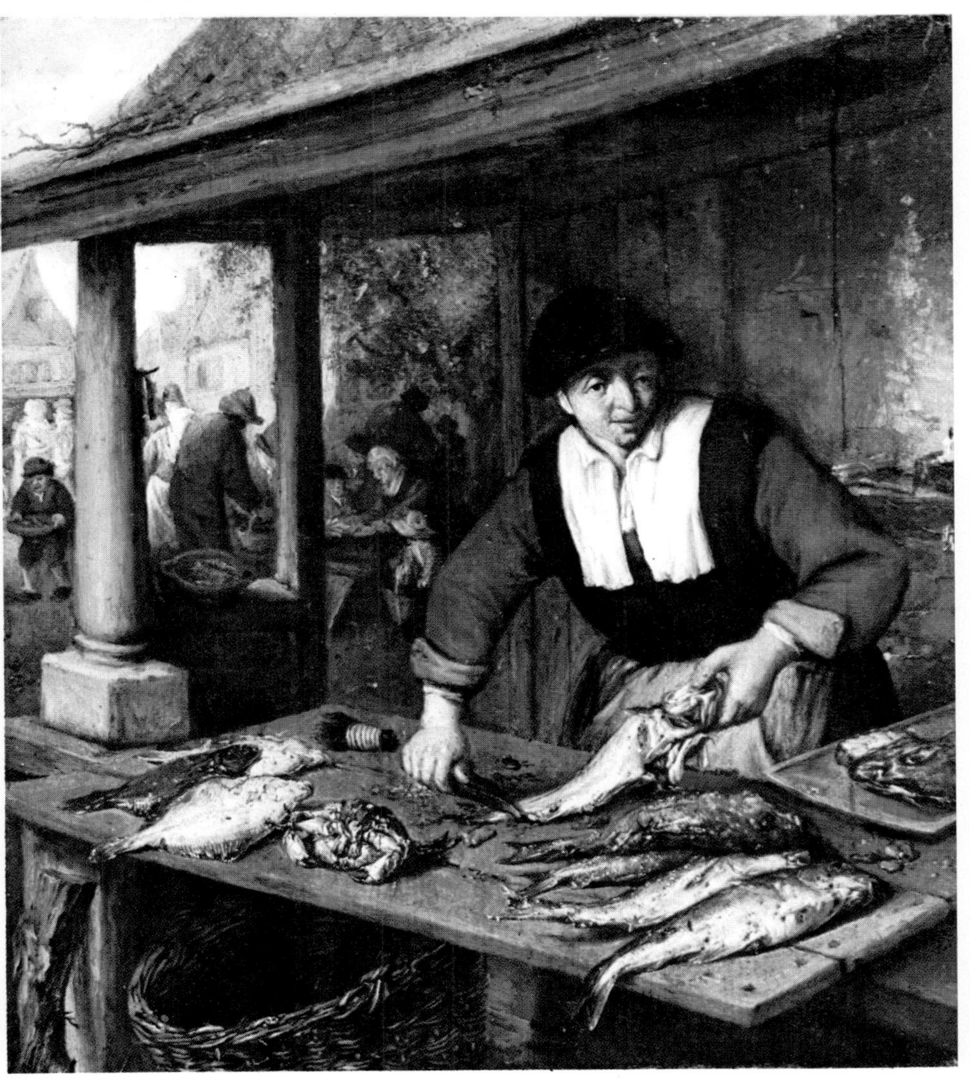

JAN STEEN Dutch, 1626–79
A Merry Party
Canvas 59″ × 58 1/4″ (150 × 148 cm.) Inv. No. 337
Signed at bottom left: J. Steen

Jan Steen, born in Leyden, was one of the most popular of the Dutch masters of the seventeenth century. His gay and animated genre-scenes were highly appreciated, both by his contemporaries and by collectors in the eighteenth and nineteenth centuries. He was a pupil of Nicolaus Knüpfer in Utrecht and of his father-in-law, Jan van Goyen, and lived and worked for varying periods of time in nearly every large town in Holland.

His range of subjects was extremely wide; he painted both villages and towns, peasants and well-to-do citizens; his vividly coloured, broadly constructed compositions depict taverns, sick-rooms, fairs, workshops and weddings, mythological and historical scenes in the spirit of the Dutch oratorical groups of his time, as well as character figures and a few portraits.

Steen often depicted his family and himself, as indeed he has done in this picture, where he, his wife and his children are seen carousing. The work gets its alternative title of 'The Cat Family' from the basket of new-born kittens held by the girl at the back of the circle – the sort of anecdotal and amusing touch which frequently occurs in Steen's work.

From the Esterházy collection.

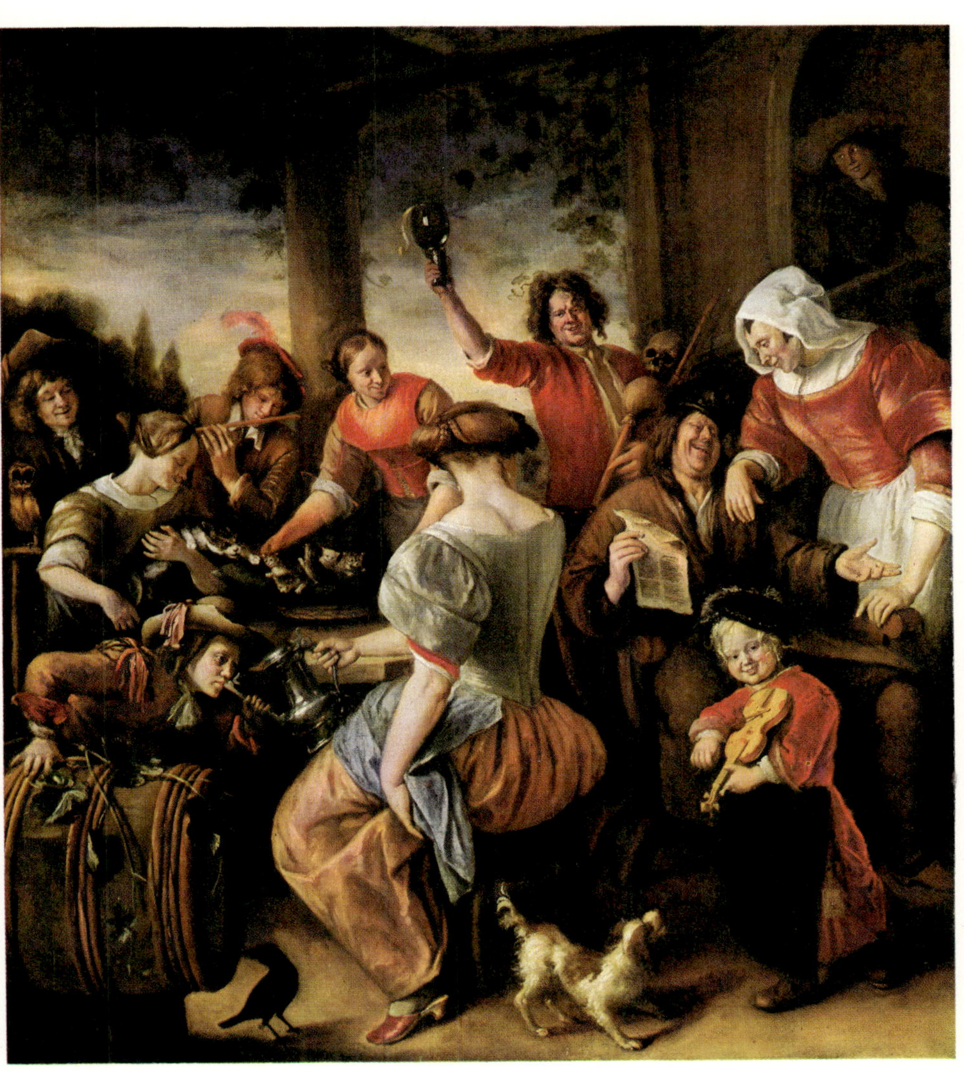

PIETER JANSZ. SAENREDAM Dutch, 1597–1665
The Interior of the Nieuwe Kerk in Haarlem
Panel 33 7/8″ × 40 1/2″ (86 × 103 cm.) Inv. No. 311
Signed at bottom right: Pr Saenredam fecit A° 1653 8/16

The Haarlem artist Pieter Jansz. Saenredam is one of those Dutch painters who specialized throughout their lives in a single field, gradually perfecting their execution of the chosen subject; he devoted himself almost exclusively to church interiors. Painters of architecture are generally rather limited in their range of motifs and their means of interpretation, but Saenredam was so deeply absorbed in his subject and gifted with such pictorial eloquence that his works must be counted as masterpieces.

This picture is typical of his calm compositions of simple, undecorated Protestant churches, their interiors occasionally enlivened by the inclusion of an awe-inspiring old tomb or statue, whose beauty and monumentality are enhanced by the painter's restraint in excluding all anecdotal detail; nothing disturbs the silence of the church. Saenredam's is an artistic vision set apart from the turmoil of the world, a harmony of perspective and light.

From the Esterházy collection.

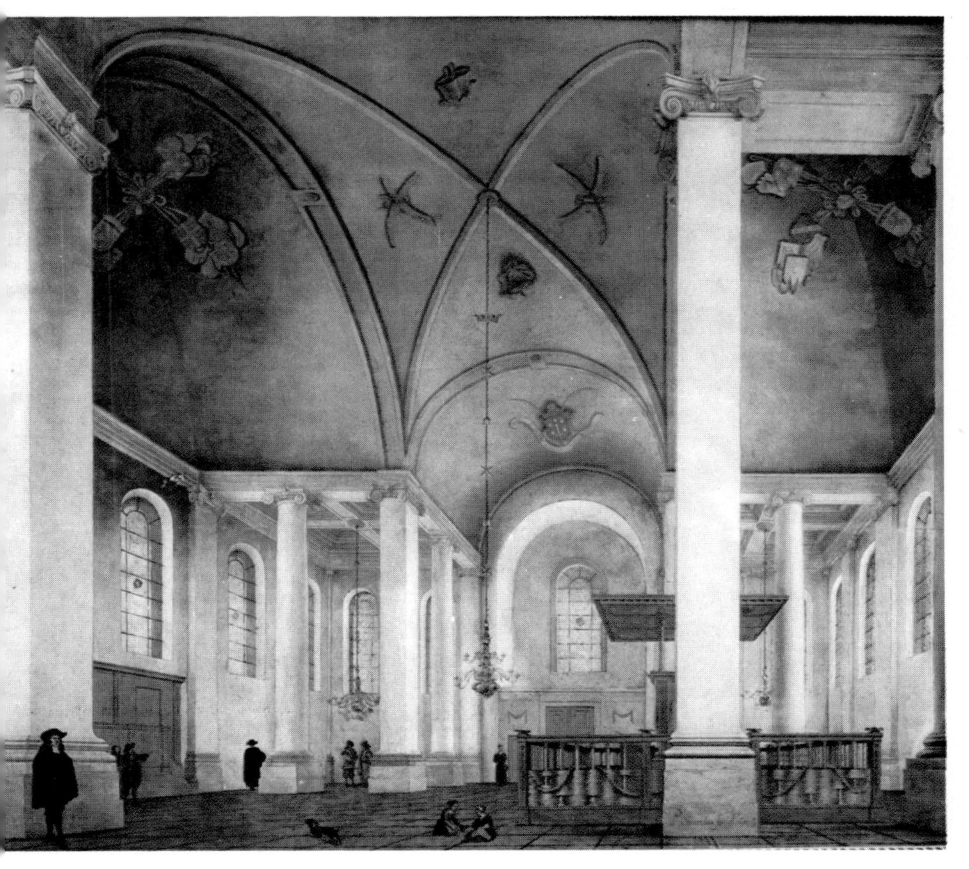

SALOMON VAN RUYSDAEL Dutch, *c.* 1602–70
After the Rain
Panel 22″ × 34″ (56 × 86.5 cm.) Inv. No. 260
Signed at bottom right: SvR 1631

Several members of the Ruysdael family of Haarlem figure in the history of Dutch painting, particularly landscape painting, the earliest of them, Salomon van Ruysdael, being inscribed in the Haarlem painters' guild in 1623. *After the Rain*, the earliest of the nine paintings by him in Budapest, contains a motif often repeated in his later paintings: a sandy road leading to a building half hidden by trees. Here and there we see breaks in the clouds which otherwise cover the sky, the air is still moist and misty after the storm, and the freshened foliage and the damp sand convey to perfection the characteristic atmosphere of the coastal countryside. In his early works, such as this, Salomon van Ruysdael used vivid greenish and yellowish colours, and it was only later that his colouring became darker and more muted. His later works, such as *The 'White Swan' Inn* (p. 265), dated 1662, and his large *Cavalry Battle* of 1659, are also more restless and animated; the landscape is peopled with figures which play a more important role in the composition as a whole and there is greater emphasis on human incident.

From the Esterházy collection.

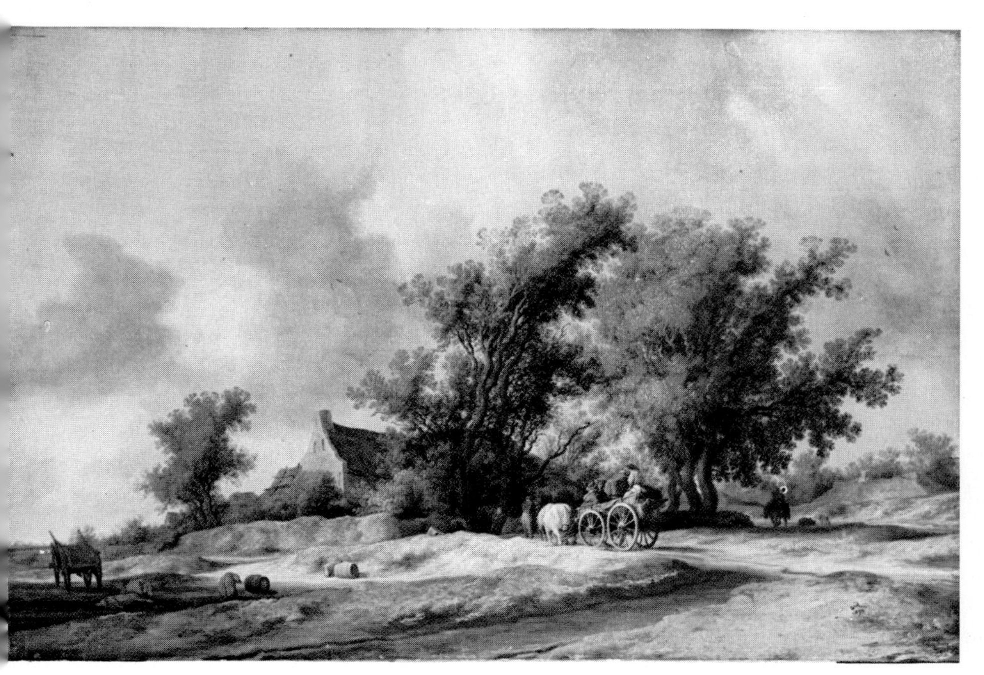

JACOB VAN RUISDAEL Dutch, 1628/9–1682
View of Amsterdam
Canvas 20 5/8" × 17 1/8" (52.5 × 43.5 cm.) Inv. No. 4278
Signed at bottom right with monogram

Jacob van Ruisdael followed in the footsteps of his uncle, Salomon, and became a landscape painter; indeed, he was one of the most prolific and important of Dutch landscape painters. His range of subjects was wider than that of his uncle and of Dutch landscape painters in general. He depicted the rather gloomy dunes and flat, green fields as well as towns, forest scenes and waterfalls; he painted a Jewish cemetery on the outskirts of a town, fishing boats at sea, tracts of marshland with trees and views of seaports, always finding the manner most suited to a particular theme, time of day, kind of weather or type of landscape. No other artist has matched the susceptibility with which he interpreted the peculiar atmospheric phenomena of the Netherlands. Unlike the Italian and French landscape painters, Ruisdael followed the practice of Dutch masters in always painting the real inhabitants of a particular landscape – for him the countryside was a setting for human beings, not mythical heroes. The farmsteads nestling among the trees housed Dutch peasants, on the fishing boats Dutch fishermen are seen earning their daily bread, and it is not disguised Greek deities but shepherds who are seen minding the sheep.

From 1656 on Ruisdael worked in Amsterdam, and this was the period when he painted the picture in Budapest – a view of the Binnenamstel, with a sandy road meandering by the water's edge, and a rosy church spire rising high above the city.

From the Pálffy bequest.

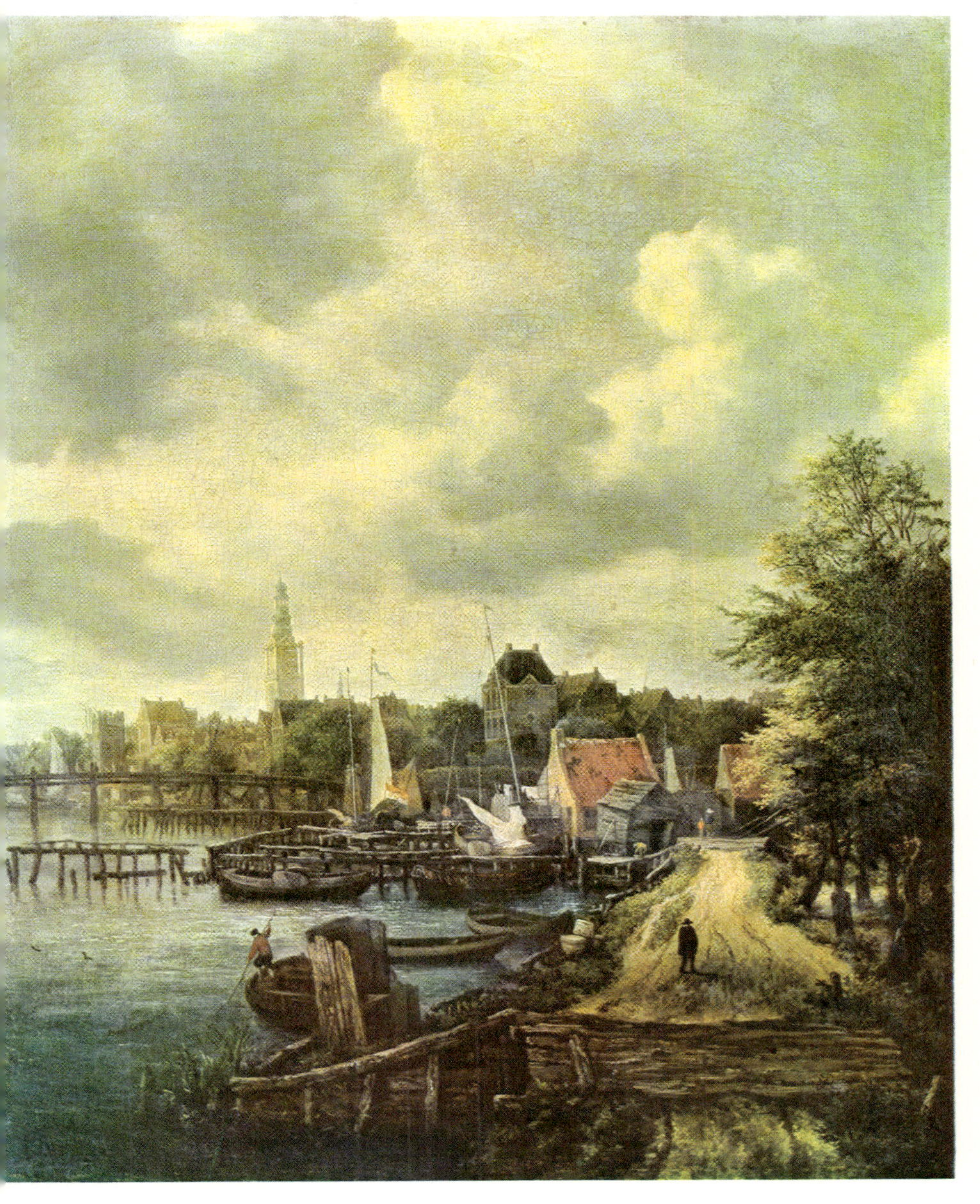

JAN VAN GOYEN Dutch, 1596–1656
Seascape with Fishermen
Panel 14 1/4″ × 12 5/8″ (36.1 × 32.2 cm.) Inv. No. 4305
Signed on the boat at bottom left: VG

In Holland in the seventeenth century it was customary for painters to specialize in one field, or even one subject. Painters who specialized in figure painting sought the help of another artist for the execution of a landscape, while the landscape painter would often ask a colleague to paint the human or animal figures or still-lifes that he wanted to include in his composition; it was very seldom that anyone who had established his name in a certain field was prepared to undertake a different kind of work. In fact specialization was carried to such lengths that some artists did not paint landscapes in general but restricted themselves to seascapes, twilight landscapes, townscapes or churches.

Such small paintings were produced comparatively quickly and in large numbers at quite modest prices. It is characteristic of the situation that Jan van Goyen, a famous painter of Dutch seascapes, was obliged to deal in tulip bulbs to make ends meet; moreover, he often got more for his tulips than for some of his paintings. During his youth Van Goyen was the pupil of Esaias van de Velde, and painted a great variety of landscapes in warm, brownish tones. Gradually, however, his interest became centred on the sea, the greyish, cloudy coast and the flat coastal plains under an enormous sky. It was in this type of scene that he created his masterpieces, among them the little gem in Budapest, a harmonious seascape with fishing boats.

From the Pálffy bequest.

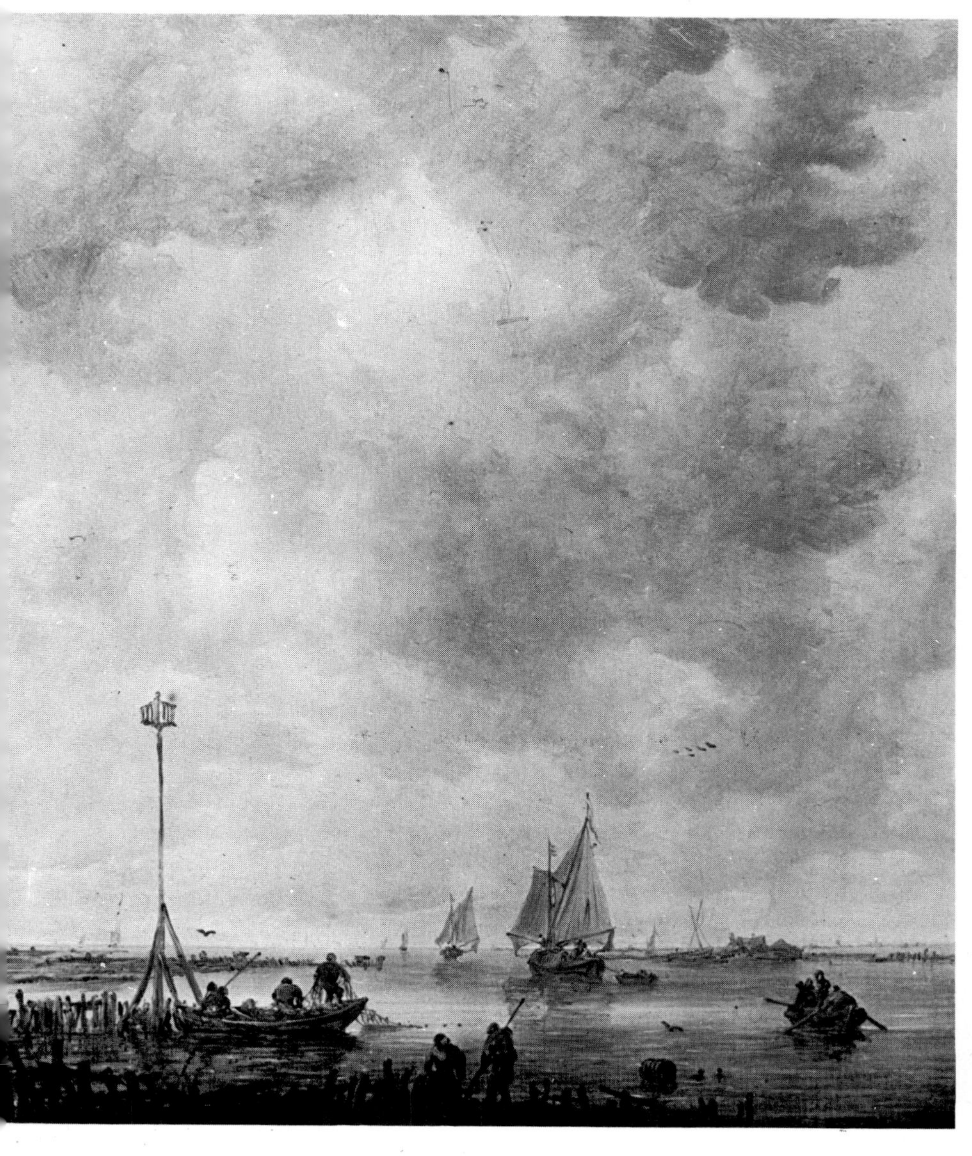

AELBERT CUYP Dutch, 1620–91
Cows in the Water
Panel 23 1/4" × 29 1/8" (59 × 74 cm.) Inv. No. 408
Signed at bottom left: A. cuÿp

The Dordrecht painter Aelbert Cuyp was not only a landscape painter, although there is no doubt that his most attractive and significant works belong to this genre. His range covered conversation pieces, seascapes, portraits and group portraits – an example of the last being the picture of a Dutch family in the Budapest Museum (p. 266) – but he most frequently depicted animals and landscapes with human figures engaged in fishing, hunting or riding. The setting is generally the countryside around his native town of Dordrecht, and his pictures show us the Meuse estuary with its low coastline, boats at their moorings and cattle grazing. The pictures are characterized by an atmosphere of serenity and calm, with glistening water, soft clouds, gentle landscape, cattle whose smooth coats shine in the evening light and human figures engrossed in work, all combining in a peaceful harmony.

From the Esterházy collection.

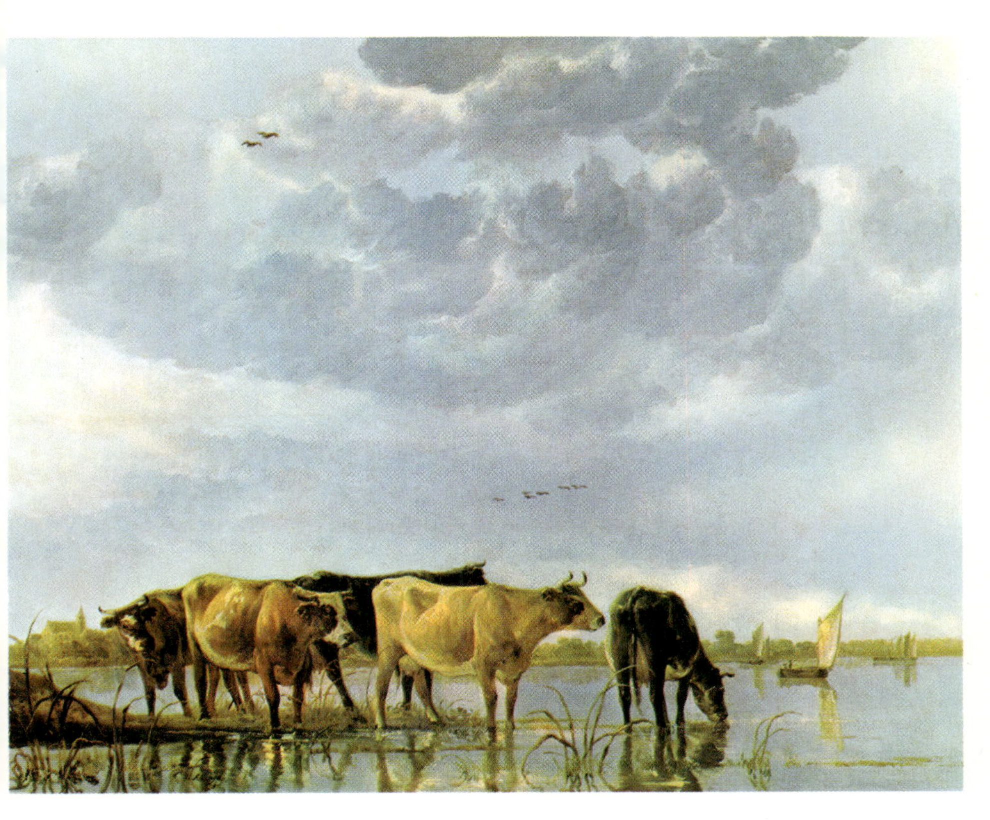

HANS HOLBEIN THE ELDER German, 1460/5–1524
The Death of the Virgin
Panel 59″ × 90″ (150 × 228.5 cm.) Inv. No. 4086
Signed on the censer: HANS. HOLPAIN.

At the turn of the sixteenth century Hans Holbein the Elder, famous painter of altar-pieces and portraits, was the leading painter of the rich merchant city of Augsburg. The painting in Budapest is one of his finest works and, indeed, one of the most significant works of German painting at that time. The inscription tells us that it was commissioned by Wolfgang Preu, Canon of Rottenbuch between 1490 and 1500 and that it originally decorated the tomb of the Preu family in the Church of St James at Straubing.

The death of the Virgin is placed in a contemporary domestic setting. Mary, represented as a middle-class woman of Augsburg and wearing the clothes of the period, is seen lying on her canopied bed with the Apostles grouped about her like her family – one of them, wearing spectacles, is reading from the Bible. The artist follows the medieval tradition of simultaneous narration by depicting the sequel in the same picture: at the top we see the Virgin's soul, in the form of an innocent young girl in white, ascending to heaven to be received by God the Father. In this painting Holbein, with exquisite taste and force, blends the traditional, late Gothic approach with a new style of representing nature and reality adopted from Netherlandish painting.

Donated by F. Kleinberger in 1911.

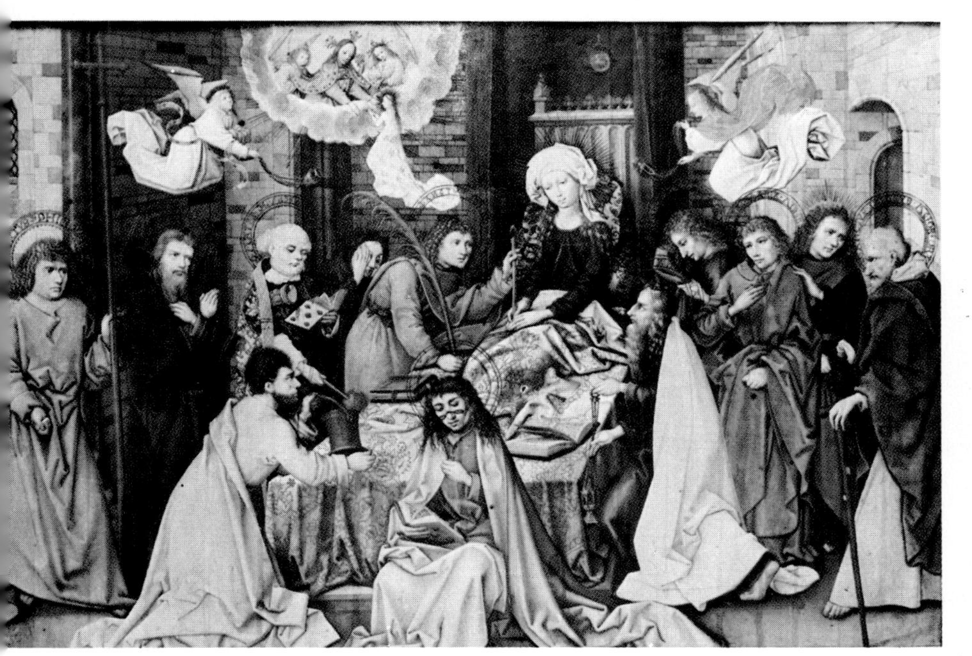

ALBRECHT DÜRER German, 1471–1528
Portrait of a Man
Panel 17″×11 3/8″ (43×29 cm.) Inv. No. 142

Albrecht Dürer, the greatest master of Renaissance art in Germany, began his career as an apprentice goldsmith in his father's workshop in Nuremberg, but in 1486 he was sent to study under Michael Wolgemut, the most gifted painter in Nuremberg at that time. His development as an artist was, however, most decisively influenced by two visits to Venice in 1494–5 and 1505–7, and by the time he visited the Netherlands in 1520–1 he had already developed a mature style of his own. A versatile artist with a broad range of interests, he was fascinated by the theoretical aspects of art and wrote a treatise on the subject in 1528. Besides being a painter he was an industrious and brilliant graphic artist, whose woodcuts and engravings contributed greatly to popularizing German art of the sixteenth century. His paintings include altarpieces, religious pictures and some outstanding portraits. Although he began by working in the German late Gothic tradition, Dürer was to introduce the Renaissance to Germany with his pure compositions in which the sure touch of the draughtsman is always evident. With his workshop and followers he marked out the lines of development of the new style for later years.

This small picture now in Budapest – a portrait of a youth, painted in brilliant, warm colours – is sometimes ascribed to Dürer's pupils Hans Süss von Kulmbach or Hans Baldung Grien. Some scholars believe to recognize in the sitter Dürer's brother Andreas; however, the smooth features and simple attire hardly provide enough clues for identifying the sitter.

Transferred in 1848 from Buda Castle to the Hungarian National Museum. Formerly in Archduke Leopold Wilhelm's collection and the Imperial collection in Vienna.

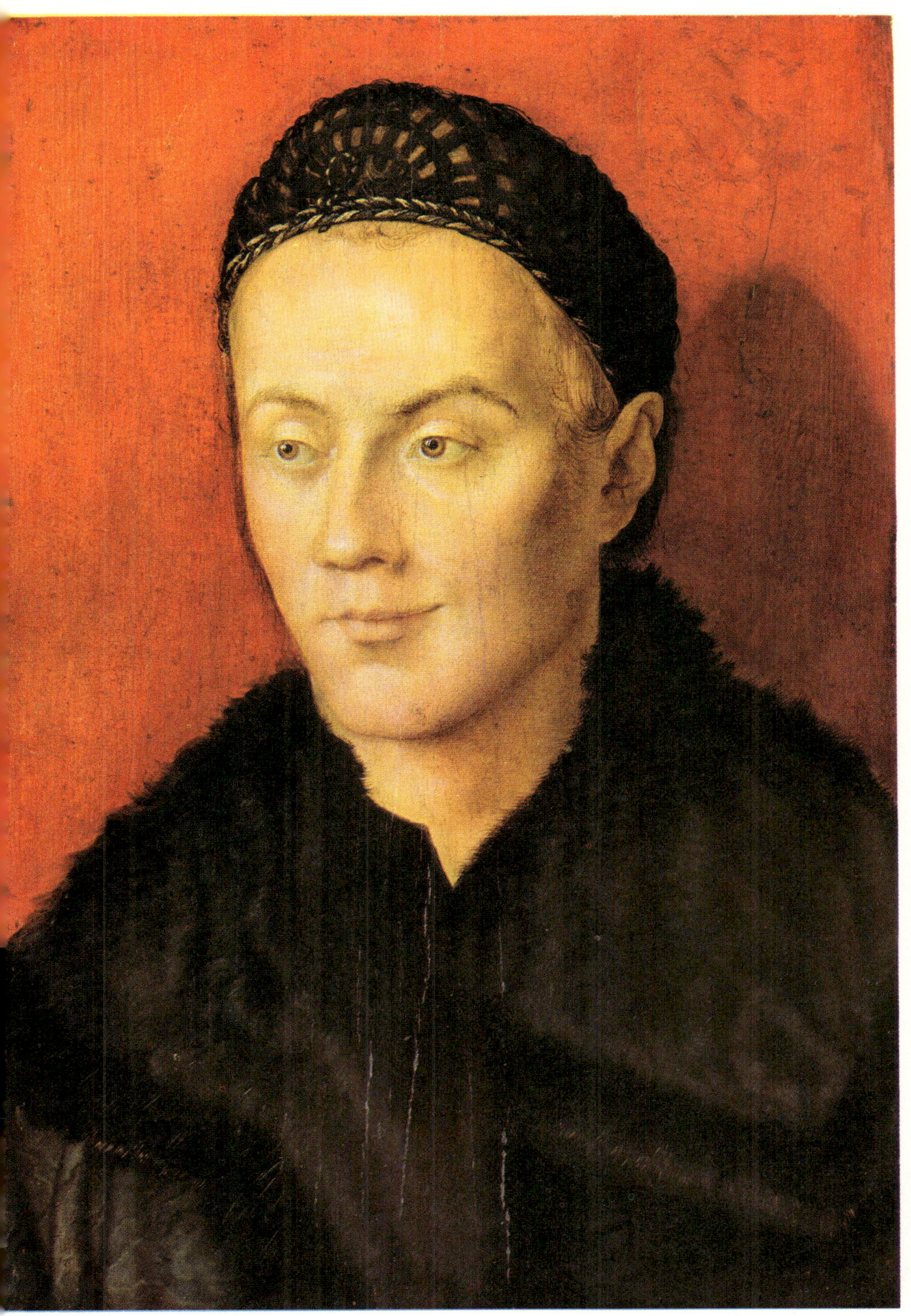

HANS BALDUNG GRIEN German, 1484/5–1545
Adam and *Eve*
Two panels, each 81 7/8″ × 32 7/8″ (208 × 83.5 cm.) Inv. Nos. 1888–9

Hans Baldung Grien represents an interesting and individual trend in the history of German painting in the sixteenth century. Although he began his career as a painter in Nuremberg very much under the influence of Dürer, during his activity in Strasbourg and Freiburg he developed his own ideas and revealed in his altar-pieces, historical compositions and portraits, as well as his prolific output of graphic work, an exceedingly rich imagination and a growing predilection for characterization.

Vigorous lines, clear and plastic forms and bold presentation are the characteristic features of his pictures in Budapest, the *Mater Dolorosa* (p. 271) and the two companion-pieces *Adam* and *Eve*. The latter appear to have belonged to a series consisting of four nudes, and it is recorded that in 1641 four paintings by Hans Baldung, representing Adam, Eve, Judith and Venus, found their way from Strasbourg into the possession of a Basle merchant. The full-length *Judith*, now in the Germanisches Museum in Nuremberg, and the *Venus* in the Kröller-Müller Museum at Otterlo are panels of the same structure and dimensions as the pictures in Budapest and, since the former is dated 1524, it may be assumed that the whole series, including the two pictures in Budapest, was painted in that year.

Purchased in Vienna in 1900; formerly in the Schönborn collection in Vienna.

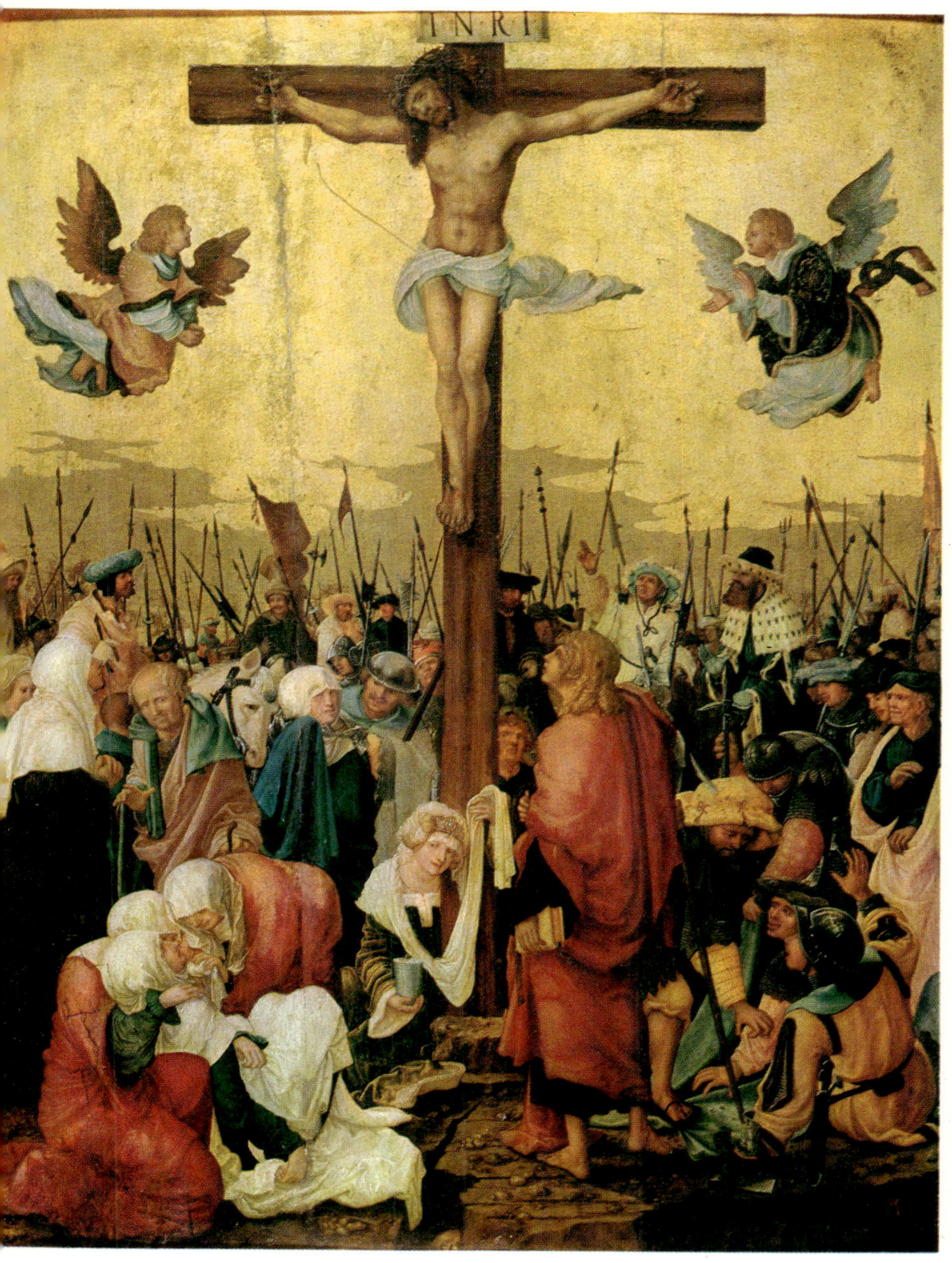
I·N·R·I

JOHANN KUPETZKY German, 1667–1740
The Artist and His Family
Canvas 43 3/4″ × 35 7/8″ (111 × 91 cm.) Inv. No. 3922

The son of Czech parents, Kupetzky was born at Bazin in Hungary in 1667. He studied in Vienna under the Swiss artist Benedikt Klaus in 1684–6 and then lived in Italy until 1709. He worked in Vienna and then in Nuremberg, where he remained from 1723 until his death in 1740. Although he painted some religious compositions, he was primarily a portrait-painter. He was especially popular with the wealthy bourgeois and merchants of Nuremberg, of whom he usually painted half-length or three-quarter-length likenesses, posing his sitter against a simple background, either with the tools of his trade or engaged in a favourite pastime. He looked to Rembrandt as his ideal and tried to follow the master's example not only in the arrangement of his pictures and in his colouring but also in painting innumerable variants of portraits of himself and members of his family.

The most remarkable work of these last is the great family portrait that found its way after the painter's death to the ducal gallery of Ansbach. The family is seen in intimate grouping, indicative of a quiet domesticity which was shortly afterwards disrupted by his wife's infidelity. The weary painter, no longer young, gazes at us with short-sighted eyes over the shoulder of his little son; his wife, past her prime, is on the left, her eyes revealing a determined character. The Museum of Fine Arts owns about twenty works by Kupetzky, of which this family group, with its deep insight and vigorous execution, is by far the most powerful and effective.

Given to the Museum by Marcell Nemes in 1910.

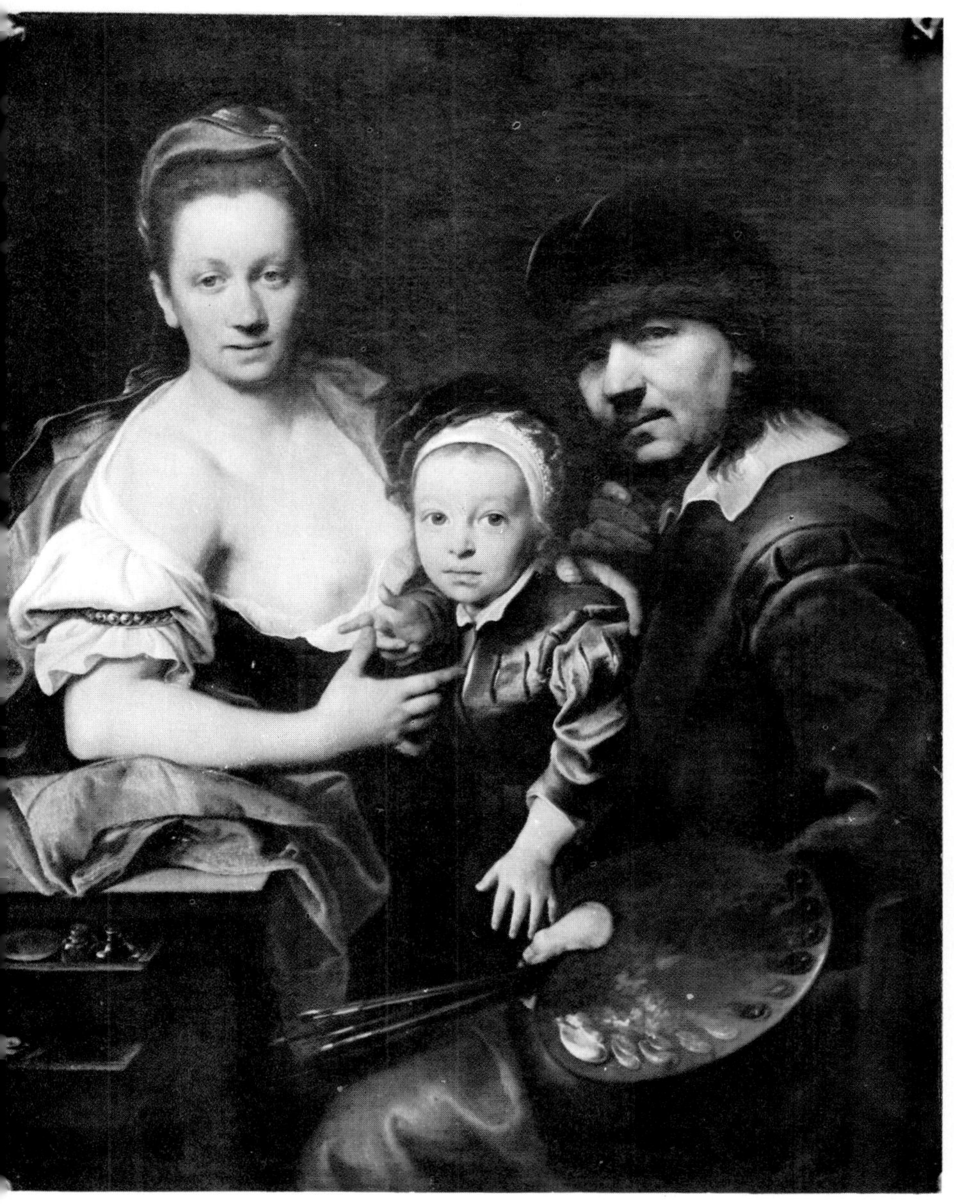

JOHANN LISS German, *c.* 1597–1629/30
A Country Wedding Procession
Canvas 25 3/4″ × 32 1/8″ (65.5 × 81.5 cm.) Inv. No. 3844
Inscribed bottom right: JO

The life of Johann Liss reflects clearly the strange and complex circumstances of art in seventeenth-century Europe. He was born in Oldenburg, in North Germany, but soon left his native country and, indeed, his art is hardly connected with contemporary German painting. He studied in Amsterdam, possibly under Hendrik Goltzius, the most important Dutch graphic artist of the period, then moved to Italy and worked in Venice up to his death at the age of about thirty. In his singular and individual art Dutch and Venetian features are blended and he greatly influenced the development of Venetian painting in the seventeenth century.

Of the two pictures by Liss in the Museum of Fine Arts, the *Country Wedding Procession* reflects the spirit of Netherlandish genre-painting, both in its theme and in its approach, while *Judith with the Head of Holofernes* (p. 272) is a dramatic composition in the Italian manner. The picture of the gay and drunken wedding procession was formerly one of a pair, and its companion-piece, depicting peasants fighting, is now in the Germanisches Museum in Nuremberg. These paintings may possibly date from the beginning of Liss's stay in Venice, when he was still strongly influenced by Flemish and Dutch art.

Purchased in 1908 from an art dealer in Vienna.

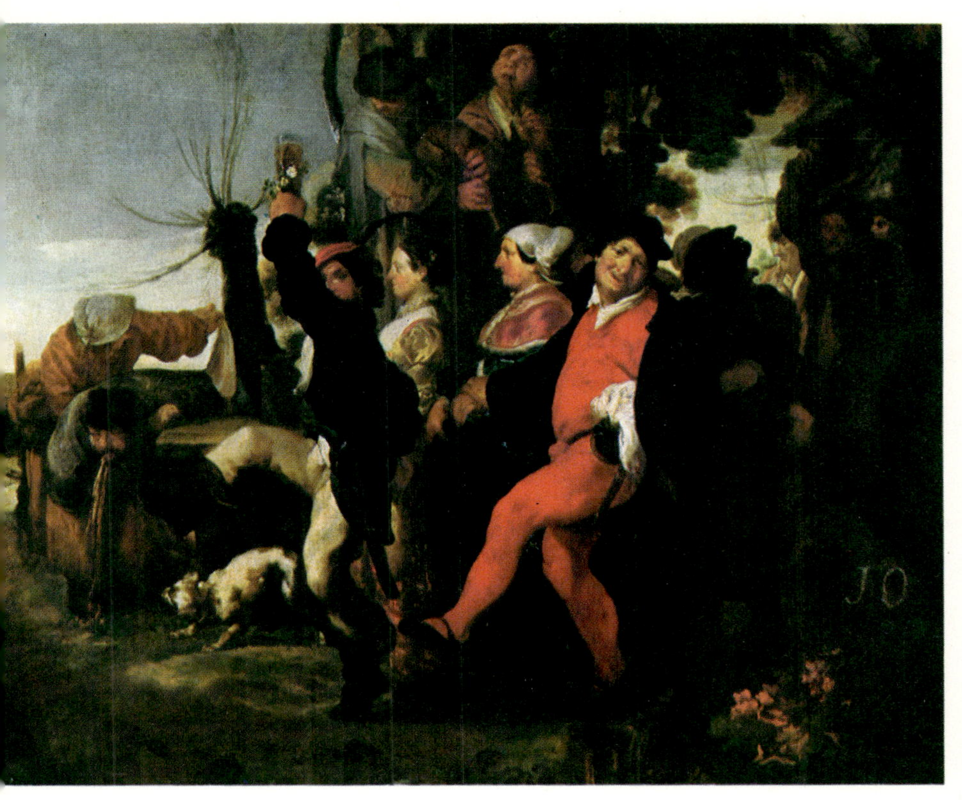
JO

FRANZ ANTON MAULBERTSCH Austrian, 1724–96
The Holy Trinity
Canvas 24 5/8″ × 13″ (62.5 × 33 cm.) Inv. No. 6503

It was as a master of fresco-painting and as a most prolific decorator of churches and palaces in Austria, Czechoslovakia and Hungary that Franz Anton Maulbertsch was most appreciated by his contemporaries. Perhaps nowadays greater value is placed on his surviving *bozzetti* – sketches painted in gloriously fresh colours with brilliant technique. The Budapest Museum is fortunate in possessing a comprehensive collection of his works. The stylistic features of his early work may be studied in some recent acquisitions which include two large and brilliantly coloured Biblical compositions in bright colours, *Joseph and His Brothers* and *Rebecca at the Well* (p. 273), while the two altar-pieces, *The Death of St Joseph* and *The Martyrdom of St Paul*, as well as some sketches, give an idea of his achievements as a mature artist in the 1750s and 1760s. The late works, such as *The Holy Trinity*, a sketch for an altar-piece, are fluid in their handling, and the light colours give a silvery effect. In these sketches Maulbertsch captured his subjects with a few unbelievably light strokes of the brush and some spots of colour permeated with light. When he elaborated these sketches in their final form, however, particularly in the case of the later altar-pieces, the spontaneity was often lost, the forms becoming heavier and the hues muted.

Acquired in 1931. Formerly in the Glück collection in Budapest.

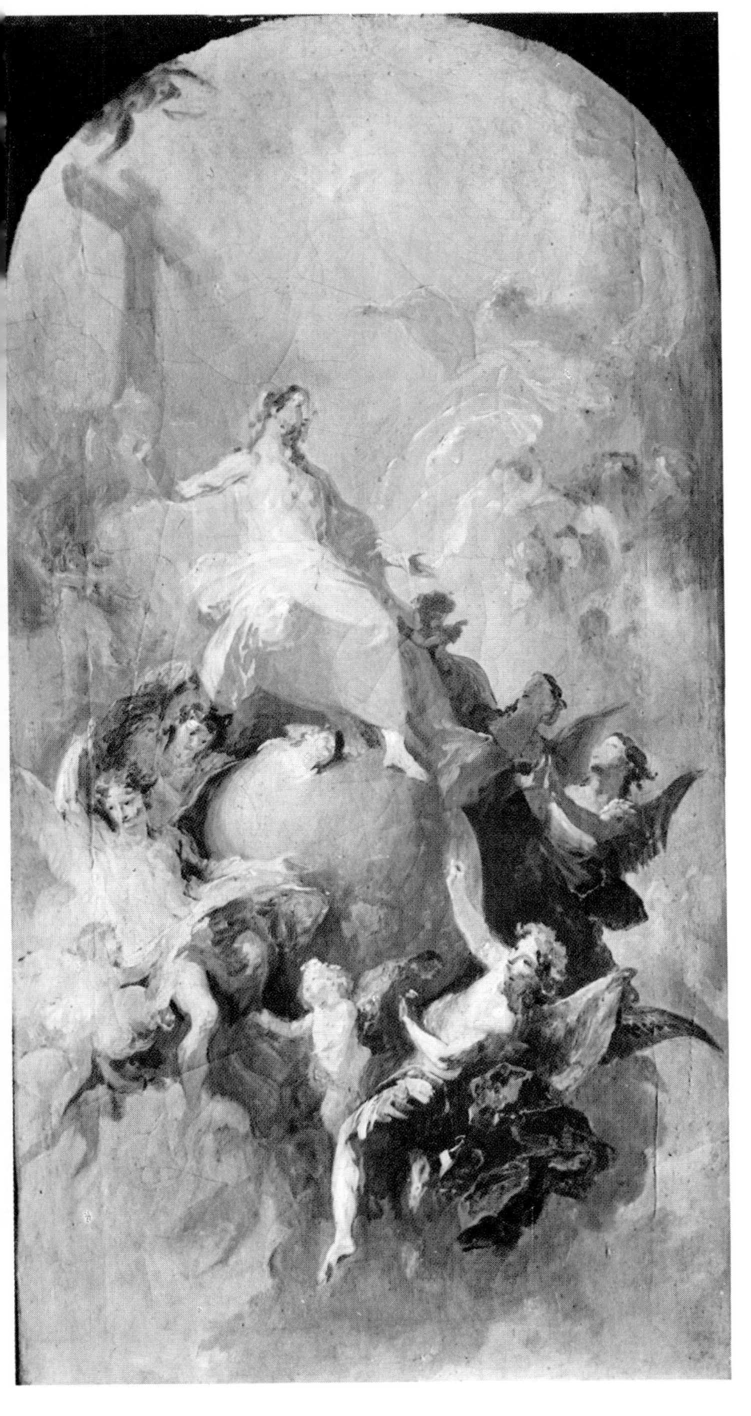

ANGELICA KAUFFMANN German, 1741–1807
Portrait of a Woman
Canvas 51 5/8″ × 40 1/2″(131 × 103 cm.) Inv. No. 444
Signed at left: Angelica Kauffmann. Pinx: Romae a° 1795.

Angelica Kauffmann was one of the most fêted artists of her time, winning high praise from Goethe (whose portrait she painted), Herder and other literary figures. Her popularity was not entirely due to the fact that by the end of the eighteenth century women had been to some extent emancipated by the Enlightenment, for her surviving pictures, particularly her portraits, show that she was an exceptionally gifted artist who consistently and effectively expressed in her works the approach of the new era of Neo-classicism. Most of her historical compositions are based on classical and literary themes, while her portraits are characterized by lucidity of form, noble poses and cool, limpid colours.

This portrait of a middle-aged woman in front of her dressing-table was for many years believed to be a self-portrait, but comparison with authentic self-portraits disproves this. The inscription tells us that the portrait was painted in Rome in 1795, so it is more likely to have been a likeness of Princess Esterházy, for whom Angelica Kauffmann is known to have worked at that time.

From the Esterházy collection.

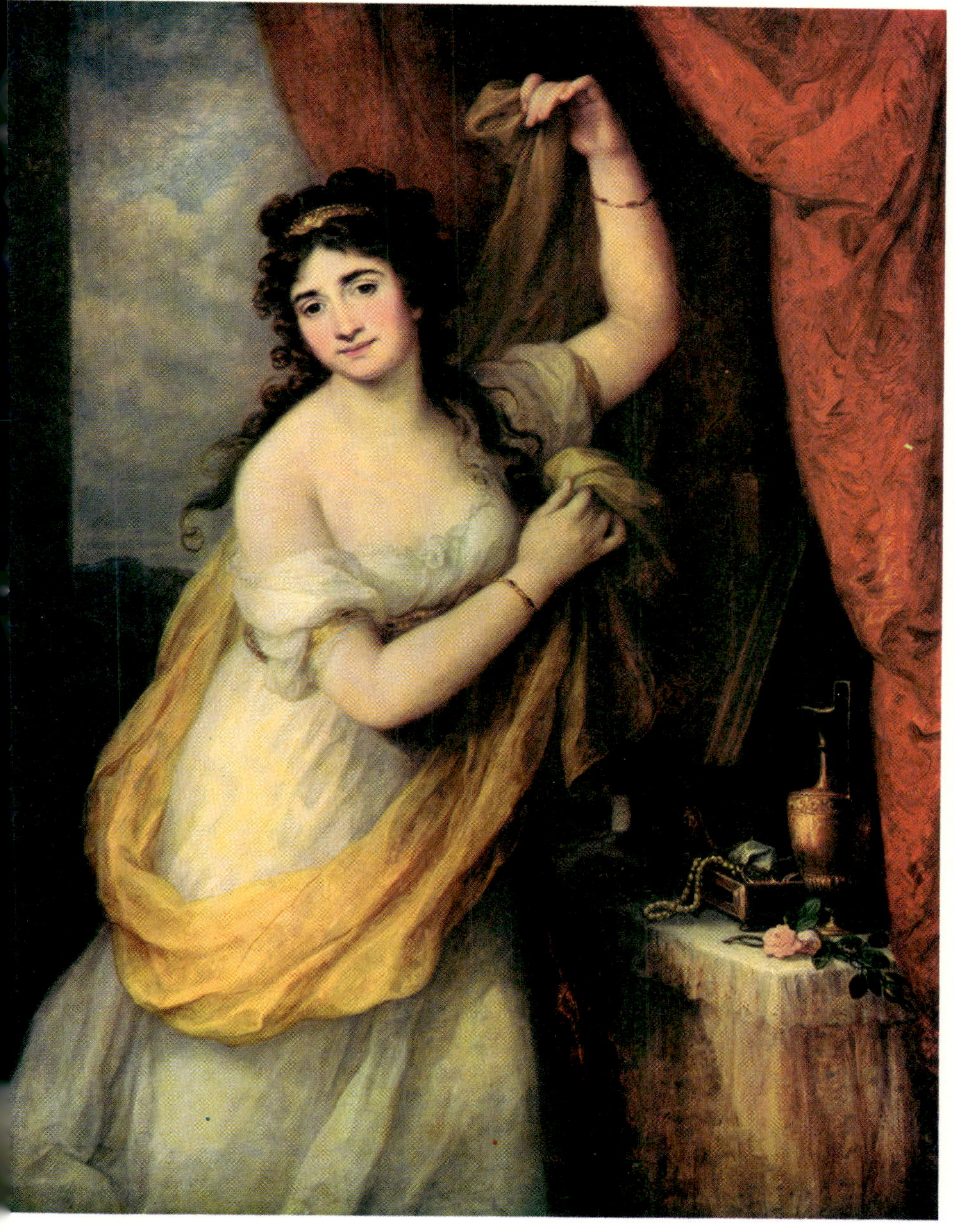

NICOLAS POUSSIN French, 1594–1665
The Rest on the Flight into Egypt
Canvas 22 1/2″ × 29 1/8″ (57 × 74 cm.) Inv. No. 57.18

One of the most splendid of the Museum's recent acquisitions is Nicolas Poussin's early work *The Rest on the Flight into Egypt*, bought in 1957, which dates from the artist's early years in Italy.

Born in Les Andelys in Normandy, Poussin ran away from home in 1612 to escape the lawyer's life his parents planned for him. He may have gone briefly to Rouen and studied under Noël Jouvenet, before reaching Paris, where he probably frequented the studios of Ferdinand Elle and Georges Lallemand. In 1624 he went to Rome, where, except for a two-year return to France in the 1640s, he spent the rest of his life. Poussin was inspired by the art of Antiquity as well as that of the great Renaissance masters, and his own works are characterized by a severe and deliberate structure and clear lines. His colours, particularly in the early and mature works, are fiery and brilliant, and he succeeded in creating a wonderful harmony between the content, the gesture and the means of expression.

In this picture there is a close-knit unity between the charming young Madonna, the *putti* playing among the trees and St Joseph, absorbed in his reading. The tenderness of the drawing – which nevertheless reveals an absolute surety of touch – the fascinating play of colour and expression, are features of Poussin's early work.

Purchased in 1957 from a private collection in Budapest.

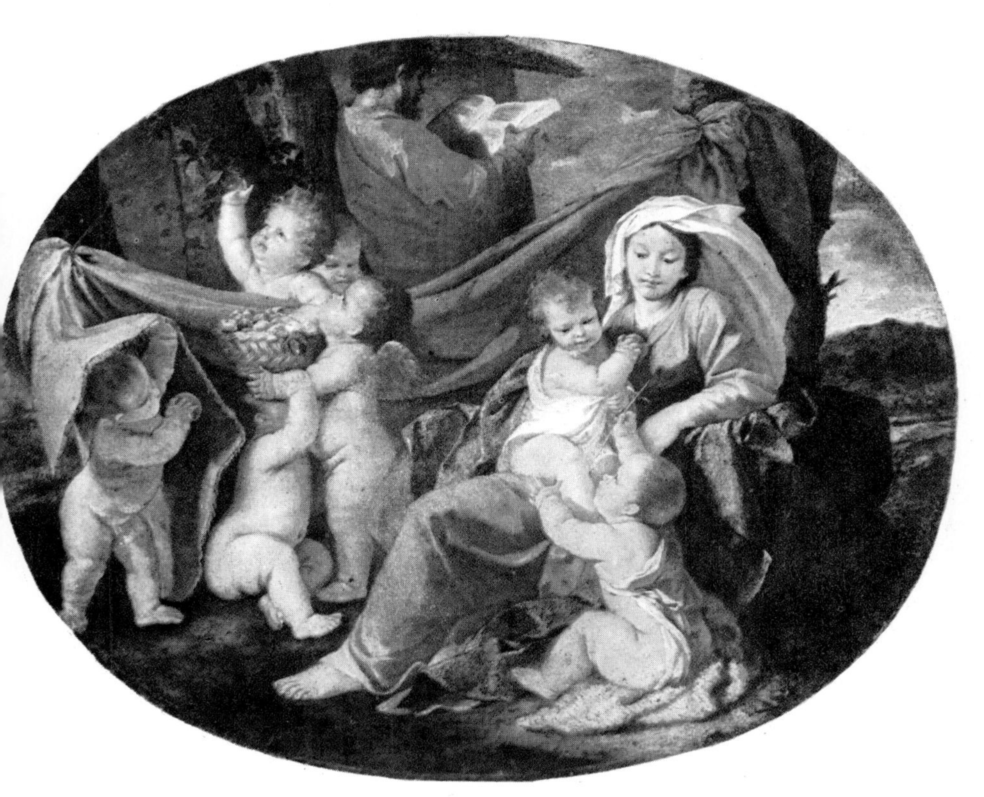

CLAUDE LORRAIN (CLAUDE GELLÉE) French, 1600–82
Villa in the Roman Campagna
Canvas 27 1/8″ × 35 7/8″ (68.8 × 91 cm.) Inv. No. 708

Like Nicolas Poussin, Claude Gellée, a native of Lorraine, went to Italy while still young and lived and worked in Rome as an honoured member of the artists' colony. Italian painters being on the whole not greatly attracted towards the painting of pure landscapes, the genre was first explored in the North and was introduced into Italy by painters from the Netherlands, Germany and France. The French painters, Poussin, Claude and Poussin's nephew, Gaspard Dughet, created a specific kind of landscape, known as the 'ideal landscape', introducing mythological or legendary figures and often creating a pleasing harmony by blending elements of reality with antique ruins or classical buildings. To all this Claude added a specific quality of his own – a magic evocation of mood, an exquisite shading of atmospheric elements and subtlety of lighting.

The painting in Budapest depicts a villa in the country near Rome, the house and the landscape bathed in the gentle light of the late afternoon sun; in the foreground, where the shadows have already lengthened, the surface of the water reflects the figures of the shepherd and his flock. The drawing for this picture is in the Duke of Devonshire's collection at Chatsworth; the inscription on the back of the drawing tells us that the picture was painted for Prince Pamphili, probably some time in the 1640s.

From the Esterházy collection.

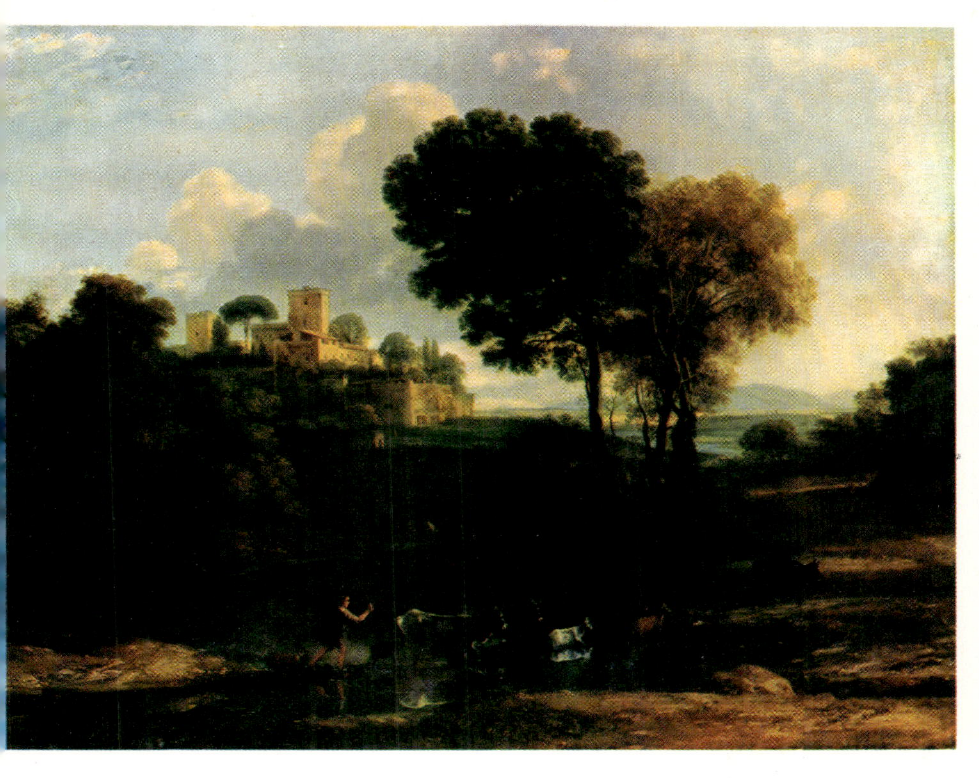

SIMON VOUET French, 1590–1649
Apollo and the Muses
Canvas 31 1/2″ × 87 1/4″ (80 × 221.5 cm.) Inv. No. 707

Like his great compatriots, Poussin and Claude, the Parisian Simon Vouet began his career in Italy. His early works reflect the influence of Caravaggio and Lanfranco; Baroque animation, heavy forms and dramatic contrast of light and shadow are characteristic of the paintings he produced in Rome and Naples. In 1627 Vouet returned to France to become one of the leading masters and a favourite painter of official circles. He gradually adapted his subjects and style to suit the new requirements, painting decorative compositions for the palaces in Paris and for castles in the country. They were usually allegorical or mythological compositions with noble and pure forms rendered with light colours and harmonious lines.

The long and narrow composition now in Budapest probably adorned the salon or library of a country house, and was painted in the 1630s. It was acquired as part of the Esterházy collection together with a full-length painting of Venus, formerly attributed to Vouet.

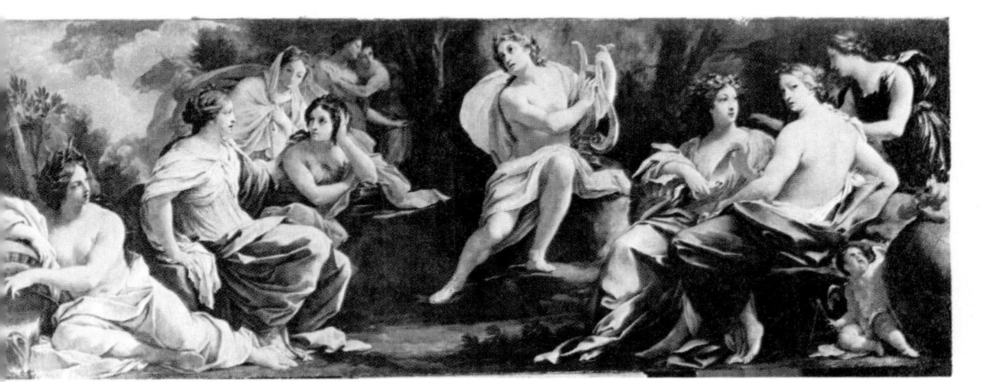

LAURENT DE LA HIRE French, 1606–56
Theseus and Aethra
Canvas 55 1/2″ × 46 5/8″ (141 × 118.5 cm.) Inv. No. 693

This is a representation of Plutarch's story in which, in the presence of his mother, the young Greek hero Theseus finds the sword and sandals his father Aegeus has buried under a heavy stone. Seventeenth-century French masters often chose to depict some fairly recondite theme from Graeco-Roman history or legend, and Laurent de La Hire, a popular Parisian artist of the period, excelled in paintings of this kind. There is another picture by him in Budapest which depicts a historical scene: *King Ninus Offering the Crown to Semiramis* (p. 269). This latter painting, signed and dated 1646, is stricter in its composition and cooler in its colour than the more animated and picturesque representation of Theseus, which was probably produced earlier and in which the influence of Poussin is still strongly felt.

The two historical compositions by La Hire and his *Virgin and Child* came to the Museum from the Esterházy collection.

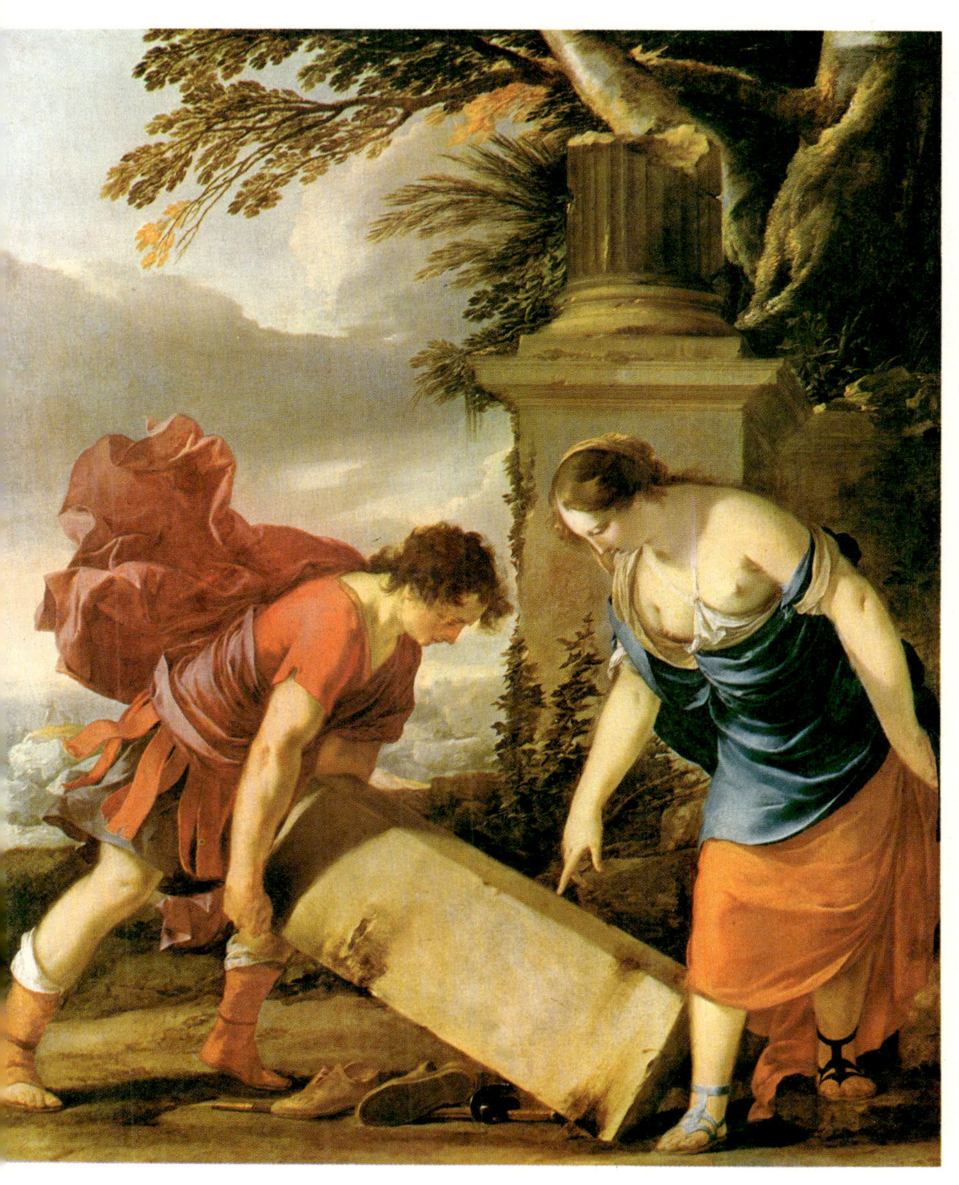

JEAN-BAPTISTE GREUZE French, 1725–1805
Randon de Boisset
Canvas 28 3/4 × 22 7/8″ (73 × 58 cm.) Inv. No. 1345
Signed: peint. par J Greuze 177[3 or 5]

Appreciated by his contemporaries for his moralizing compositions, such as *The Village Bride* or *A Father's Curse*, Jean-Baptiste Greuze's tremendous popularity was also due to his sentimental pictures of young girls (p. 270). Later generations, however, have been more attracted by his surviving portraits, which testify to his unquestionable pictorial talent. Like his contemporaries, Greuze first began to paint in Rococo style but was very soon influenced by the Enlightenment and he became one of the favourites of the writers of the movement, and especially of Diderot.

His portraiture is rooted in the Rococo, the influence of Nattier and Peronneau being unmistakable, but, as we can see here, his sitters' poses were more intimate and their expression more human and immediate than anything found in the work of his predecessors, the court painters. By depicting his subjects in half-length portraits, with no indication of the setting, he succeeded in bringing the sitter closer to the spectator. Randon de Boisset, collector of taxes, was a connoisseur and one of Greuze's patrons; his collection, sold in 1777, contained many of the artist's works.

Bought in 1894 from the Bourgeois Brothers in Cologne.

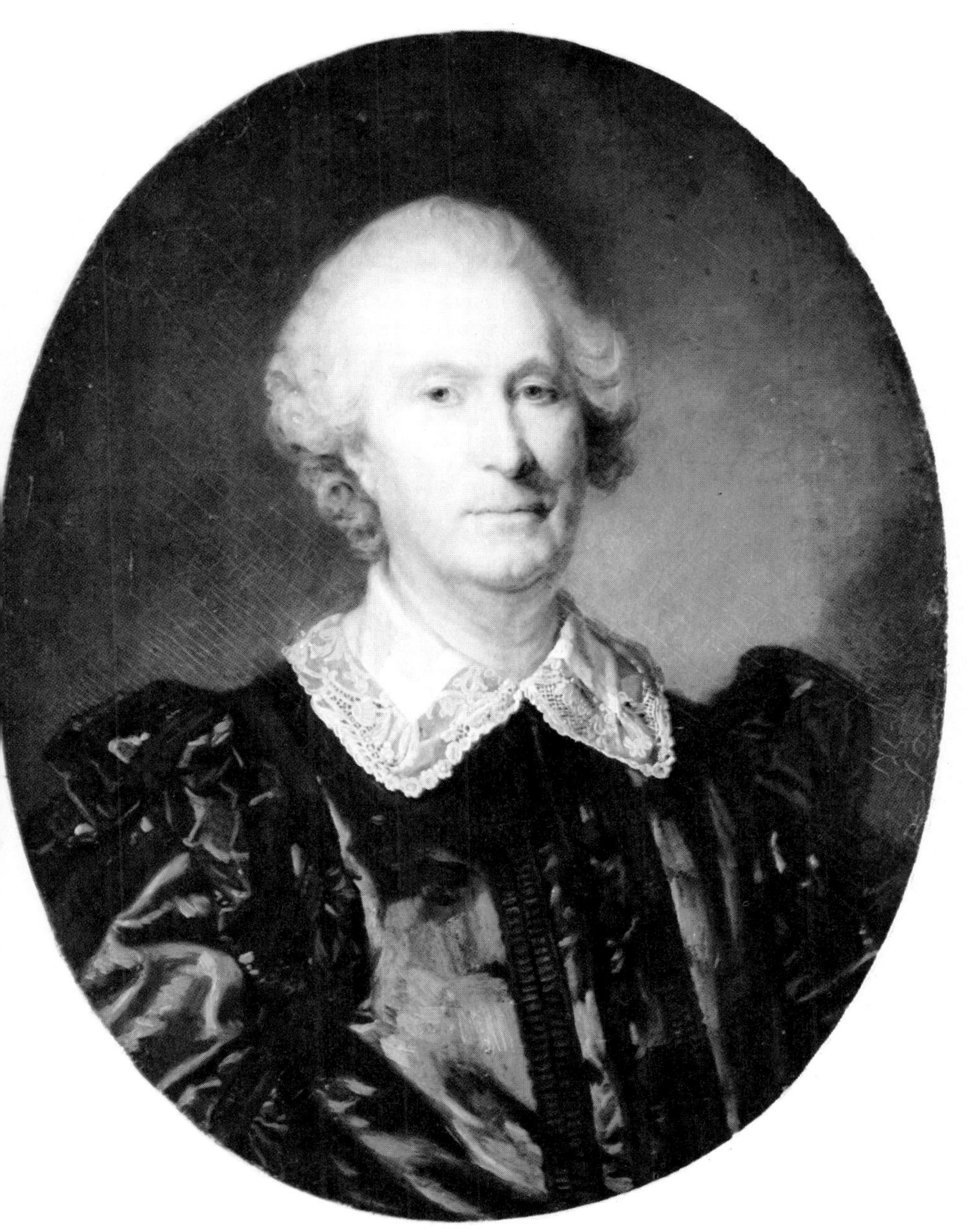

SIR JOSHUA REYNOLDS British, 1723–92
Admiral Sir Edward Hughes
Canvas 29 7/8″ × 24 3/4″ (76 × 63 cm.) Inv. No. 458

Joshua Reynolds, the most important painter in England in the eighteenth century, was the first President of the Royal Academy on its foundation in 1768 and was knighted the following year. Utilizing the pictorial teachings of the past, the compositional principles of Baroque art and the colouring of the Venetian painters of the Renaissance, he became the foremost portrait-painter of his time. The members of the English aristocracy and the wealthy middle classes who commissioned him usually expected him, as their official painter, to produce dignified and flattering likenesses, and indeed, by lavish use of external trappings and a truly brilliant capacity for selecting the most becoming pose, he was able to do what was required of him. But he could penetrate beneath the elegant surface and had the power to suggest character and individuality without marring the pleasing overall picture.

Plump, serene and ruddy of face, with an evident partiality for good food and drink, there is something reminiscent of Falstaff in the portrait of Admiral Hughes now in Budapest. The fiery garnet tint of the coat and the gold of the braid and the order on the sitter's breast create a brilliant harmony which marvellously demonstrates the principal virtue of Reynolds's art: his glowing colour. The picture was painted in 1786 and, according to Reynolds's notes, became the property of the Imperial Ambassador in 1787. This Imperial Ambassador was none other than Prince Esterházy, and the picture was acquired by the Museum as part of the Esterházy collection. There is another version in the Painted Hall at Greenwich.

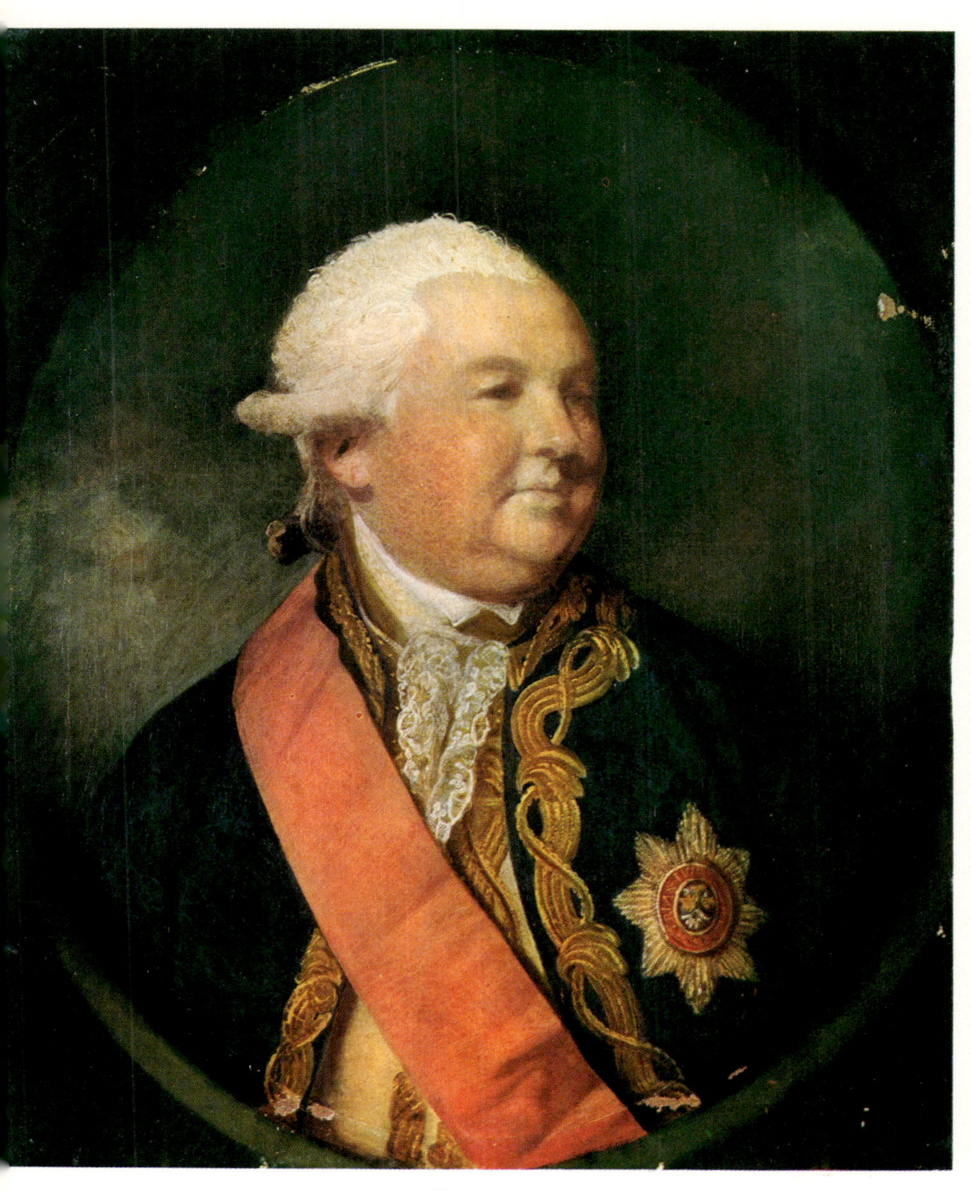

SIR HENRY RAEBURN British, 1756–1823

Mrs Kenneth Murchison

Canvas 35 3/8″ × 27 1/2″ (90 × 70 cm.) Inv. No. 3401

The development of portrait painting is the dominant feature of British painting in the eighteenth century; contemporary social conditions created a situation in which members of the court and aristocracy, the country gentry and the wealthy bourgeoisie, actors and writers, all wanted to have their likenesses painted by British or foreign masters. The resulting pictures, in all their variety, provide a fascinating panorama of the upper reaches of the society of the period. Men and women are depicted singly, in pairs or in an intimate family group, in stately and idealized portraits, full-length or half-length. Landscape played an important role in these portraits, for Gainsborough and Reynolds, as well as Romney and Raeburn, liked to create atmosphere by placing their figures in a landscape setting, often beneath the rich, green foliage of trees. They had a preference for romantic motifs, pensive or emotional postures and intimate moods.

It is because of his sincerity and reticent simplicity that Scotsman Raeburn has a special place among these famous portraitists. He lived and worked in Edinburgh, depicting his Scottish compatriots in serious vein with warm, fluidly handled colours.

Bought in London in 1906.

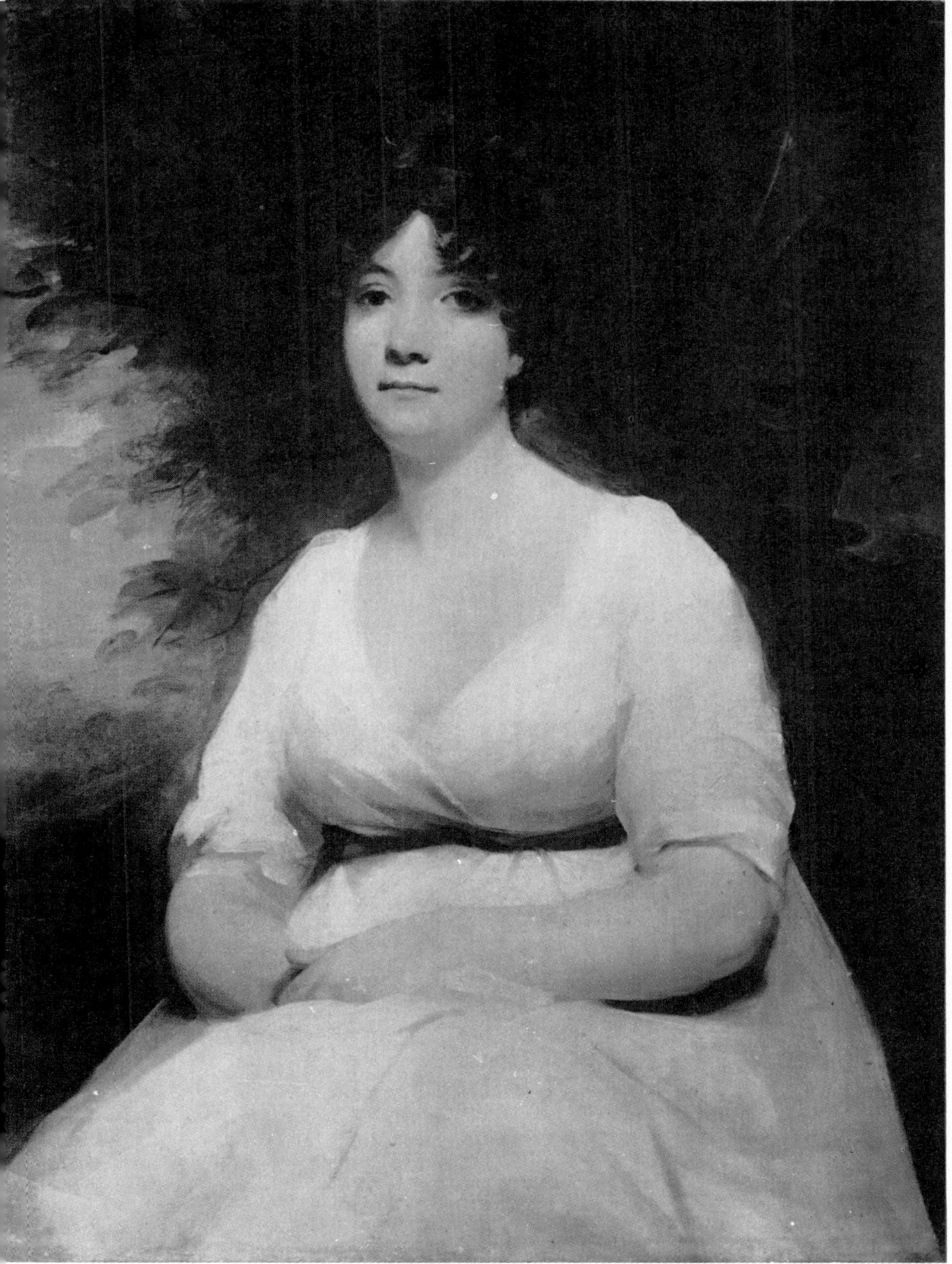

JOHN CONSTABLE British, 1776–1837
Waterloo Celebrations at East Bergholt
Canvas 9″ × 13 1/8″ (23 × 33.5 cm.) Inv. No. 4624

John Constable is perhaps the greatest painter of the English countryside. He depicts the soaring Gothic spire of a cathedral beyond the trees, a hay wain trundling along a winding lane, or a solitary horseman homeward bound, capturing with a wonderful immediacy the ever-changing clouds racing across the sky and the landscape below, brilliantly illuminated in the rays of the emerging sun. No other painter has conveyed with such painterly susceptibility the unique landscape of England in all its changing moods and atmospheric conditions. He began his career under the influence of the Dutch landscape painters of the seventeenth century, but he brought the art of landscape painting to a new perfection by studying and recording directly and humbly the ever-changing face of nature. He was sensitive to every impression, and his grasp of transient phenomena was the reason for his profound influence on the artists who came after him – the painters of the Barbizon School and the Impressionists.

This painting is a small gem, a lively representation of the celebrations held in Constable's native village of East Bergholt after the victory of Waterloo. The assembled villagers watch as an effigy of Napoleon is hung on the gallows.

Purchased in Vienna in 1913.

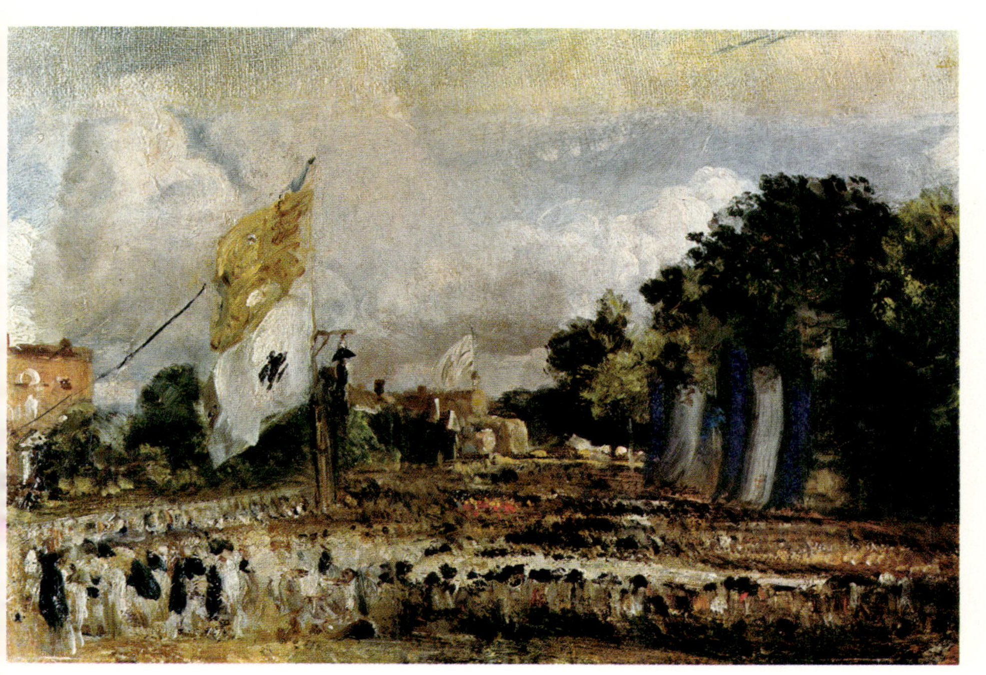

EUGÈNE DELACROIX French, 1798–1863
Horse Frightened by Lightning
Paper 9 1/4″ × 12 5/8″ (23.6 × 32 cm.) Inv. No. 1935–2698
Signed at bottom right: Eug. Delacroix

At the Delacroix Exhibition held in Paris in 1963, the most comprehensive exhibition of his work to date, considerable interest was aroused by this vital and beautiful watercolour, in which we see the most individual features of Delacroix's art as well as the characteristics of Romanticism in general. Passionate and full of life, the work has a bold structure which runs counter to past conventions and combines with its spontaneity to create a splendid example of the new movement through which artists freed themselves from the fetters of academicism.

In this small masterpiece vision and reality, action and change, colour and light are blended into a unique harmony. Alarmed by a thunderbolt, a white horse stands dramatically outlined against a dark background of storm clouds. The head is thrown sideways as the animal rears in alarm; the mane is swept by the gale, the nostrils quiver and the eyes vividly reflect overwhelming terror. The violence of the movement and the brilliant light in which the animal is bathed create the illusion that it is about to burst through the surface of the picture; the horse thus becomes a symbol of ungovernable force and irresistible movement.

This watercolour was given by the painter to his friend, Baron Switer in 1824. It then passed into the Chéramy and Kann collections in Paris and was later bought from the dealer Bernheim by a Budapest collector, Pál Majovszky, whose collection was acquired by the Museum of Fine Arts in 1935.

The watercolour is kept in the Department of Prints and Drawings. In the permanent exhibition of oil-paintings Delacroix's art is represented by *A Moroccan and His Horse* (p. 275), a signed work of the master's mature period.

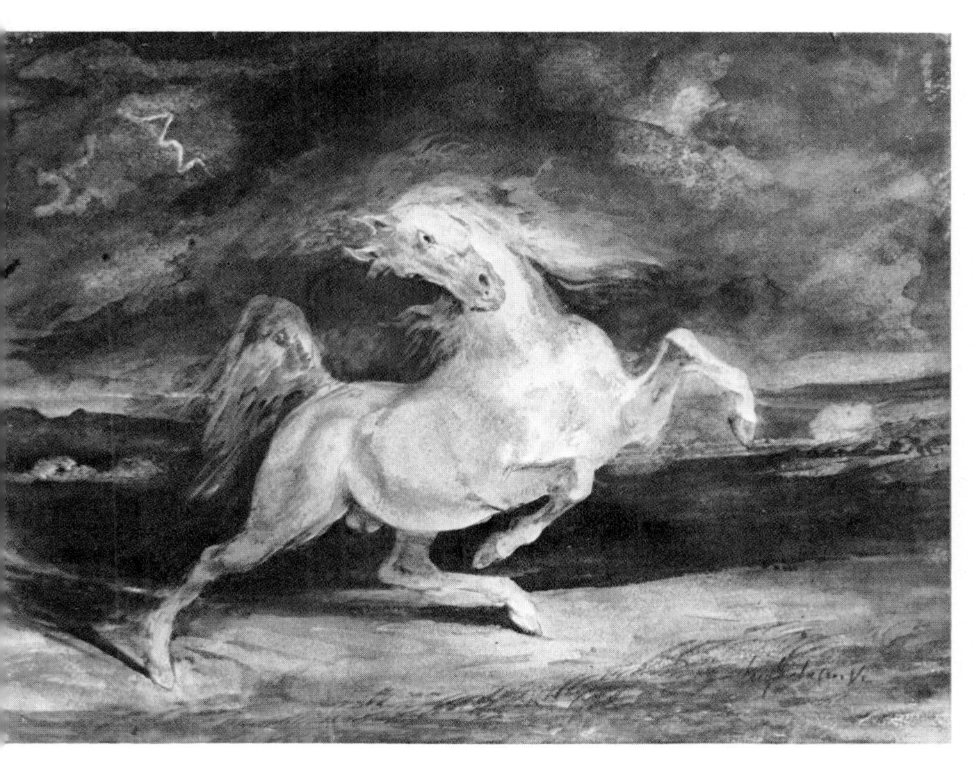

CAMILLE COROT French, 1796–1875
Woman with Daisies
Canvas 30 3/4″ × 22 7/8″ (78 × 58 cm.) Inv. No. 501 B

Corot achieved popularity and success as an artist mainly on account of his landscapes – paintings of misty dawns, green valleys and groves of trees with silvery foliage – which marked a new departure in European landscape painting from the second quarter of the nineteenth century onwards. Some of these, *Souvenir de Coubron* (p. 275) among others, may be seen in the Museum of Fine Arts. Gifted as he was as a creator of poetic landscapes, Corot was nevertheless also a competent figure painter, though his portraits are much more rarely seen than his landscapes.

In 1946 the Museum of Fine Arts acquired an important and beautiful portrait, known as *Woman with Daisies*, which represents a young woman wearing a garland in her long hair. The dark tones of the background are painted with broad strokes of the brush, an admirable foil for the monumental outlines of the light-bathed figure with its brilliant blue sleeves, red bodice and fresh white chemise. The picture is unfinished; the right hand was no more than a sketch when the painter gave the canvas to his friend, Gaspard Lacroix.

Formerly in the Dollfuss collection in Paris; acquired from the Herzog collection in 1946 for the Museum of Fine Arts.

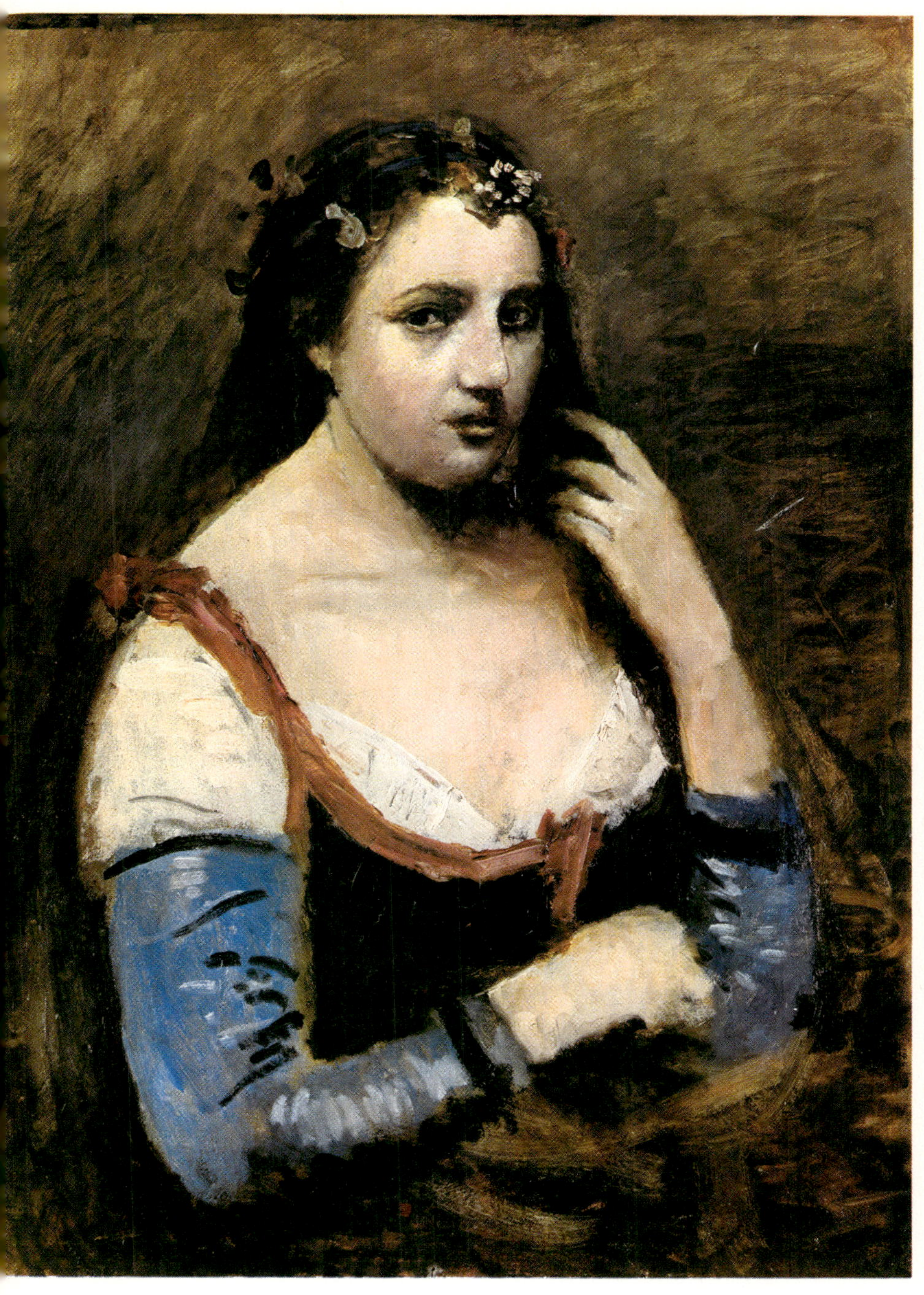

GUSTAVE COURBET French, 1819–77
The Wrestlers
Canvas 99 1/4″ × 78″ (252 × 198 cm.) Inv. No. 502 B
Signed at bottom left: G. Courbet 1853

Courbet, pioneer of nineteenth-century Realism, deliberately set himself the task of depicting the stark realities of everyday life. He painted men engaged in hard physical work or peasants wearied by long years of tilling the soil, and his pictures reflect the dark, unidealized side of life.

The Wrestlers, painted in 1853, is a characteristic work, both in theme and execution. The two muscular athletes grapple with each other, panting and straining, filling the foreground of the picture so that the spectator is given as it were a front seat from which to watch their stupendous efforts. This dramatic episode is effectively outlined against the fresh green of the background, the stand, caught in the sunshine and the contented and indifferent crowd. This composition, in which Courbet struck a new and powerful note, shocked and alarmed those of timid academic tastes and aroused much interest among his contemporaries. Traces of an earlier painting are discernible on the canvas; Courbet has mercilessly used the canvas of his earlier picture *Walpurgis Night*, painted in 1848.

In 1882 *The Wrestlers* was put up for auction at the Hôtel Drouot in Paris; through the Berlin art dealer, Cassirer, it was acquired by the Budapest collector Ferenc Hatvany.

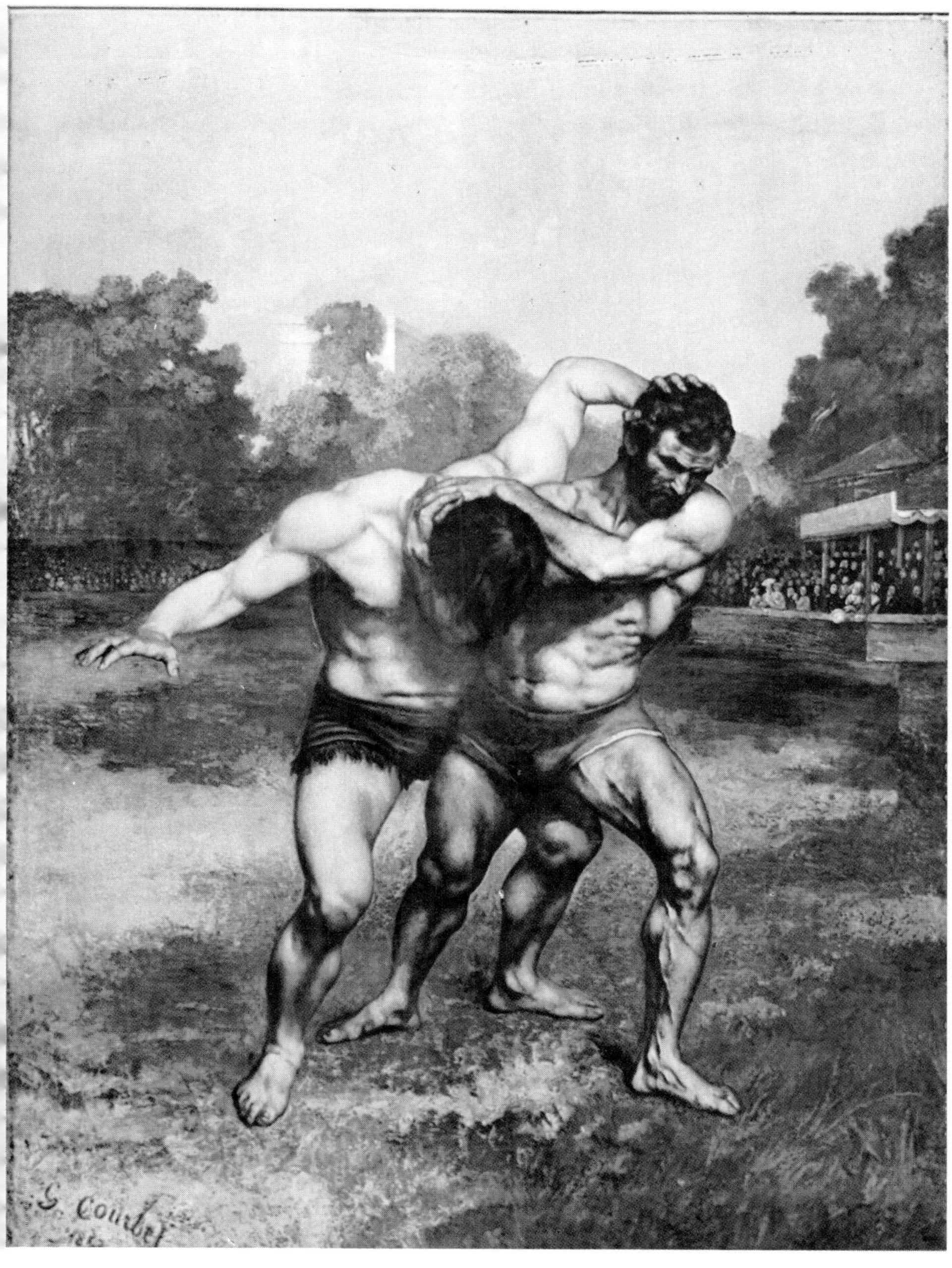
G. Courbet

CLAUDE MONET French, 1840–1926
Fishing Boats
Canvas 28 3/4″ × 36 3/8″ (73 × 92.5 cm.) Inv. No. 436 B
Signed at bottom right: Claude Monet 86

Claude Monet survived by several decades Manet and Pissarro, the fellow Impressionists with whom he had fought for the renewal of French painting. He was a prolific painter who created a formidable number of works from the 1870s up to the 1920s. Three phases of his development are represented by the works now in the Budapest Museum: the early *Harbour at Trouville* (p. 276), dated 1870, *Apple Trees in Blossom*, painted in 1879, and *Fishing Boats*, produced seven years later, in 1886.

With its boldness of expression and painterly *bravura*, this work is a dramatic and powerful version of a subject the artist had already depicted several times before. Here he uses broad, impasted brush-strokes to depict a sandy stretch of the shore with three heavy, weatherbeaten boats and a menacing background of green waves, white-crested and storm-tossed. The scene is viewed from above so that restless diagonals, as well as the handling which first dissolves the colours and then unites them again, combine to convey the singular susceptibility to the phenomena of nature which is the unique contribution of the Impressionists. The picture was painted at Étretat on the Normandy coast north of Le Havre.

From the Herzog collection.

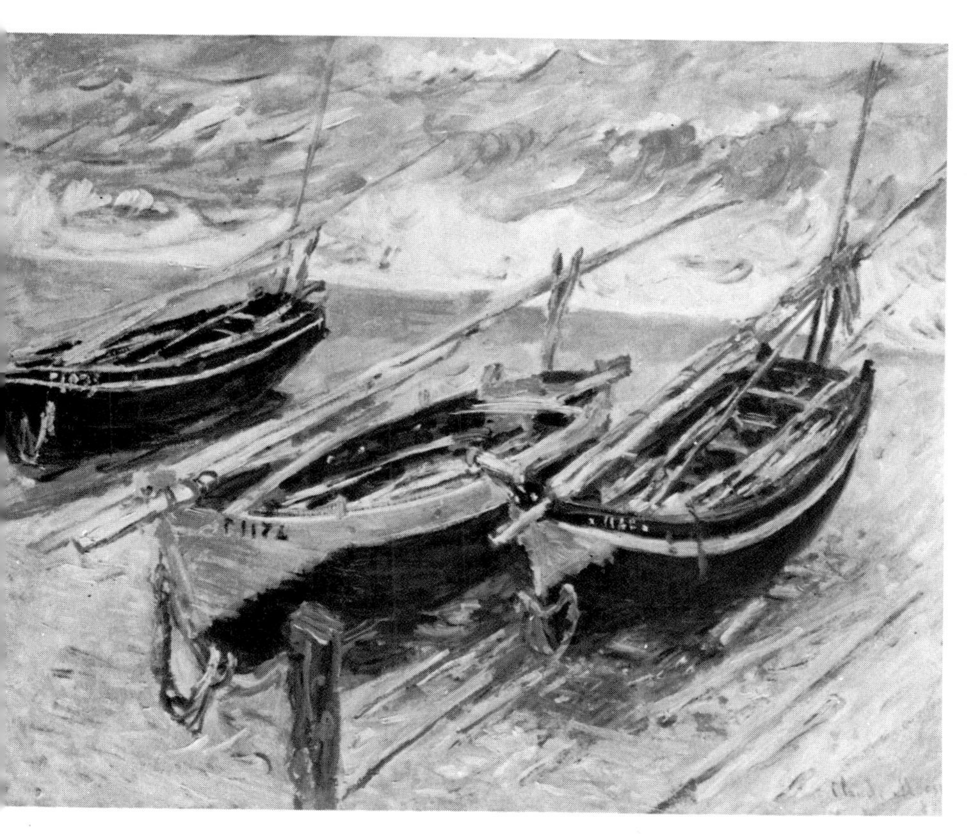

EDOUARD MANET French, 1832–83
Lady with Fan
Canvas 35 3/8″ × 44 1/2″ (90 × 113 cm.) Inv. No. 368 B
Signed at bottom left: Manet

Edouard Manet painted this portrait of Jeanne Duval in 1862 in his studio in Paris. The creole sitter, a native of San Domingo, was Baudelaire's mistress and the muse to whom he dedicated many of his verses. *Lady with Fan*, which depicts her reclining on a sofa with a closed fan in her hand, is one of the finest examples of Manet's Spanish period, a worthy counterpart to such works as *Lola de Valence* and *Spanish Guitarist*. This youthful work is full of vigour and shows a remarkable degree of maturity – witness the execution of the gossamer-like lace curtain in the background, the magnificent colour harmonies of green and white, the melancholy face and expressive hands. The watercolour sketch for this painting is in the Museum of Bremen.

Formerly in Berlin as part of Manet's bequest; bought for the Budapest Museum of Fine Arts in 1916.

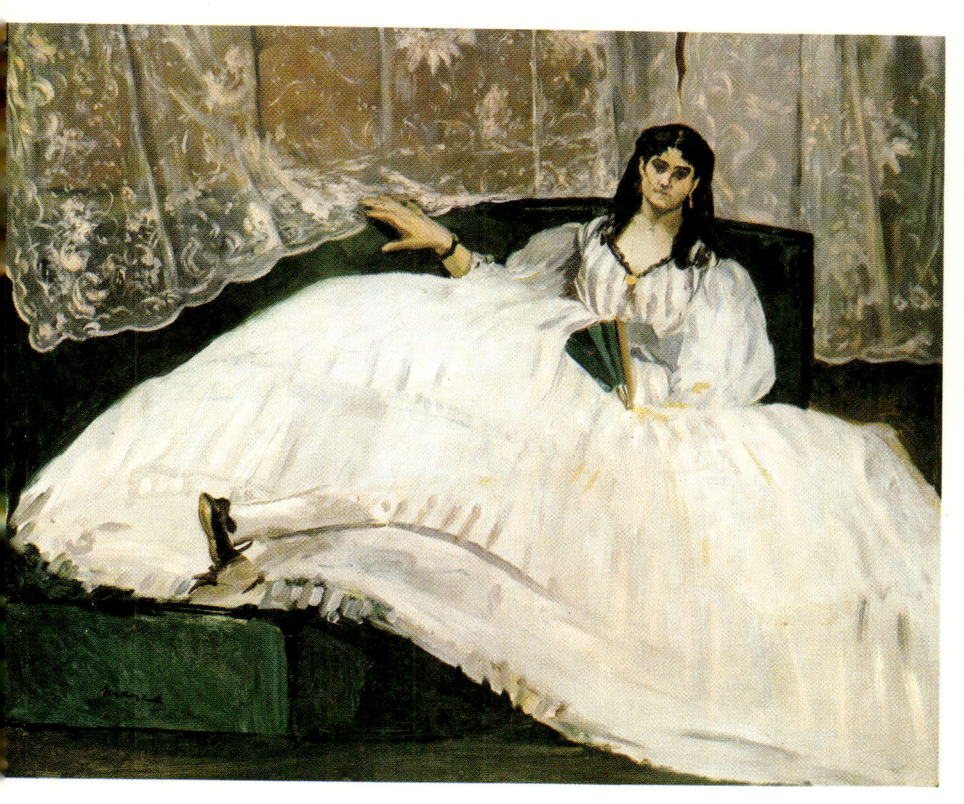

CAMILLE PISSARRO French, 1831–1903
The Pont-Neuf
Canvas 21 5/8″ × 18 1/4″ (55 × 46.5 cm.) Inv. No. 205 B
Signed at bottom left: C. Pissarro, 1902

Before 1872, when the artistic aims of the Impressionists were embodied in Monet's famous picture *Impression, Sunrise*, artists associated with the new movement worked to a greater or lesser extent in the traditional style, and certainly the early works of Monet and Pissarro were unquestionably influenced by Corot. From the early 1870s onwards, however, French painters began to break away from the traditional approach to landscape painting, gradually abandoning the Barbizon School.

The picture by Pissarro now in Budapest, *La Varenne-de-St-Hilaire* (p. 276) was painted about 1863 and cannot be described as an Impressionist work, but this view of the Pont-Neuf in Paris, on the other hand, a late work dated 1902, is a true Impressionist painting. The artist has dissolved the scene into tiny, vibrating spots of colour which fuse into optical unity only in the eye of the spectator. Everything is motion, lively and fresh, and the artist represents with equal skill the traffic on the old bridge, the damp and steamy atmosphere and the bustle of life in a modern city. Pissarro lived near the bridge, on the Place Dauphine, and from his window several times painted the eternal yet ever changing view of the Seine as it flows under the oldest bridge in Paris.

Purchased in 1907.

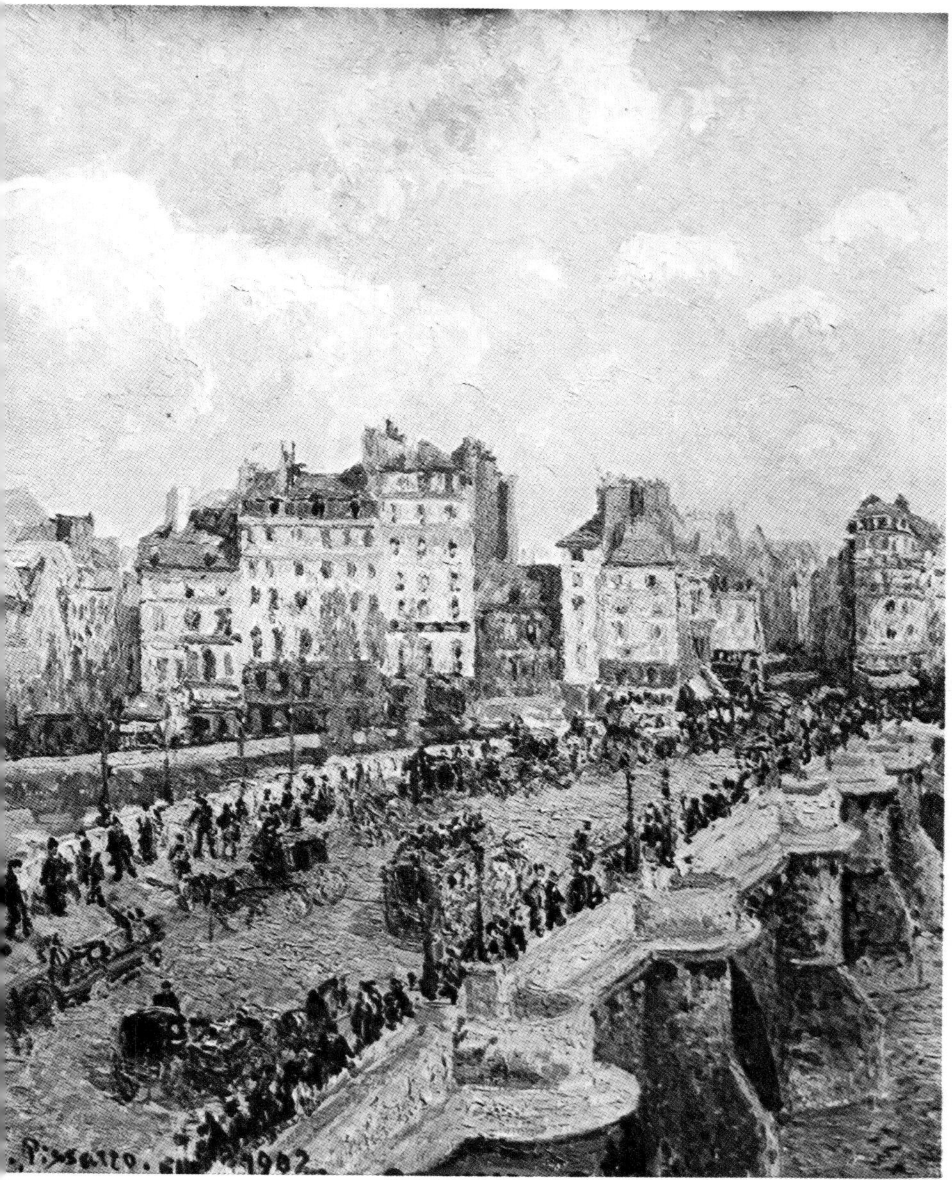
Pissarro. 1902

PAUL GAUGUIN French, 1848–1903
Black Pigs
Canvas 35 7/8″ × 28 3/8 (91 × 72 cm.) Inv. No. 355 B
Signed at bottom right: P. Gauguin 91

In 1891, weary of conventional life in a civilized society, Gauguin, who had been a stockbroker before becoming a painter, forsook Europe for the South Seas. He settled in Tahiti where he recorded, with enthusiasm and a tremendous upsurge of his imaginative powers, the fiery tropical landscape and its simple inhabitants. It was in this paradise of peace and beauty, so full of glowing colours, that he discovered his true message, his new and individual manner of expression.

It is most illuminating to compare the picture painted on Tahiti with an early work of 1879, *Winter Landscape*, also in Budapest (p. 276). The picture painted on Tahiti is a harmonious composition made up of broad areas of colour – dazzling greens, glowing yellows and reds. In the pale and luminous view of Normandy there is clear evidence of the painter's talent (though he was virtually unknown at the time he painted it), but here the painter had not yet ventured to depart from the traditional approach. *Black Pigs*, painted twelve years later, is a liberated, triumphant creation; with its broad forms, courageous simplicity and decorative values it points the way for artists of the twentieth century.

Bought at the 1913 Gauguin Exhibition in Budapest.

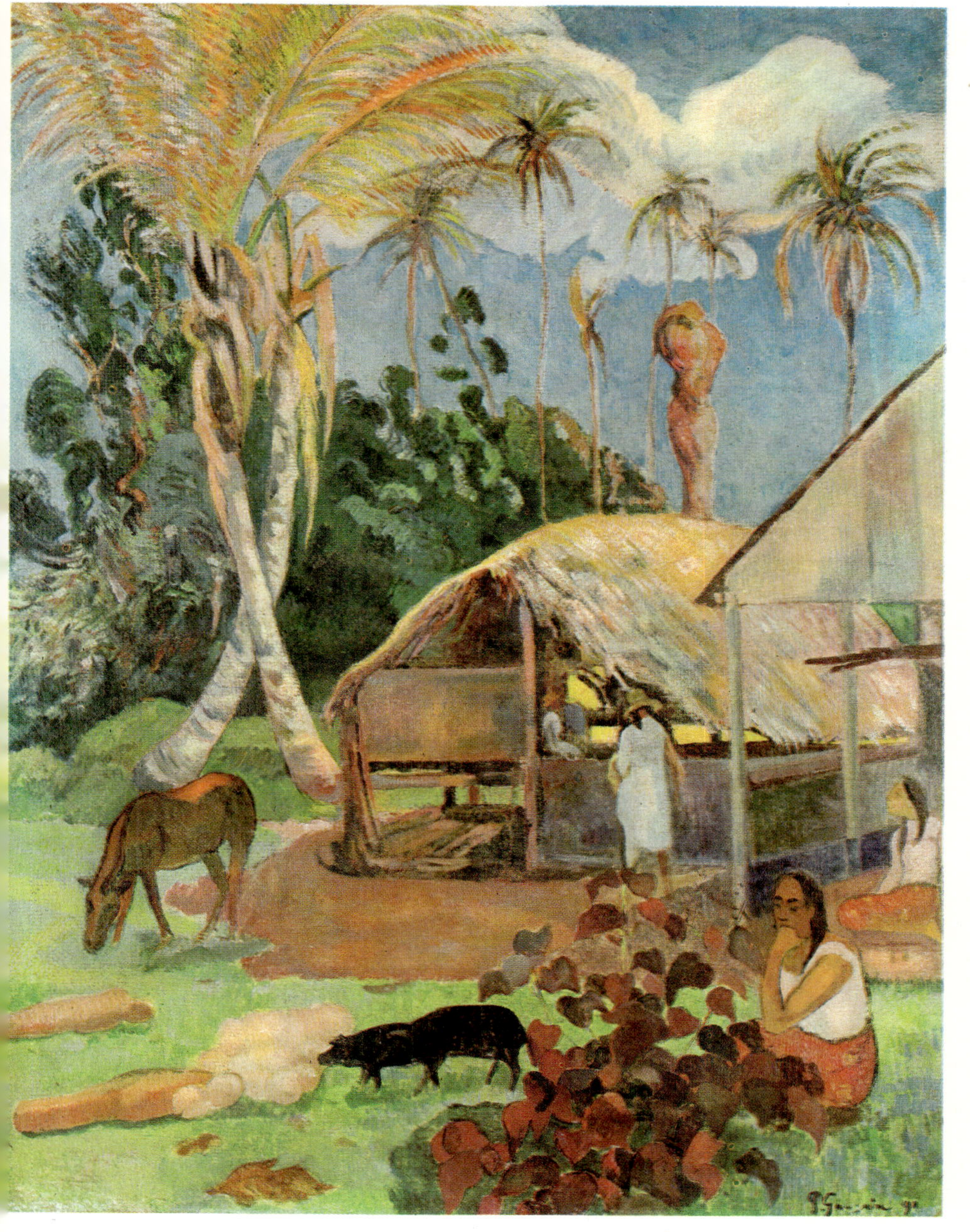

AUGUSTE RENOIR French, 1841–1919
Portrait of a Girl
Canvas 22 1/4" × 18 1/2" (56.5 × 47 cm.) Inv. No. 435 B
Signed bottom left: Renoir

The early work of Auguste Renoir has many links with Impressionism. For a time he exhibited together with the Impressionists, with whom he shared the wish to achieve a new and liberated pictorial vision, but he differed from them in temperament and aim, and was soon developing in another direction. Although, like Monet and Pissarro, he was engrossed in the representation of trees and fields seen in intense sunshine, his interest was focused on the human figure, on living beings of flesh and blood, sensuous and active. His spontaneous, plastic representations depict people in interiors, in the open air, alone or in groups, at the piano in the drawing-room or by the cradle, in a box at the theatre or in a restaurant on the river bank; an endless succession of human figures, clothed or nude. The plump, honey-blonde girl in this picture, painted in the 1890s, was the model for a good many of his portraits. The tender forms harmonize with the fresh colours to create a work of extraordinary beauty.

Purchased from the Herzog collection in 1945.

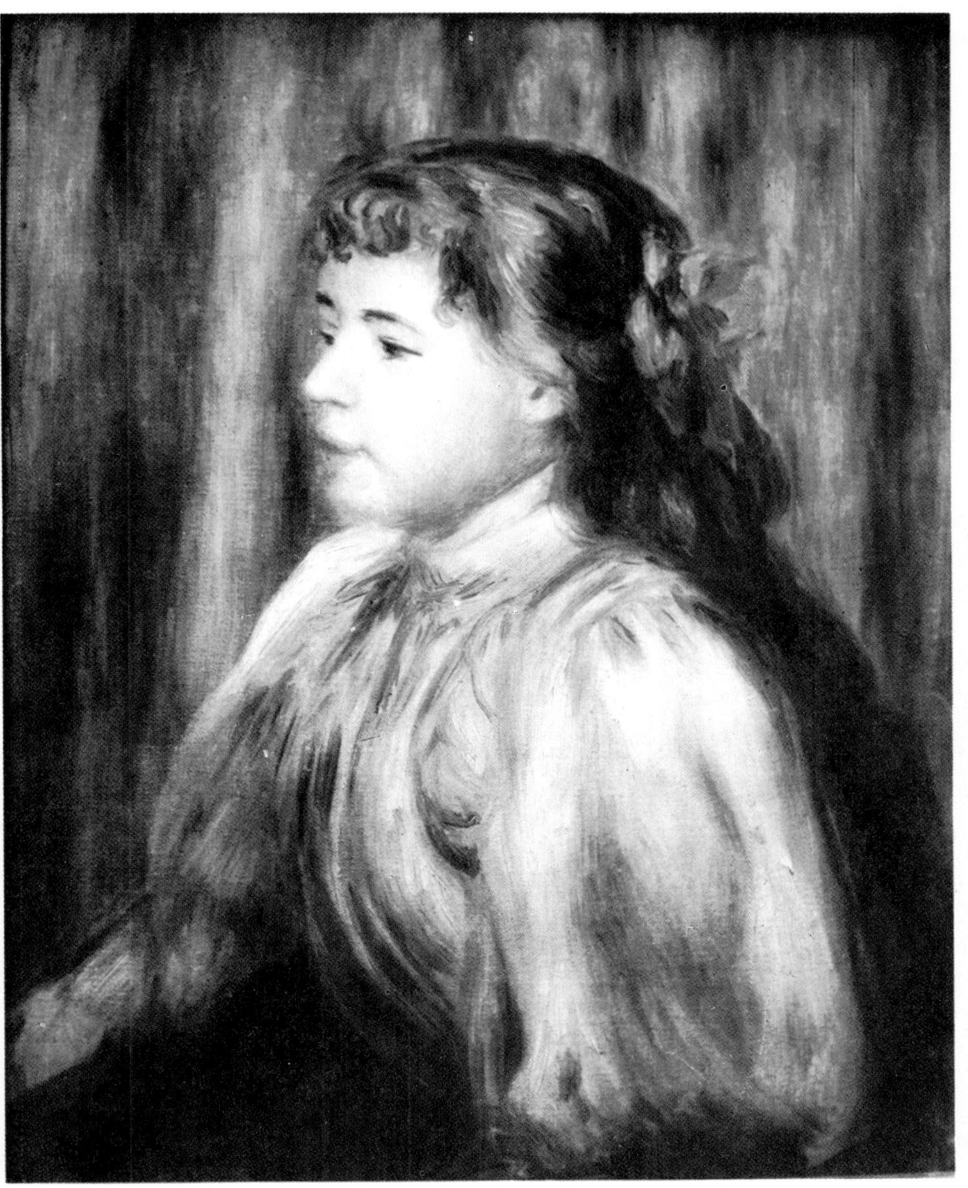

HENRI DE TOULOUSE-LAUTREC French, 1864-1901
Ces Dames
Cardboard 23 3/4″ × 31 3/4″ (60.3 × 80.5 cm.) Inv. No. 356 B
Signed at bottom left: T. Lautrec

The *fin de siècle* mood of Paris, gay or wretched, has never been recorded with such vividness and animation as in the works of Toulouse-Lautrec. He records with swift lines the figures of the *demi-monde:* dancers whose past was as doubtful as their future was likely to be bitter, faded beauties, gamblers and jockeys.

The painting in Budapest, *Ces Dames*, dates from the last decade of the century and presents a devastating interpretation of character and, at the same time, thanks to its fresh pastel tints, makes a charming picture. The ladies, sharp-featured women past their prime, are to be seen in a great many of his works; they were attached to the Moulin Rouge or to neighbouring brothels. Here the artist shows them at their ease, chatting together in intimate fashion.

Purchased at the exhibition of works by Toulouse-Lautrec held in Budapest in 1913.

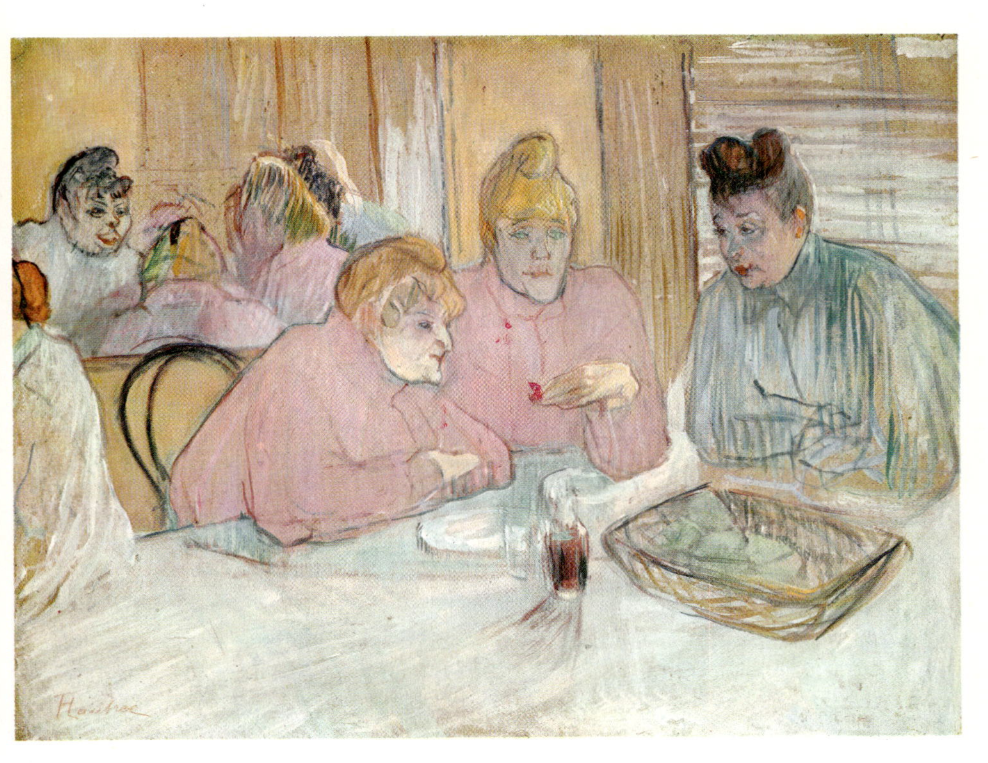

PAUL CÉZANNE French, 1839–1906
The Sideboard
Canvas 25 5/8″ × 31 7/8″ (65 × 81 cm.) Inv. No. 371 B

Cézanne's struggle for recognition was as bitter as that of the Impressionists. He lived and worked in seclusion in Provence, and only since his death has he been acknowledged as one of the greatest masters of all time. His early work was in the style of Impressionism, but he broke away and created an artistic idiom that was all his own; in fact, he gave a new direction to modern painting. While the Impressionists dissolved forms into light and colour, with an artistic vision focused on motion and change, the principle features of Cézanne's landscapes, still-lifes and figure compositions are a firm structure and clear, definite forms. In his work form found its rightful place once more, colour served the creation of structural unity.

The Sideboard, with its lucid construction and its blue-green and white colouring, is a characteristic example of Cézanne's art, enchanting in its harmonies. The arrangement – the white napkin, the placing of the apples and the crockery – clearly conveys depth, the dimensions of the objects and, at the same time, constitutes a well-poised and logical unity of form.

Acquired for the Museum from the collection of Marcell Nemes in 1917.

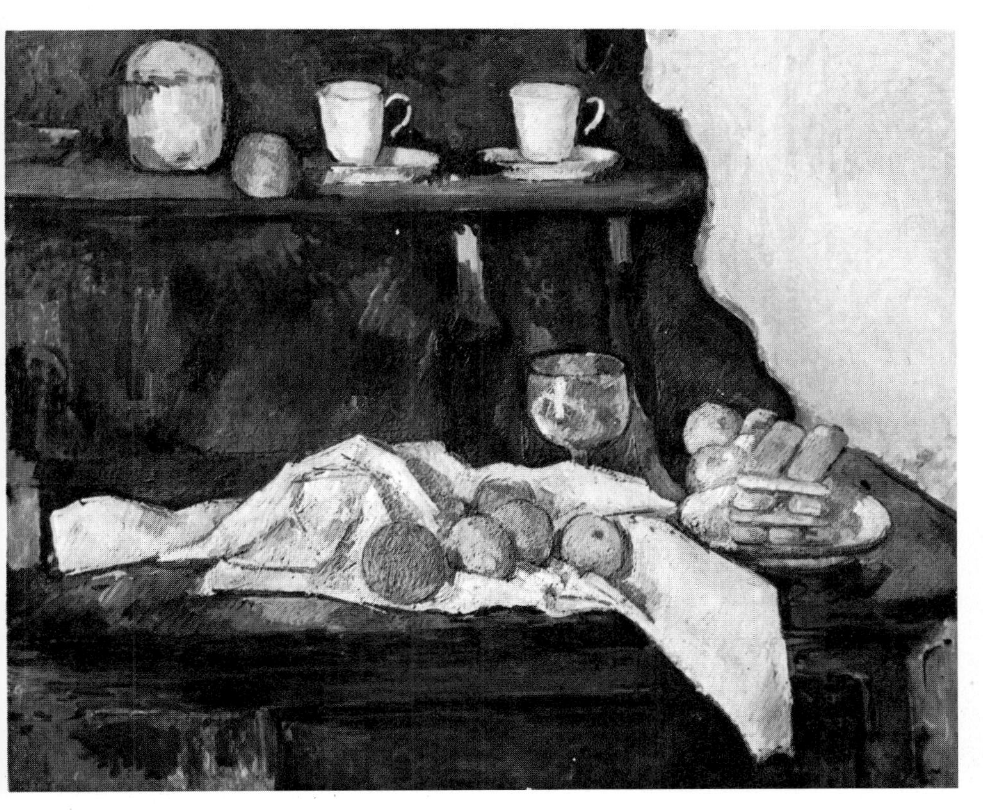

PIERRE BONNARD French, 1867–1947
The Luncheon
Canvas 21 1/8″ × 24″ (53.5 × 61 cm.) Inv. No. 400 B
Signed: Bonnard

The art of Pierre Bonnard, so rich in pictorial values, so lyrical in its approach, covers a period extending from the end of the last century almost to the present time. Gauguin, Japanese prints and (distantly) Art Nouveau were the dominating influences in his early work, especially evident in his striving for decorative effect and richness of colour. There is in the Budapest Museum a small picture by Bonnard which dates from this early period, *Mother and Child*, painted in 1894.

The Luncheon, a later work, shows a greater refinement of expression and maturity of imagination. The painting conveys the quiet atmosphere of a gas-lit interior, in which figures move vaguely about among gay, colourful objects. The details, as if depicted at random, the mingling of stationary and moving elements, the structure and choice of images, are characteristic of Bonnard's at first sight arbitrary compositional structures, which are held together and heightened by his use of colour. From 1890 until 1899 Bonnard belonged to the group of artists known as the Nabis who were keenly interested in a variety of decorative tasks, including the creation of posters and stage sets, but always emphasized the two-dimensionality of the picture plane. Their influence is detectable in this picture where the lines of demarcation between the different planes of the perspective are in dissolution.

The two paintings by Bonnard were acquired by the Museum of Fine Arts with the Baron Kohner collection in the 1930s.

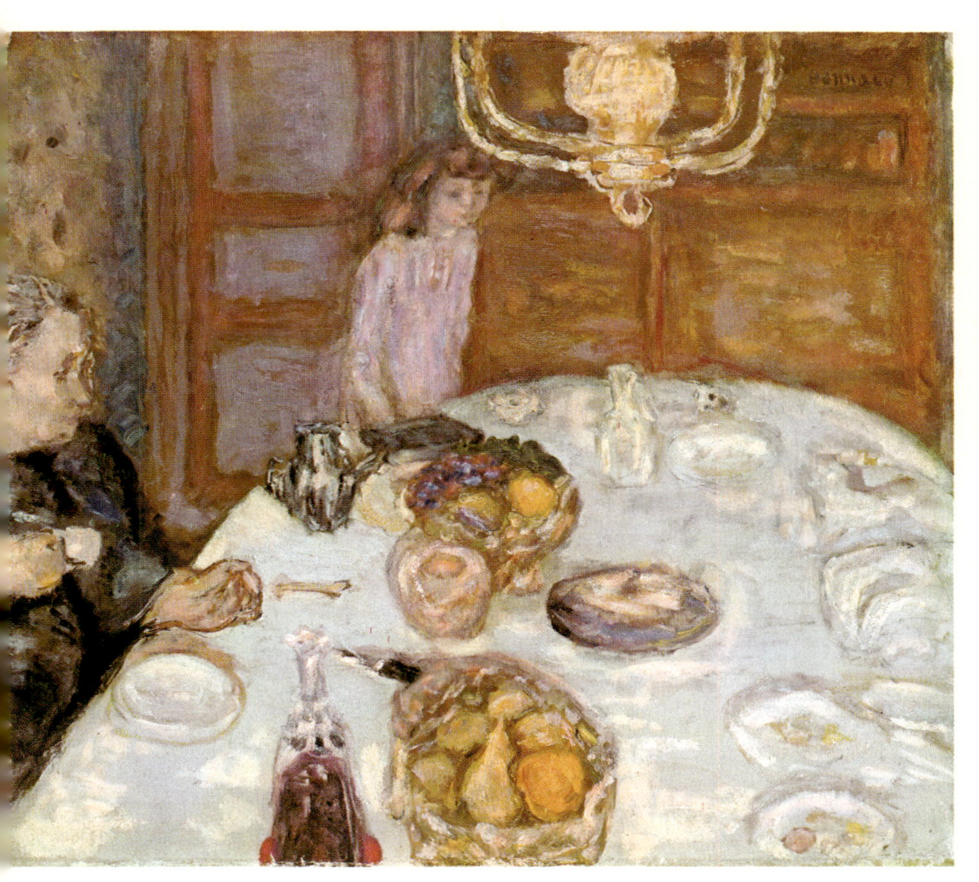

ITALIAN PAINTING

Thirteenth to eighteenth centuries

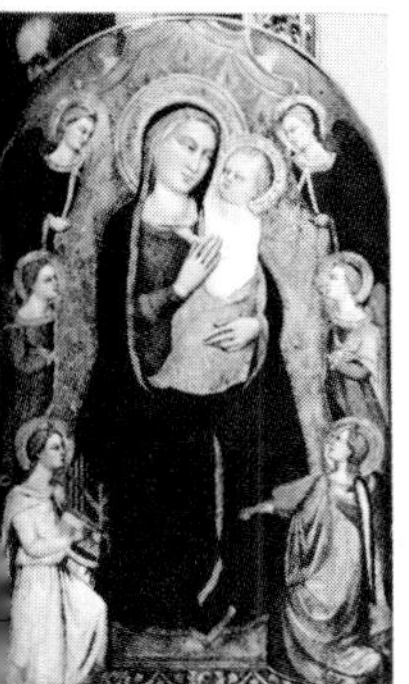

Jacopo di Cione
Virgin and Child Enthroned with Angels

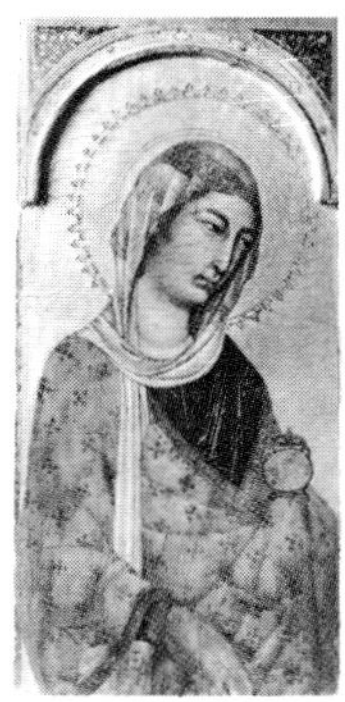

Segna di Buonaventura
St Lucy

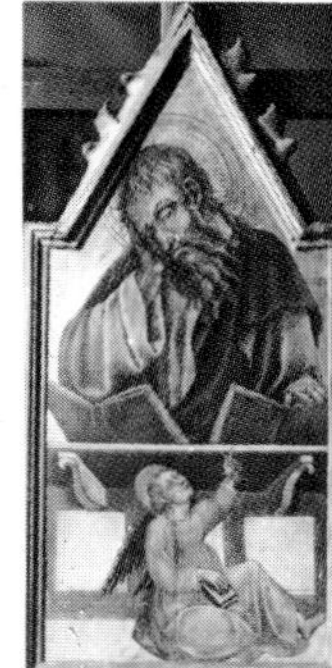

Giovanni di Paolo
St Matthew

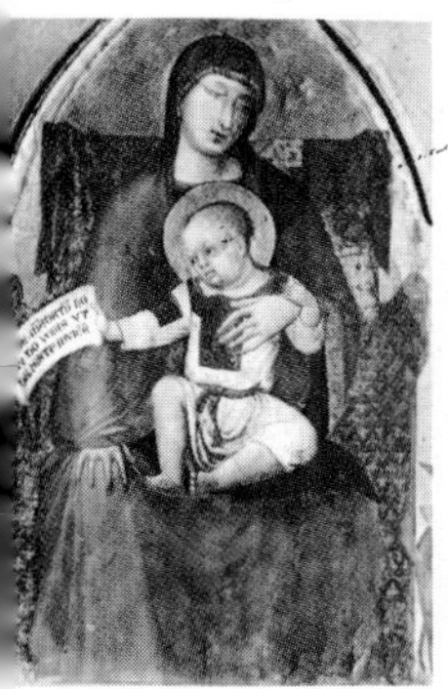

Ambrogio Lorenzetti
Virgin and Child Enthroned

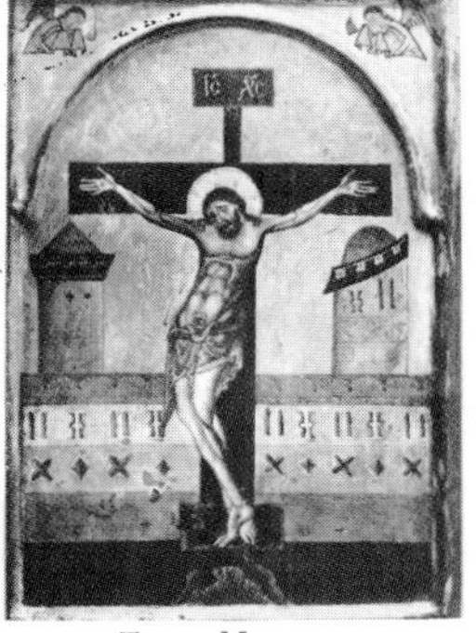

Tuscan Master
(thirteenth century)
Christ on the Cross

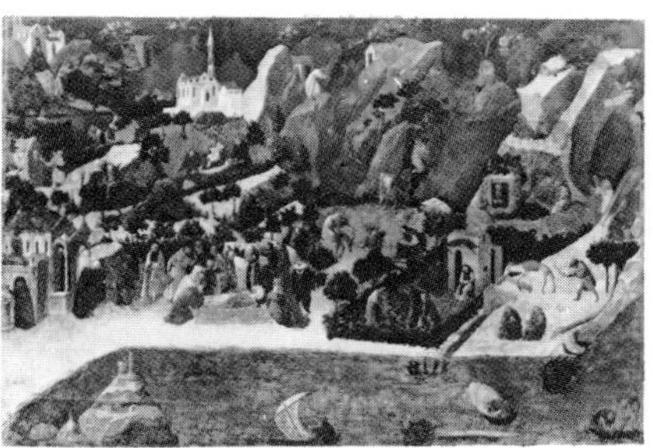

Lorenzo Monaco
Scenes from the Lives of the Hermits

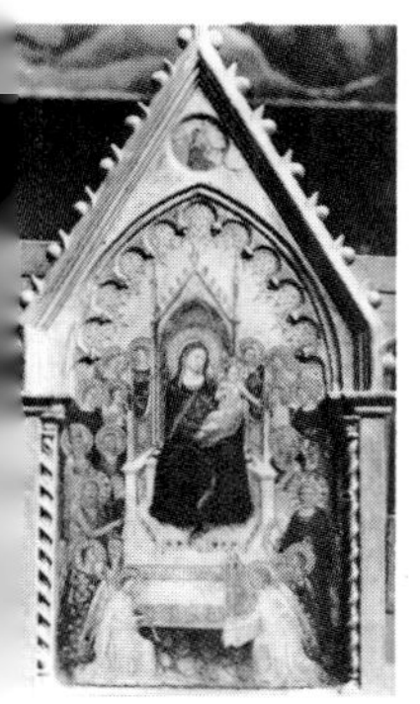

Jacopo del Casentino
Virgin and Child with Saints and Angels

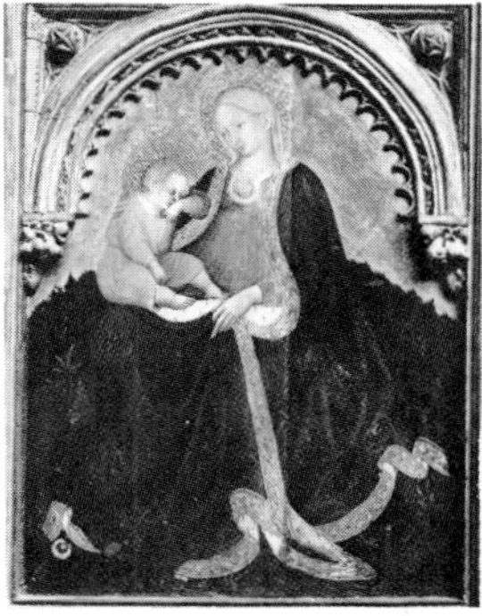

Jacobello del Fiore
The Virgin and Child

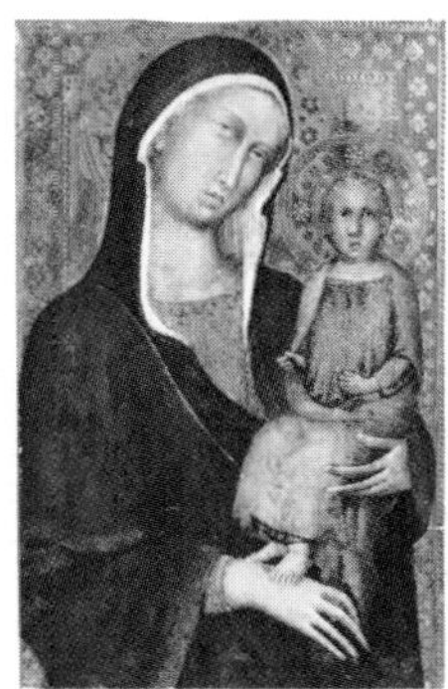

Naddo Ceccarelli
The Virgin and Child

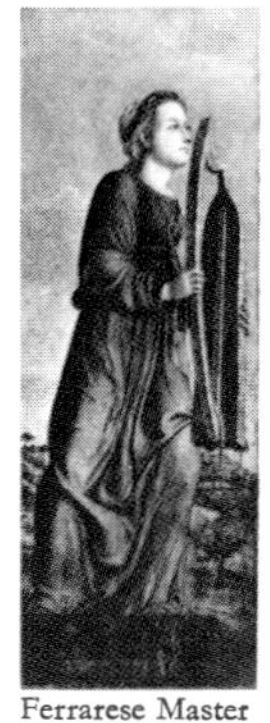
Ferrarese Master
fifteenth century)
Figure with Harp

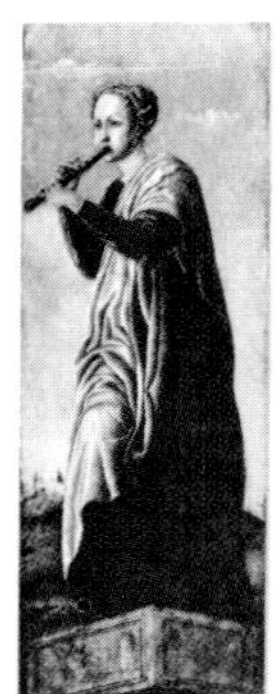
Ferrarese Master
(fifteenth century)
Figure with Flute

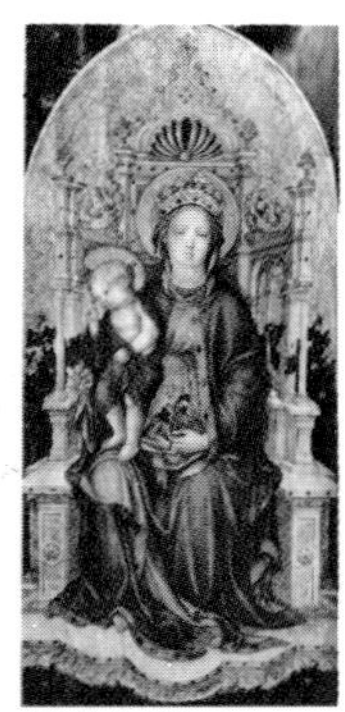
Michele Giambono
Virgin and Child Enthroned

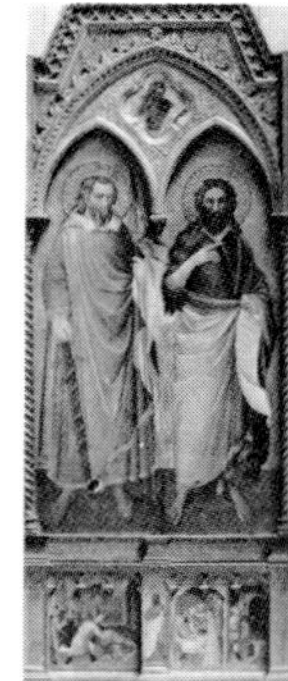
Spinello Aretino
St Nemesius and St John the Baptist

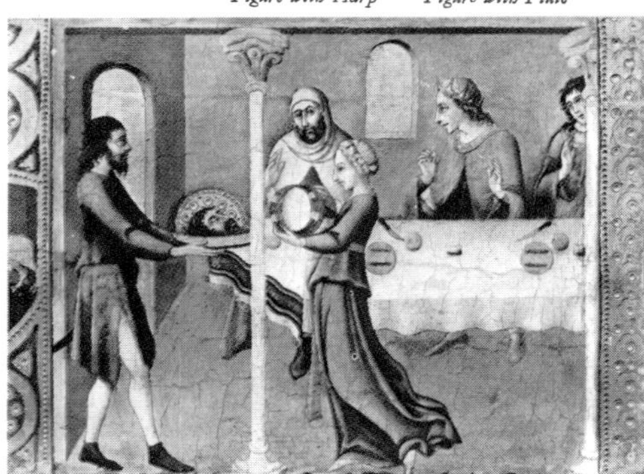
Sano di Pietro *The Dance of Salome*

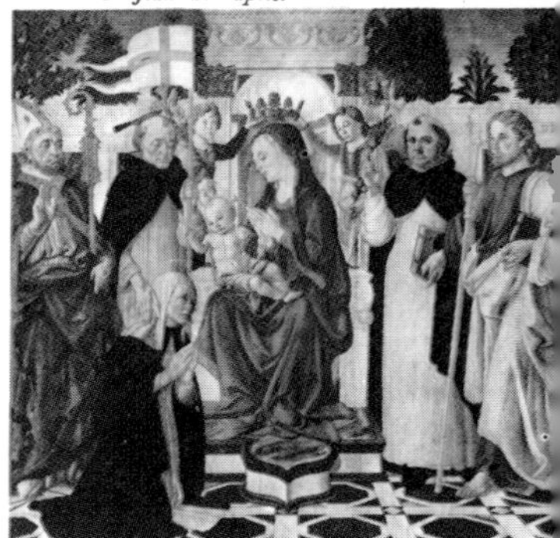
Workshop of Verrocchio
Virgin and Child Enthroned with Saints

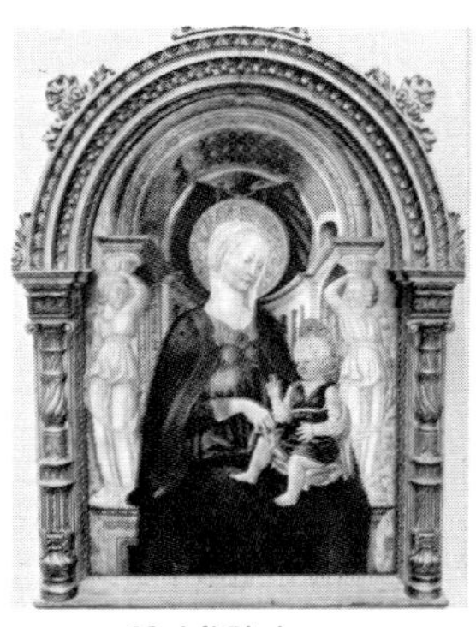
Neri di Bicci
Virgin and Child Enthroned

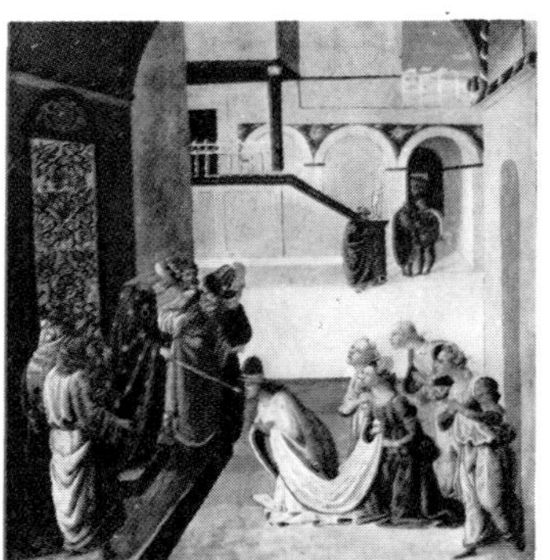
Jacopo del Sellaio
Esther and Ahasuerus

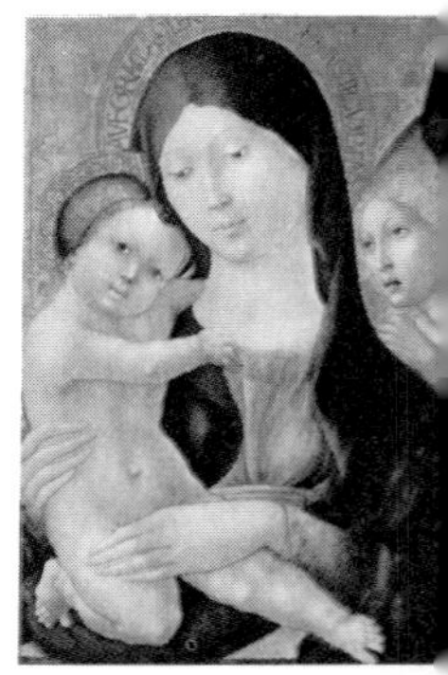
Liberale da Verona
The Virgin and Child

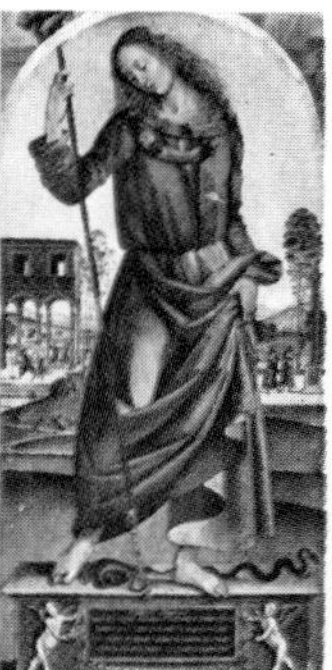
Luca Signorelli
Tiberius Gracchus

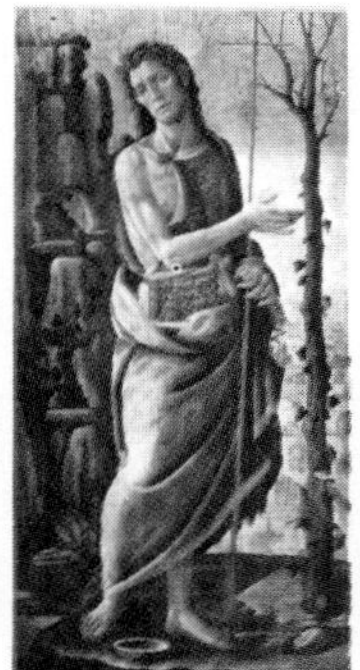
Follower of Botticelli
St John the Baptist

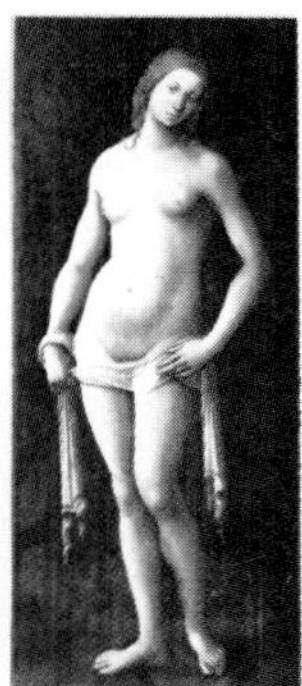
Lorenzo Costa
Venus

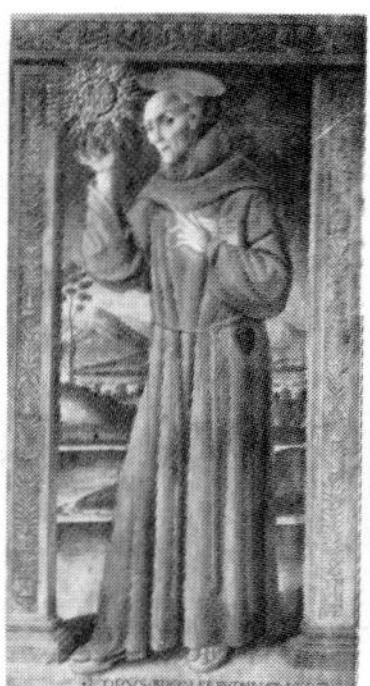
Niccolò da Foligno
St Bernardino of Siena

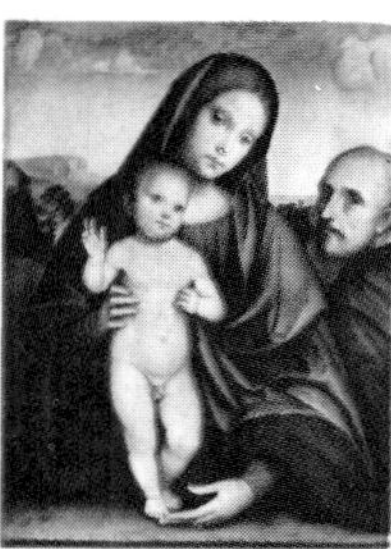
Francesco Francia
The Holy Family

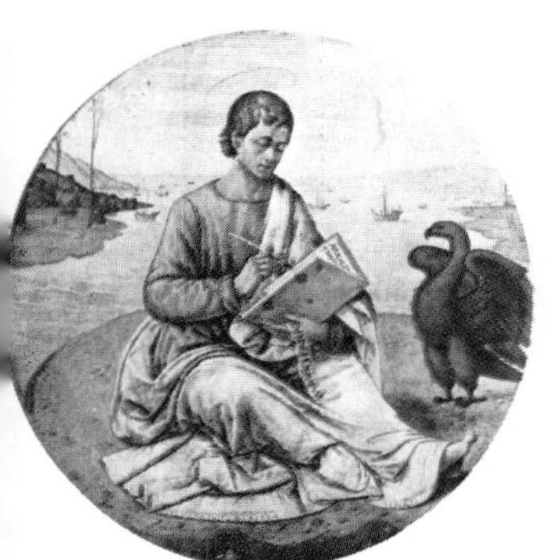
Attributed to
Francesco Granacci
St John on Patmos

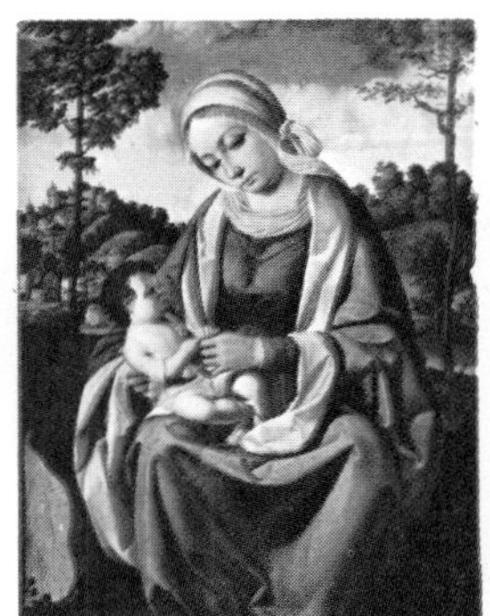
Andrea Previtali
The Virgin and Child

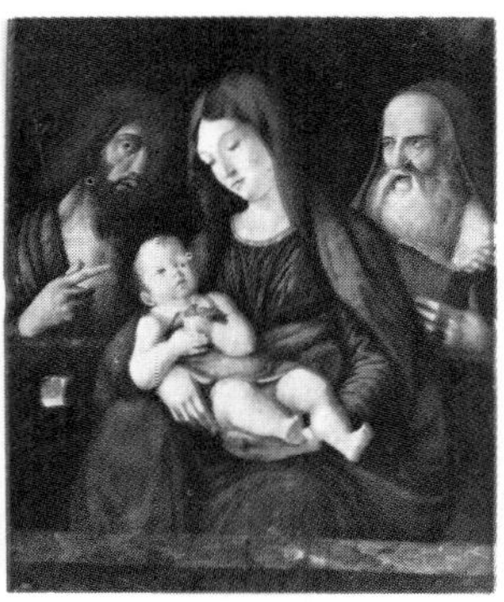
Alvise Vivarini
Virgin and Child with St John the Baptist and St Jerome

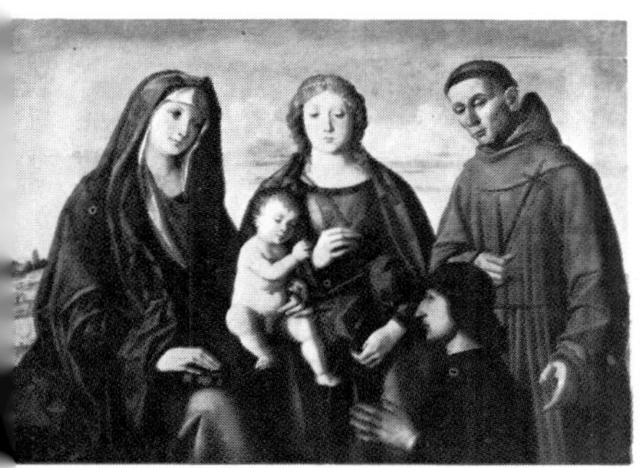
Vincenzo Catena
Virgin and Child with St Francis, a Female Saint and Donor

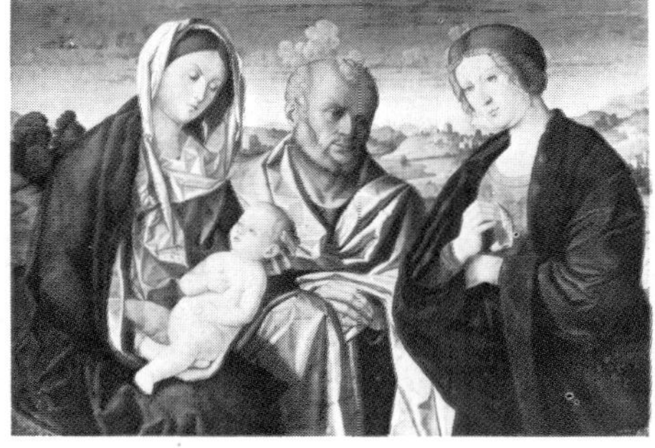
Vincenzo Catena
The Holy Family with a Female Saint

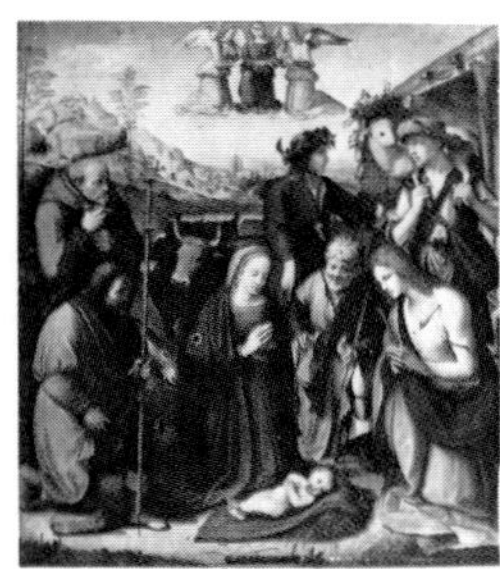

Ridolfo Ghirlandaio
The Adoration of the Shepherds

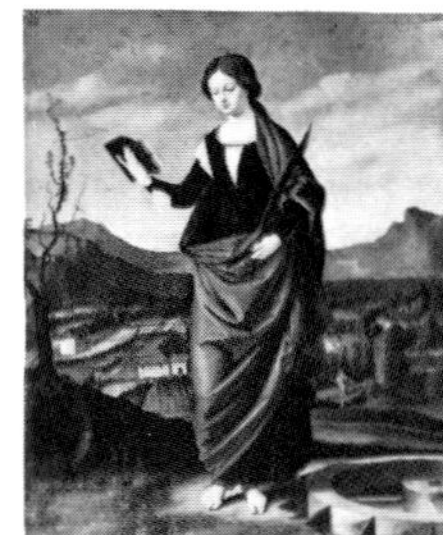

Marco Basaiti
St Catherine

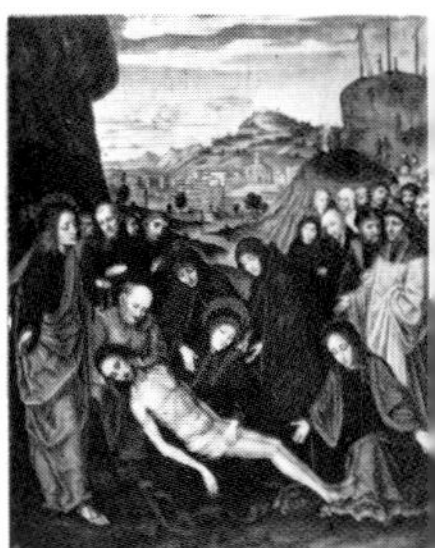

Borgognone
The Lamentation

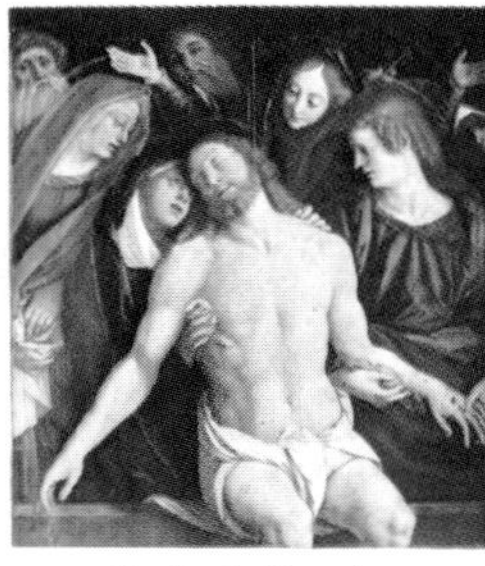

Gaudenzio Ferrari
The Dead Christ with the Virgin and Saints

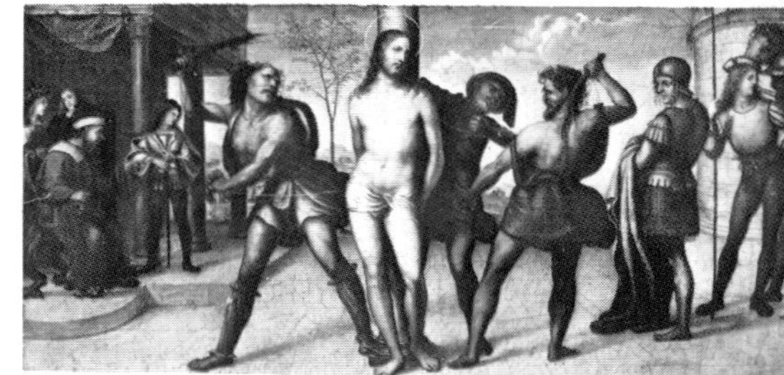

Sodoma *The Scourging of Christ*

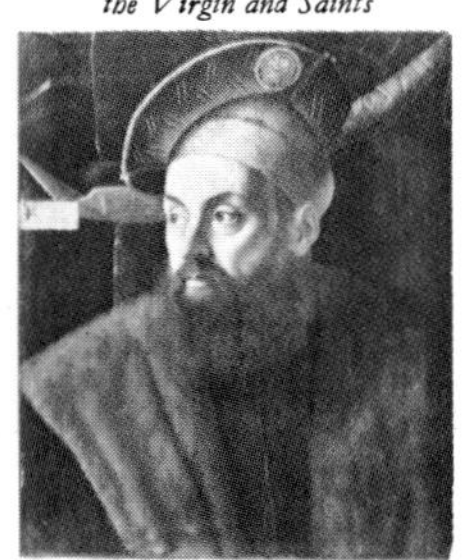

Bartolommeo Veneto
Portrait of a Man

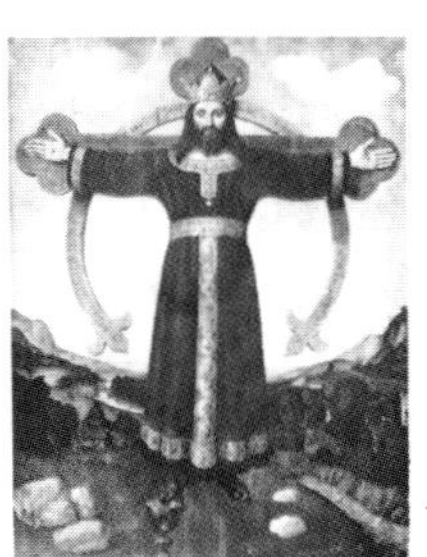

Piero di Cosimo
Christ on the Cross

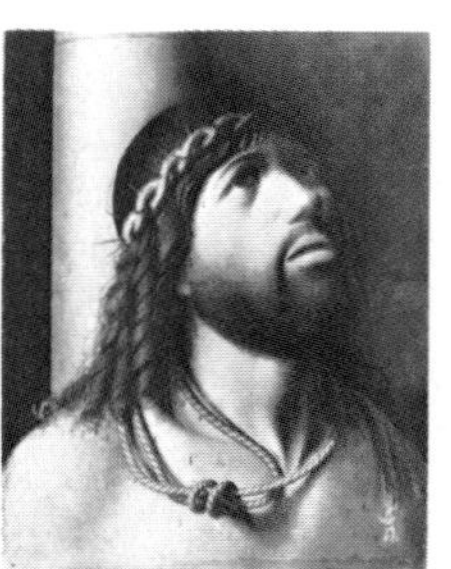

Pietro da Messina
Christ at the Column

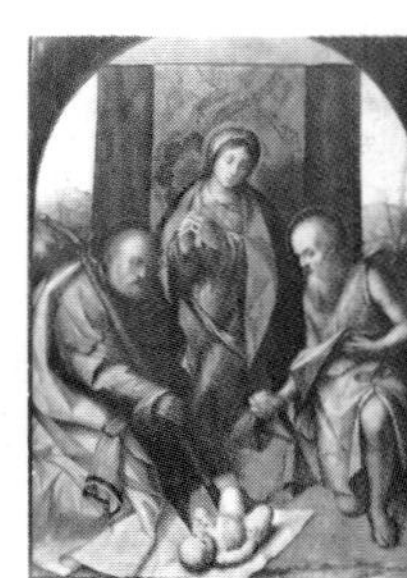

Boccaccio Boccaccino
The Holy Family with St Jerome

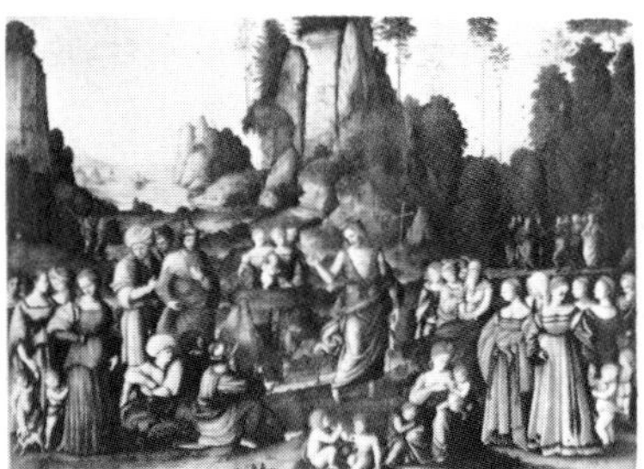

Bacchiacca *St John the Baptist Preaching*

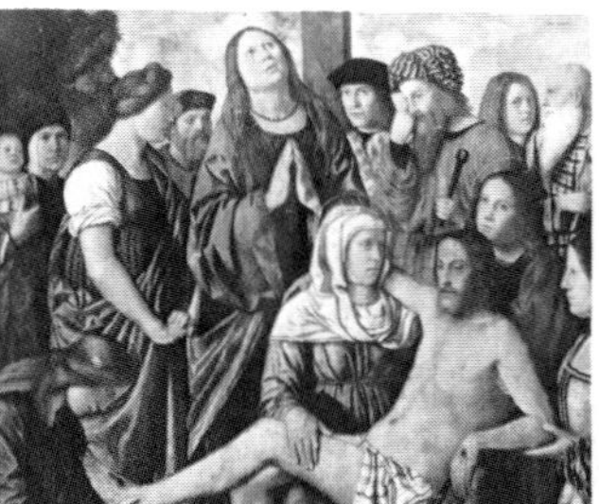

Marco Marziale *The Lamentation*

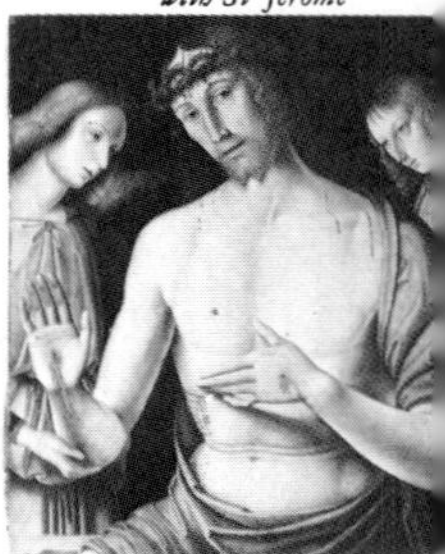

Giovanni Santi, *The Risen Chris*

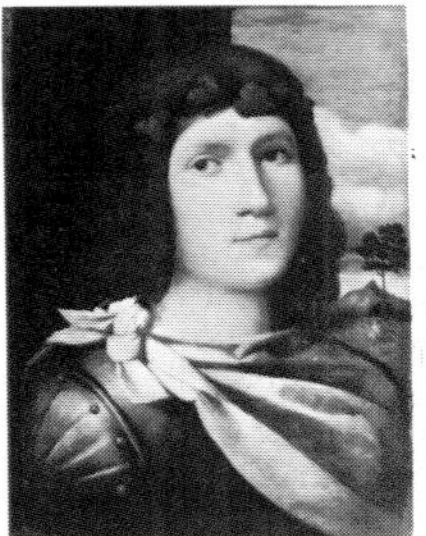

Palma Vecchio
Bust of a Youth

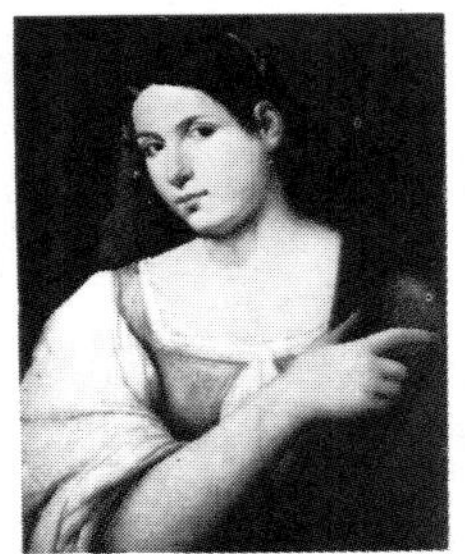

Sebastiano del Piombo
Portrait of a Girl

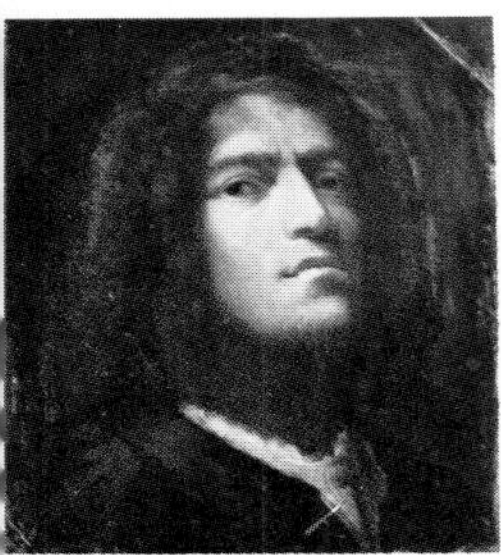

Giorgione *Self-portrait*

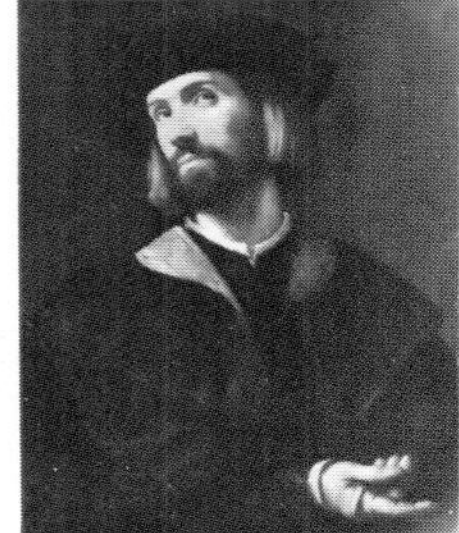

Lorenzo Lotto *Portrait of a Man*

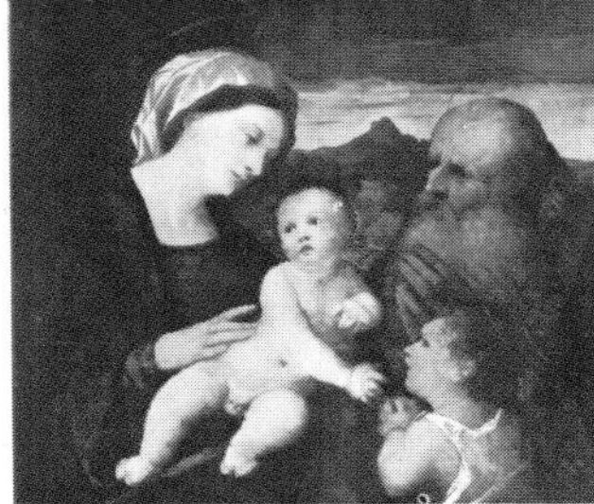

Palma Vecchio *Virgin and Child with the Young St John the Baptist and another Saint*

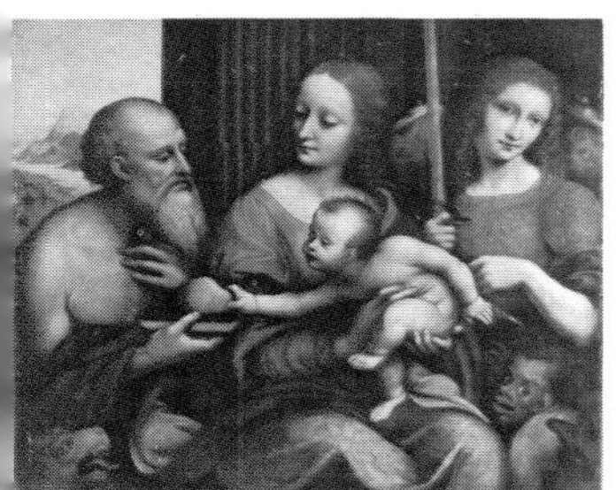

Giampietrino *Virgin and Child with St Jerome and the Archangel St Michael*

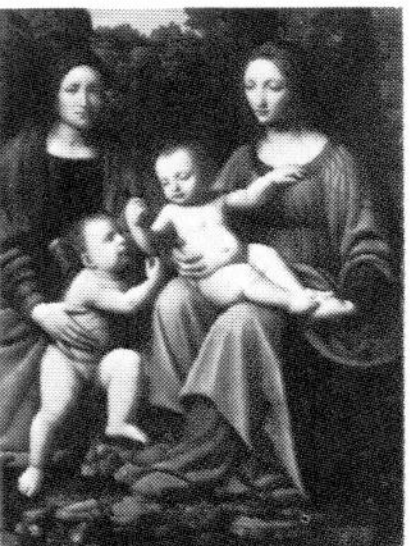

Bernardino Luini *Virgin and Child with St Elizabeth and the Young St John the Baptist*

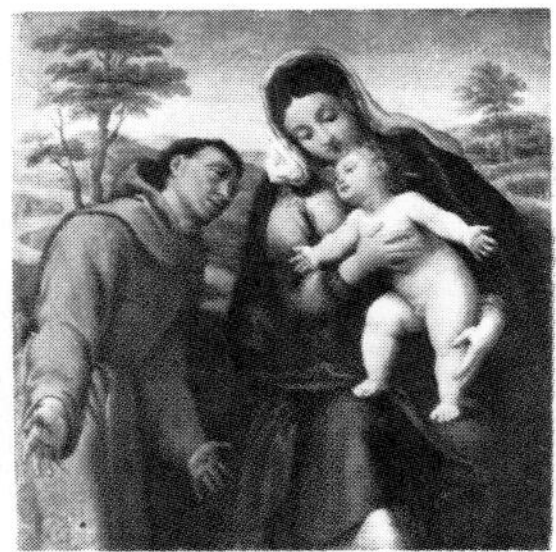

Lorenzo Lotto *Virgin and Child with St Francis*

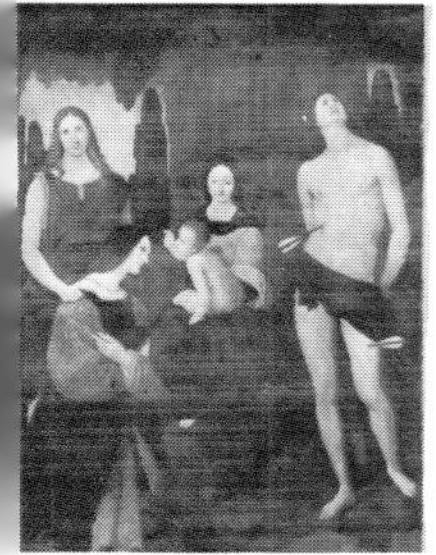

Giovanni Antonio Boltraffio
The Lodi Madonna

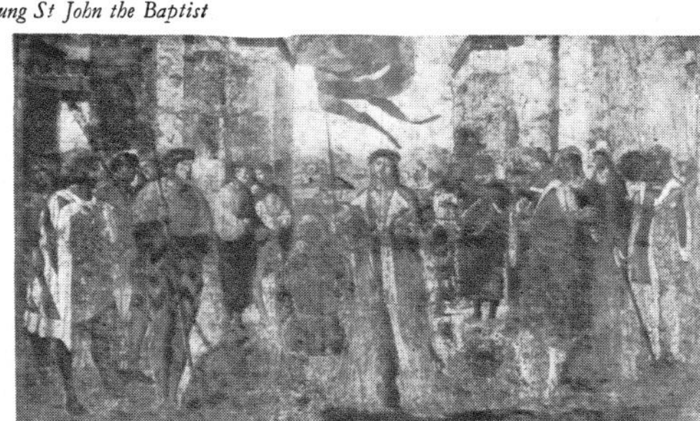

Bartolommeo Montagna
Alfonso II, King of Naples, Gives Niccolò Orsini a Banner

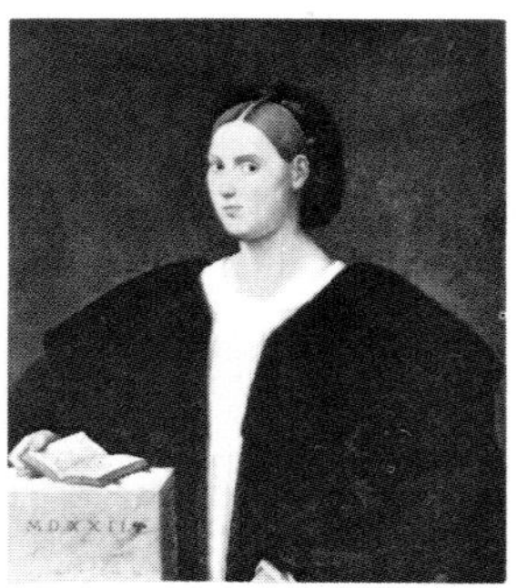

Bernardino Licinio *Portrait of a Woman*

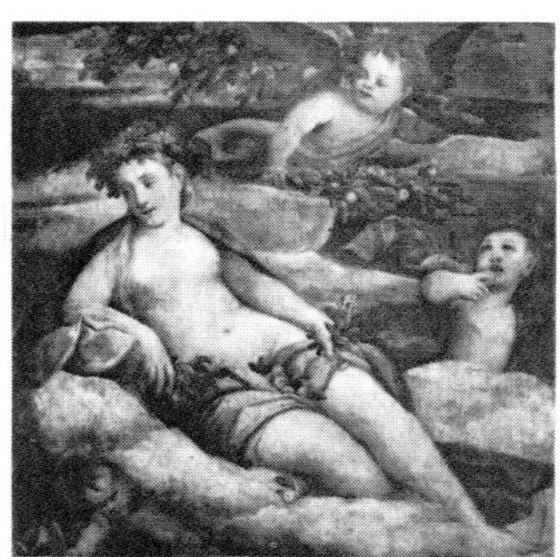

Bonifazio Veronese *Summer*

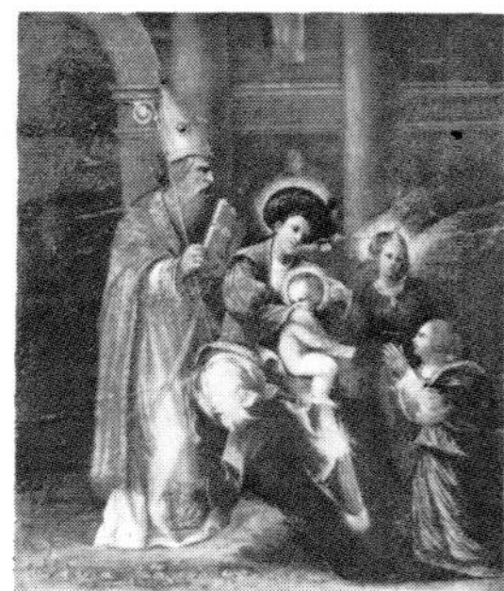

Dosso Dossi
Virgin and Child with Angel, Saint and Donor

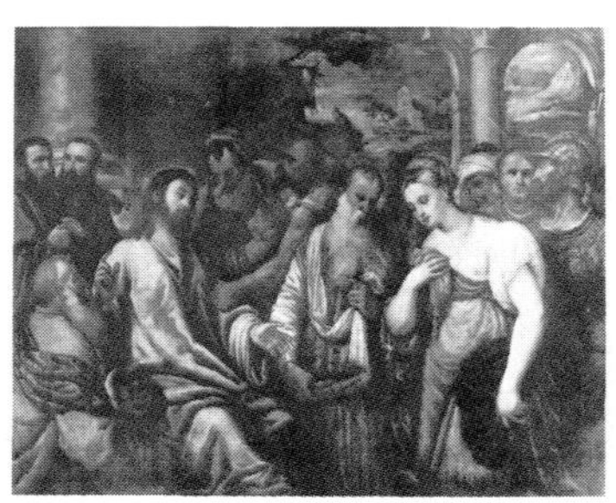

Bonifazio Veronese
Christ and the Woman Taken in Adultery

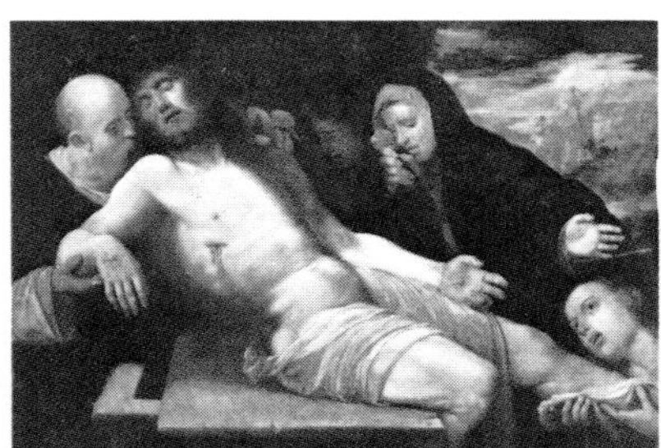

Girolamo Savoldo *The Entombment*

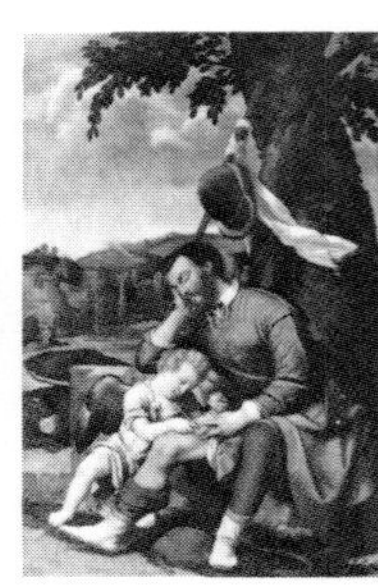

Moretto da Brescia
St Roch with an Angel

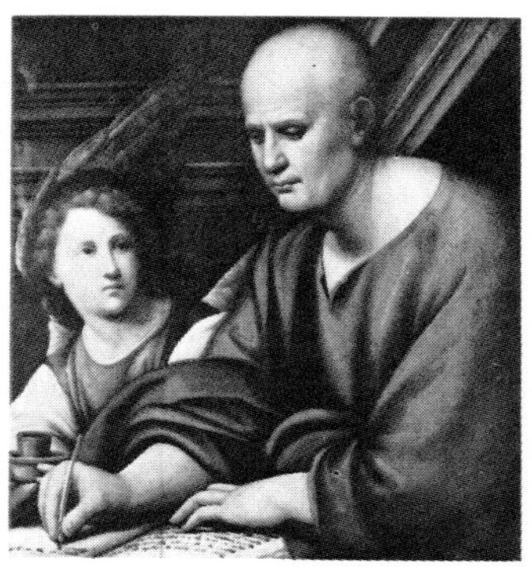

Giovanni Antonio da Pordenone *St Matthew*

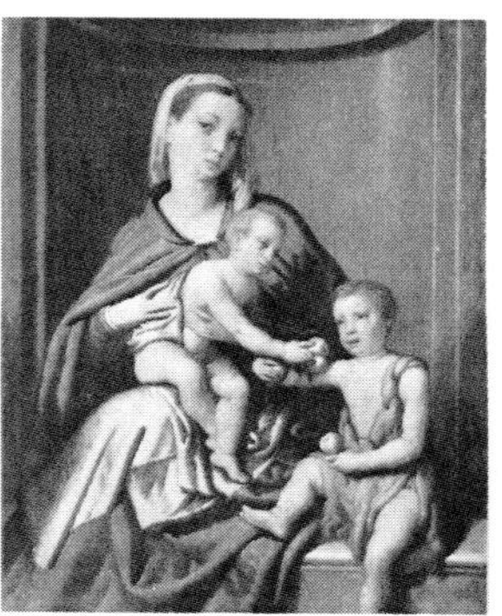

Giovanni Battista Moroni
Virgin and Child with the Young St John the Baptist

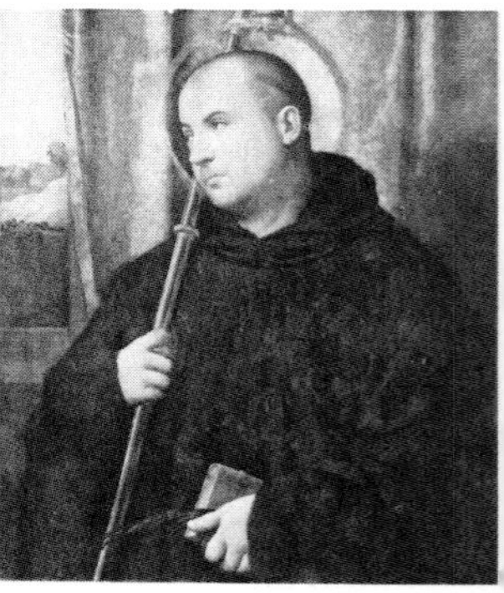

Moretto da Brescia *A Martyr Saint*

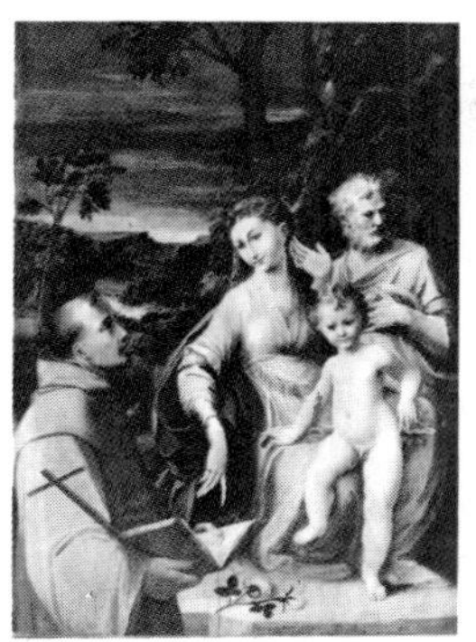

Girolamo Mazzola Bedoli
The Holy Family with St Francis

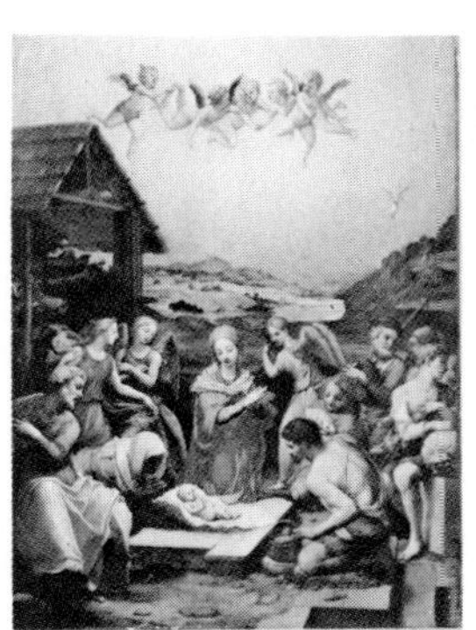

Angelo Bronzino
The Adoration of the Shepherds

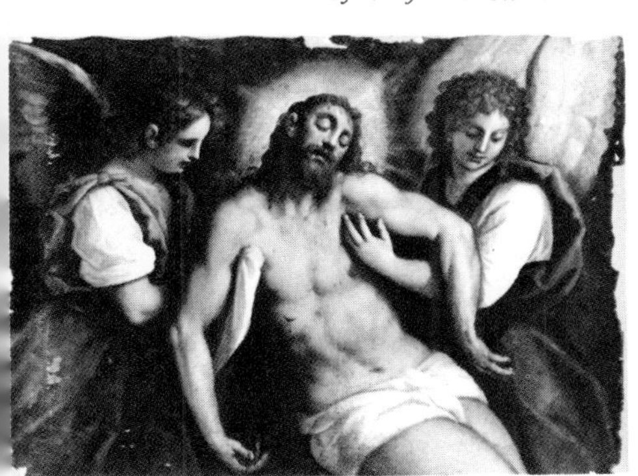

Palma Giovane *The Dead Christ*

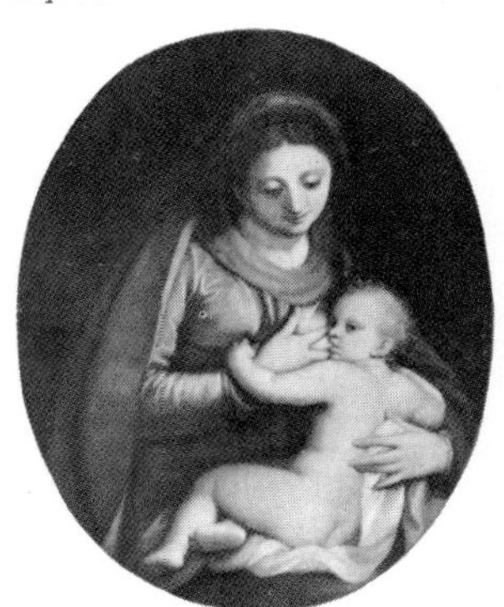

Sofonisba Anguisciola
The Virgin and Child

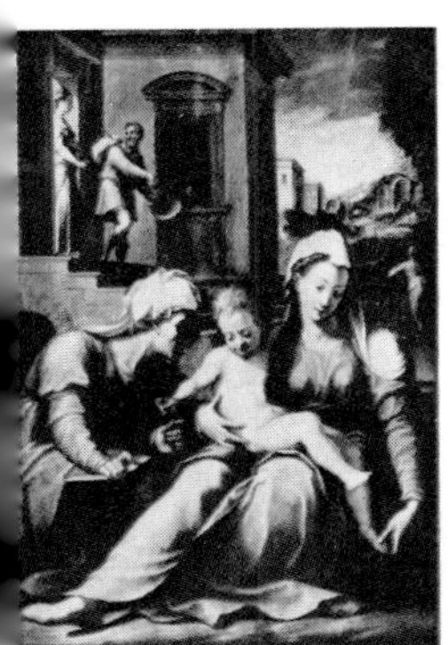

Girolamo Macchietti
Virgin and Child with St Anne

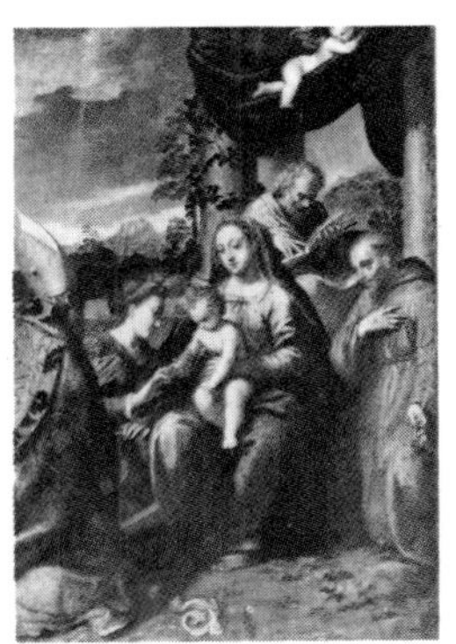

Scarsellino
The Mystic Marriage of St Catherine

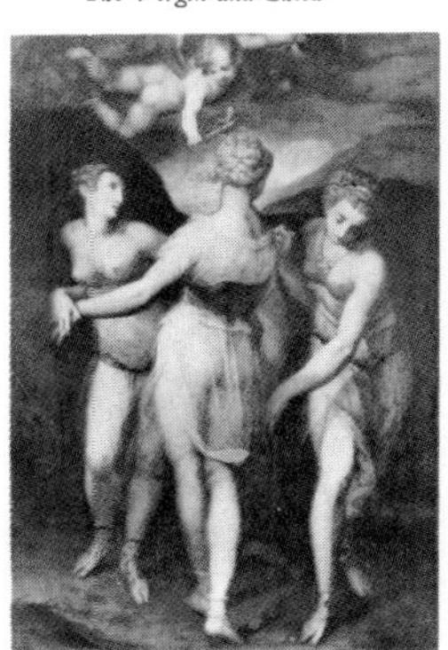

Battista Naldini
The Three Graces

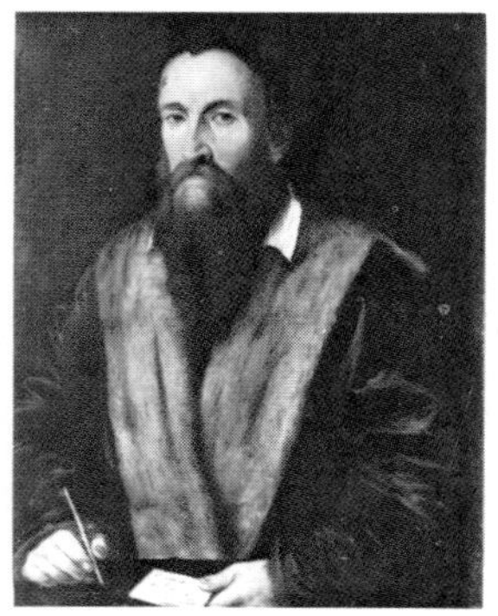
Romanino *Self-portrait*

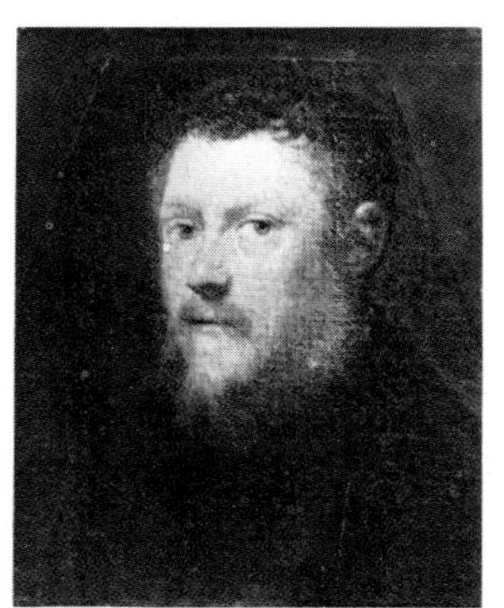
Tintoretto *Portrait of a Man*

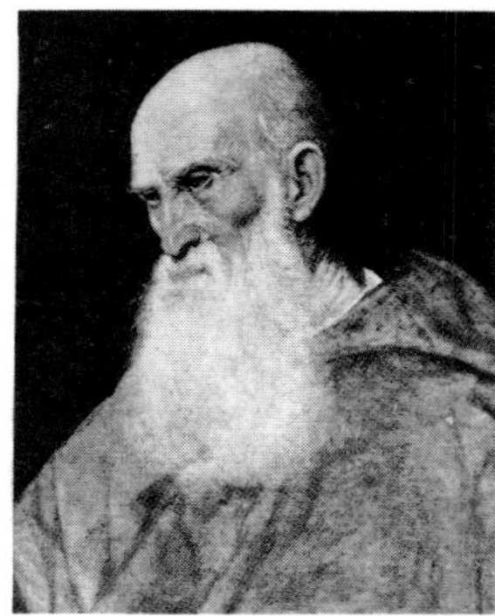
Titian *Cardinal Pietro Bembo*

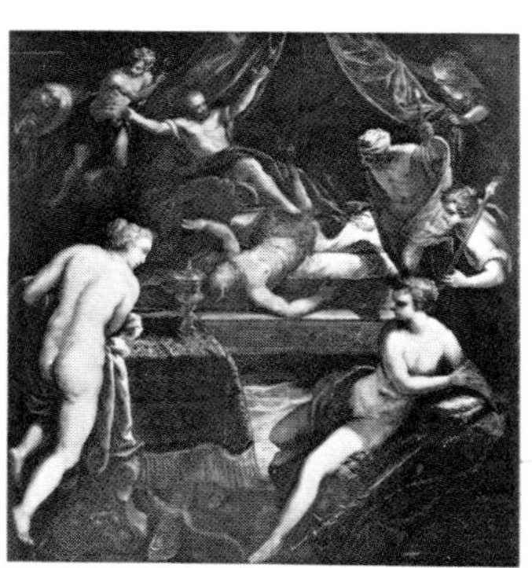
Tintoretto
Hercules Expelling the Faun from Omphale's Bed

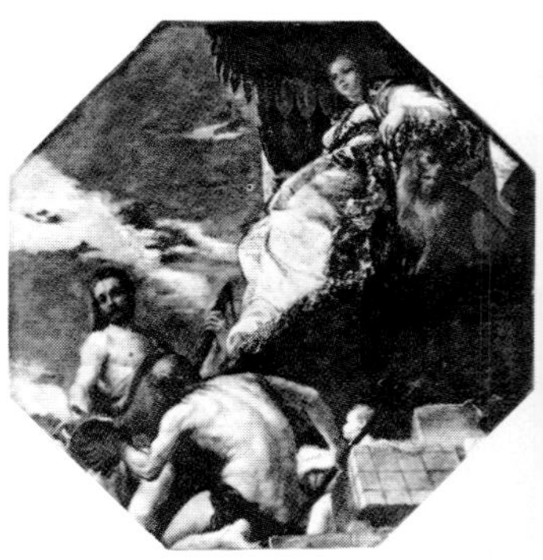
Veronese *Allegory of Venice*

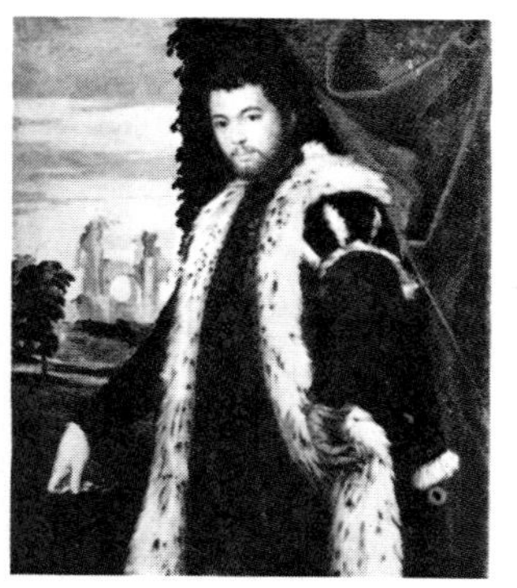
Veronese *Portrait of a Man*

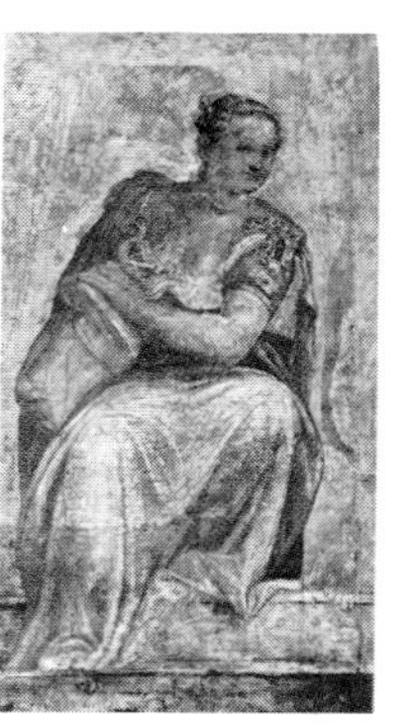
Giambattista Zelotti
Allegorical Figure: Courage

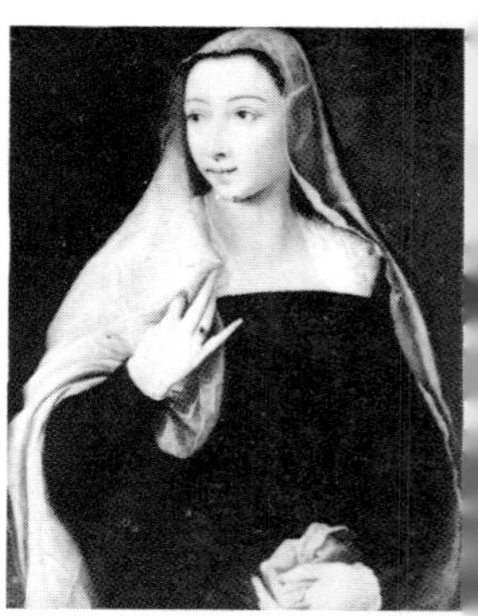
Italian Master (sixteenth century)
Vittoria Farnese

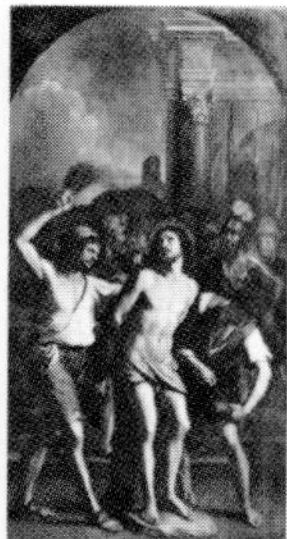
Guercino
The Scourging of Christ

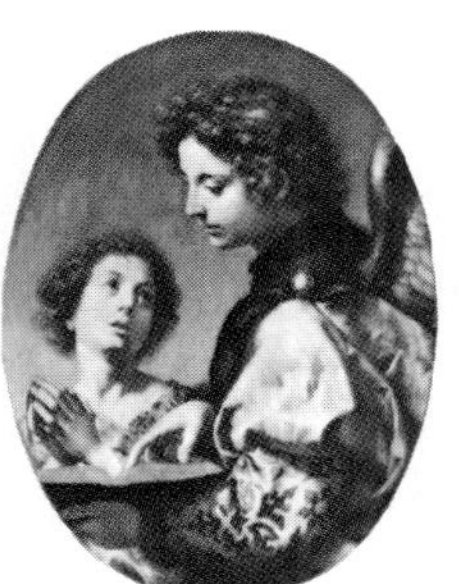
Carlo Dolci
The Guardian Ange

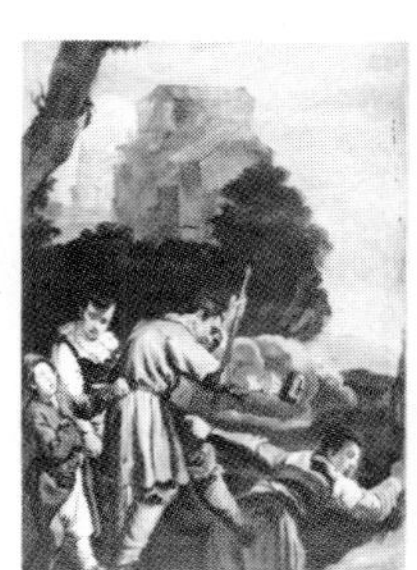
Domenico Fetti
The Blind Leading the Blind

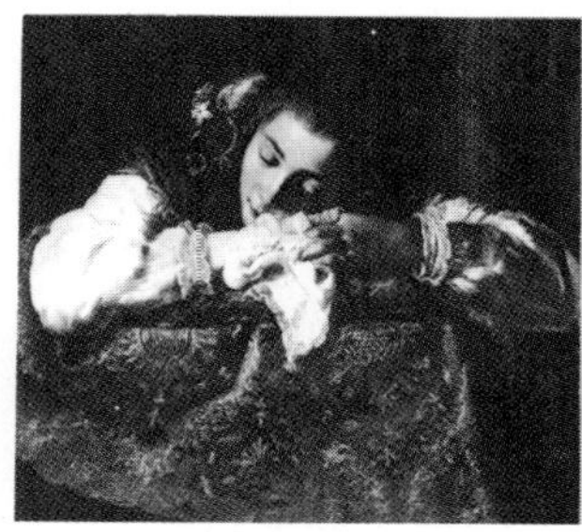
Domenico Fetti
Sleeping Girl

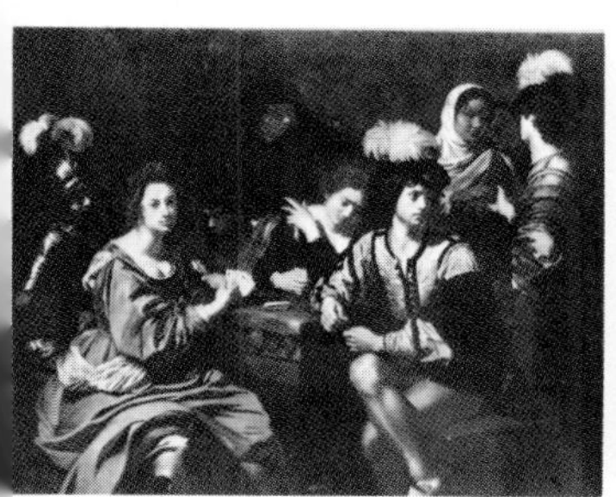
Attributed to
Bartolomeo Manfredi
The Card Players

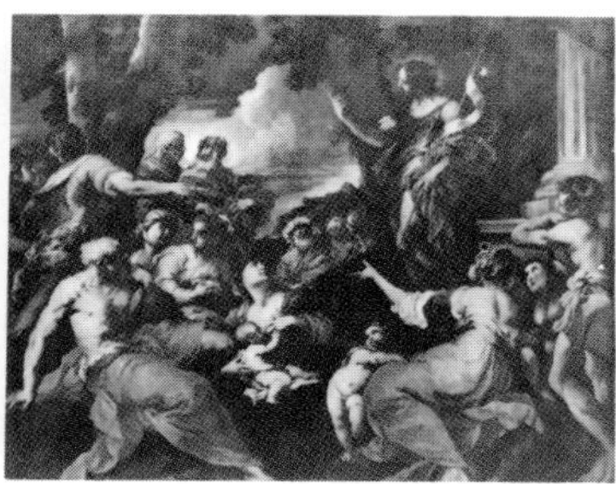
Valerio Castello
St John the Baptist Preaching

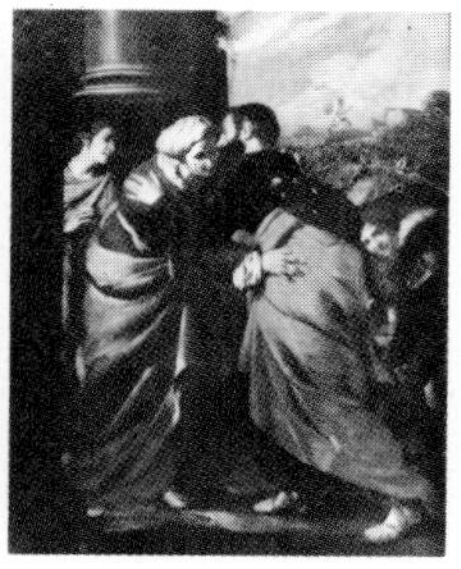
Massimo Stanzioni
Joachim and Anne Meeting at the Golden Gate

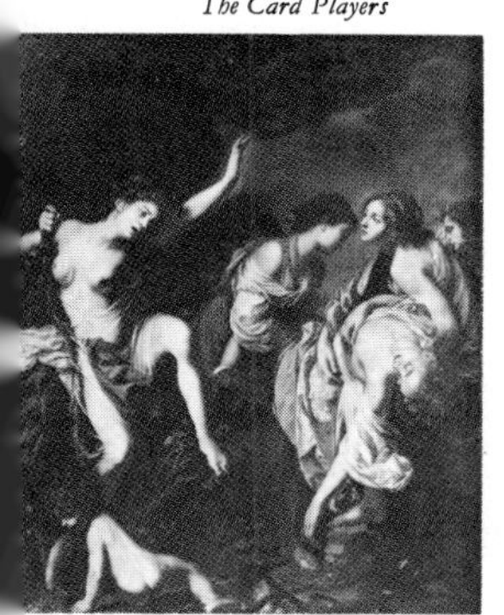
Francesco Furini *Venus Mourning Adonis*

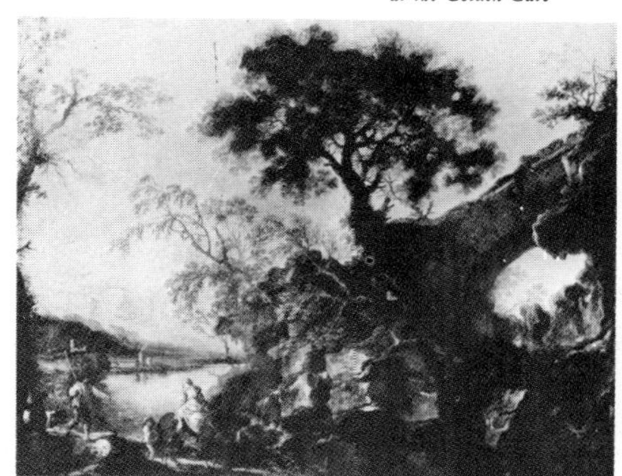
Salvator Rosa *Rocky Landscape with Waterfall*

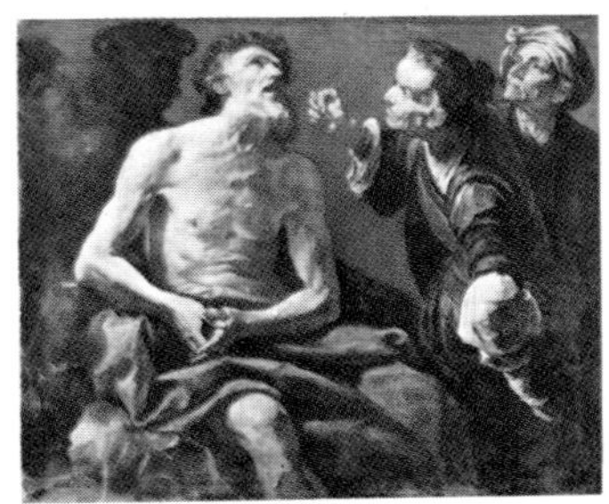
Gioacchino Assereto
The Mocking of Job

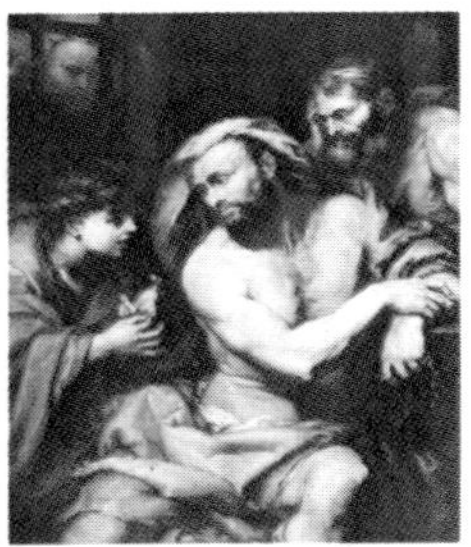
Giovanni Battista Langetti
Joseph in Prison Interpreting Dreams

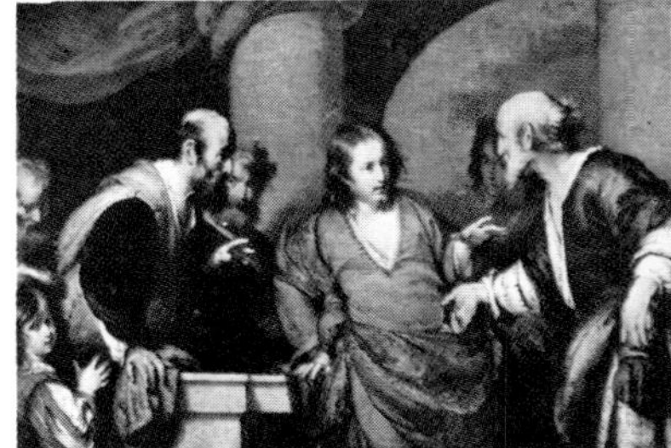
Bernardo Strozzi
The Tribute Money

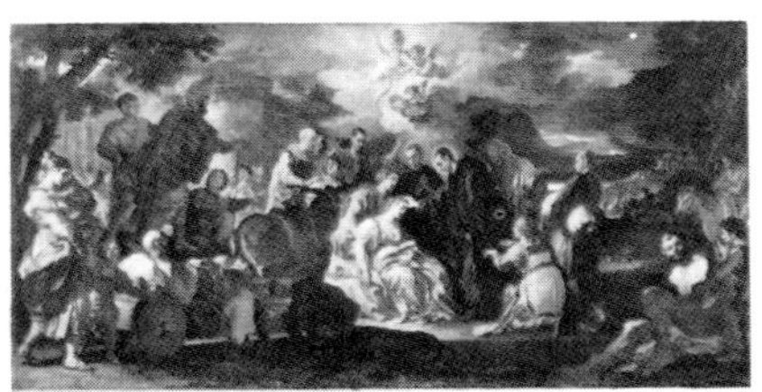
Francesco Solimena *St Maurus Healing the Sick*

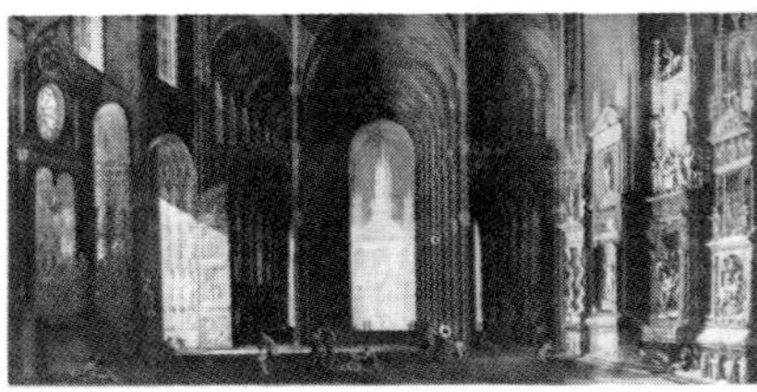
François Nomé *Church Interior*

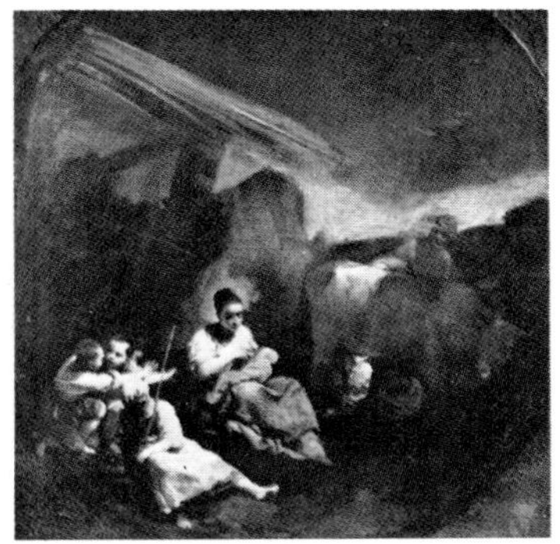
Giuseppe Maria Crespi *Peasant Family Resting*

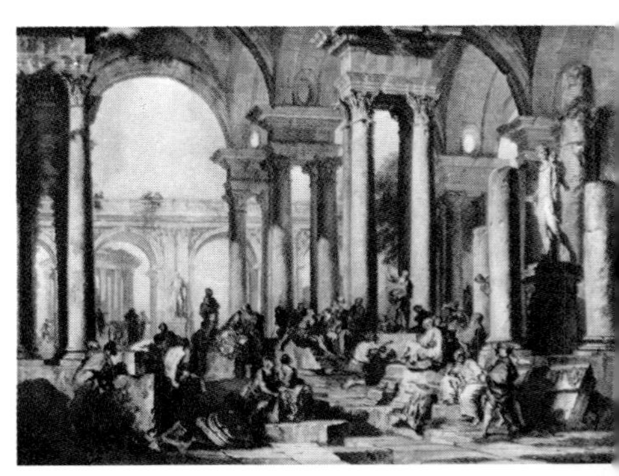
Giovanni Paolo Pannini *St Paul Preaching at Athens*

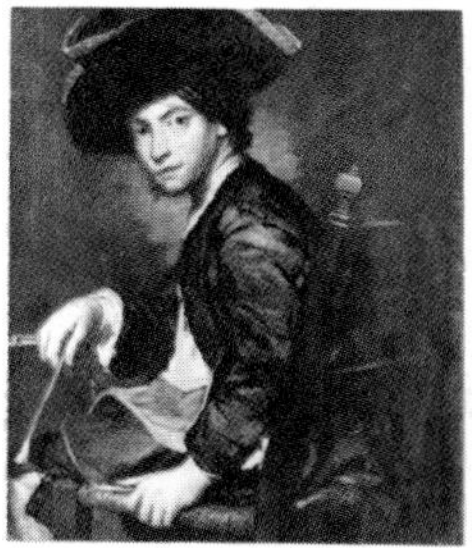

Vittore Ghislandi
Portrait of a Young Painter

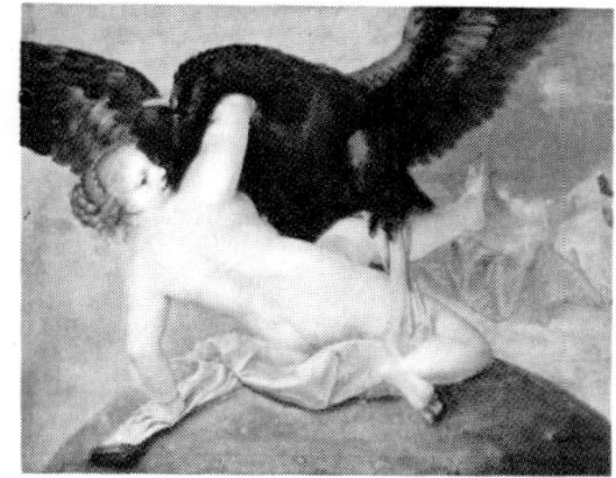

Marco Liberi *Jupiter and Mnemosyne*

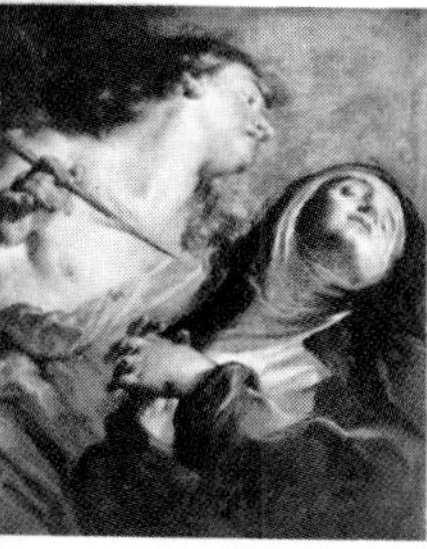

Giuseppe Bazzani
The Vision of St Theresa

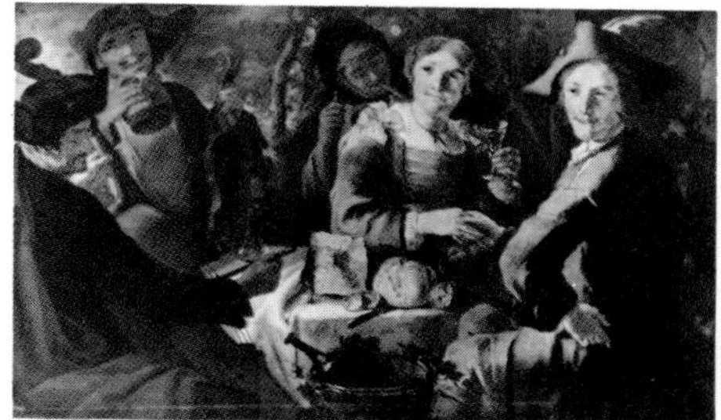

Giacomo Francesco Cipper
Young Couple with Musicians

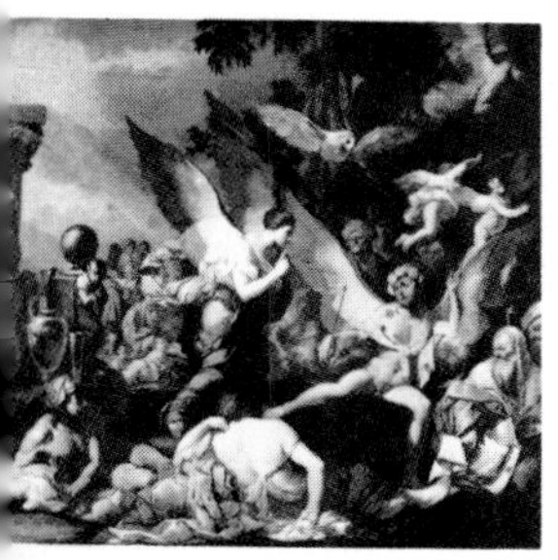

Giulio Carpioni
Iris in the Realm of the God of Dreams

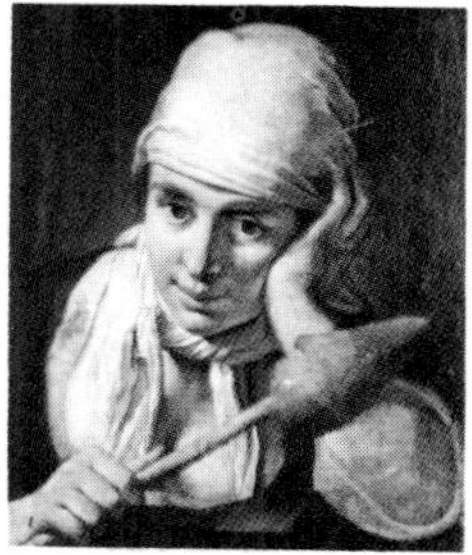

Pietro Rotari *Girl with Distaff*

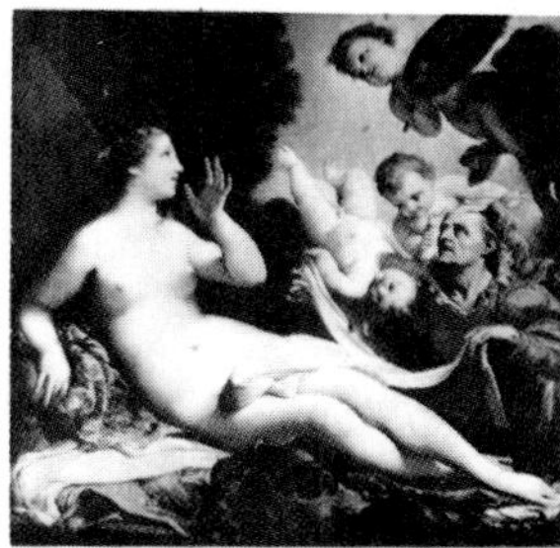

Antonio Bellucci *Danaë*

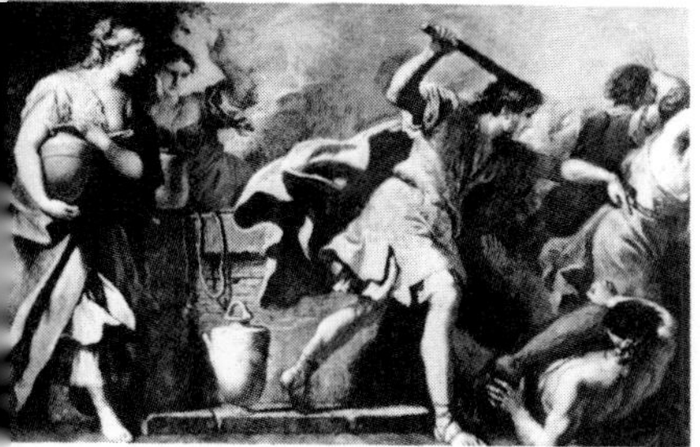

Sebastiano Ricci
Moses Defending the Daughters of Jethro

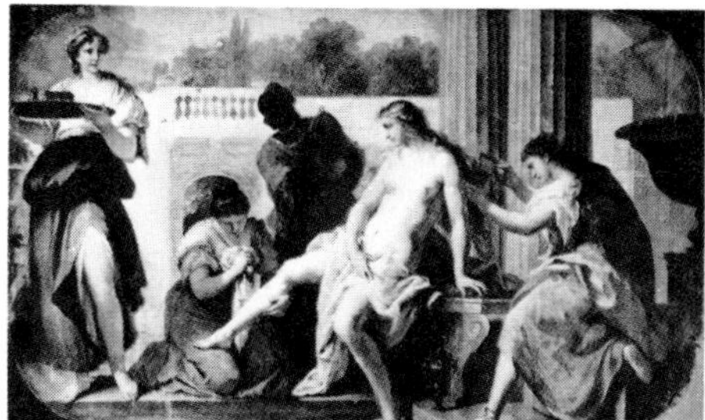

Sebastiano Ricci *Bathsheba Bathing*

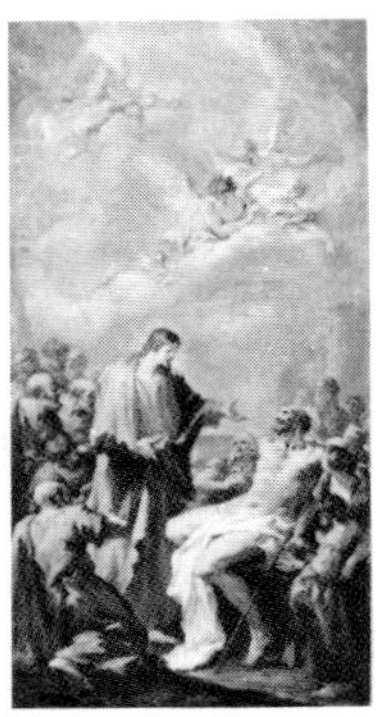

Giovanni Antonio
Pellegrini
Christ Healing the Paralytic

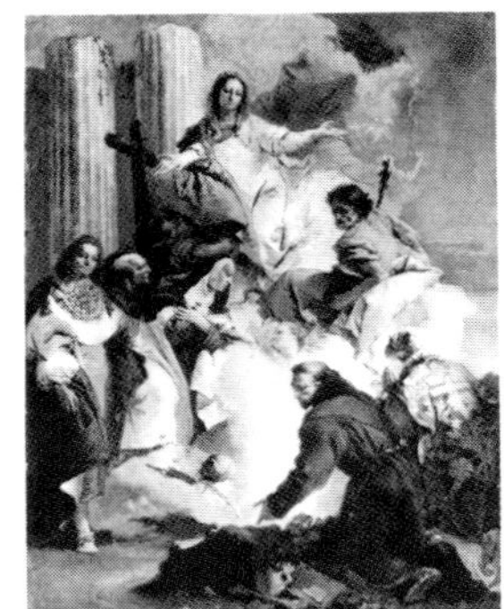

Giovanni Battista Tiepolo
The Virgin with Six Saints

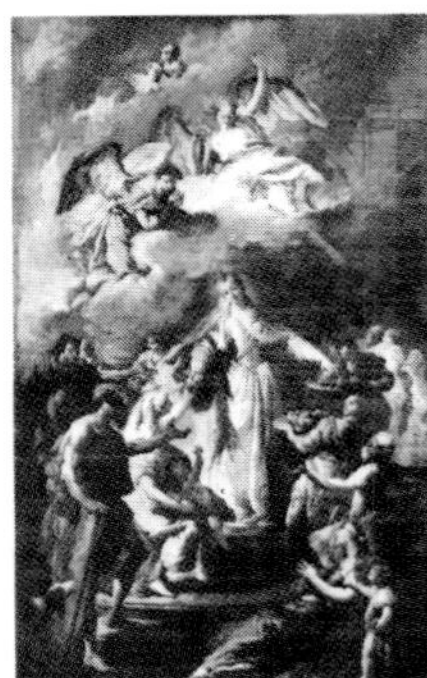

Giovanni Battista Pittoni
St Elizabeth of Hungary Distributing Alms

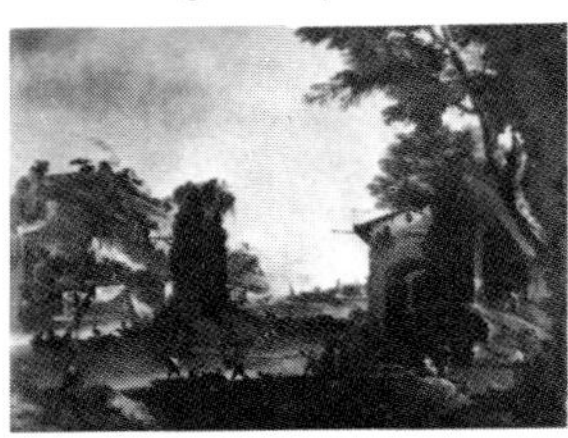

Marco Ricci
Riverside Scene

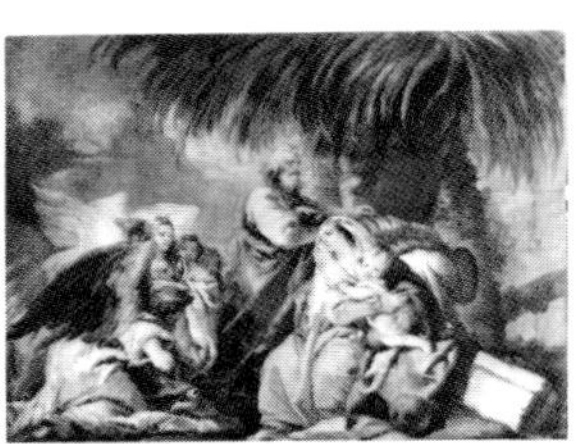

Giovanni Domenico Tiepolo
The Rest on the Flight into Egypt

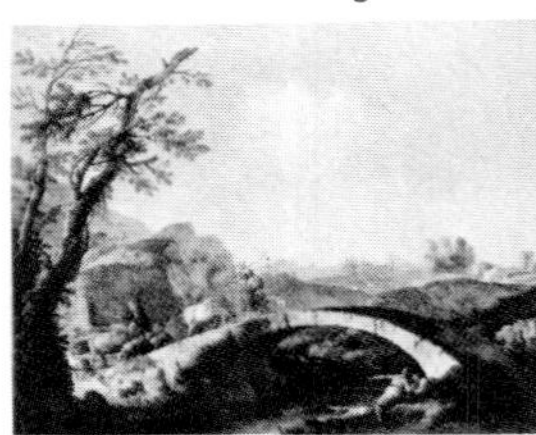

Francesco Zuccarelli
Landscape with Bridge

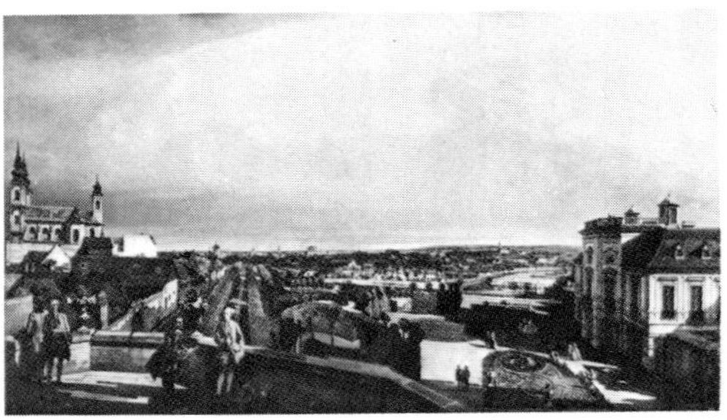

Bernardo Bellotto
The Kaunitz Palace and Garden in Vienna

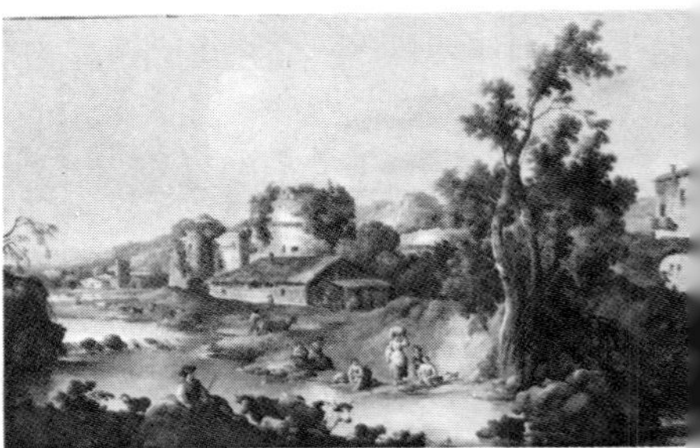

Giuseppe Zais *Landscape with River*

SPANISH PAINTING

Fifteenth to nineteenth centuries

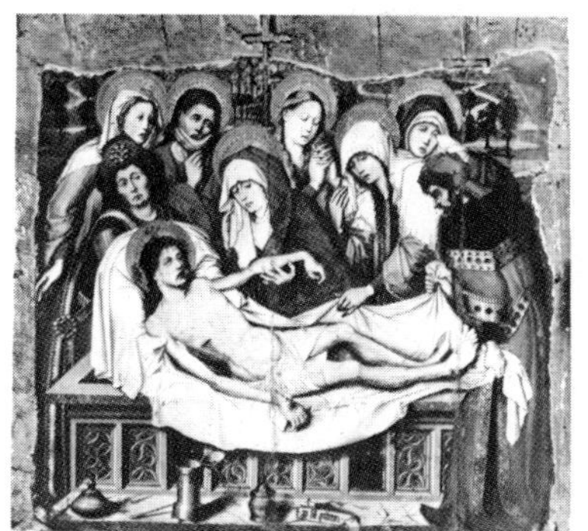

Pedro Sánchez *The Entombment*

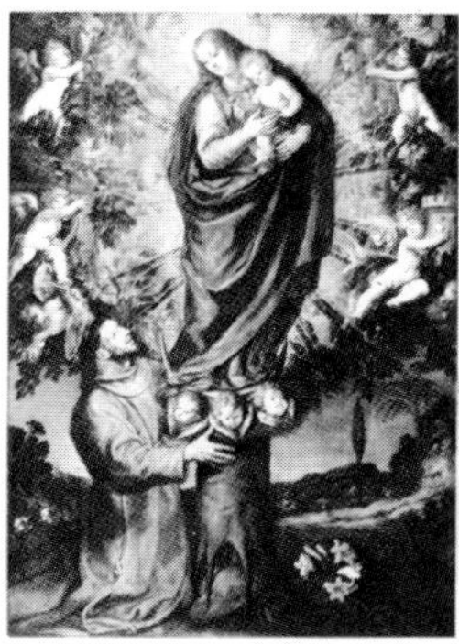

Vicente Carducho
The Vision of St Francis

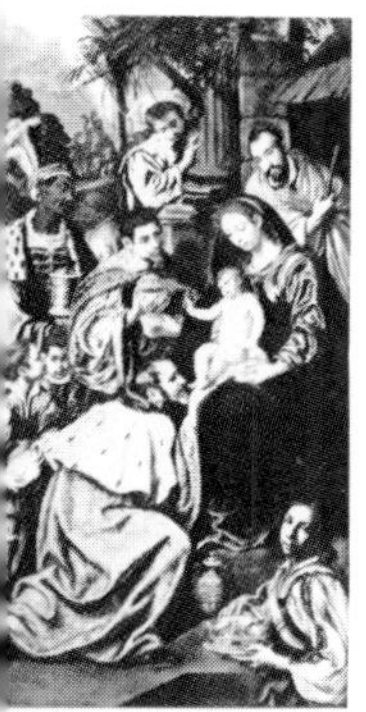

Luis Tristán
The Adoration of the Magi

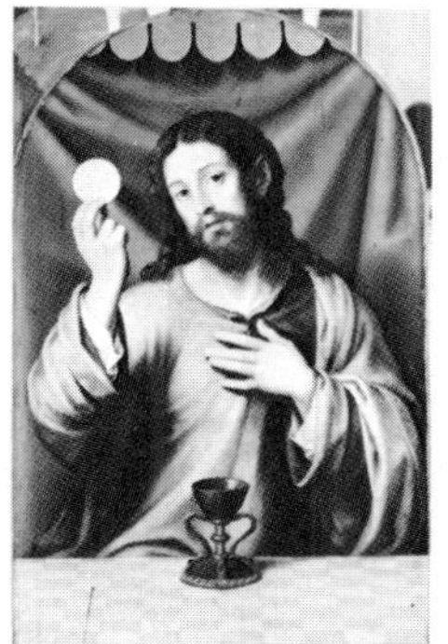

Juan de Juanes
Christ with the Eucharist

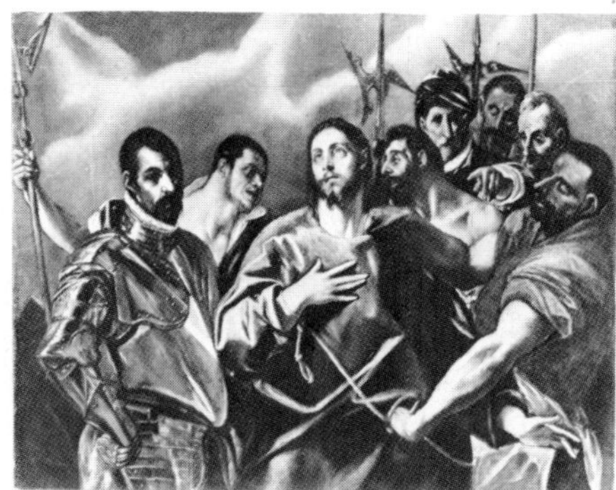

El Greco
The Disrobing of Christ

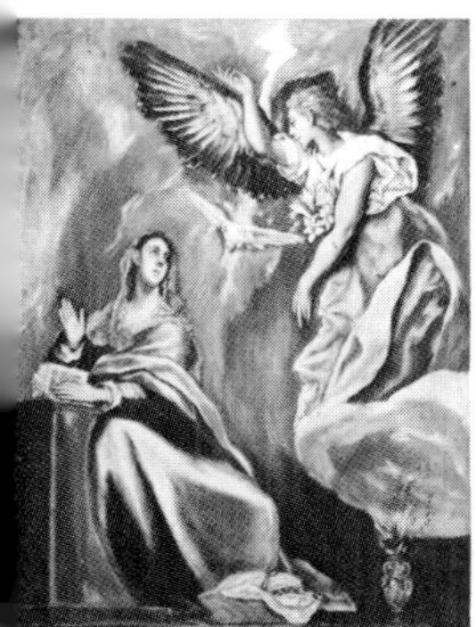

El Greco *The Annunciation*

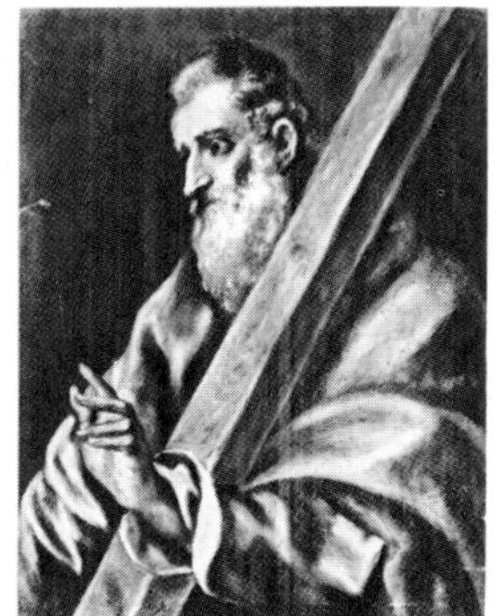

El Greco *St Andrew*

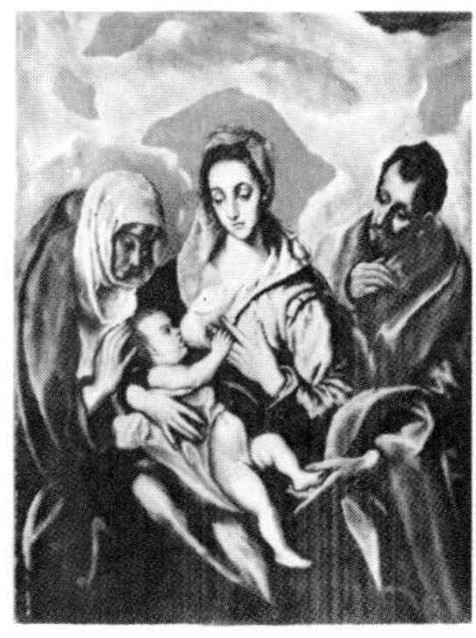

El Greco
The Holy Family with St Elizabeth

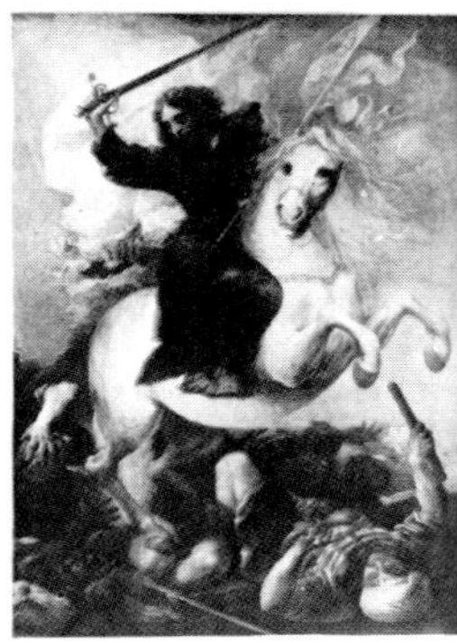
Juan Carreño de Miranda
St James the Greater

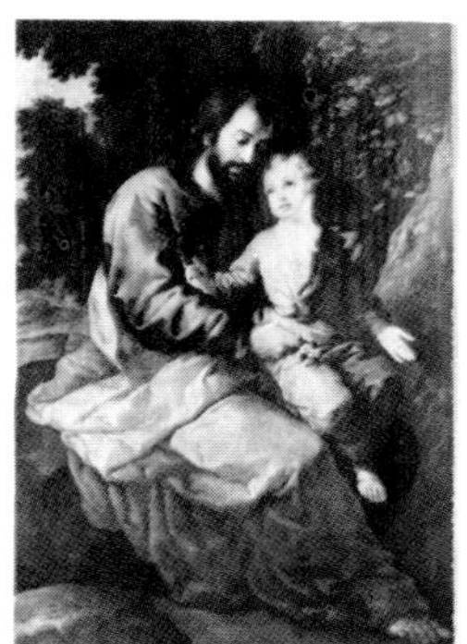
Francisco de Herrera the Elder
St Joseph with the Infant Christ

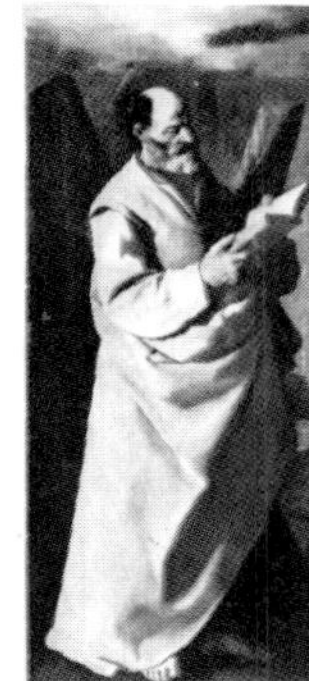
Francisco de Zurbarán
St Andrew

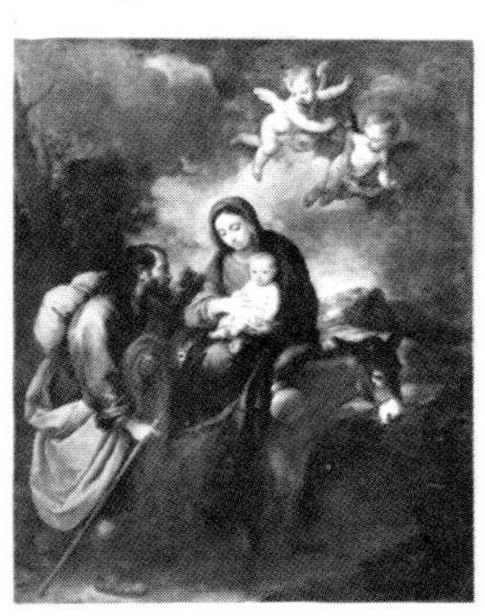
Bartolomé Esteban Murillo
The Flight into Egypt

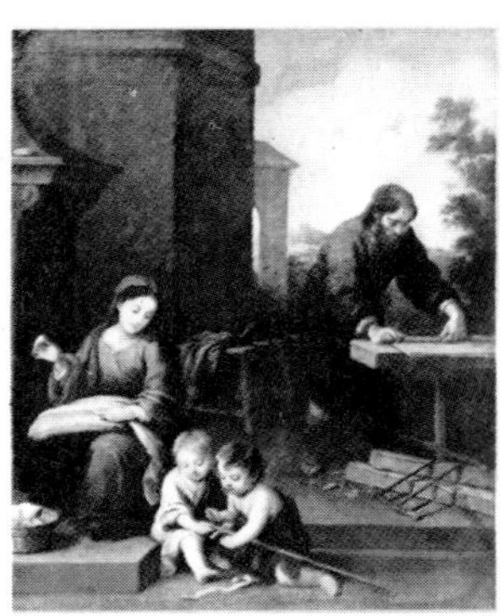
Bartolomé Esteban Murillo
The Holy Family with the Young St John the Baptist

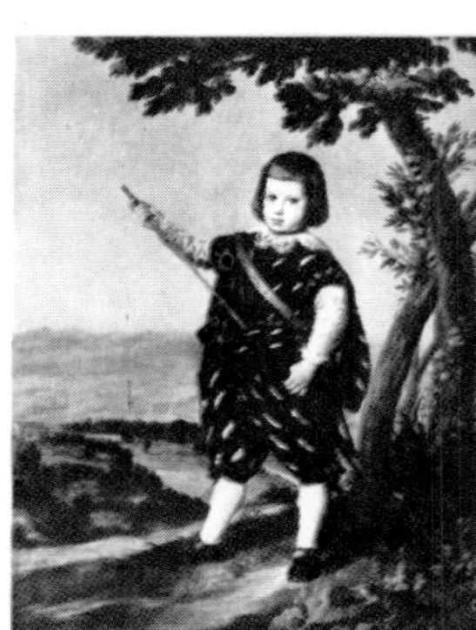
Juan Bautista del Mazo
The Infante Baltasar Carlos

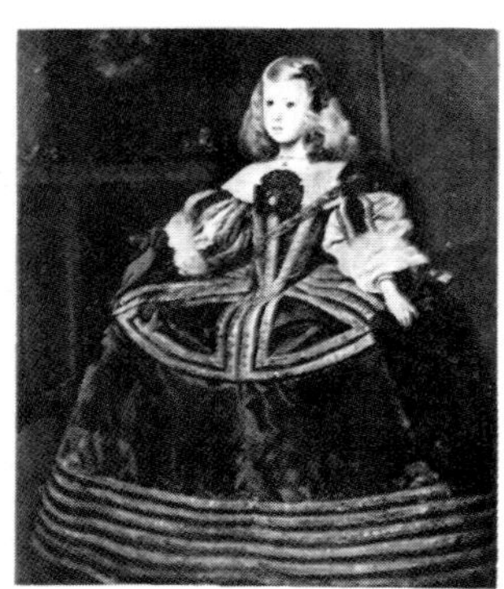
Juan Carreño de Miranda
The Infanta Margarita Teresa

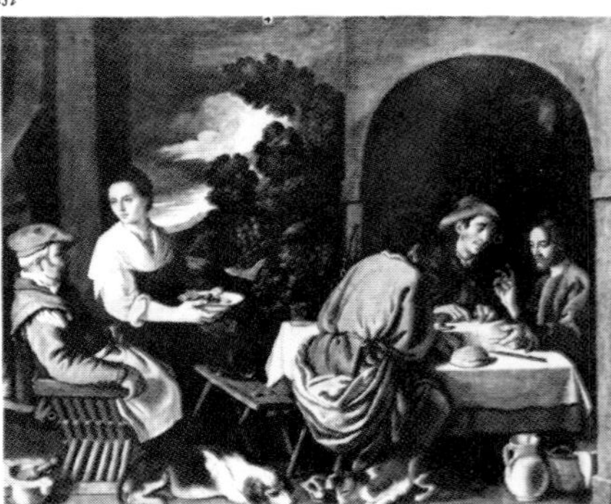
Pedro Orrente *The Supper at Emmaus*

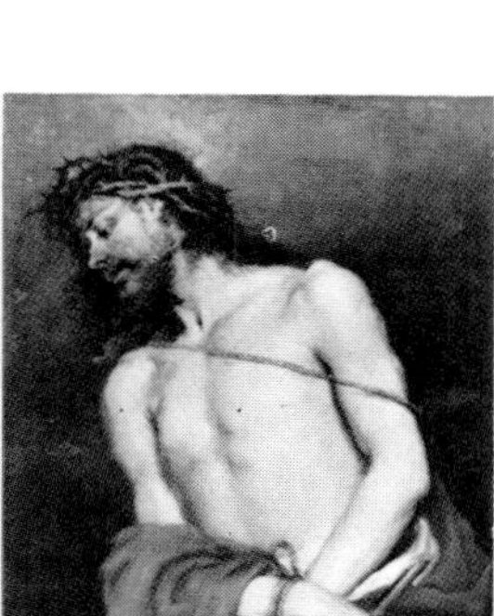

Mateo Cerezo the Younger *Ecce Homo*

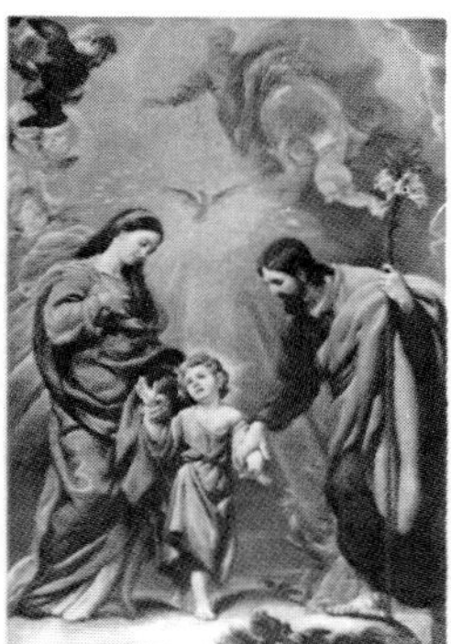

Claudio Coello *The Holy Family*

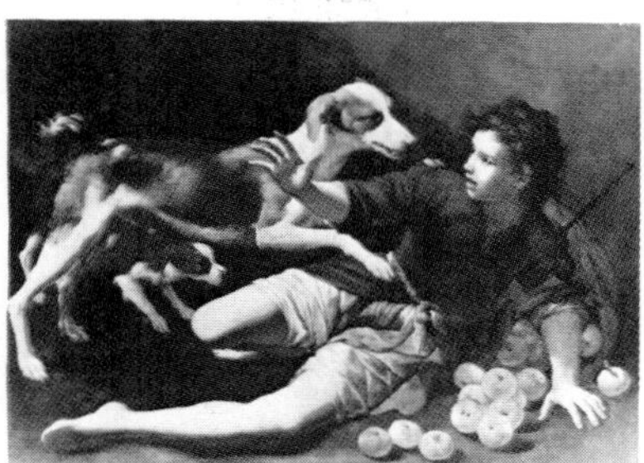

Pedro Núñez de Villavicencio *Spilt Apples*

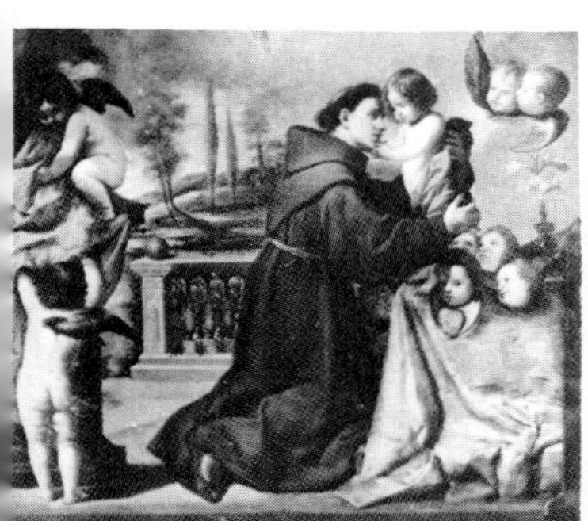

Antonio Pereda
St Anthony of Padua Worshipping the Infant Christ

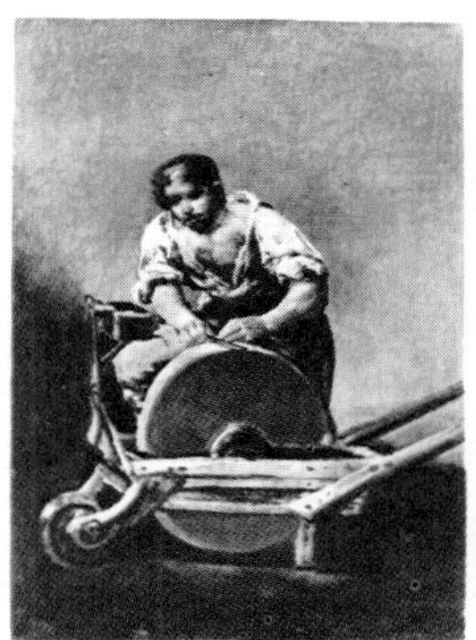

Francisco de Goya
The Knife-Grinder

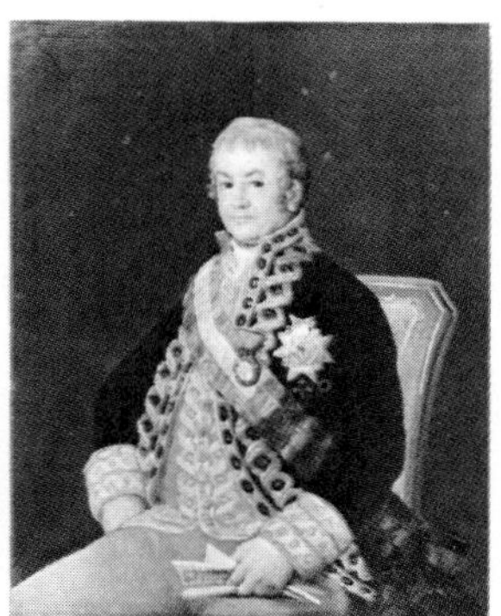

Francisco de Goya
The Marqués Caballero

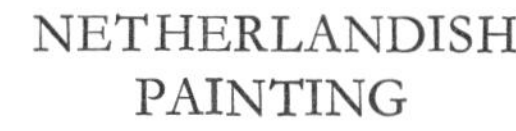

NETHERLANDISH PAINTING

Fifteenth to eighteenth centuries

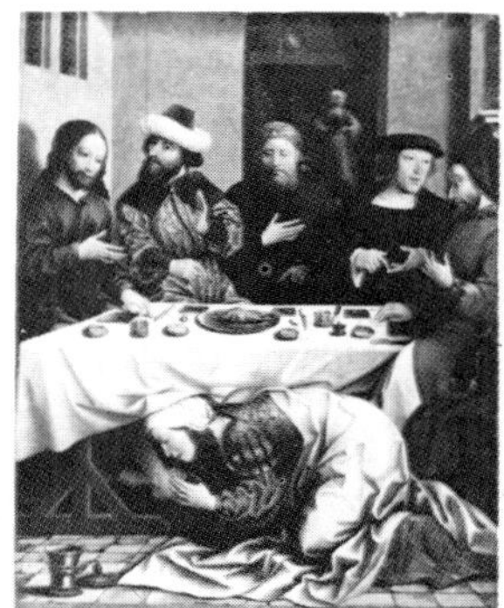

Master of the Legend of Mary Magdalene
Christ in the House of Simon the Pharisee

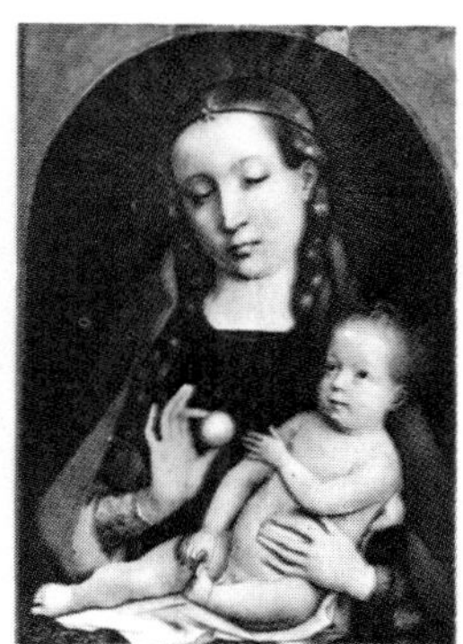

Michel Sittow
The Virgin and Child

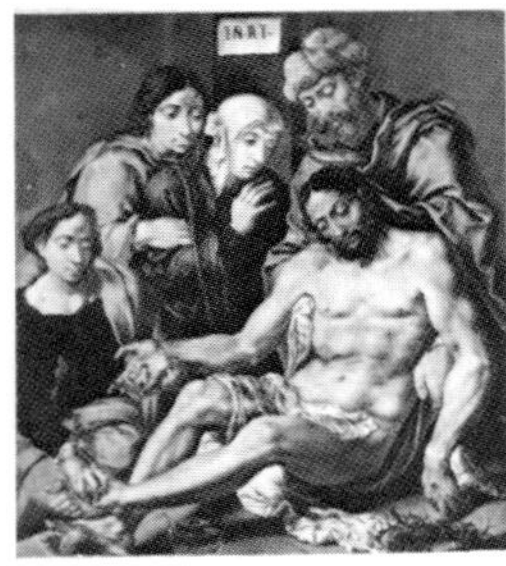

Maerten van Heemskerck
The Lamentation

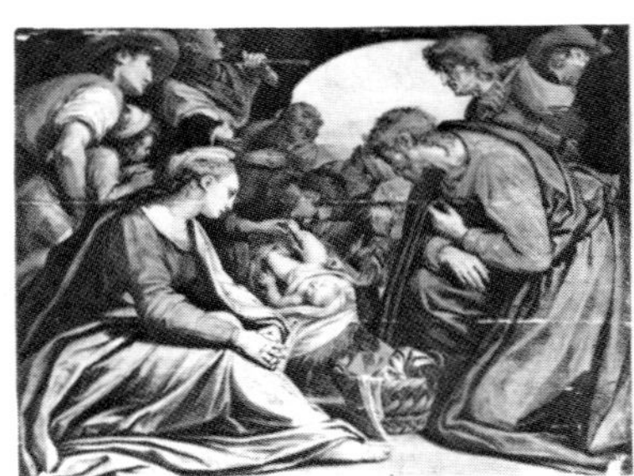

Anthonie van Blocklandt
The Adoration of the Shepherds

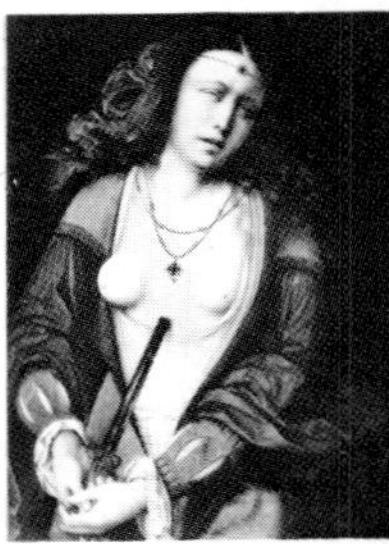

Master of the Holy Blood
Lucretia

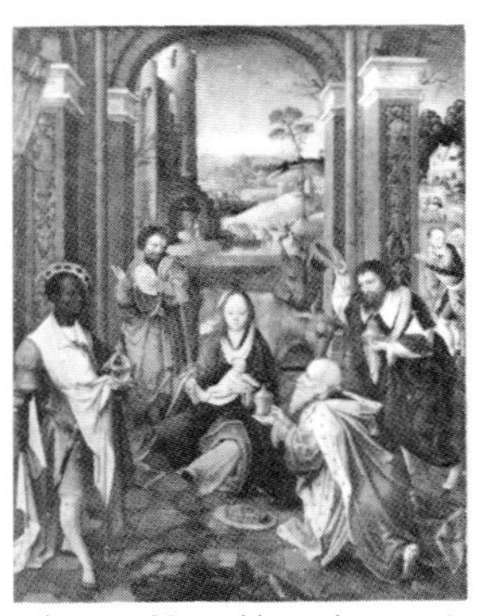

Antwerp Master (sixteenth century)
The Adoration of the Magi

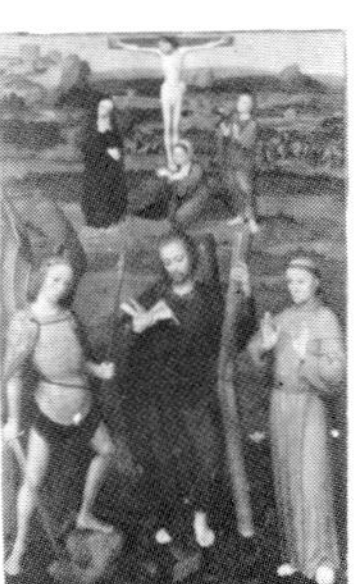

Adriaen Isenbrant
Crucifixion with St Andrew, St Michael and St Francis

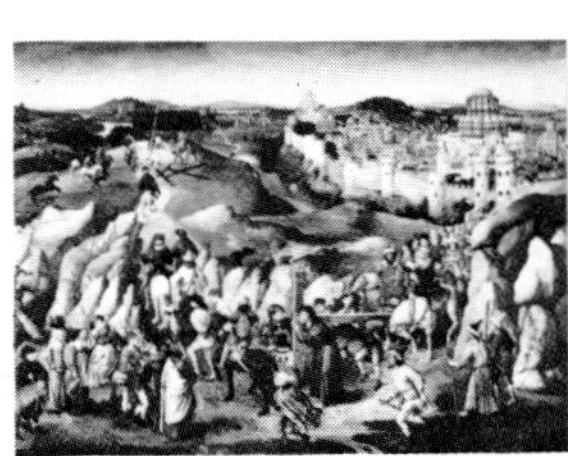

After Jan van Eyck
The Road to Calvary

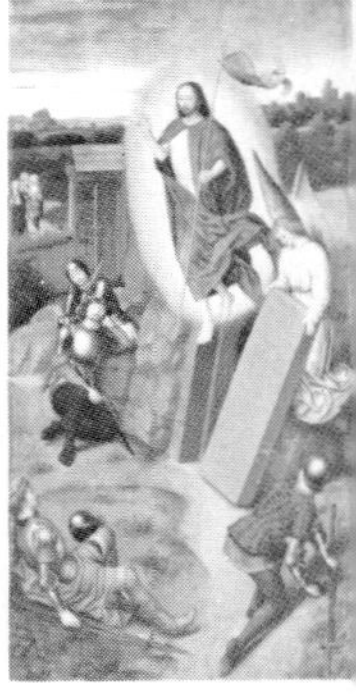

Hans Memling
The Resurrection

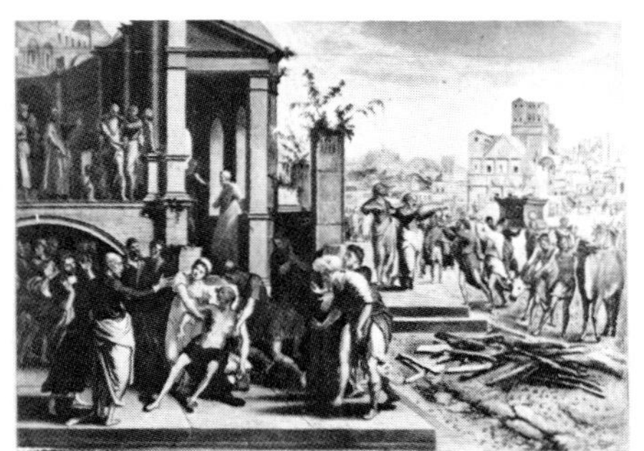

Jan van Hemessen
St Paul and St Barnabas Healing a Cripple at Lystra

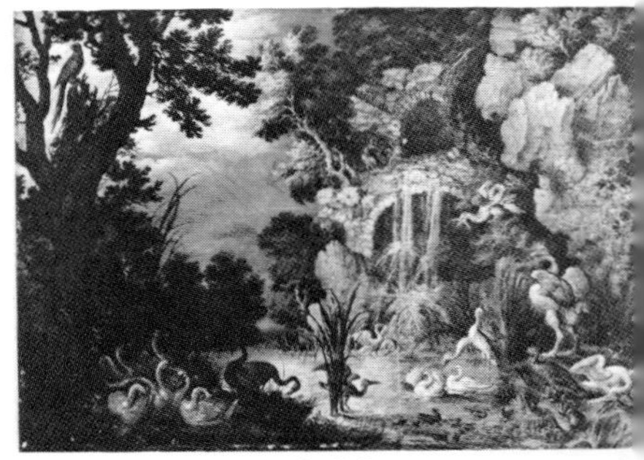

Roelandt Savery
Landscape with Birds

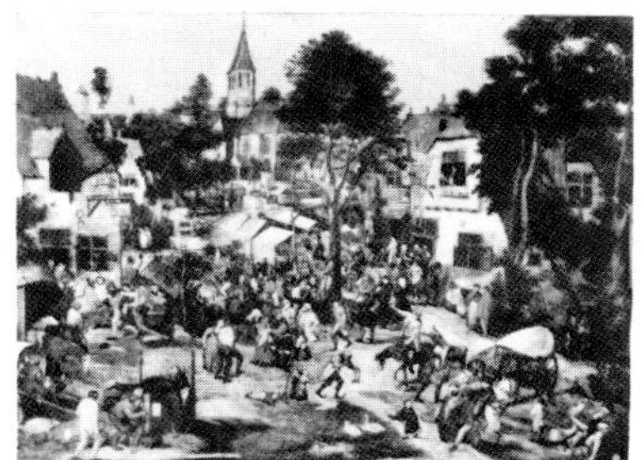

Pieter Brueghel the Younger *Village Fair*

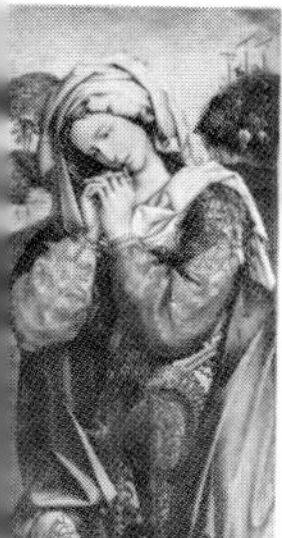

Colijn de Coter
Mary Magdalene

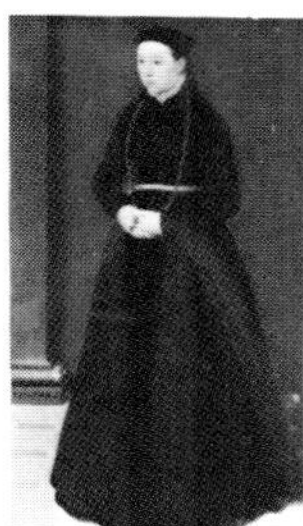

Nicolas Neufchatel
The Wife of Hendrik Pilgram

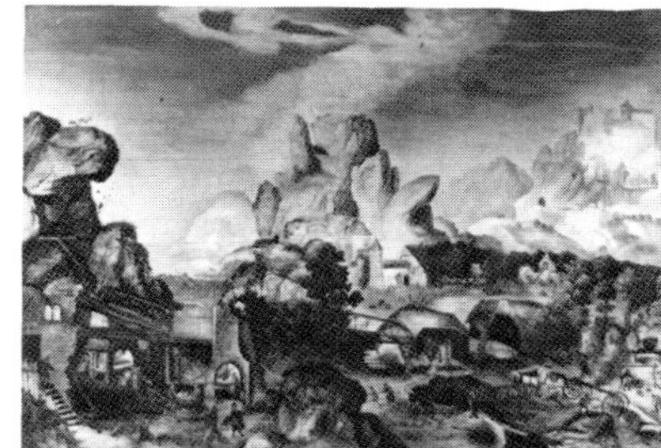

Herri met de Bles
Rocky Landscape with Ironworks

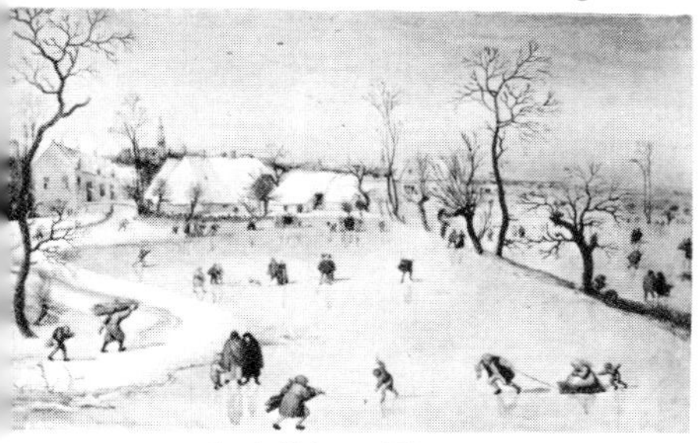

Jacob Grimmer *Winter*

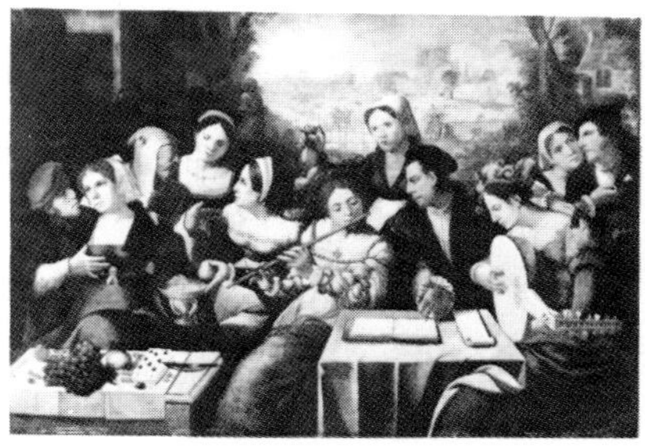

Jan Vermeyen *The Prodigal Son Wasting His Substance*

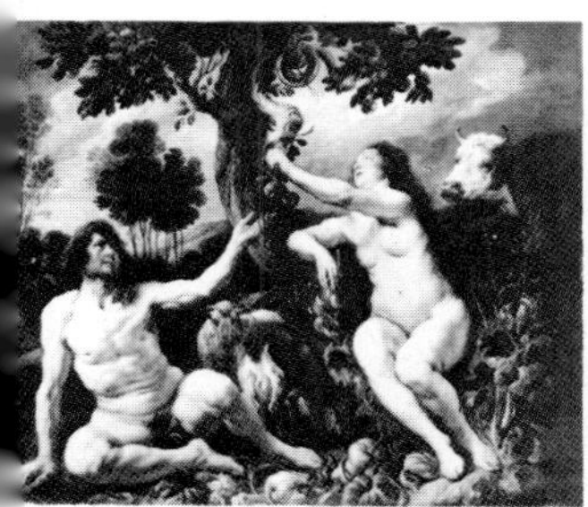

Jacob Jordaens
The Fall of Man

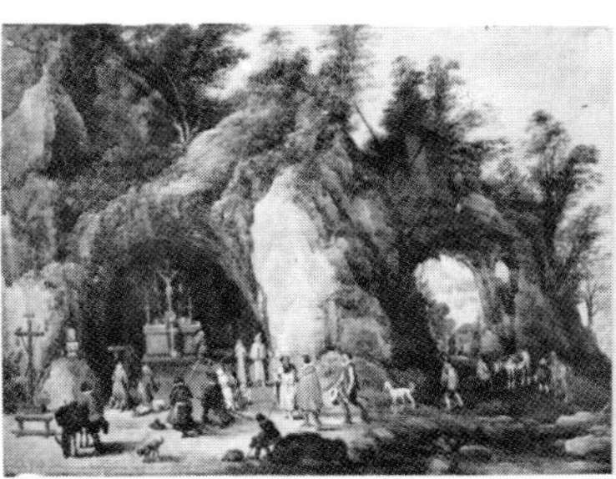

Josse de Momper
Divine Service in a Cave

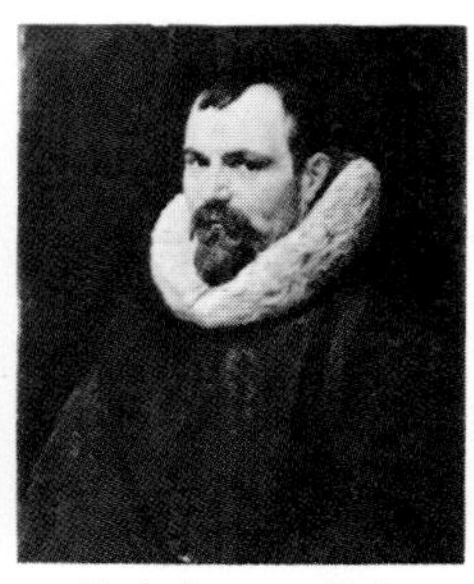

Sir Anthony van Dyck
Portrait of a Man

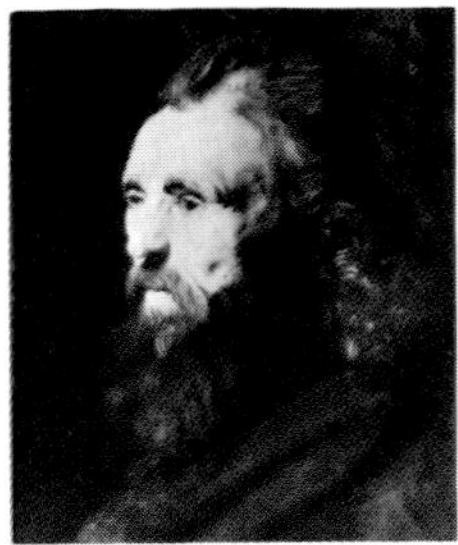

Peter Paul Rubens
Study of a Man's Head

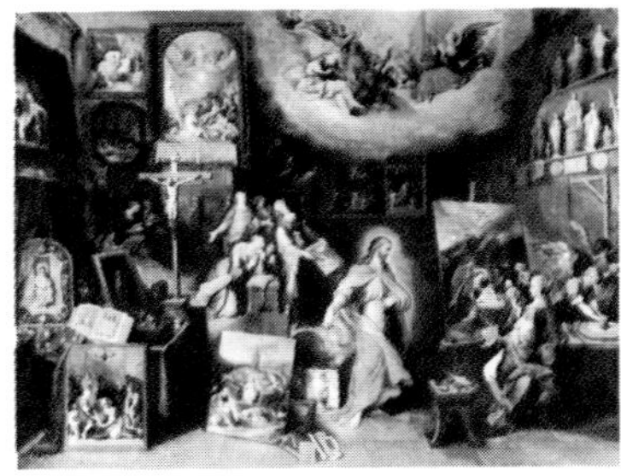

Frans Francken the Younger
The Imitation of Christ

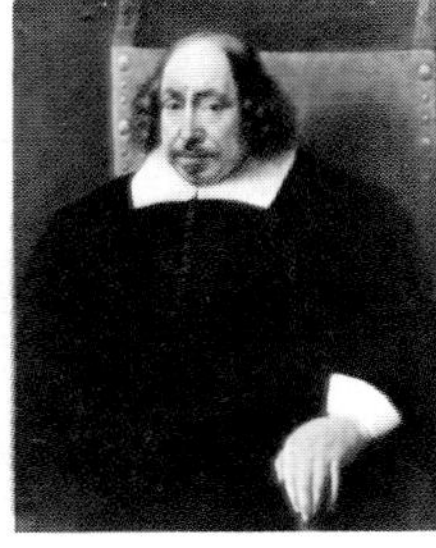

Jacob Jordaens
Portrait of a Man

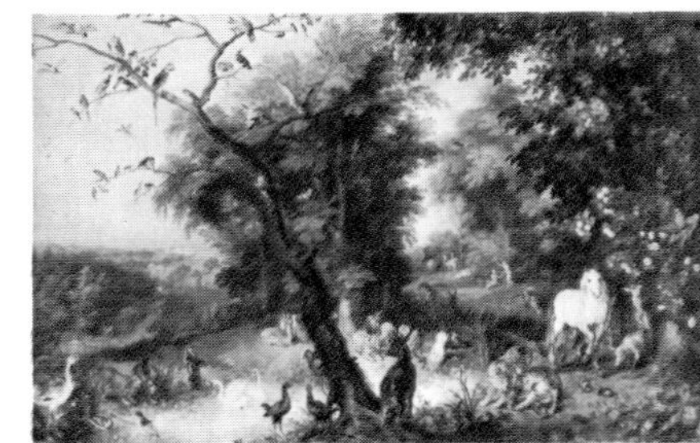

Jan Brueghel the Elder
The Fall of Man

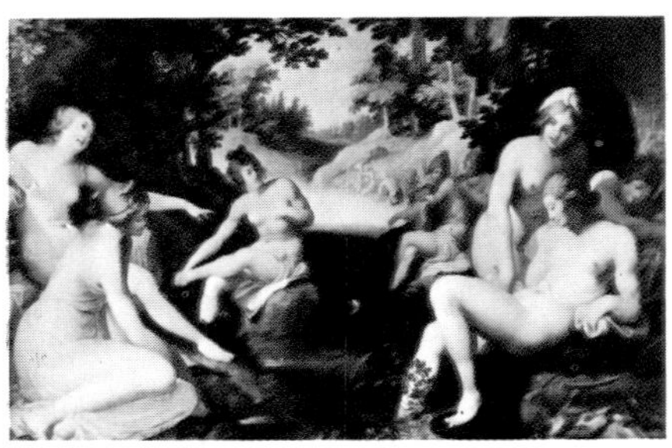

Abraham Janssens the Elder *Diana and Callisto*

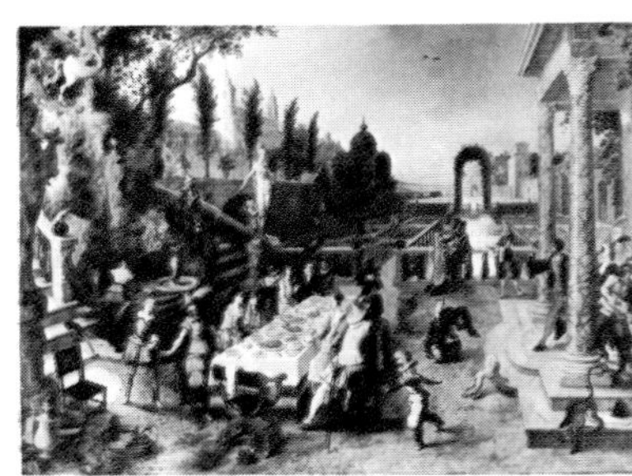

Sebastian Vrancx *An Alfresco Banquet*

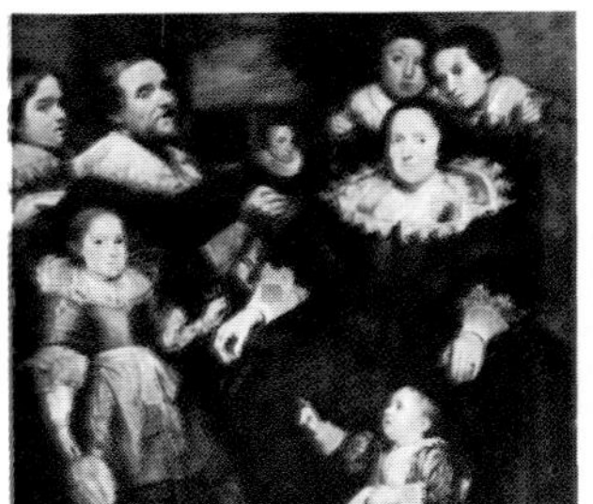

Cornelis de Vos *A Family Portrait*

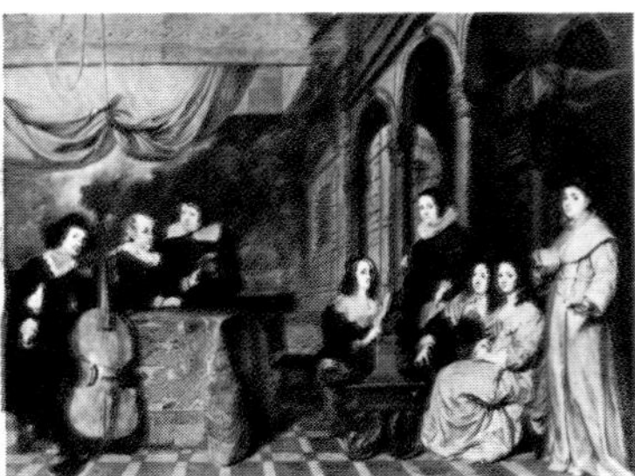

Gonzales Coques *A Family from Antwerp*

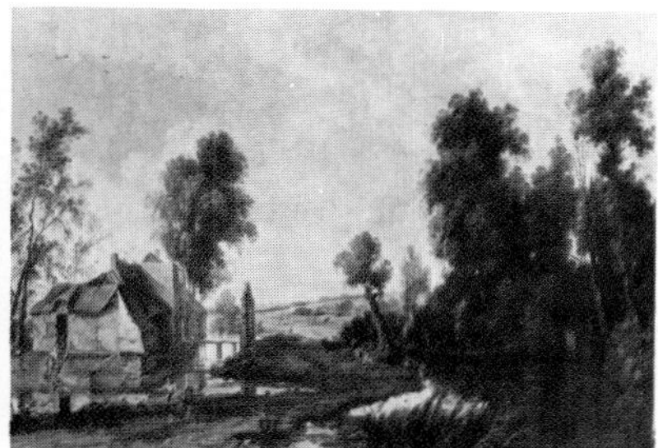

Jan Wildens *Landscape with Farm*

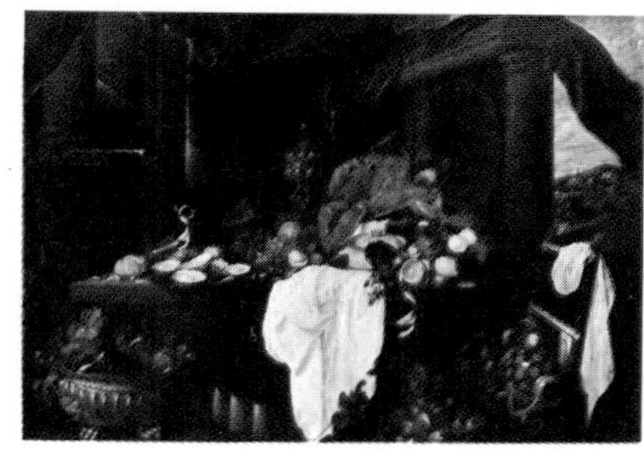

Andries Benedetti *Still-life with Fruit*

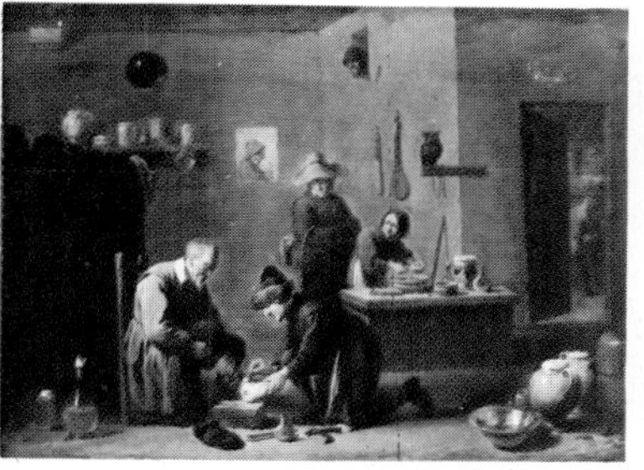

David Teniers the Younger
The Barber-Surgeon's Shop

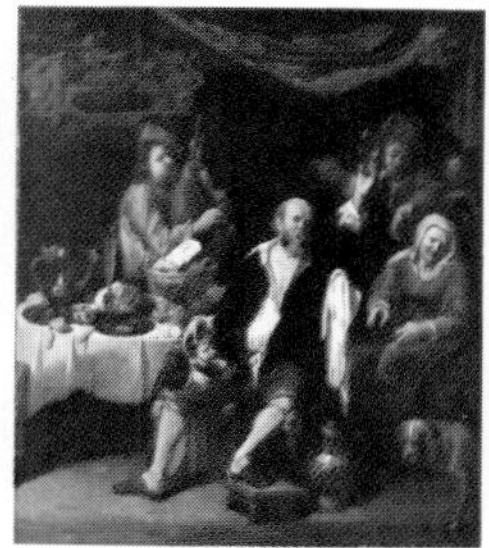

David Ryckaert III
A Merry Party

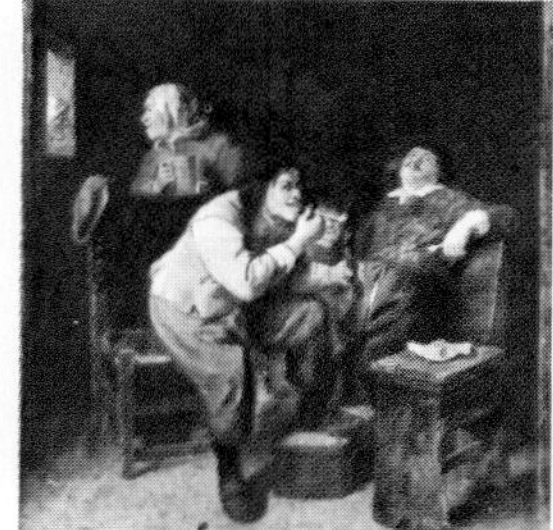

Adriaen Brouwer
Peasants Smoking

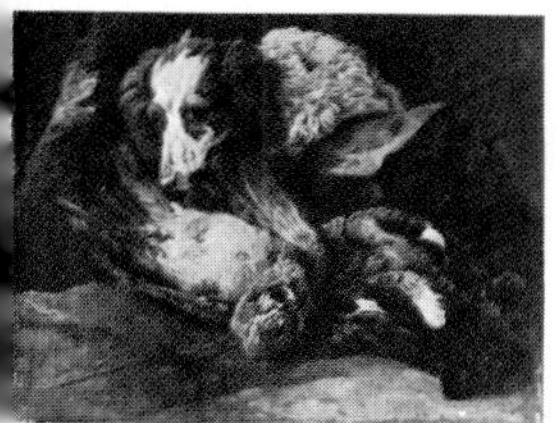

Jan Fyt
Dog with Dead Birds

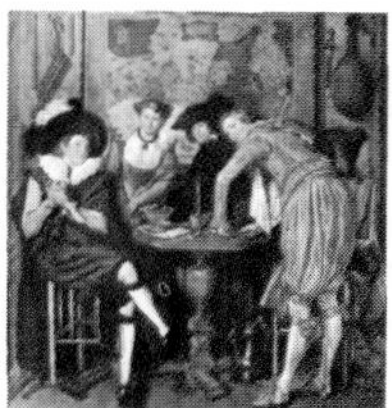

Willem Pietersz. Buytewech
A Merry Party

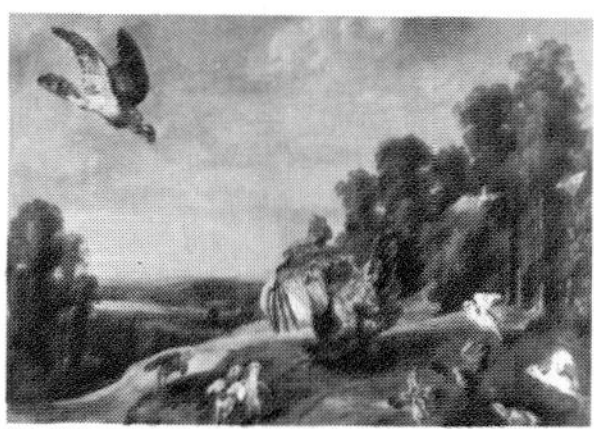

Frans Snyders *The Hawk and the Hen*

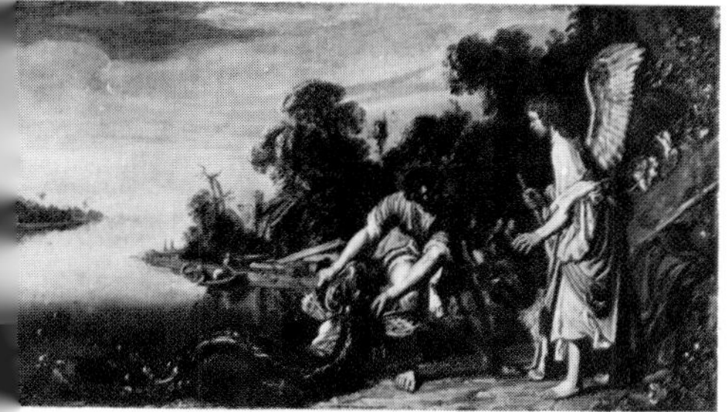

Peter Lastman
Tobias and the Angel with the Fish

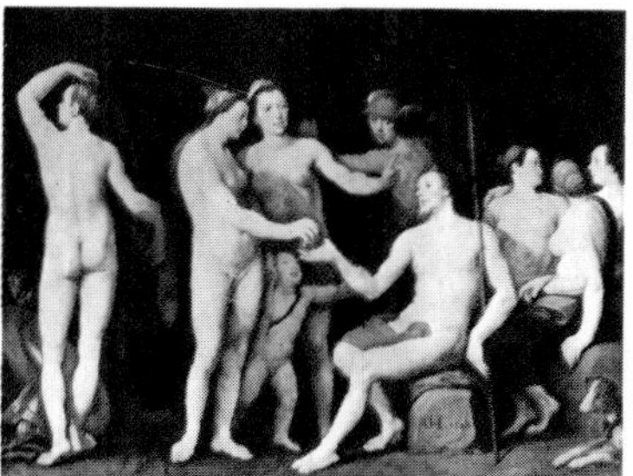

Cornelis van Haarlem *The Judgment of Paris*

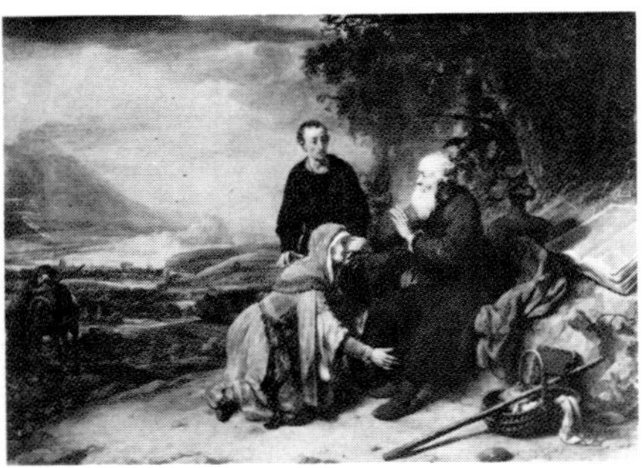

Gerbrandt van den Eeckhout
Elisha and the Shunammite Woman

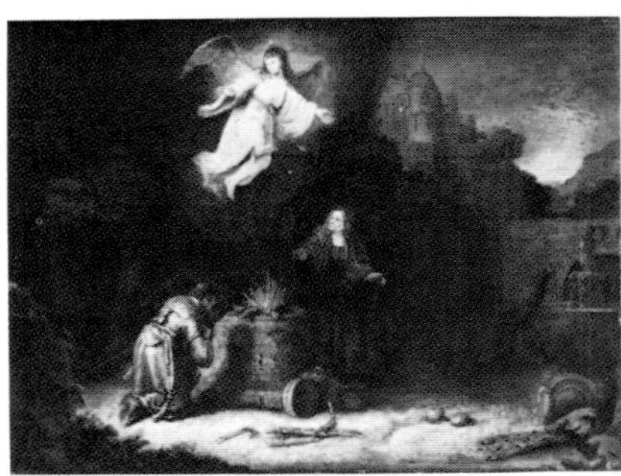

Govaert Flinck
The Offering of Manoah

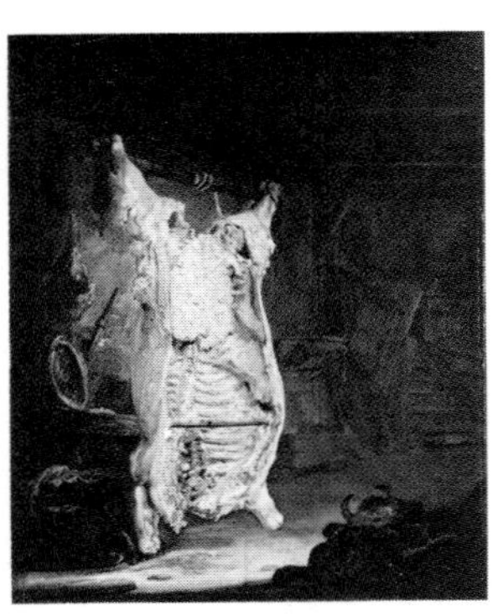

Rembrandt *The Slaughtered Ox*

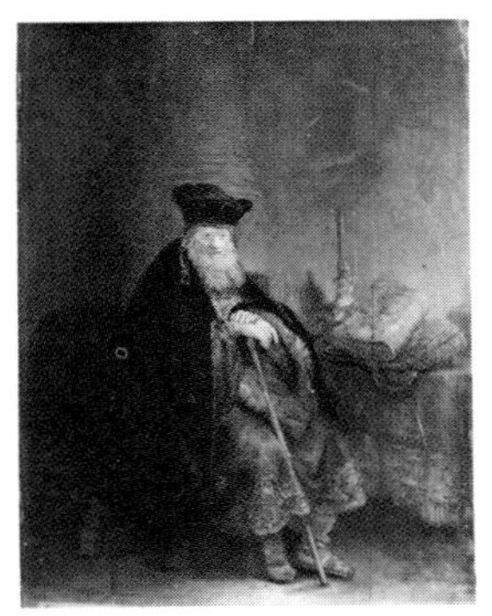

Rembrandt *The Old Rabbi*

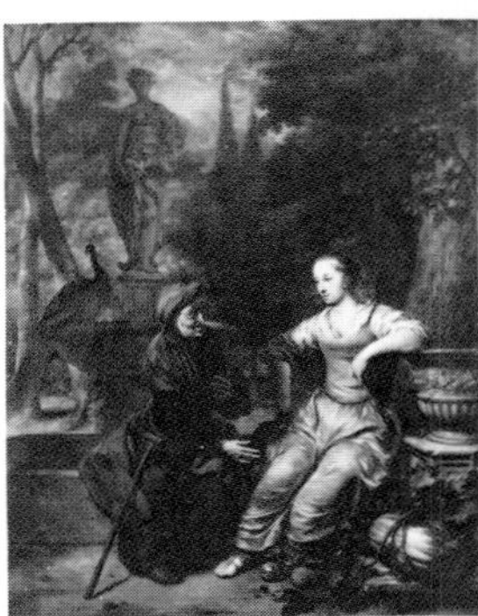

Gerbrandt van den Eeckhout
Vertumnus and Pomona

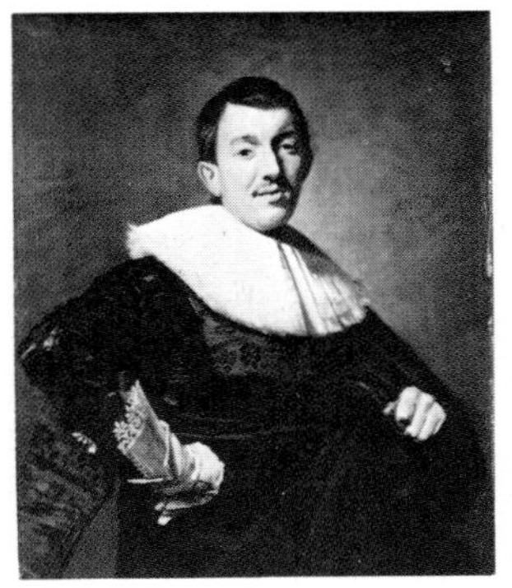

Frans Hals *Portrait of a Man*

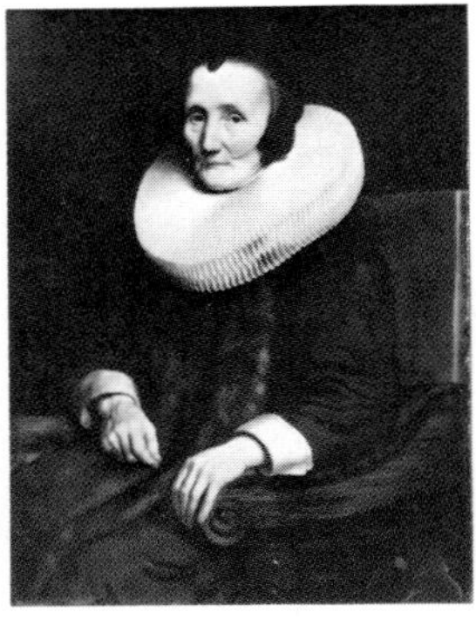

Nicolaes Maes *The Wife of Jacob Trip*

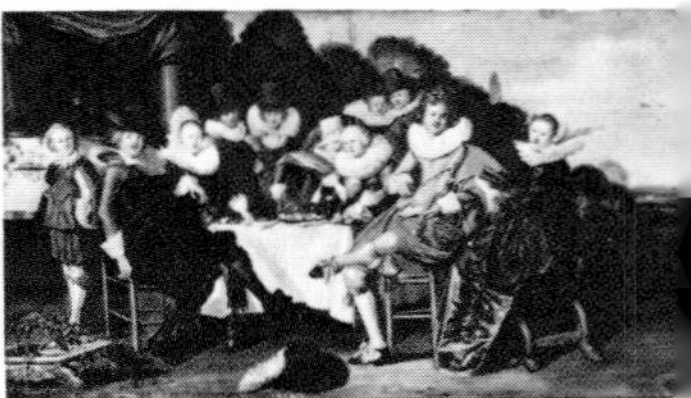

Dirck Hals *A Merry Party*

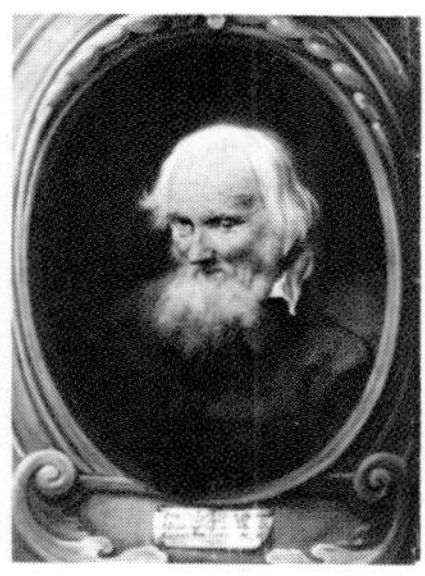
Jan Lievens
Petrus Egidius de Morrion

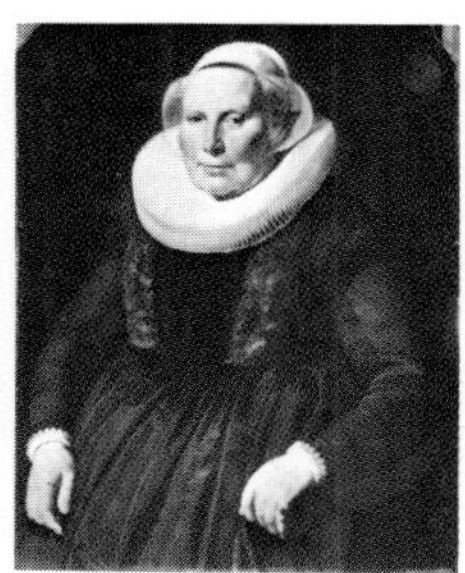
Thomas de Keyser
Portrait of a Woman

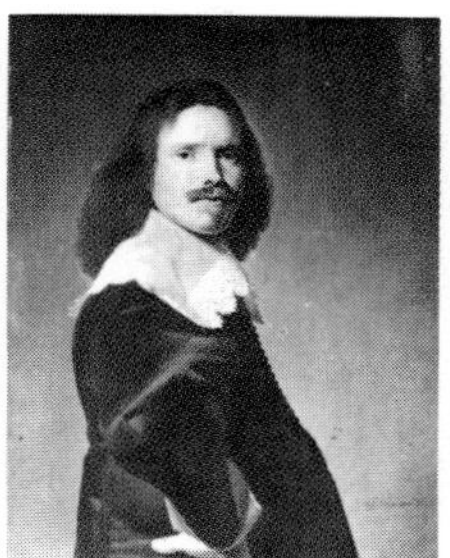
Jan Cornelisz. Verspronck
Portrait of a Man

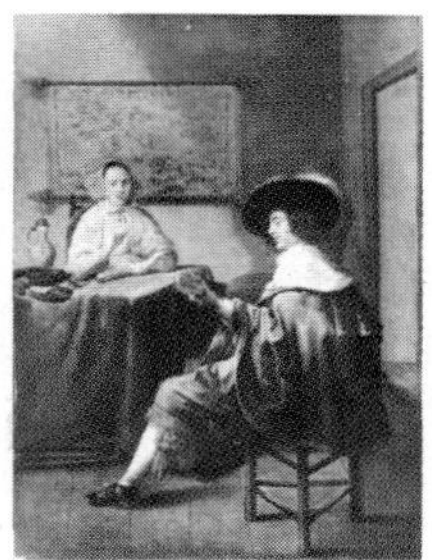
Jan Miense Molenaer
The Music Makers

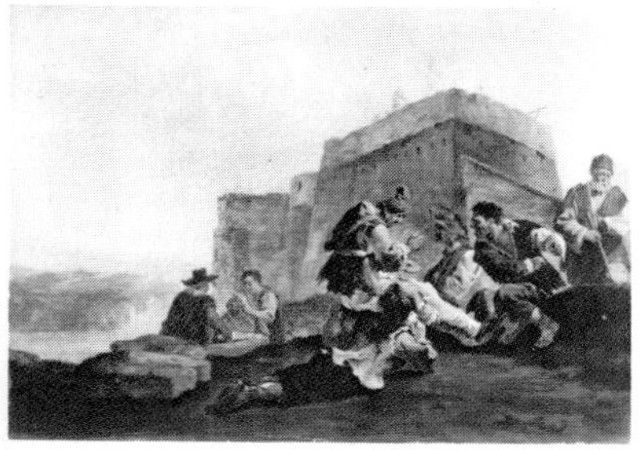
Pieter van Laer
Landscape with Peasants Playing Morra

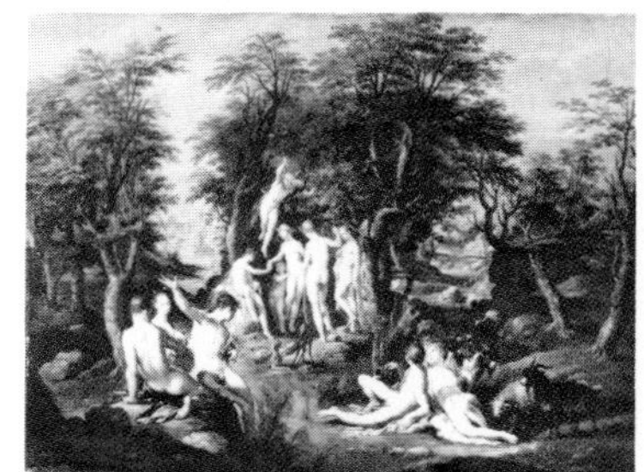
Joachim Wtewael
The Judgment of Paris

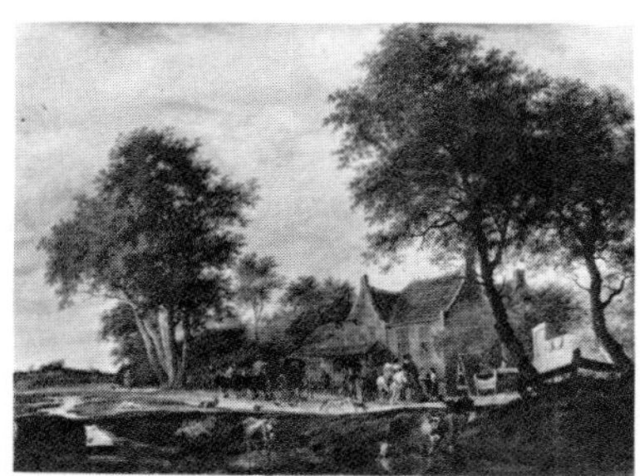
Salomon van Ruysdael *The 'White Swan' Inn*

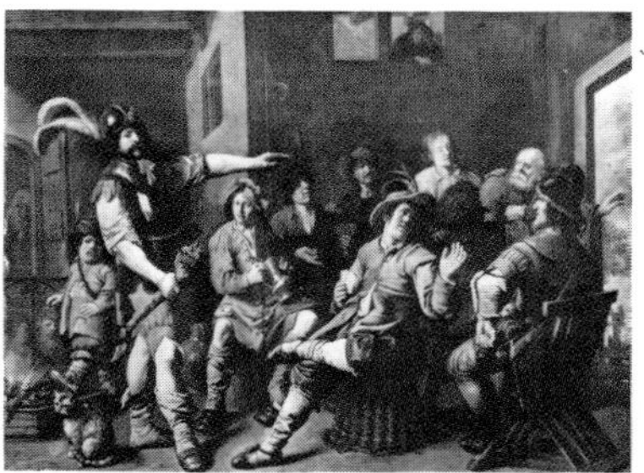
Jan Miense Molenaer *St Peter's Denial of Christ*

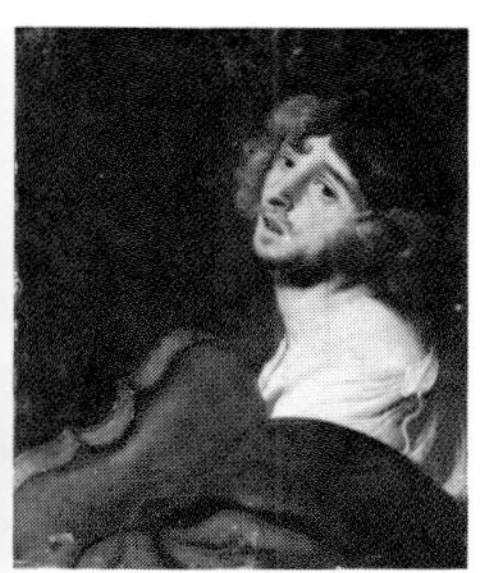
Jacob Adriaensz. Backer
Young Man with Violin

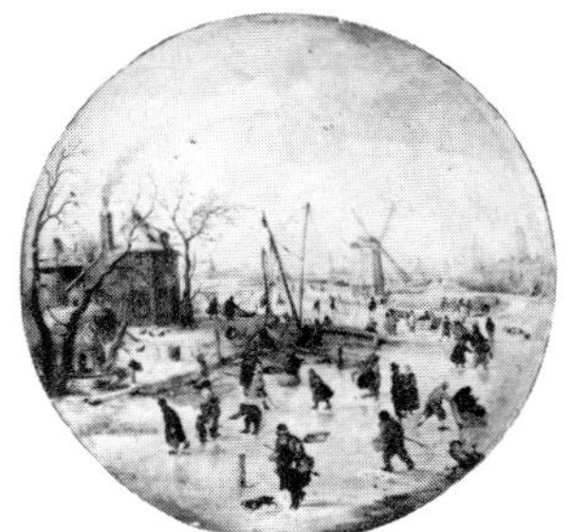
Hendrick Avercamp
Winter Scene with Skaters

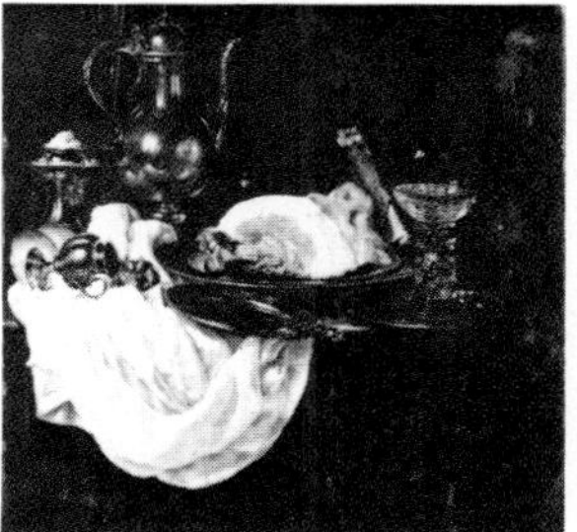
Willem Claesz. Heda
Still-life with Ham

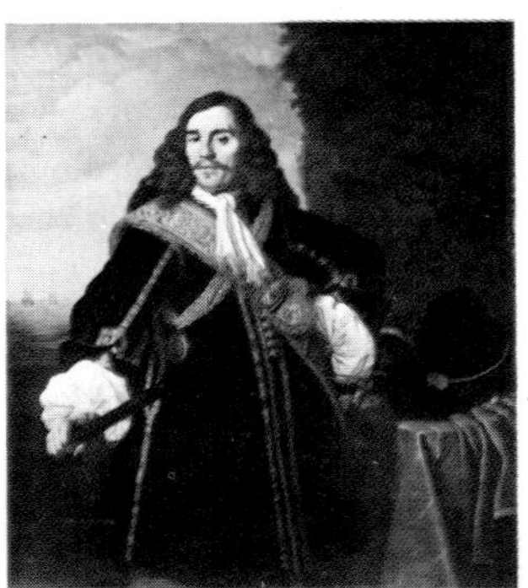

Bartholomeus van der Helst
Admiral Gideon de Wildt

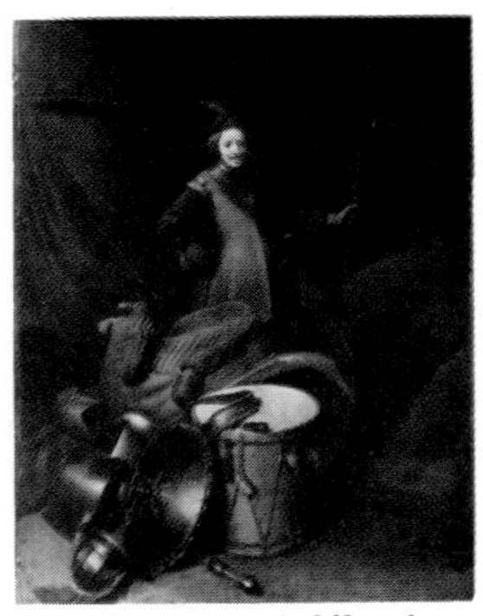

Gerard Dou *An Officer of the Leyden Civic Guard*

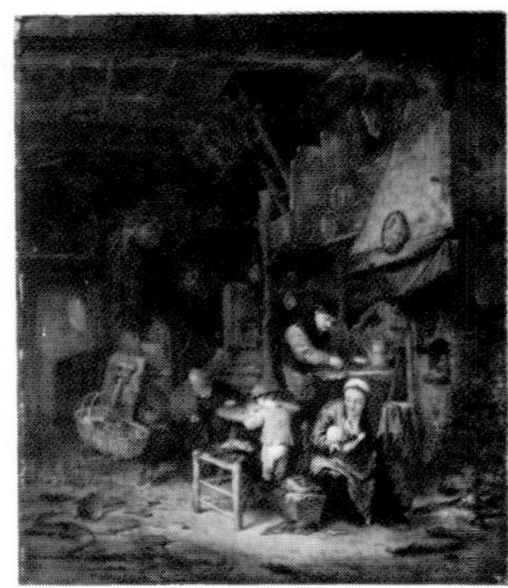

Adriaen van Ostade
Interior with a Peasant Family

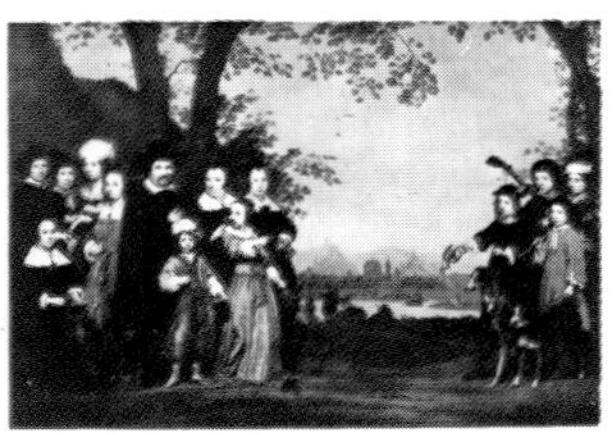

Aelbert Cuyp *Family Portrait*

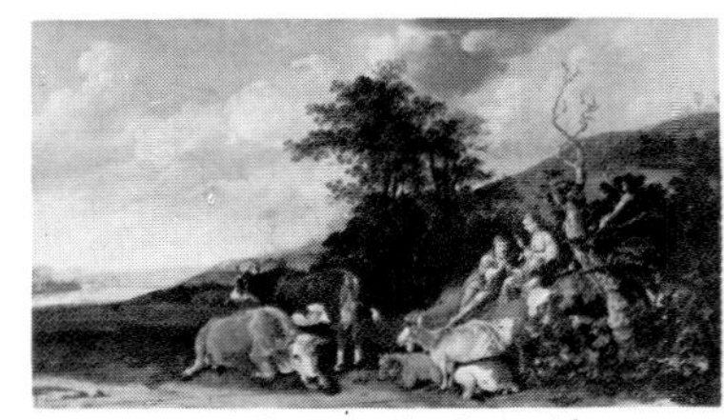

Paulus Potter *Landscape with a Shepherd and Shepherdess*

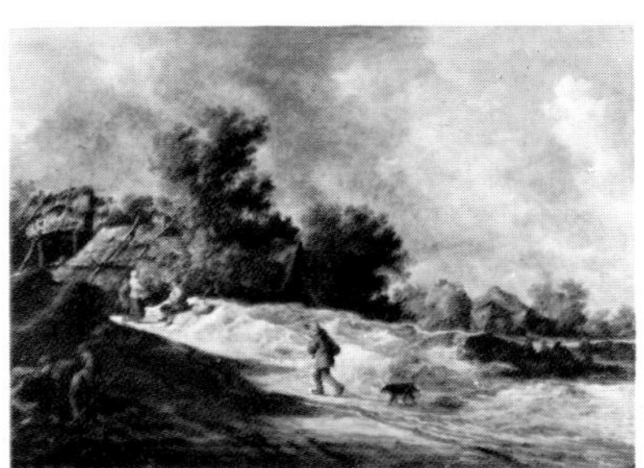

Jan van Goyen
Landscape with Peasants

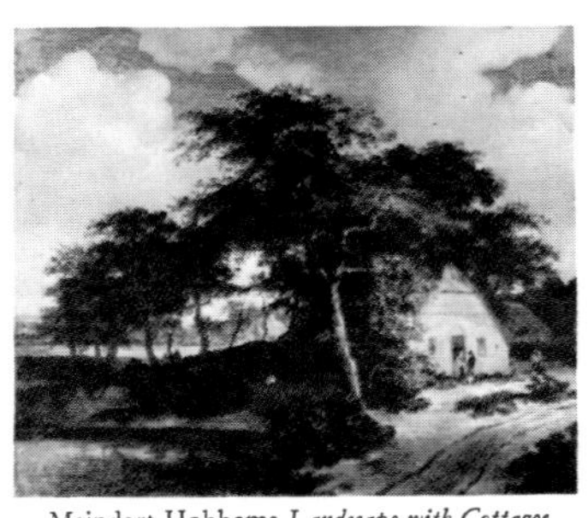

Meindert Hobbema *Landscape with Cottages*

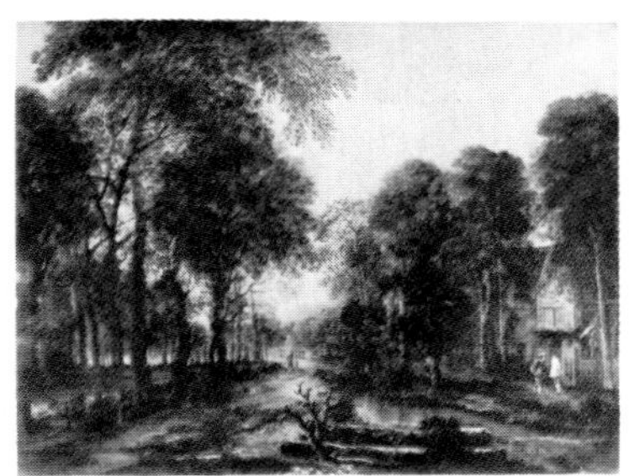

Aert van der Neer
Wooded Landscape with Houses

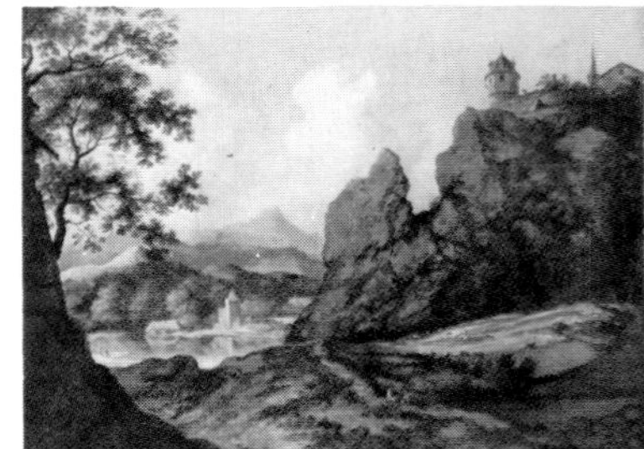

Allaert van Everdingen
Rocky Landscape

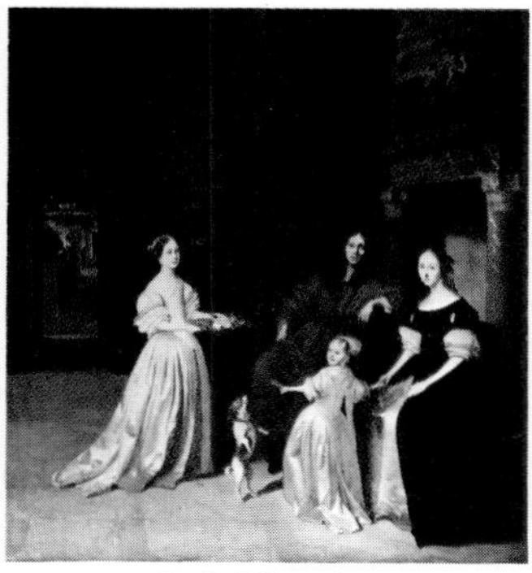

Jacob Ochtervelt
A Dutch Family

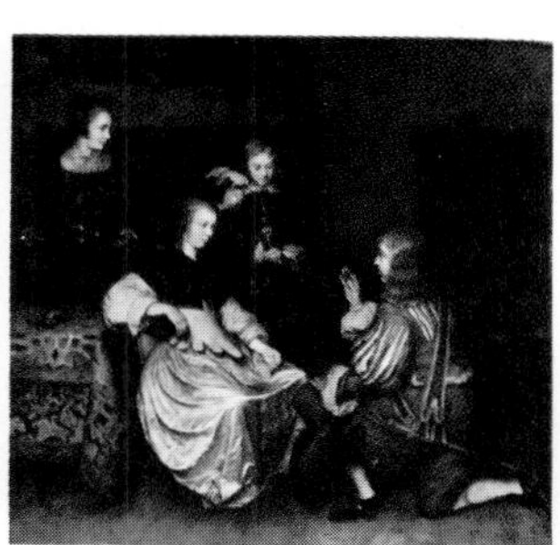

Caspar Netscher
The Presentation of a Locket

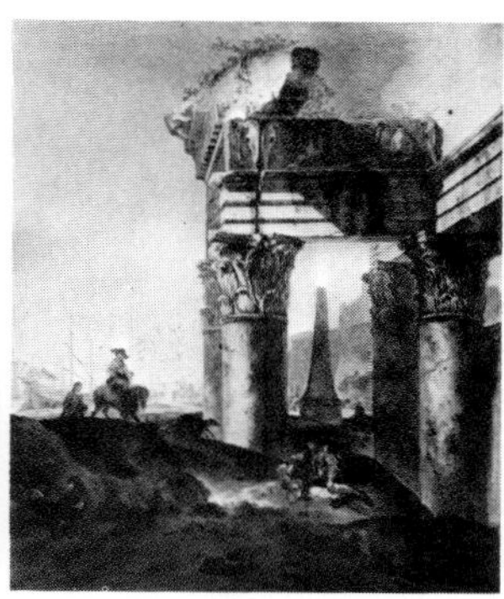

Jan Baptist Weenix *The Ruins of the Temple of Vespasian in Rome*

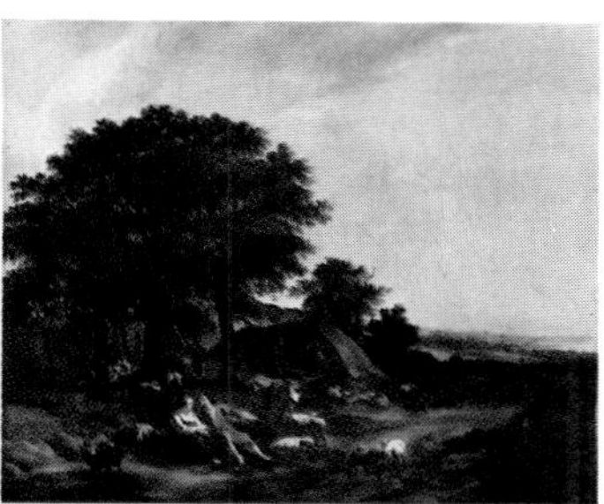

Claesz. Berchem
Landscape with Shepherds Resting

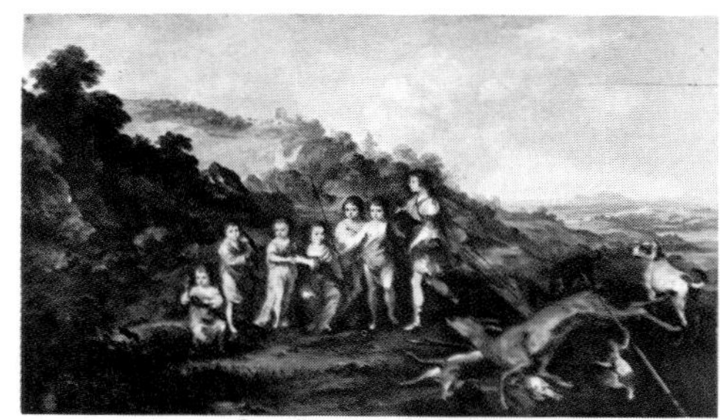

Cornelis van Poelenburgh
The Children of Elector Palatine Frederic V, King of Bohemia

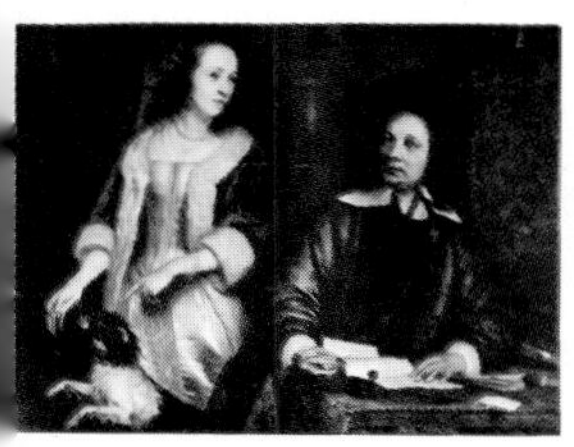

Abraham van den Tempel
Portrait of a Married Couple

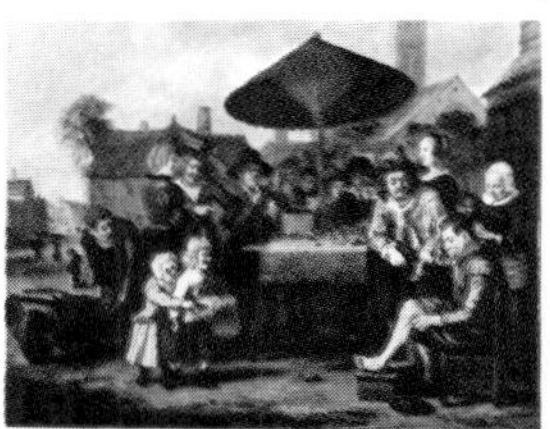

Jan Victors
A Quack at His Stall

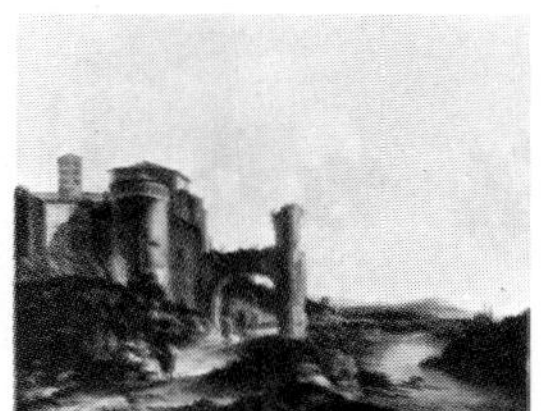

Jan Asselyn
Italian Landscape

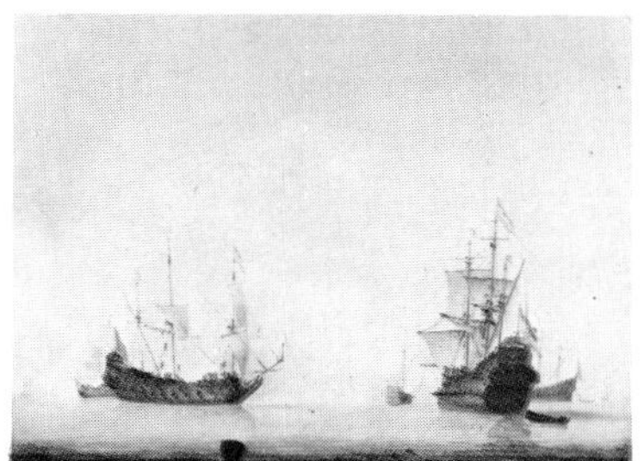

Willem van de Velde the Younger
Warships on a Calm Sea

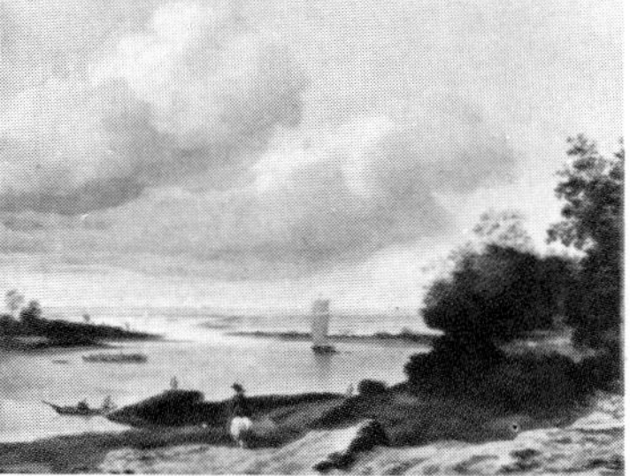

Anthonie van Borssom
River-bank with a Horseman

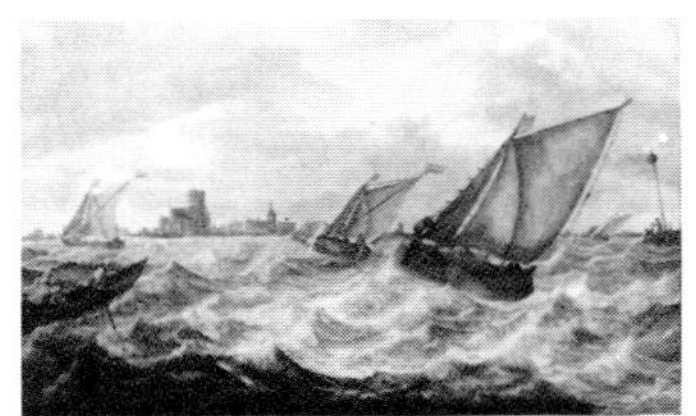

Abraham van Beyeren
Rough Sea

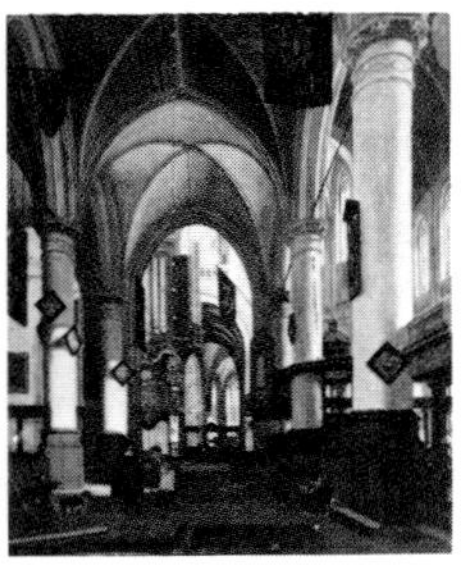

Emanuel de Witte
Interior of the Oude Kerk in Amsterdam

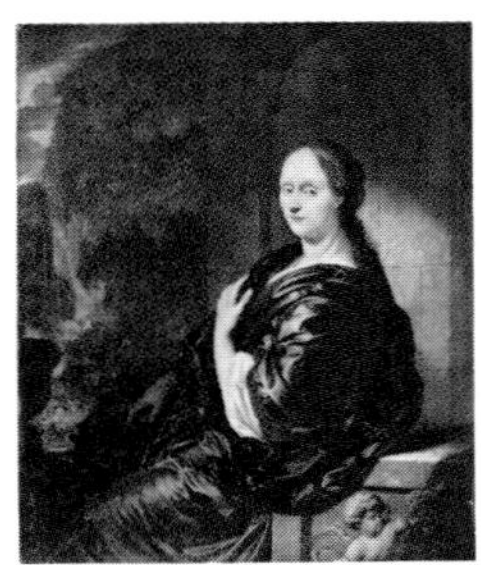

Adriaen van der Werff
Portrait of a Woman

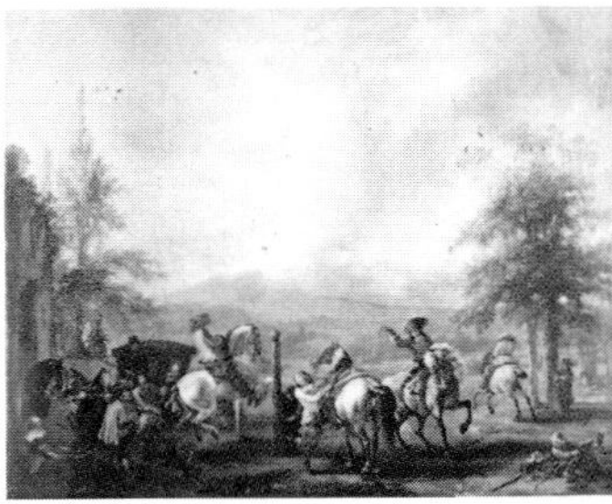

Philips Wouwerman
The Riding School

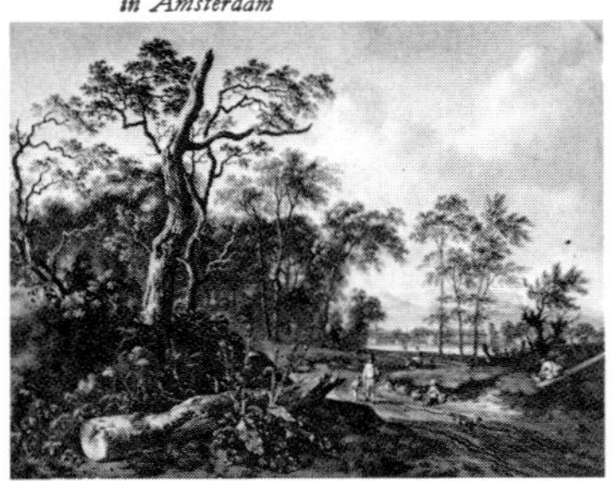

Jan Wynants
Road by a Wood

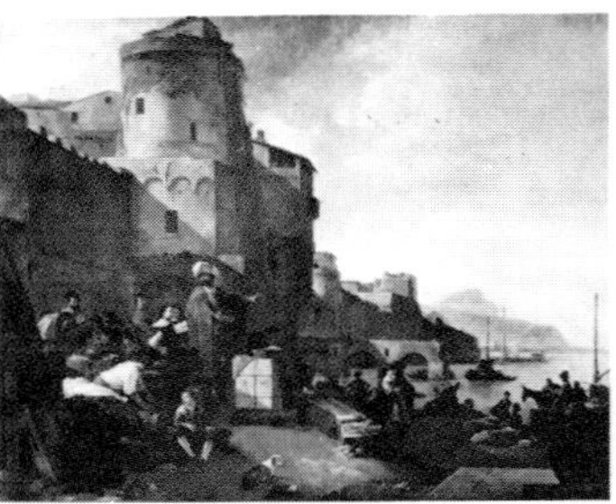

Thomas Wyck
Italian Port

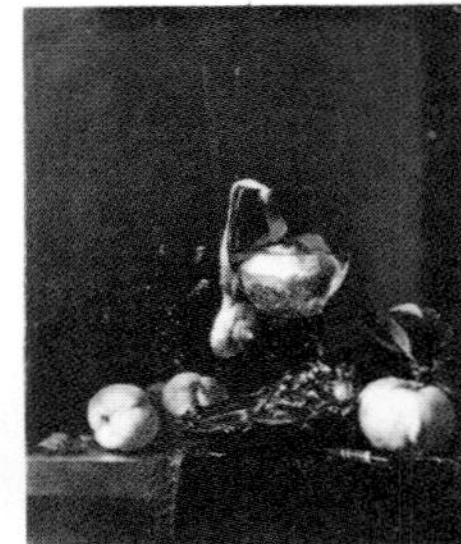

Willem Kalf
Still-life with Fruit

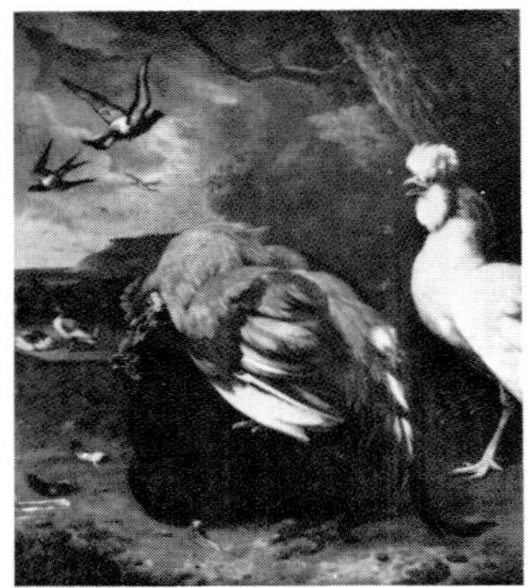

Melchior de Hondecoeter
The Farmyard

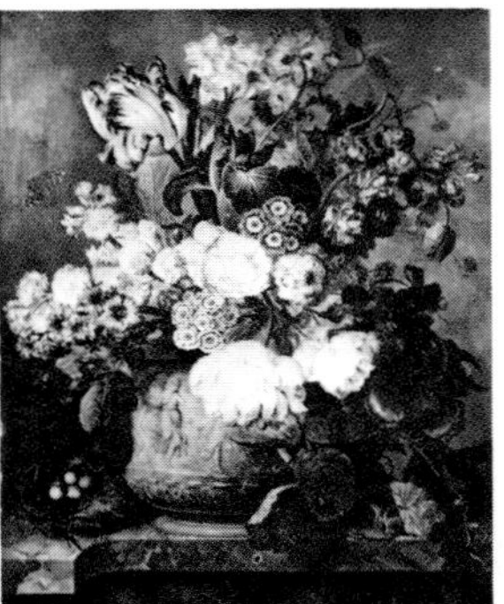

Jan van Huysum
Flowers in a Vase

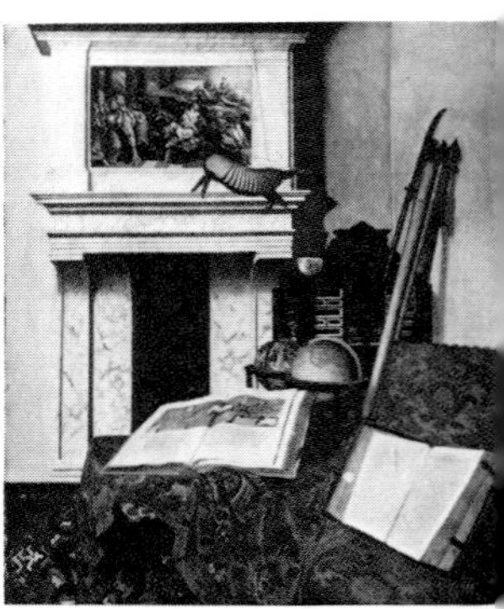

Jan van der Heyden
Interior with Curios

FRENCH PAINTING

Seventeenth and eighteenth centuries

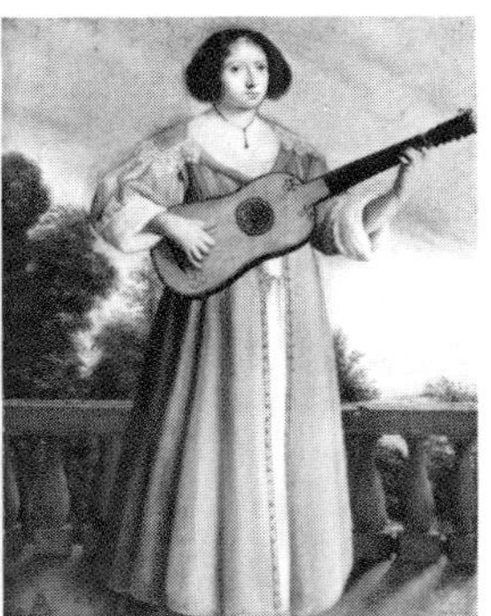

Augustin Quesnel the Younger
Woman Playing the Guitar

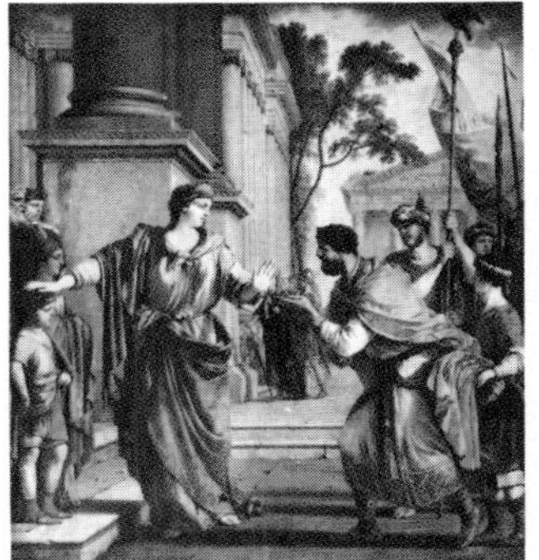

Laurent de La Hire
King Ninus
Offering the Crown to Semiramis

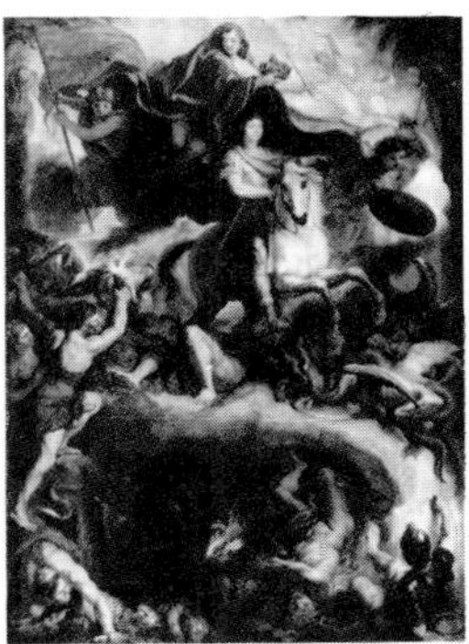

Charles Lebrun
The Apotheosis of Louis XIV

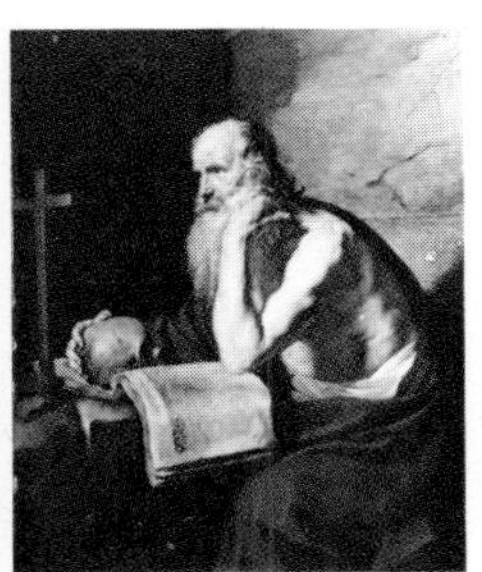

Jacques Blanchard
St Jerome

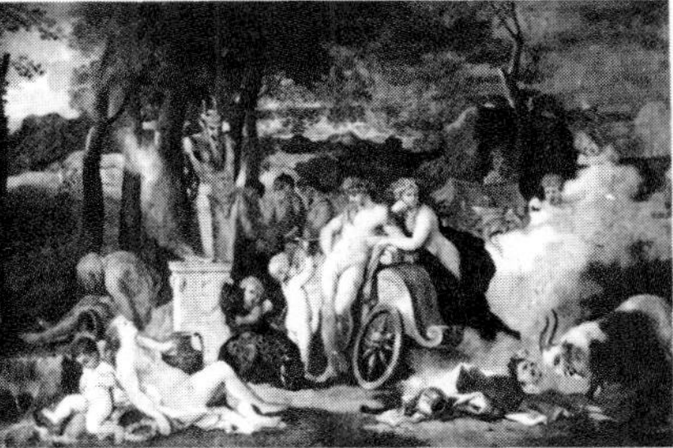

Sébastien Bourdon
Bacchus and Ceres with Nymphs and Satyrs

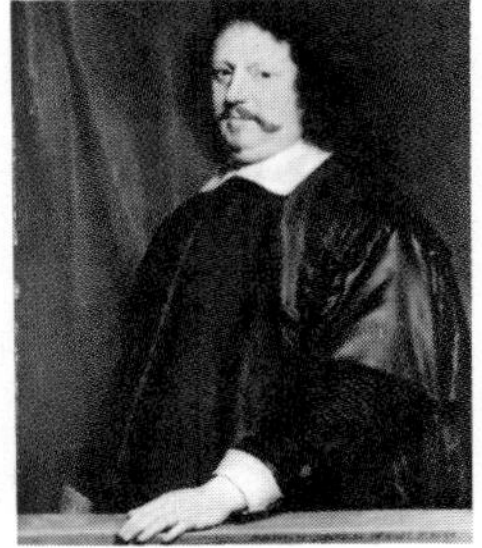

Philippe de Champaigne
Portrait of I. Gronlart

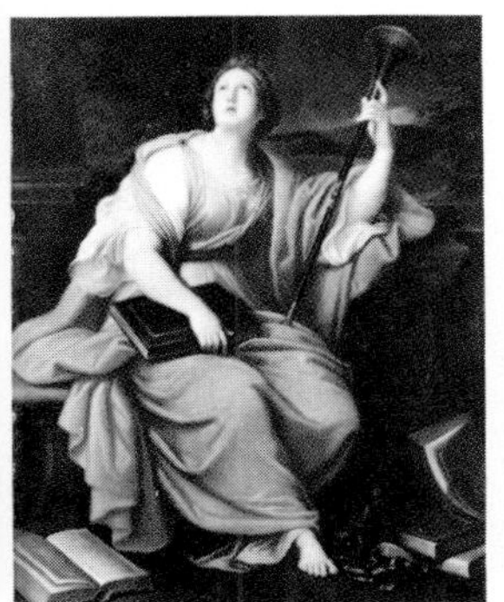

Pierre Mignard *Clio*

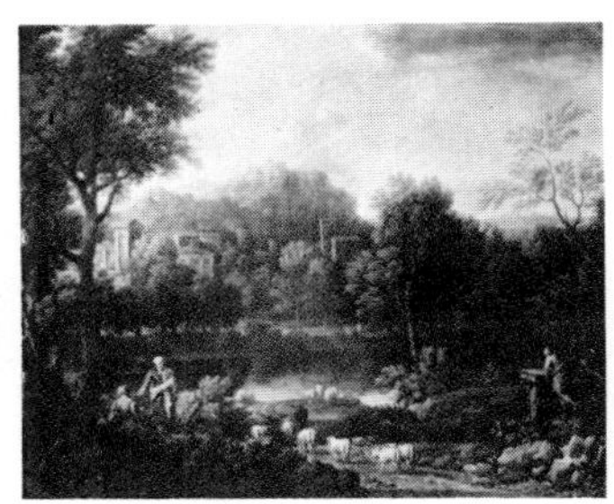

Gaspard Dughet *Imaginary Landscape*

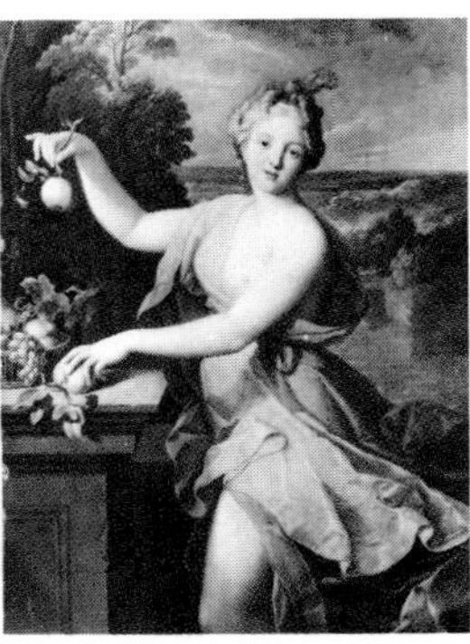

Nicolas Fouché *A Lady as Pomona*

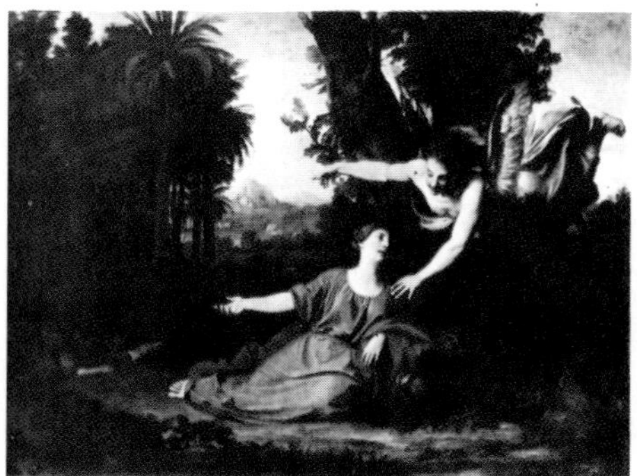
Nicolas Colombel *Hagar and the Angel*

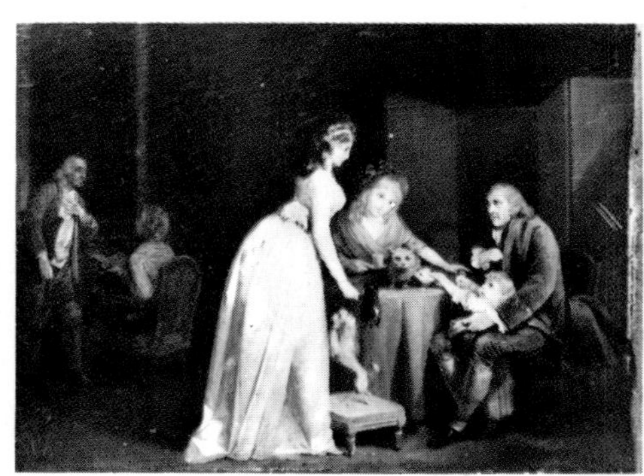
Louis Léopold Boilly *Visiting Grandfather*

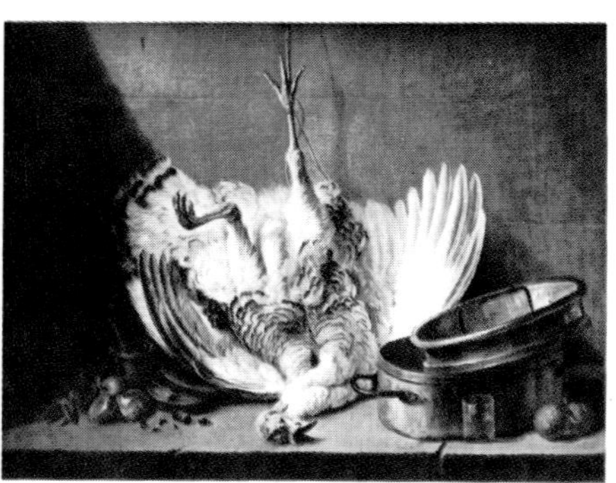
Jean-Baptiste Siméon Chardin *Still-life with Turkey*

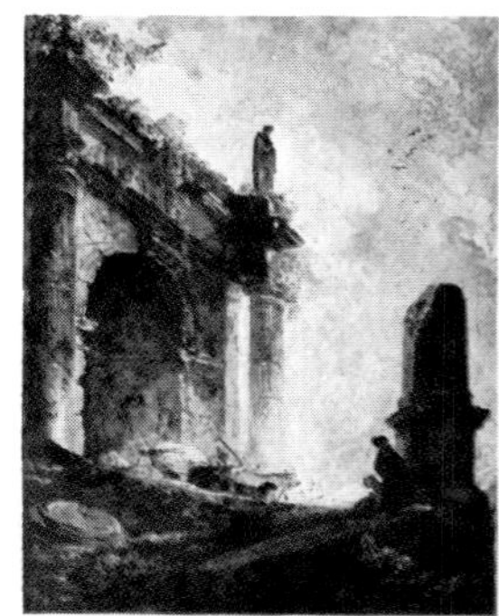
Hubert Robert *Ruins with Figures*

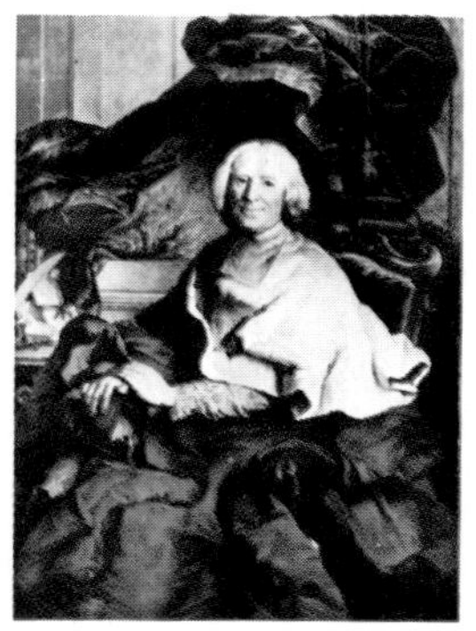
Hyacinthe Rigaud
Cardinal Fleury

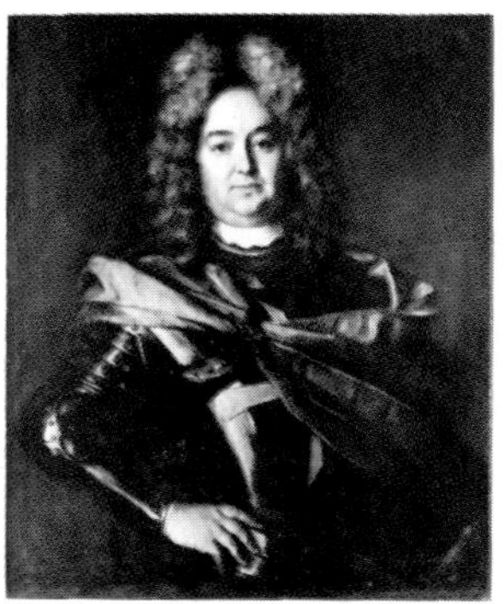
Nicolas de Largillière
Portrait of a Man

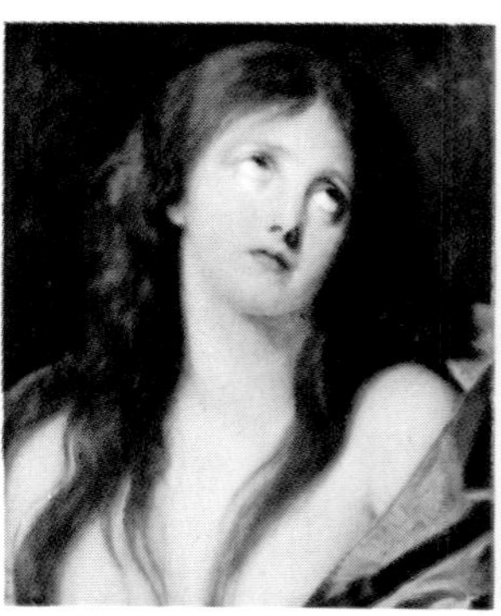
Jean-Baptiste Greuze
Portrait of a Girl

GERMAN PAINTING

Fifteenth to twentieth centuries

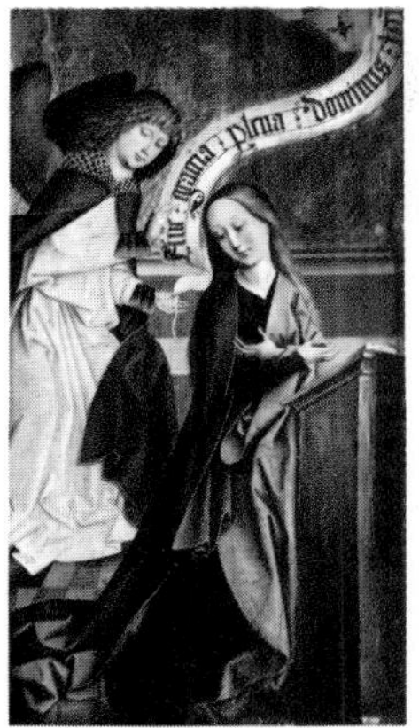

Rueland Frueauf
The Annunciation

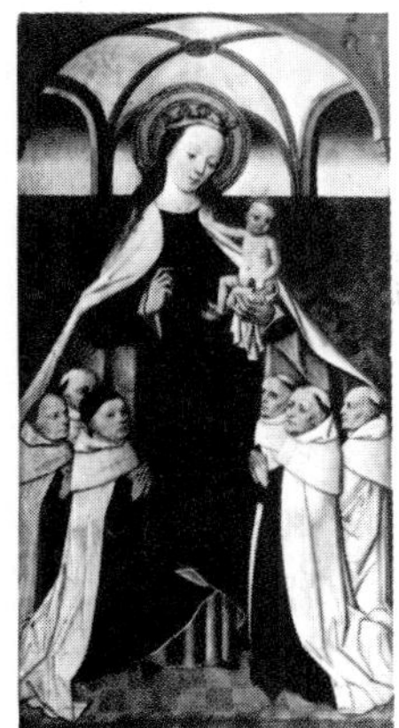

Master of the Life of the Virgin
Virgin and Child with Six Carmelites

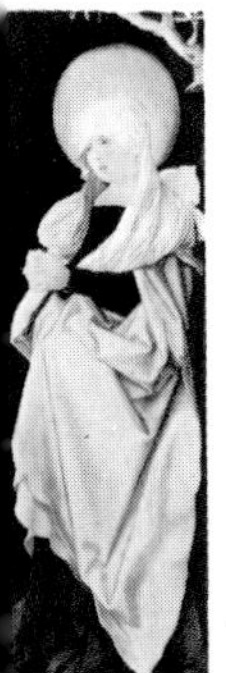

Hans
Baldung Grien
Mater Dolorosa

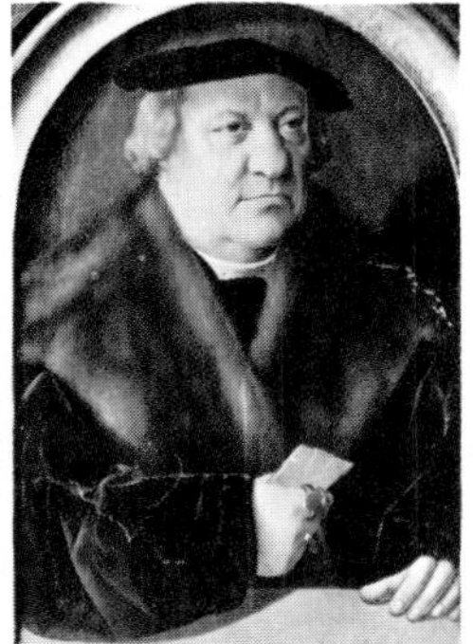

Barthel Bruyn
Petrus von Clapis

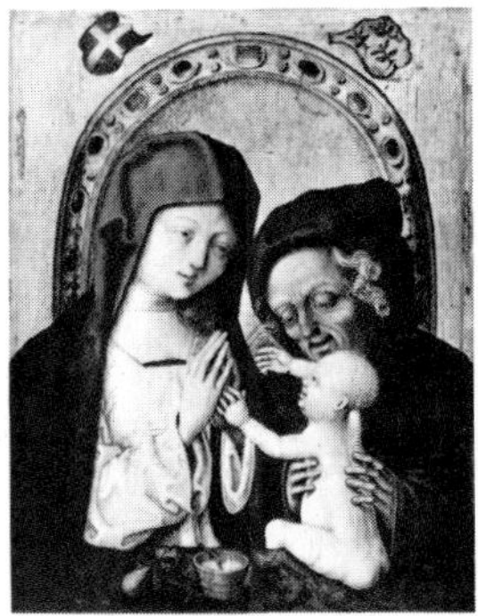

Master of the St Bartholomew
Altar-piece *The Holy Family*

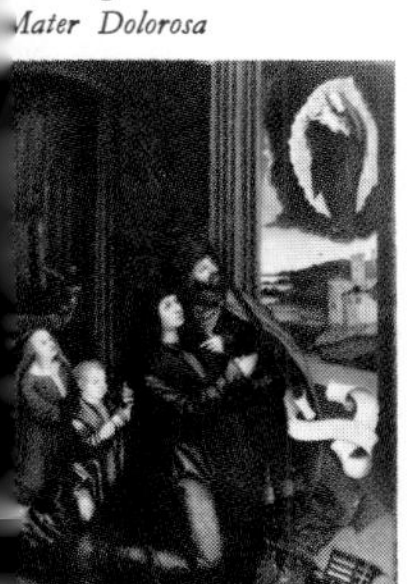

Bernhard Strigel
St Ladislas Commends
Ladislas II to the Virgin

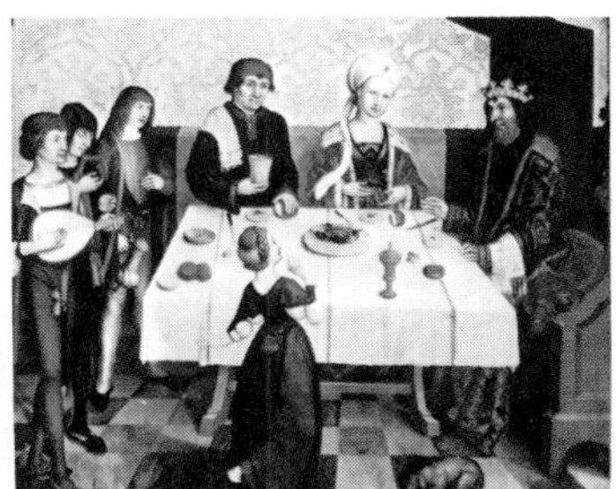

Berne Carnation Master
The Dance of Salome

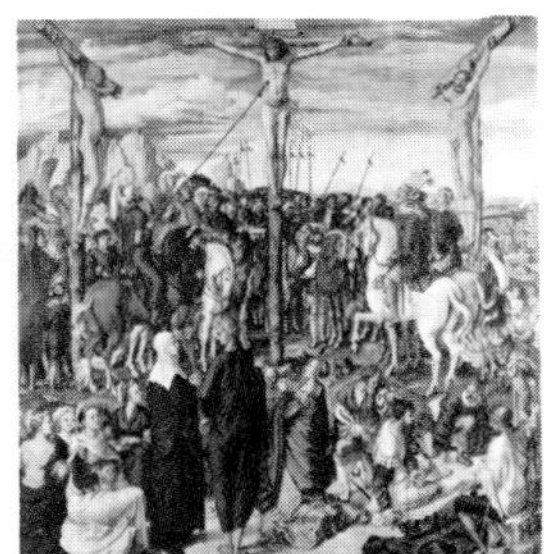

Anton Woensam
The Crucifixion

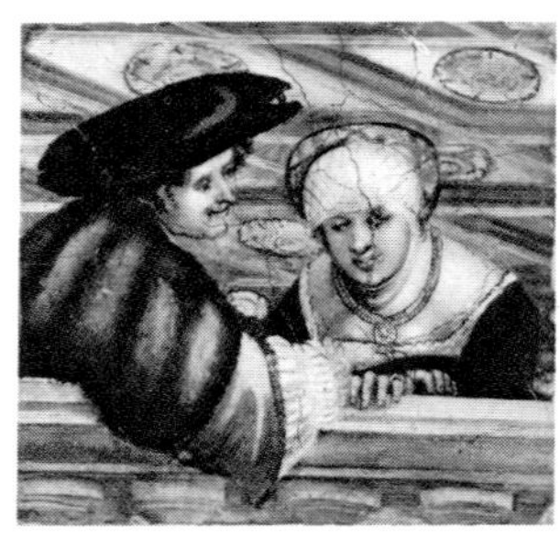

Albrecht Altdorfer *Lovers*

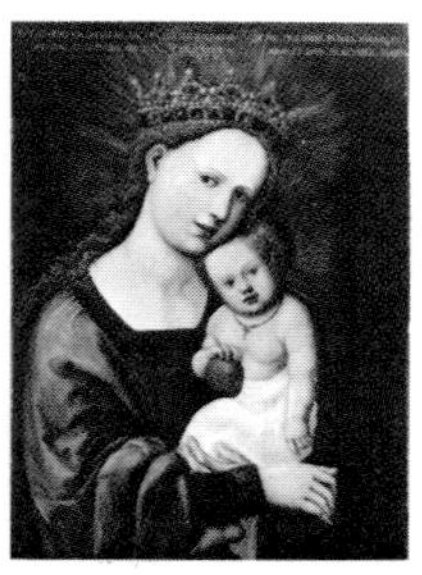

Albrecht Altdorfer
The Virgin and Child

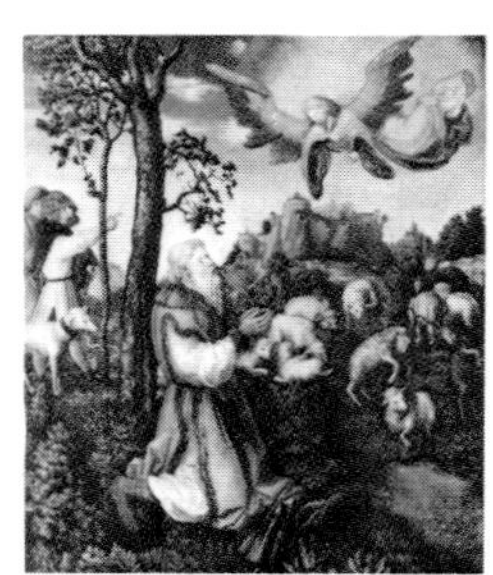

Lucas Cranach the Elder
The Angel Appearing to Joachim

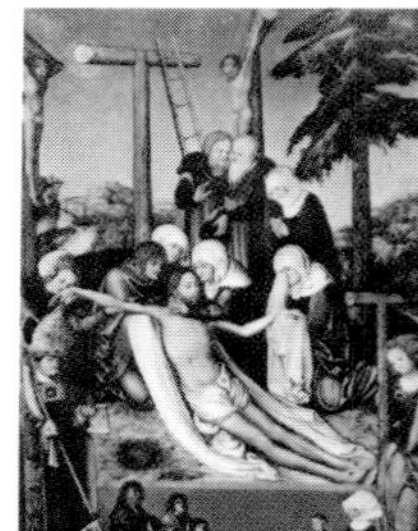

Lucas Cranach the Elder
The Lamentation

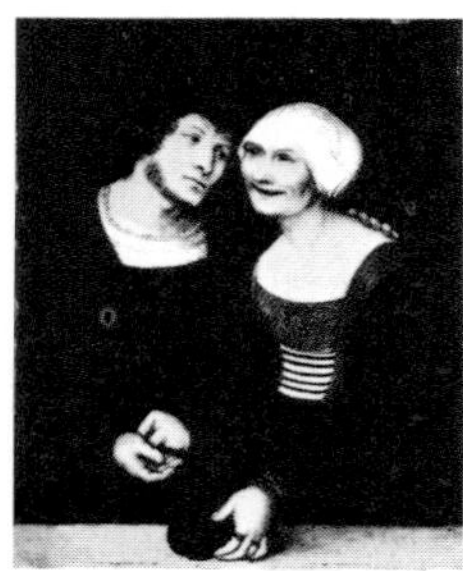

Lucas Cranach the Elder
The Infatuated Old Woman

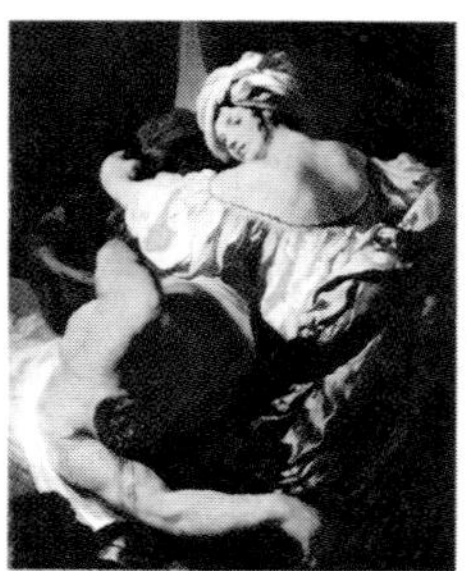

Johann Liss *Judith with the Head of Holofernes*

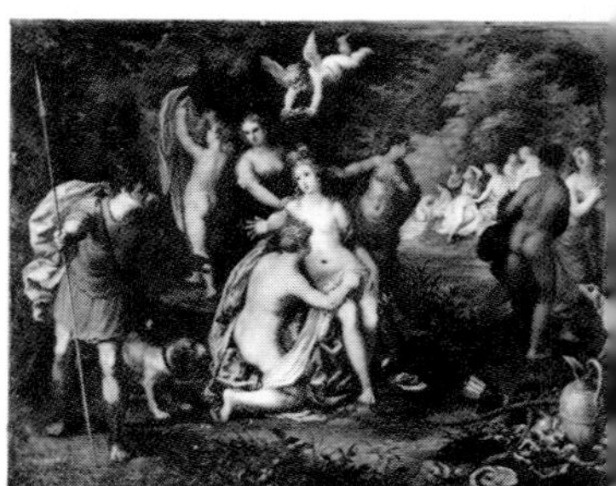

Johann Rottenhammer
Diana and Acteon

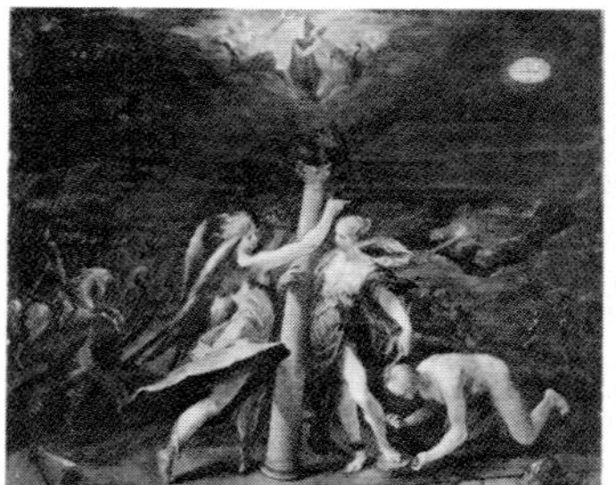

Hans von Aachen
The Liberation of Hungaria

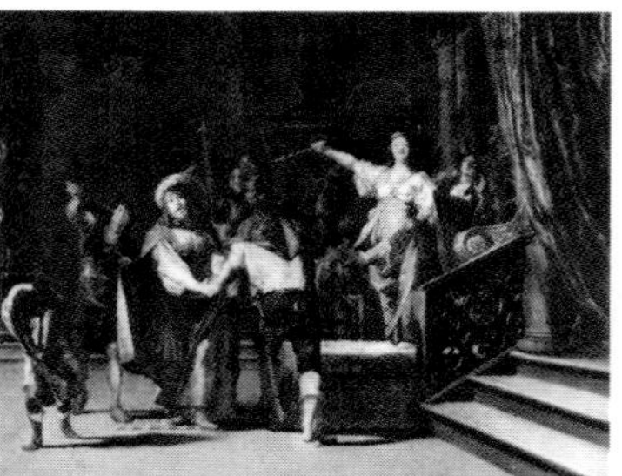

Nicolaus Knüpfer
Semiramis Has Her Husband Ninus Slain

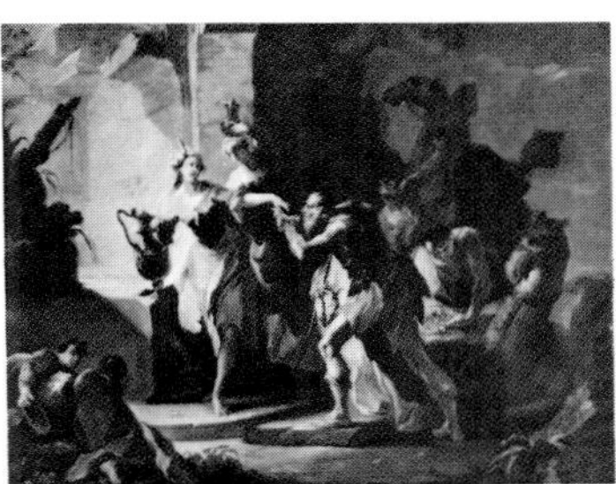

Franz Anton Maulbertsch
Rebecca at the Well

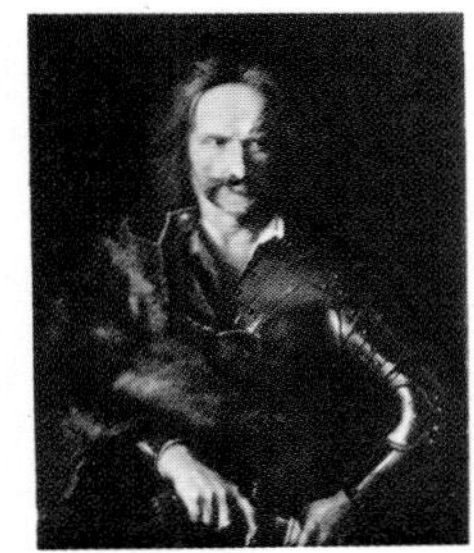

Johann Kupetzky
An Old Warrior

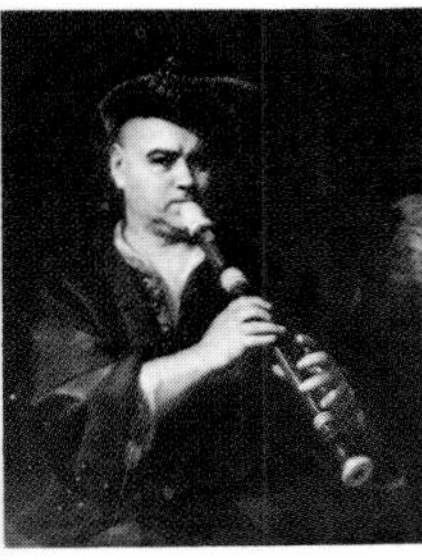

Johann Kupetzky
Man Playing the Shawm

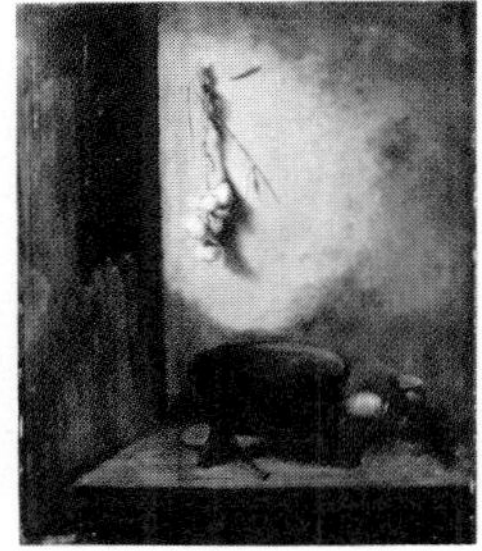

Christoph Paudiss
Still-life: Garlic Hanging on a Wall

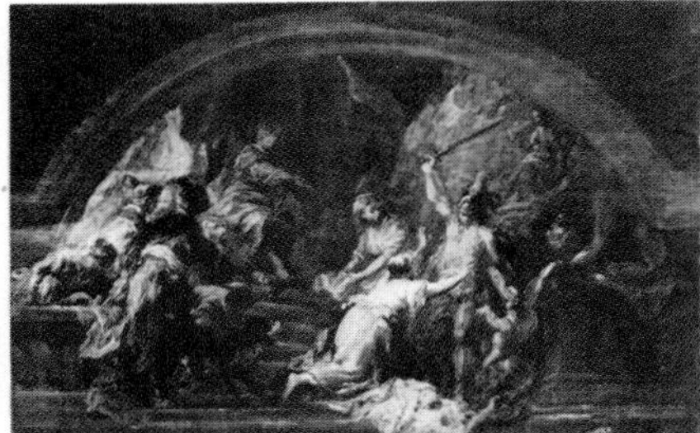

Martin Johann Schmidt
The Judgment of Solomon

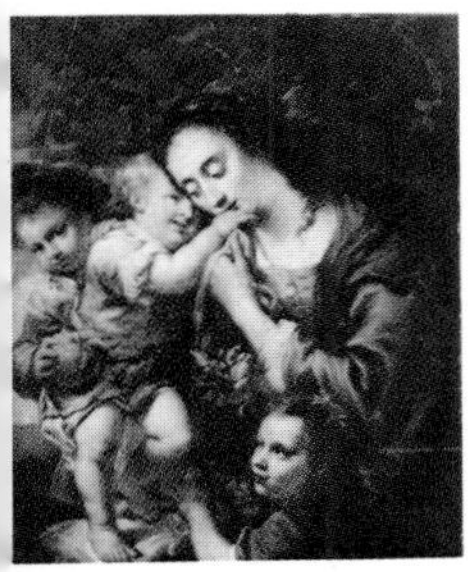

Jürgen Ovens
A Mother and Her Children

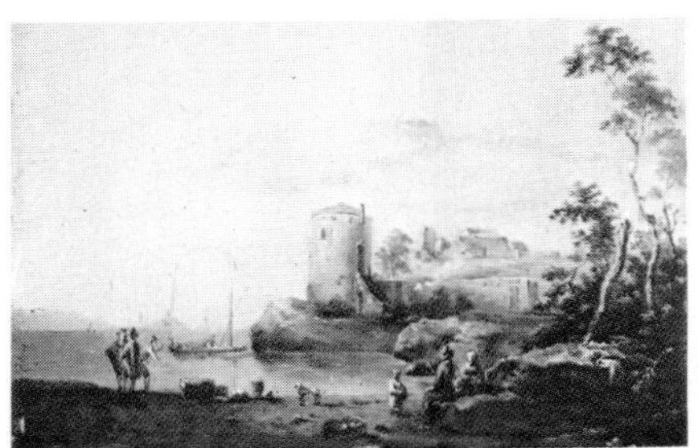

Norbert Grund *River Landscape with a Tower*

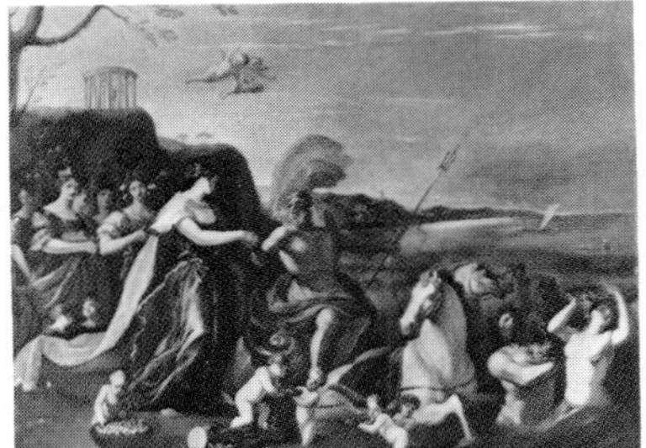

Johann Heinrich Schönfeld
Neptune and Amphitrite

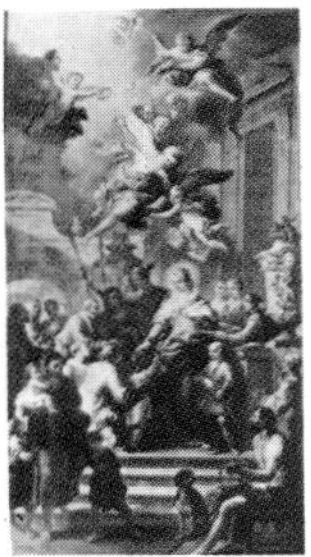

Daniel Gran
St Elizabeth of Hungary Distributing Alms

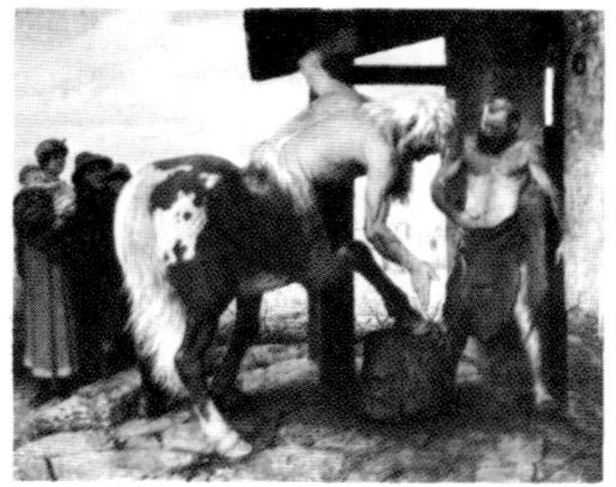

Arnold Böcklin *The Centaur at the Smithy*

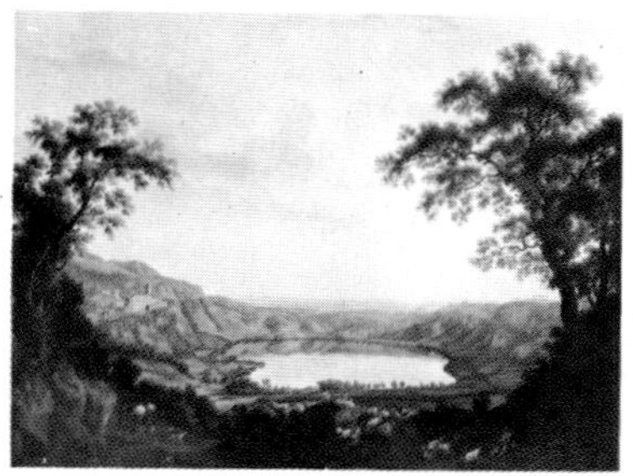

Jacob Philipp Hackert *Lake Nemi*

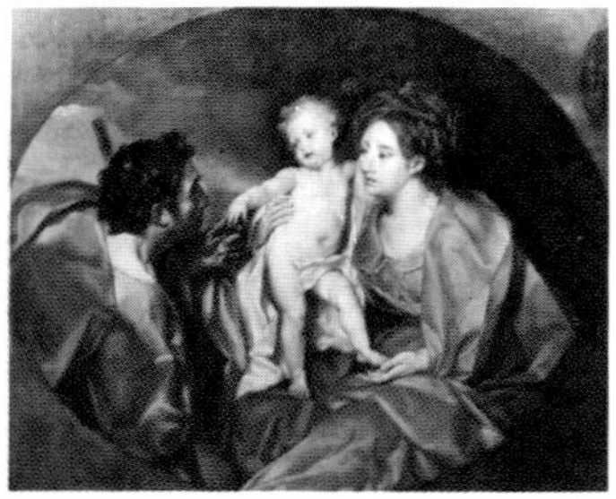

Anton Raphael Mengs
The Holy Family

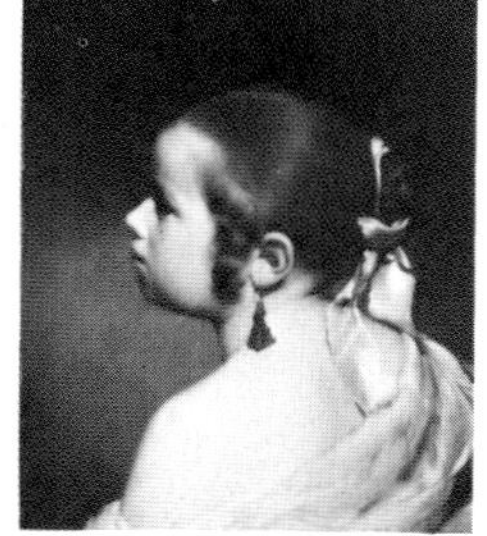

Franz Eybl
Portrait of a Girl

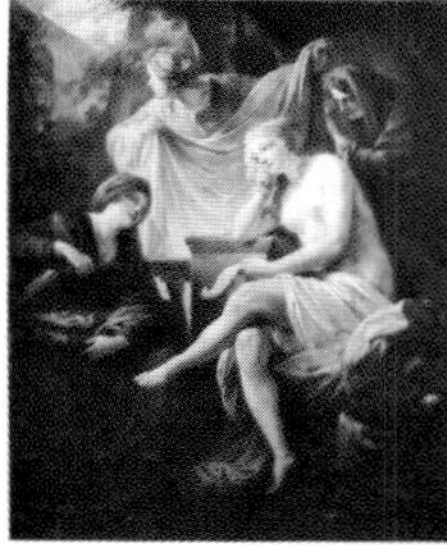

Friedrich Heinrich Füger
Bathsheba

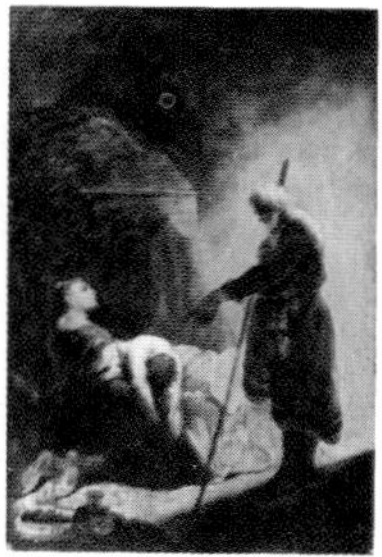

Januarius Zick *Elisha and the Shunnamite Woman*

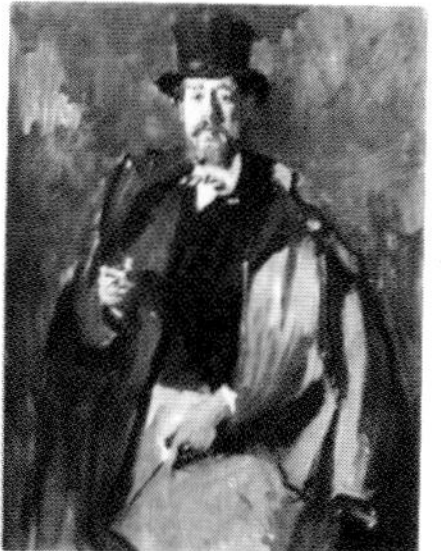

Wilhelm Leibl
Pál Szinyei Merse

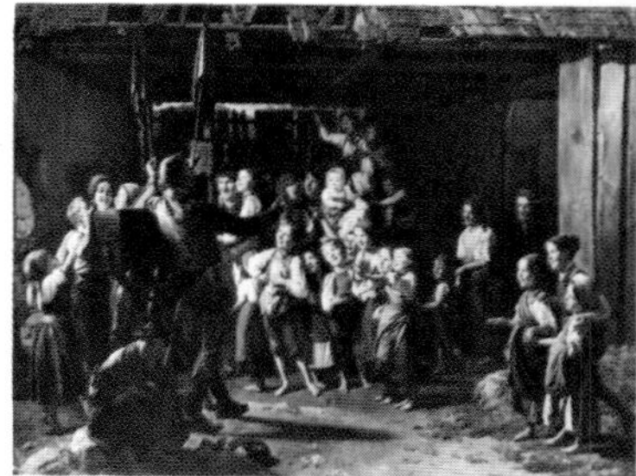

Ferdinand Georg Waldmüller
The Peep-show

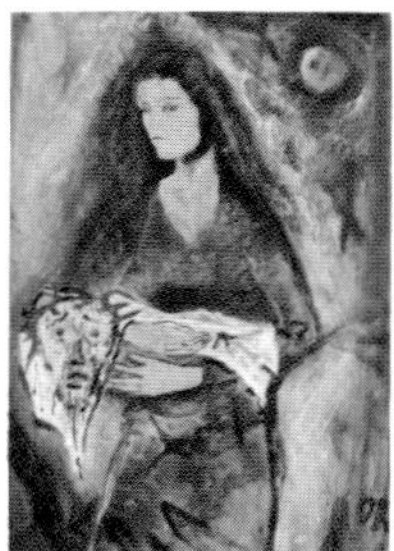

Oskar Kokoschka
Veronica

ENGLISH AND FRENCH PAINTING

Seventeenth to twentieth centuries

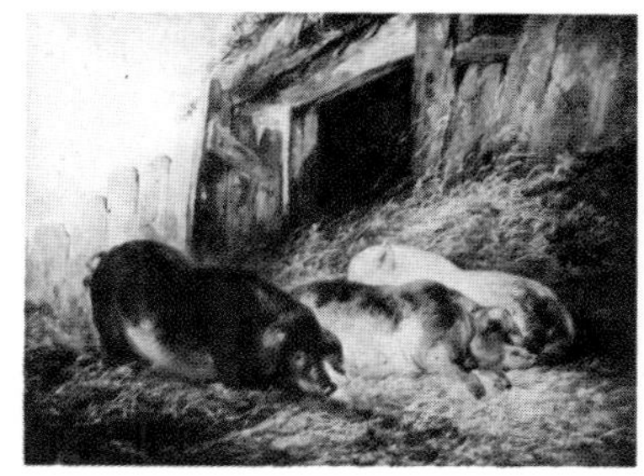

George Morland *The Pigsty*

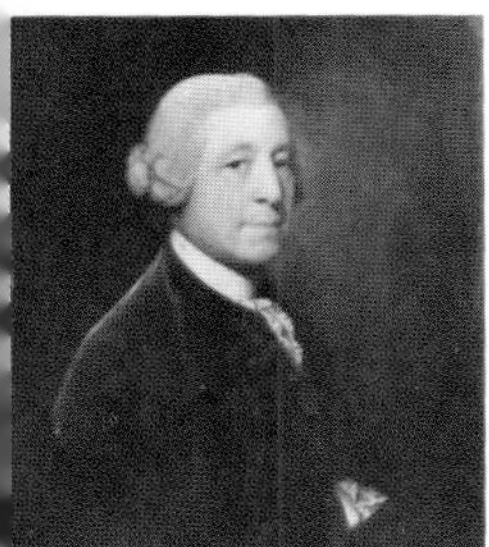

Thomas Gainsborough
Charles Hotchkiss

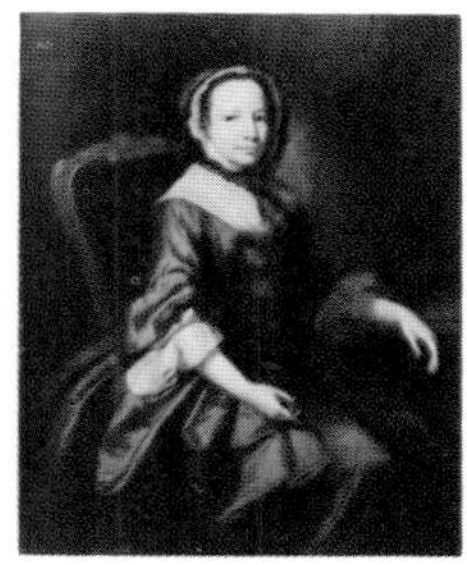

William Hogarth
Lady Thornhill

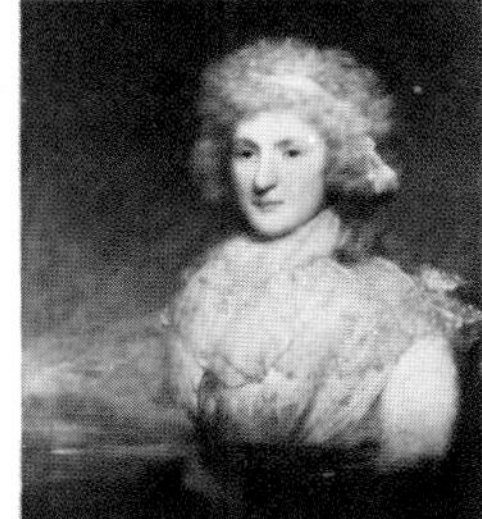

John Hoppner
Mrs Batt

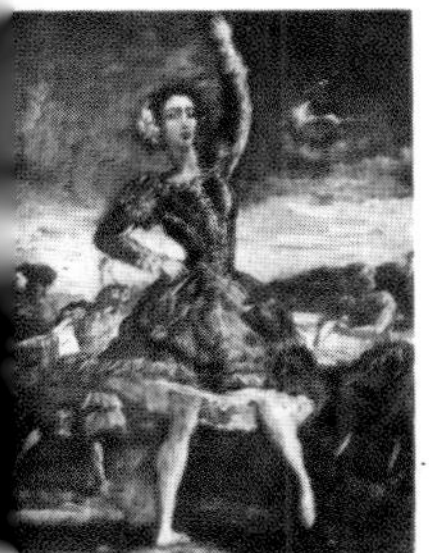

Théodore Chassériau
La Petra Camara

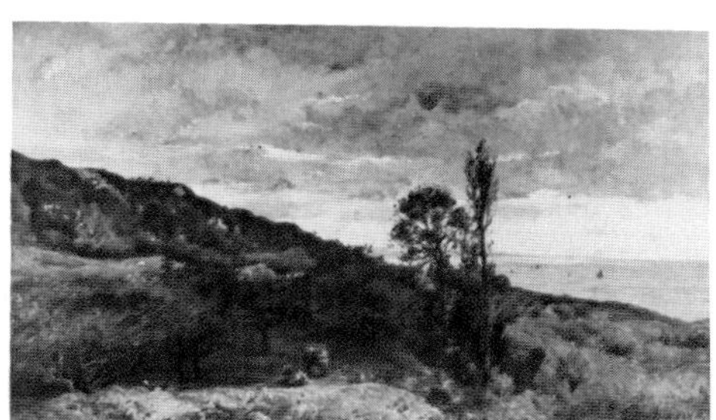

Charles-François Daubigny *Landscape near Villerville*

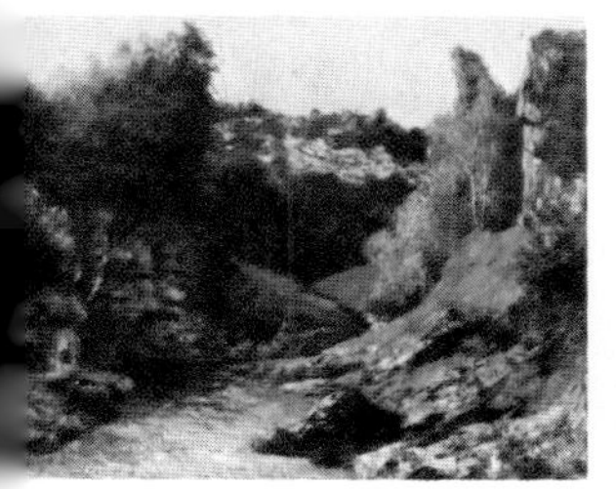

Gustave Courbet *Rocky Landscape*

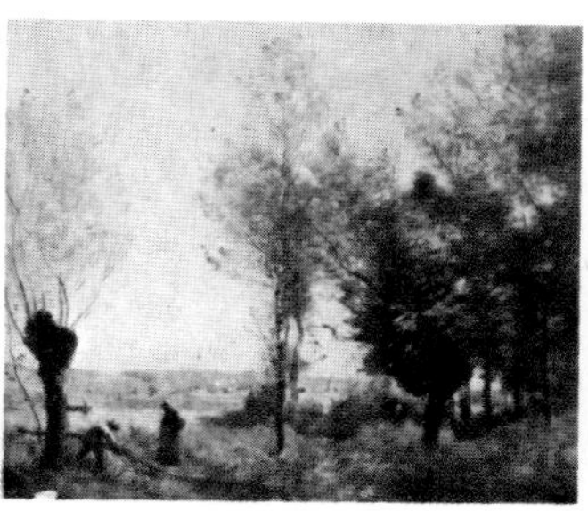

Camille Corot *Souvenir de Coubron*

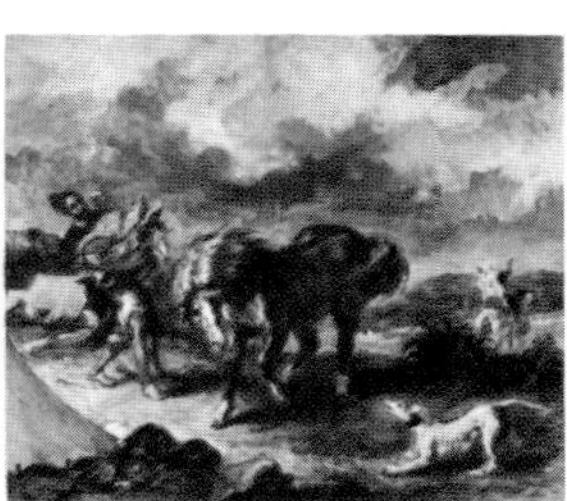

Eugène Delacroix
A Moroccan and His Horse

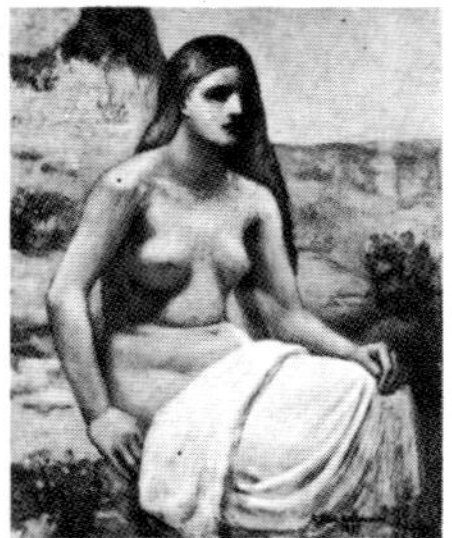

Pierre Puvis de Chavannes
Mary Magdalene

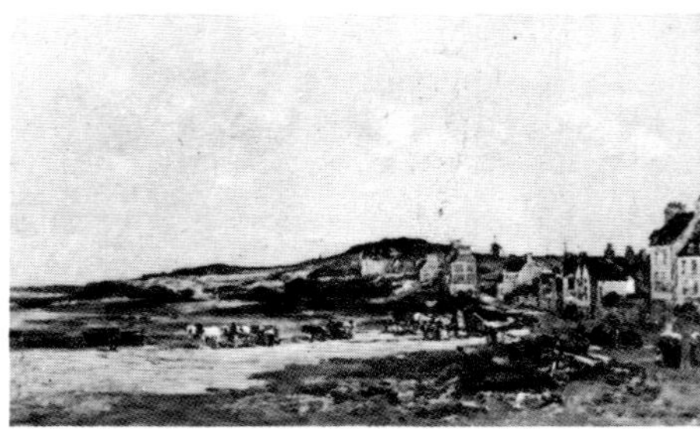

Eugène Boudin *Portrieux*

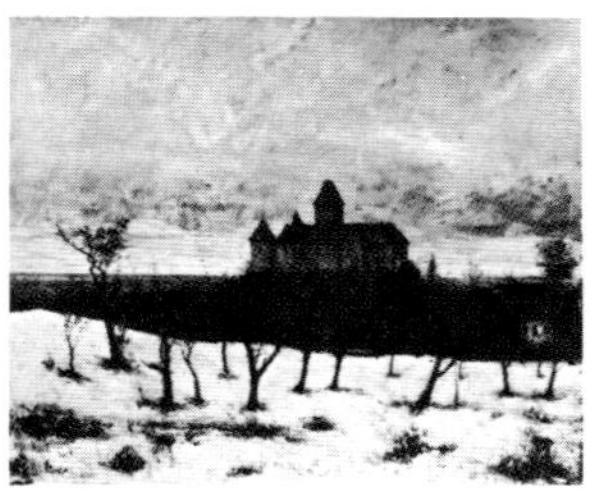

Gustave Courbet *Lake of Neufchâtel*

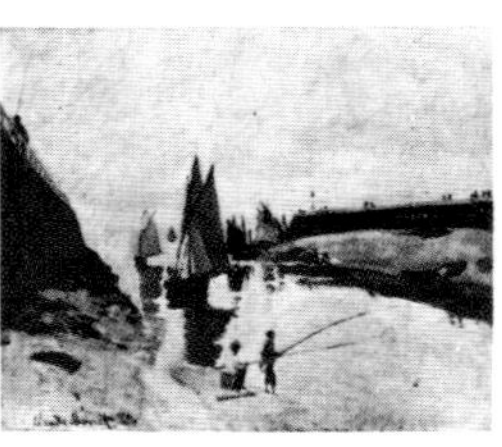

Claude Monet
The Harbour at Trouville

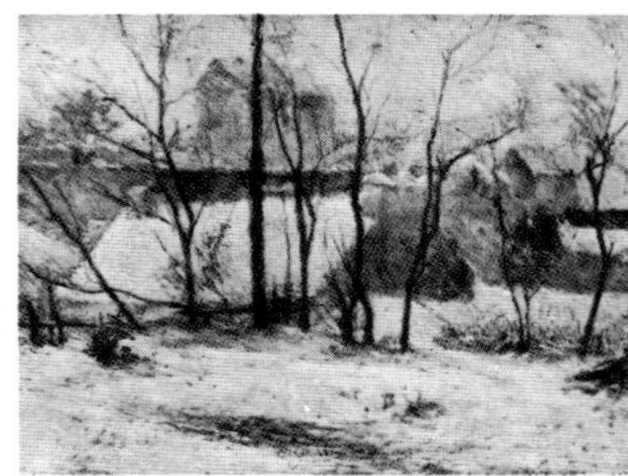

Paul Gauguin *Winter Landscape*

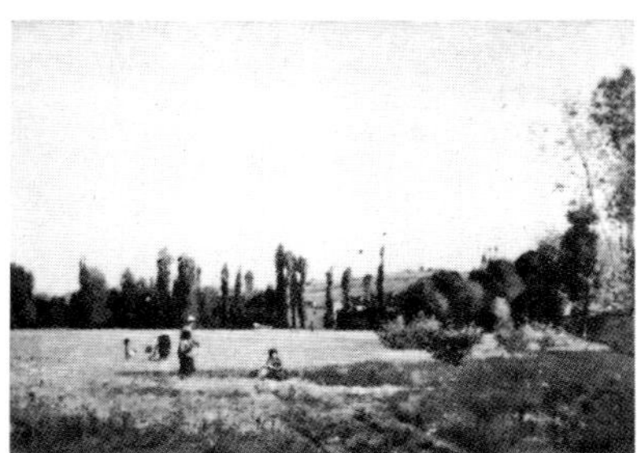

Camille Pissarro *La Varenne-de-St-Hilaire*

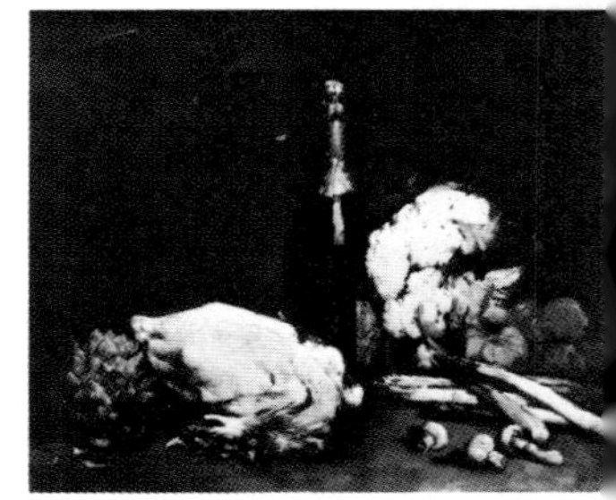

Théodule Ribot *Still-life*

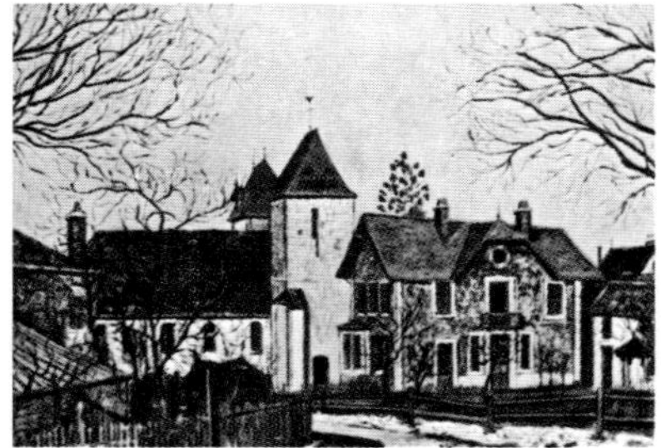

Maurice Utrillo *The Street*

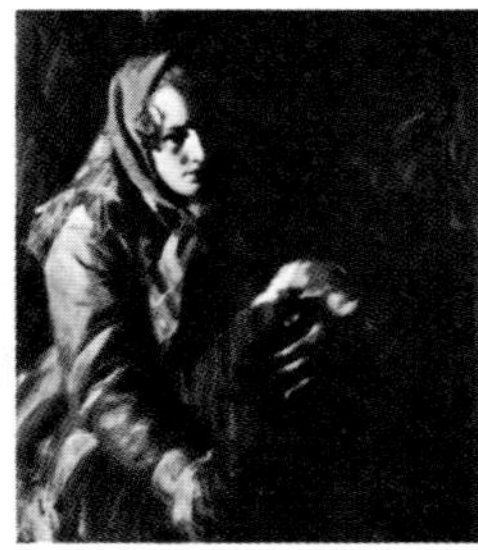

Anders Leonard Zorn
Mother and Child

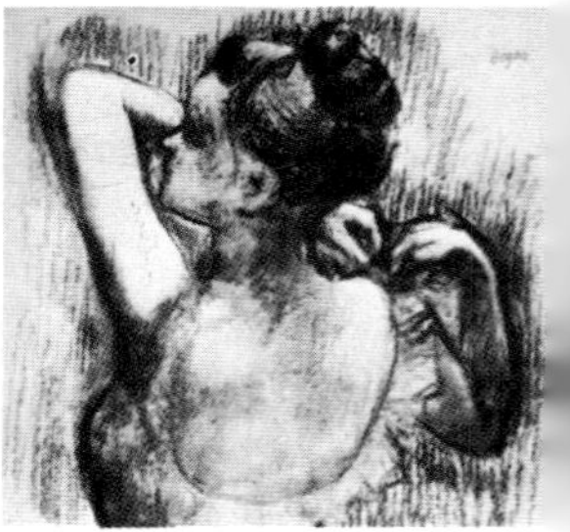

Edgar Degas *The Dancer*

LIST OF ILLUSTRATIONS

The numbers in *italics* indicate reproductions in colour